T0385150

PRAISE FOR *EMPTY VESSEL*

'A thrilling, meticulous and wondrously original journey, told with a flair and reverence for detail that captures all the joys, travails and horrors of life across time, place and water. A fabulous book'
Philippe Sands, author of *East West Street*

'If you've ever struggled to understand what terms like "globalisation" or "financialisation" actually mean, *Empty Vessel* is the book for you. Kumekawa combines in depth research with powerful storytelling to show the reader, in concrete terms, how modern capitalism really works – and how it has changed over the last several decades'
Grace Blakeley, author of *Vulture Capitalism*

'In the astonishing trajectory of a humble barge, *Empty Vessel* delivers an ambitious history of the global economy, linking everything from oil-drilling and offshore finance to military deployments and mass incarceration. I've rarely read a book that so deftly entwines a single, accessible story with the broad forces of globalization. A stunningly original history, as phenomenally well-researched as it is eloquently told'
Maya Jasanoff, author of *The Dawn Watch*

'When the world went on lockdown, Kumekawa took a different tack, tracking a single barge through its journey across the planet. What he discovers is the hidden material life and labor that make the global economy possible. A brilliant, unforgettable tale of our modern times'
Eric Klinenberg, co-author of *Modern Romance*

'A compelling voyage in and of itself, taking the reader on a journey around the global economy that illuminates the systemic blind spots of the late twentieth century and early twenty-first century global economy. A trip on a barge that takes you further than you imagined'
Kojo Koram, author of *Uncommon Wealth*

'Kumekawa is an excellent guide to this half a century moment in the history of capitalism. By focusing on something small and very local he allows us to see something big and very global: the forgoing of new inequalities, the retooling of global economic hierarchies, the refashioning of trade and industry, the feverish burning of fossil fuels and the violence and coercions embedded into the neoliberal order supervised by a powerful but recast state. The many-headed hydra of neoliberalism has found its chronicler'

Sven Beckert, author of *Empire of Cotton*

'An ingenious, marvelous book. Kumekawa has captured the big economic stories of the past half-century in the perambulations of a single ship. His vessel drifts across the globe from one major upheaval to the next, a floating, steel witness to extraction, mass production, deindustrialization, incarceration, and war. The result is a high seas picaresque through the systems that tie the modern world together'

Henry Grabar, author of *Paved Paradise*

'A gripping tale – of a floating prison, the worlds of global and offshore capital in which such ships are moored, and the maritime and legal infrastructures that keep such worlds afloat, even amidst the tidal waves of economic and ecological disaster'

Surabhi Ranganathan, Professor of International Law, University of Cambridge

'Kumekawa's tale of the Barge . . . is an imaginative and beautifully written allegory of the decades of globalization and the fugitive wealth it supported. What an eye-opening read!'

Charles S. Maier, Leverett Saltonstall Professor of History, Emeritus, Harvard University

'A captivating story – I read it like a detective novel – and at the same time a profound contribution to the history of economic, financial and material life in the contemporary globalized world'

Emma Rothschild, Jeremy and Jane Knowles Professor of History, Harvard University

'*Empty Vessel*, both the book and the accommodation container ship whose checkered history it unfolds, brilliantly illuminates the workings of a global offshore economy that would prefer to remain in the shadows, lingering on the margins of the law, thriving on secrecy, sleight of hand and tax avoidance. By following in the vessels' wake Kumekawa's riveting story reveals not just its physical use and functions-as accommodation for British troops, New York prisoners, oil workers, asylum seekers-but explains how the Vessel became an exemplary object caught up in global skeins/schemes of capital and finance'

John Brewer, Professor Emeritus,
Caltech Division of Humanities and Social Sciences

'Brilliantly traces the history of one vessel to make the historical forces of globalization concrete. A riveting and important read that shows the strange ties between tax havens and trade, prisons and ports. Offshore is more than a concept; it is a place. Kumekawa is the ideal guide to that place and its complicated inner workings'

Heidi Tworek, Professor of History and Public Policy and
Canada Research Chair, University of British Columbia

EMPTY VESSEL

ALSO BY IAN KUMEKAWA

*The First Serious Optimist: A. C. Pigou and
the Birth of Welfare Economics*

EMPTY VESSEL

THE STORY OF THE GLOBAL ECONOMY IN ONE SHIP

IAN KUMEKAWA

JOHN MURRAY

First published in Great Britain in 2025 by John Murray (Publishers)

1

Copyright © Ian Kumekawa 2025

The right of Ian Kumekawa to be identified as the Author of the Work has been asserted by him in accordance with the Copyright, Designs and Patents Act 1988.

A CIP catalogue record for this title is available from the British Library

Hardback ISBN 9781399816229
Trade Paperback ISBN 9781399816236
ebook ISBN 9781399816250

Typeset in Adobe Garamond Pro

Printed and bound in Great Britain by Clays Ltd, Elcograf S.p.A.

John Murray policy is to use papers that are natural, renewable and recyclable products and made from wood grown in sustainable forests. The logging and manufacturing processes are expected to conform to the environmental regulations of the country of origin.

Carmelite House
50 Victoria Embankment
London EC4Y 0DZ

www.johnmurraypress.co.uk

John Murray Press, part of Hodder & Stoughton Limited
An Hachette UK company

The authorised representative in the EEA is Hachette Ireland, 8 Castlecourt Centre, Dublin 15, D15 XTP3, Ireland (email: info@hbgi.ie)

*To SGL, who inspired this book
and anchored its author*

I can no more, bathed in your langours, O waves,
Sail in the wake of the carriers of cottons,
Nor undergo the pride of the flags and pennants,
Nor pull past the horrible eyes of the hulks.

Final stanza of "Le Bateau Ivre" (The Drunken Boat),
by Arthur Rimbaud, translated by Oliver Bernard

CONTENTS

TIMELINE OF THE VESSEL
AND ITS SISTER VESSEL

	The Vessel	**The Sister Vessel**
1978	Finnboda Varv, a Swedish shipbuilder, begins planning to construct two new barges, referring to them as Nybygge ("Newbuild") 408 and Nybygge 409. The latter is the Vessel.	The Sister Vessel is referred to as Nybygge 408.
1979	The *Balder Scapa* is constructed at Finnboda Varv outside of Stockholm, Sweden, and delivered to Parley Augustsson's Balder Group in Norway. It is then towed to the Scapa Flow in Scotland.	The *Balder Floatell 1* is constructed at Finnboda Varv for the Balder Group, but never delivered.
1981	The *Balder Scapa* is sold back to Finnboda and returns to Sweden, where it is reregistered. The Vessel is renamed the *Finnboda 12*. It is then sold to Consafe Offshore.	The Sister Vessel is renamed the *Finnboda 11* and is registered in Sweden. It is then sold along with the Vessel to Consafe Offshore.
1981–1983	Consafe renovates the barge in Gothenburg, Sweden, adding an accommodation block, and renames it the *Safe Esperia*.	Consafe renovates the barge in Gothenburg, Sweden (ending in 1982), adding an accommodation block, and renames it the *Safe Dominia*.
1982		The *Safe Dominia* is reregistered in Jersey and then transported to Stanley in the Falkland Islands, where it serves as a barracks for British troops under the name COASTEL 1.

	The Vessel	The Sister Vessel
1983	The *Safe Esperia* is acquired by the Bibby Line and reregistered in the United Kingdom. It is transported to Stanley in the Falkland Islands, where it serves as a barracks for British troops under the name COASTEL 3.	
1985	The Vessel is renamed the *Bibby Resolution*.	The Bibby Line buys the Sister Vessel outright and renames it the *Bibby Venture*.
1987		The *Bibby Venture* leaves Stanley and is reregistered in the Bahamas. It is refurbished outside of London and then delivered to the New York City Department of Correction. It is moored at Pier 36 in the East River and called the Maritime Facility I.
1988	The *Bibby Resolution* leaves Stanley and is reregistered in the Bahamas. It is refurbished outside of London and then delivered to Volkswagen in Emden, West Germany.	The *Bibby Venture* is moved to Pier 1 in Brooklyn.
1989	The *Bibby Resolution* is transported to New York, where it is leased by the New York Department of Correction. It opens as a jail at Pier 36 off Manhattan, officially called the Maritime Facility II.	The *Bibby Venture* is moved to Pier 40 in Manhattan, on the Hudson River.
1994	The *Bibby Resolution* ceases operation as a detention facility and is moved to Brooklyn. New York City buys the Vessel.	The *Bibby Venture* ceases operation as a detention facility. New York City buys the Sister Vessel.
1997	The Vessel is acquired by the British government and transported to Portland, England, where it begins service as a prison under the new name HMP *The Weare*.	
2005	HMP *The Weare* closes. The Vessel is renamed *The Weare*.	
2006	*The Weare* is acquired by Pacific Maritime (Asia) Ltd. and then by Holystone Overseas Ltd. The two firms dispute their contract in English court.	

	The Vessel	The Sister Vessel
2008	The Vessel, still in Portland, is renamed the *Jascon 27* and registered in St. Vincent and the Grenadines by the Sea Trucks Group, the parent company of Holystone.	
2010	The *Jascon 27* is towed to Onne, Nigeria, where it begins service as an accommodation vessel for offshore oil workers.	
by 2013		The Sister Vessel is renamed the *Venture* and is registered in St. Vincent and the Grenadines. It is owned by the British shipowner Intership, and is used as an accommodation vessel off the Nigerian coast.
2016	The *Jascon 27*'s status is "laid up."	The *Venture* is purchased by an Indian shipping group, Halani.
2018	The Sea Trucks Group's leadership splits. One faction, operating under the name West African Ventures, takes possession of the *Jascon 27.*	The *Venture* is operating off the coast of Namibia when its crew is abandoned by Halani, prompting intervention by the International Maritime Organization and the International Labour Organization. It is deregistered from the shipping registry of St. Vincent and the Grenadines.
2021		The Sister Vessel is renamed the *High Ocean IV* and reregistered in St. Kitts and Nevis. It is towed to Gujarat in India, via Port Louis, Mauritius.
2022		The *High Ocean IV* is scrapped in Alang, Gujarat.

PREFACE

Early in 2020, I first learned that New York City operated a prison ship, known colloquially as "the Boat," moored off the South Bronx. My future wife, a public defender then working in the South Bronx, had a client who had just been incarcerated there: a squat gray vessel on which the novel coronavirus was rapidly spreading. Perhaps because I am a historian trained in British imperial history, "the Boat" immediately called to mind images of prison hulks, the notorious facilities that were a hallmark of the British penal system of the eighteenth and nineteenth centuries. I thought of Pip peering at the looming hulks over the marshes of the Thames estuary with fear and horror at the beginning of Charles Dickens's *Great Expectations*.

Intrigued, I began to investigate the history of the ship moored in the East River. I discovered that though "the Boat" itself had a fairly straightforward origin story, the story of the jail barge that it had replaced in the early 1990s was full of twists and turns. That story turned out to be a remarkable narrative of the economic life of globalization and privatization, themes that were at the center of my previous work on state capture in the early twentieth century.

I began spending more and more time tracing the first barge's journey, from a dockyard in Sweden to the South Atlantic, Lower Manhattan, England, and finally West Africa. As the pandemic descended, closing archives and forcing people to stay home, I conducted oral history interviews over Zoom with people who had built, worked on, and been incarcerated on the barge. I had these conversations with people all over the world at a time when the world felt simultaneously disconnected and entirely in sync. Cities were locked down and borders were closed, but billions of people were experiencing the same phenomena of disease, uncertainty, and loss. Billions of people were disconnected but found themselves disconnected *together*. Speaking with people over Zoom, peering into their homes as they peered into mine, it was hard to escape how small the world was and how global an experience could be.

At the same time, the pandemic brought physical boundaries and physical infrastructure out of the shadows and into the limelight. The breakdown of global supply chains and the inability to source face masks or toilet paper exposed how quotidian life depended on a whole hidden world. As everyday activities became fraught with danger, it became impossible to avoid considering how important grocery store workers were. It was impossible to ignore how vital buses were, and airplanes, and ships. I learned about the barge against this backdrop. The more I learned, the more I became convinced that a "barge's-eye view" provided a fascinating and vital perspective onto our global world and the changing global economy over the past forty years. The result is *Empty Vessel*.

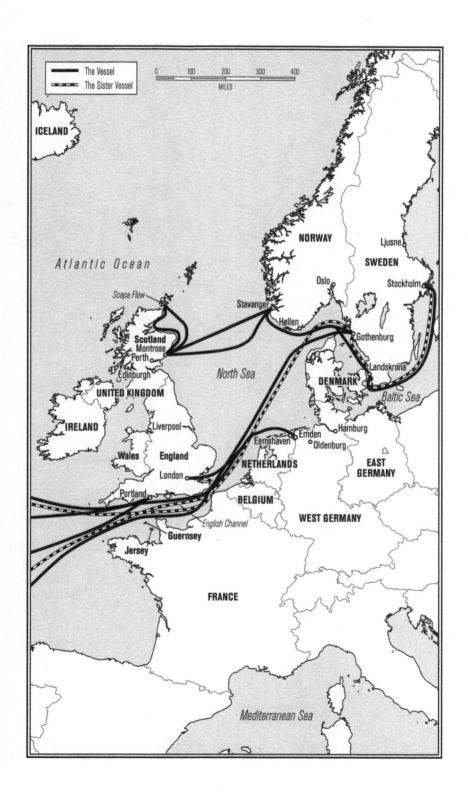

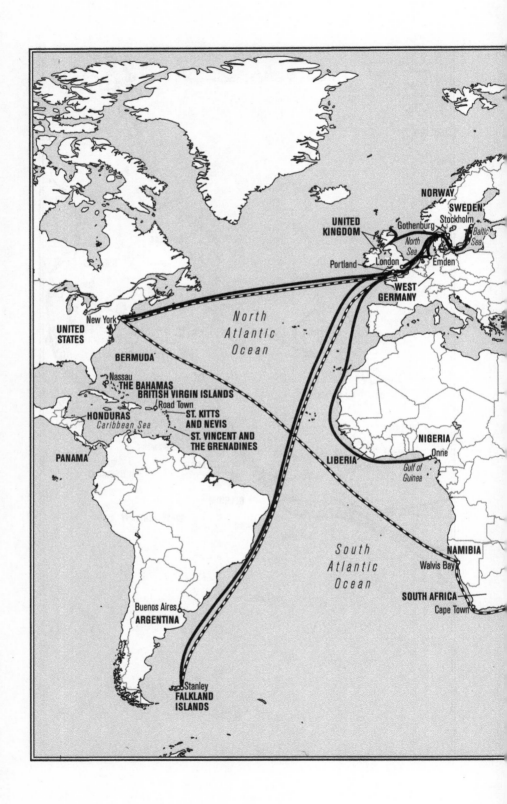

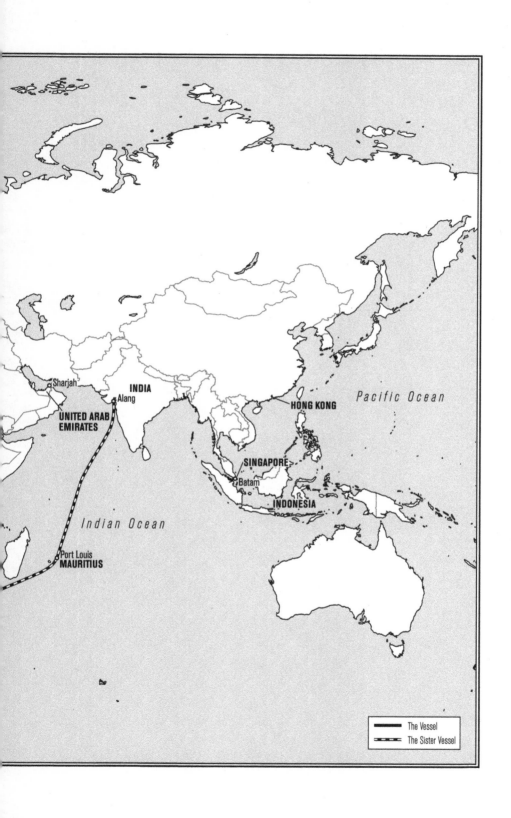

	Sharjah
UNITED ARAB EMIRATES	INDIA
	Alang

Pacific Ocean

HONG KONG

SINGAPORE

Batam

INDONESIA

Indian Ocean

Port Louis
MAURITIUS

▬▬▬▬	The Vessel
◄▬◄▬	The Sister Vessel

EMPTY
VESSEL

INTRODUCTION

On a spring day in 1989, a container ship arrived in New York harbor from Eemshaven, a deepwater port in the Netherlands. The Vessel, named the *Bibby Resolution*, belonged to a well-established Liverpool shipping line, one whose founder had invested in the Atlantic slave trade two hundred years before. But while the company that owned it had a history that went back centuries, the ship itself was unmistakably a product of the late twentieth century. The Vessel was assembled out of standardized parts developed for streamlining oceanic trade. It was a global polyglot: manufactured in Sweden, it had a British owner and an international crew. In the decade since its launch, it had been registered in four different countries. At the time it moored in New York, the Vessel was listed in the Bahamas, though it had never physically been close to Bahamian waters. Like other container ships, the *Bibby Resolution* was a creature not so much of a single country but of a global economic order.

The *Bibby Resolution* was an unusual container ship. For one thing, it did not have an engine; it had been transported to New York from Europe on the back of another ship. For another, the containers the Vessel carried were never intended to be unloaded, nor were they meant to contain merchandise. The Vessel was an accommodation ship: in the various descriptions of its owners, a "hotel ship," a "coastel," or a "floatel." These designations were meant to evoke comfort, if not luxury. But they did not change the fact that the Vessel was a simple ninety-four-meter-long flat-bottomed hull with a modular five-story steel "accommodation block" mounted on its deck.

For though the Vessel was built to house *people* rather than to transport goods, it was still very much a container ship. Its cabins and galleys, its gathering spaces and recreation rooms, were assembled out of modified steel shipping containers. And it had been brought to New York quite literally to *contain*. The New York City Department of Correction had leased the *Bibby Resolution* to serve as a floating jail.

• • •

And so, in addition to being a ship, the Vessel was also a jail, at least for the five years that it was in New York. At other points in its history, it was a barracks for troops in the Falkland Islands, temporary housing for assembly line workers in West Germany, and a home away from home for oilmen off the coast of Nigeria. Over the past four decades, the Vessel has been called many names: the *Bibby Resolution*, the *Safe Esperia*, Her Majesty's Prison *The Weare*, even "The Love Boat." Today, it goes by the unassuming name of the *Jascon 27*, a reference to a company that once had title to it. It has flown the flags of five different countries, known a litany of owners, and, though it has never had a motor of its own, traveled tens of thousands of miles. The ship at the heart of this story has both lived and contained many lives.

In and of itself, the Vessel is uncharismatic. In the description of one of its early owners, it looks "like a big shoebox."[1] Even its technical classification—"dumb pontoon"—evokes a hulking, silent presence. But although it may outwardly appear stolid and static, the Vessel's story offers a window onto the profound and dynamic changes that have buffeted and shaped the world economy over the past forty years. Moreover, it has been a repository for the effects of such changes, as well as a stage on which they have played out.

The barge was manufactured to be modular and adaptable. It is this adaptability that has given it value. As Britain's former chief inspector of prisons, Ann Owers, noted in the early 2000s, the barge was first and foremost a "container." Its meaning and function changed depending on what, or who, it contained. In the North Sea and in Nigeria, it was an offshore oil service vessel; in the Falklands it was a barracks; in New York it was a jail. The fact that the Vessel could be filled allowed it to be transformed and take on meanings that fit its setting. In this way, its emptiness has been its defining characteristic.

For this reason, throughout its existence, the barge has always been passive. It has been forged and reforged, swept along and buffeted by a set of profound and interrelated economic transformations: the growth of the carbon economy, globalization, financialization, mass incarceration. In the process, it has also become the setting against which such sweeping processes played out. Built to service the global, multinational energy industry, it was deployed in the South Atlantic as part of an effort to shift British political attention away from the widespread unemployment caused by Margaret Thatcher's government. Later, it was rushed to New York to accommodate a swelling jail population, itself precipitated by the rising unemployment and shrinking social services of the Reagan years. All the while, the Vessel was privately owned, successively registered in tax haven after tax haven.

The barge has been an abstract financial object; its ownership was divided up and leveraged, used to guarantee international corporate bonds. It has also been an abstract legal object: haggled over in arbitration tribunals in London and the British Virgin Islands and the subject of an important case in English commercial law. It was built largely because of an innovation in the international law of the sea, and first acquired as a way to circumvent Norwegian tax laws. Its registration and ownership depended on other international treaties and national tax codes. As a penitentiary and workplace, the Vessel became a stage for the enactment of other kinds of law. As such, it became a site of the abstract forces that have transformed our world over the past forty years.

• • •

So much of the language around globalization and economic transformation is abstract. It "extends" markets; it "deregulates" oversight; it "financializes" physical goods. Not coincidentally, in the United States and western Europe, one of the effects of a wide range of disparate policies and agendas often lumped together as "neoliberal" has been to drive traditional manufacturing jobs overseas while undergirding the growth of the financial sector. And financialization itself necessarily involves abstraction; it did so when grain traders developed the futures market in Chicago in the late nineteenth century, and it still does so today.[2] The vessel that this book follows belongs to this world. It is, quite literally, offshore. It was constructed from modular shipping containers, conceptualized in terms of empty, fillable volume. It is a creation of a supernational, offshore global order: registered in the Bahamas or St. Vincent and the Grenadines, owned by international consortia, leveraged by financiers in London, Oslo, and Lagos.[3]

But the barge was—and remains—fundamentally an *object*. Normally, the physical dimension of globalization remains in the background, relatively unnoticed. It usually takes catastrophe—a very physical breakdown, like the mega container ship *Ever Given* blocking the Suez Canal in 2021, or the Russian blockade of Ukrainian grain ports on the Black Sea—to cast a spotlight on the physical infrastructure that undergirds the world economy. This book attends to the extreme physicality of abstract processes. Despite the great degree to which the Vessel's story has been intertwined with the history of economic and legal abstraction over the past forty years, the barge itself is inescapably concrete. It is a physical object: a vessel made of steel weighing 9,500 deadweight tons. It took shape only as Swedish builders welded and riveted it together, piece by piece. It has gangplanks and bulkheads, a sewage treatment plant and noisy Volvo generators. Even when it was moored in New York's East River, it swayed and rocked. It housed up to nine hundred people, who ate, washed, and slept in claustrophobic proximity, using sturdy metal furniture and a vacuum toilet system that was prone to malfunction. And its physical condition deteriorated. Every few years, it needed to be removed from the water and refurbished, barnacles scraped from the hull, its decks cleaned and repainted.

The barge serves as a reminder that all economic transformations depend on material processes. And its story brings to light the very real and very physical effects of the transformation of the world economy over the past four decades. These effects are messy, far from gleaming shopping malls, glassy office blocks, and slick websites rendered in clean sans serifs. And though they are frequently hidden from public view, the physical effects are fundamental to the processes that have altered our world. Deregulation in the 1980s was enabled by the calculated exercise of military power. The economic dislocations of financialization accelerated mass incarceration and the physical detention of millions of people. The provision of global energy supplies continues to depend on the extraction of fossil fuels from deep beneath the earth and sea. Training sophisticated artificial intelligence depends on huge amounts of energy: creating a single moderately sized AI model can emit as much carbon as several cars in their lifetimes.[4]

By following a single vessel, this book offers a guide to how major global transformations were always embodied, grounded in tangible things, and, often, dependent on physical violence.[5] This book is a material history, but it is not a commodity history. It focuses on a single object. In these pages, this object is called "the Vessel," with a capital *V*.[6] For although its name changed frequently over time, the ship itself is the central, mute character of this drama. It is at once a subject and an object that highlights the importance of the physical in a rapidly changing world.

. . .

Empty Vessel relies on the barge as being a container not just in a physical but also in a metaphorical way. It treats the barge as a vessel of history. The fact that the ship has had so many different names, both officially and unofficially, speaks to the way in which it was an empty vessel, to be filled and refilled with meaning and value. By following its story, and the stories of the people who built, ran, and lived on it, it is possible to ascertain and understand similarities and linkages between seemingly disconnected processes and transformations. This ability to assemble lives and narratives, even those untethered from dry land, is a long-standing feature of maritime literature—from Richard Henry Dana's *Two Years Before the Mast* to Melville's *Moby Dick*, from B. Traven's *The Death Ship* to the maritime novels of Joseph Conrad.[7] In this book, as in other nautical stories, the ship serves as a vector that connects groups of people living thousands of miles apart, speaking different languages, practicing different trades, and confronting different challenges.

The story of the Vessel is thus a connective, global microhistory. Each chapter is centered on a particular place: a particular context in which the Vessel existed. But as a whole, the barge's story demonstrates the ways in which people and places around the world, however diverse and differentiated, *all* were shaped and affected by truly global economic transformations—offshoring in particular.[8] The Vessel is what historians call "exceptional normal"; its story is unique in its drama, but representative in kind and reflective of a larger logic.[9] In short, a simple barge can serve as a powerful vehicle in and through which to explore the global economy of the late twentieth and early twenty-first centuries and the emergent offshore world that has stitched it together.

CHAPTER 1

THE BALTIC SEA

	The Vessel	The Sister Vessel
1978	Finnboda Varv, a Swedish shipbuilder, begins planning to construct two new barges, referring to them as Nybygge ("Newbuild") 408 and Nybygge 409. The latter is the Vessel.	The Sister Vessel is referred to as Nybygge 408.
1979	The *Balder Scapa* is constructed at Finnboda Varv outside of Stockholm, Sweden, and delivered to Parley Augustsson's Balder Group in Norway. It is then towed to the Scapa Flow in Scotland.	The *Balder Floatell 1* is constructed at Finnboda Varv for the Balder Group, but never delivered.
1981	The *Balder Scapa* is sold back to Finnboda and returns to Sweden, where it is reregistered. The Vessel is renamed the *Finnboda 12*. It is then sold to Consafe Offshore.	The Sister Vessel is renamed the *Finnboda 11* and is registered in Sweden. It is then sold along with the Vessel to Consafe Offshore.

L ate in 1979, Parley Augustsson, the "limited partnership king" of Norway, fired off a Telex to the managers of the Finnboda Varv, a shipyard located just east of Stockholm.[1] It would be the last message Finnboda received from him for several months. The relationship—at first incredibly promising—had lately cooled. Augustsson, one of Scandinavia's most prominent shipowners, had purchased two barges from the struggling yard that had recently been taken over by the Swedish state. On the surface, his plan had been simple and very reasonable. He would have the barges towed along the Swedish coast and then on to Scotland, where offshore oil exploration was booming. Two sturdy barges, the idea went, would be easy to charter out at a profit.

Augustsson was a well-known figure, both in Norway and in the shipping world. He controlled a fleet of seventy ships; his fortune was vast, and his star was rising. Augustsson's stature helps explain why administrators at the small Finnboda Varv agreed to deliver the first of the two barges without any up-front payment. The fact that Augustsson and the yard's manager shared a mutual contact did not hurt either.[2] But Finnboda was also acting out of desperation. Across northern Europe, the shipbuilding industry was sinking about as fast as offshore oil was taking off. And while a contract for two simple barges certainly would not spell the end of trouble for Finnboda, it might forestall disaster for the hundreds of people employed at the yard. Thus, it was with a measure of relief that Finnboda's employees and managers delivered the first barge, the Vessel at the heart of this story, to a company owned by Augustsson on a spring day in 1979.[3] As they watched the ship, then called the *Balder Scapa*, being towed out of the Stockholm inlet toward the Baltic Sea, they had good reasons for optimism.

Unfortunately, Augustsson's contracts did not work out as intended. Securing a charter in Scotland proved unexpectedly difficult and, as Finnboda's managers reminded Augustsson of his obligation to pay for the barges, he found himself facing a slew of problems. The British salvage company interested in the ship suddenly went bankrupt. The insurance was costing too much. Other customers offered too little. Finally, toward the end of 1979, Augustsson told Finnboda's management that he had found a suitable charter. Don't repossess the barge, he cajoled, while the ship was turning a profit. The Swedish managers agreed, stipulating that they expected regular reports—"full running information."[4] But at this point, the correspondence, conscientiously kept in the Finnboda archives, dries up. The next message from Augustsson, received four months later, did not bear good news. The promised charter never panned out. In the end, Augustsson returned the barge to Finnboda without payment. Ultimately, it would be Swedish taxpayers who footed the bill for the Vessel.

How did this happen? The answer has to do with a twisted web of economic transformation and legal innovation. A large part of the explanation involves the cratering trajectory of heavy manufacturing—particularly shipbuilding—in wealthy industrialized countries. But on a more fundamental level, the answer to the question has to do with the entangled ways in which states and markets interacted in the 1970s and 1980s as the postwar economic boom ran out of steam. Governments around the world, but especially in rich Western countries, walked a fine line between protecting politically evocative industries like shipbuilding and encouraging the growth of private enterprise. As they did so, entrepreneurs like Augustsson understood that there was a lot of money to be made when states tried to change the shape of markets. The Vessel—like other projects of the mid- and late twentieth century—was a product of both public and private schemes; it depended equally on solicitous state assistance and on the entrepreneurial drive for profit.

• • •

When the *Balder Scapa* was constructed, Sweden was in economic flux. Like other wealthy European countries, its industrial future was uncertain. After decades of growth, Sweden's heavy industry was running up against the barrier of persistently high wages. Manufacturing had already entered a decades-long downward slide. In 1960, nearly half of Swedish workers were employed in the manufacturing sector; by 1980, that figure had fallen to just over a third.[5] Today, it is under a fifth. Sweden's experience reflected a wider story of deindustrialization unfolding across western Europe and the United States, where the manufacturing sector's share of total employment has fallen by more than half since 1960.[6]

In the late 1970s, industrial decline was sparking concern all over the capitalist West. It was not just that unemployment was on the rise (it was). The model of prosperity and political stability that had existed since the end of World War II also seemed to be disintegrating in real time. Economies had been anchored—socially as much as economically—by the manufacture of *physical* goods: cars and electronics, but also steel, ships, textiles, and chemicals. In the 1970s, industrial societies were confronting a new and uncertain future in which more and more people were employed by service industries, and more and more goods produced overseas. The lament, now so common, that "we used to make things here" was just beginning to emerge both in the United States and Europe.

Few productive industries in the so-called Global North, in western Europe, and in Sweden in particular, were more troubled than shipbuilding. The company that nominally owned and operated the Finnboda Varv—Götaverken—had once been the largest shipbuilder in the world by gross tons produced. Even a decade before the Vessel was assembled at Finnboda, the market for new ships was booming, driven by surging demand for new container ships. No fewer than 406 such ships entered service between 1968 and 1975, more than tripling worldwide container cargo space.[7] And though much of the growth in marine construction took place in East Asia, even in Sweden, with its relatively high labor costs, containerization buoyed the fortunes of local shipyards. Between 1970 and 1975, the number of people working in Swedish shipbuilding grew by 30 percent.[8]

But bust followed fast on the heels of boom. Though shipping capacity began to outstrip demand in the early 1970s, the real shock came in the fall of 1973, shortly after Egyptian and Syrian tanks rolled into territory occupied by Israel in a surprise attack on the Jewish holiday of Yom Kippur. As it threw the energy market into crisis, the Yom Kippur War definitively punctured the bubble in the global shipping market. Just days into the war, the Organization of Arab Petroleum Exporting Countries declared an oil embargo on wealthy countries—including the United States, Britain, and Japan—that supported Israel and Israeli policies on Palestine. As a result, global oil prices skyrocketed from three dollars a barrel to almost twelve in a matter of weeks. A political move meant to curb American support for Israel, the embargo had catastrophic impacts on businesses around the world—not least shippers.[9] The world's freight was carried over the oceans by gas-guzzling behemoths; in a day of steaming at normal speeds, a single container ship might burn through nearly one hundred tons of fuel. As the Yom Kippur War sent the price of marine diesel soaring, global shipping recoiled as if struck by a hammer.

The oil shock did far more than just pop the container ship bubble; it was a boulder hurled into the economic sea, and its effects surged outward in mighty waves. In 1975, world manufactured exports fell for the first time since World War II.[10] Suddenly, the shipping industry's plentiful supply of cargo space became an acute and glaring problem. Vessels built to contain more and more freight were left empty as global demand evaporated. Shippers around the world had borrowed and invested billions of dollars in new, ever-larger container ships. Scale was supposed to be an asset, but in a recession, it became a major liability. By the mid-1970s, with falling global exports, the massive new vessels would either have to suspend operations or operate below their cargo capacity. The result was a rate war. As supply outstripped demand, freight charges spiraled downward.[11]

This was good news for some consumers who faced lower prices, but incredibly bad news for almost anyone involved with ships. In Sweden, the outlook was particularly grim. Though existing orders for ships meant that Swedish shipyards would remain active for a few years, by 1976, the industry was on the edge of a precipice. In a vicious catch-22, by continuing to build ships, Swedish shipyards were actively contributing to the economic conditions that would throw them out of work. Each new ship that was completed exacerbated the supply glut and depressed freight rates even further, dampening future demand for new shipping. Shipyards sowed the seeds of their own destruction. As they worked through their standing orders, new work dried up. The first closure of a major shipyard in Gothenburg, the historic hub of Swedish shipping and shipbuilding, was in 1976.[12] Over the next four years, Gothenburg—a prosperous city of about 450,000 on Sweden's west coast—lost six thousand jobs in its shipyards and another two thousand or so among contracting companies. By 1982, only one of the region's four major shipyards, Götaverken Arendal, was still active.[13]

Finnboda Varv, the largest shipyard in the Stockholm area, on the other side of the country, faced the same pressures. In the mid-1970s, it produced some vessels of significant size. The largest was the 170-meter-long tanker *Libra*; a plaque in its honor still exists near its launching point. But in the late 1970s and early 1980s, Finnboda began to shrink. Its staff, some seven hundred strong in 1975, was down to a mere two hundred by 1981. Cuts were deep and difficult. The first to go were foreign workers not covered by Sweden's generous social safety net. At Finnboda's peak employment, about a third of its labor force was Finnish.[14] Very few Finns remained by the end of the 1970s.

No one wanted the cuts: not workers, not managers, and certainly not politicians. Throughout the 1970s, the governments of Social Democratic Prime Minister Olof Palme and his Centre Party successor, Thorbjörn Fälldin, both heavily subsidized shipbuilders. State funds flowed into shipyards even during the relatively rosy years at the decade's start, and as the economy worsened, state assistance intensified. The Swedish government was determined to slow the decline of domestic industry. In an effort to keep shipyards open, it stepped in to guarantee shipbuilders' existing private debt. It offered Swedish shipowners low-interest loans to acquire new Swedish-built ships. It even provided companies operating in and around Gothenburg with loans and incentives to expand employment to mop up some of the excess labor released by closing yards. All this was part of a larger initiative of industrial assistance undertaken by the Swedish government: a program that administered nearly $12 billion in direct industrial subsidies and $4 billion in loans between 1971 and 1981.[15] Those billions were dispersed all over the country of just over 8 million people, underwriting employment and ongoing manufacturing projects, especially in historically important sectors like shipbuilding. For centuries, Sweden had been a proud maritime nation. No one wanted to see—much less preside over—the country's shipyards being boarded up.

It was with this specter in mind that Stockholm opened the spigots to public funds. In 1979, the year that the Vessel was constructed, the government subsidized shipbuilders to the tune of $747 million (in 1980 U.S. dollars), some $34,420 (more than $125,000 in today's dollars) per worker.[16] By some calculations, this meant that Sweden's government was contributing more to its shipbuilding industry than the total economic value that the industry was itself creating. In other words, for every Swedish krona the government spent on supporting shipbuilding, the total Swedish economy grew by *less* than a krona. It was as though the Swedish government were pouring money down a hole. Try as it might, Stockholm was unable to prevent the slow but steady creep of unemployment in western Sweden. The government of a small country, even a rich one like Sweden, could not single-handedly turn the tide on the global shipbuilding industry.[17] Subsidies were supposed to stimulate further growth—in the words of economists, to "prime the pump." In this, they failed utterly. The problem was that Swedish labor costs were simply too high; even as global shipbuilding began to recover in the late 1970s and early 1980s, the recovery primarily benefited producers with access to much cheaper labor, particularly in South Korea and Taiwan.[18]

By 1979, there was a growing chorus of sharp warnings about the uselessness and even the dangers of mounting government intervention in the face of market pressure. Three years earlier, the Swedish Central Bank had awarded University of Chicago economist Milton Friedman the Nobel Prize in Economics. Friedman was arguably the most prominent economic critic of interventionist policies, and in his address, delivered in Stockholm on the acceptance of the award, he issued a grim warning. "The present situation cannot last," he declared. "It will either degenerate into hyperinflation and radical change, . . . or governments will adopt policies that will produce a low rate of inflation and less government intervention into the fixing of prices."[19] As it was, government meddling—however well intentioned—was compromising efficiency and overall competitiveness. In so doing, it was endangering the whole economic system.

• • •

The *Balder Scapa*—the Vessel—was built in a state-owned facility, a direct product of Sweden's generous state assistance to shipbuilders: precisely the kind of intervention that Friedman deprecated.[20] Finnboda Varv was set against a rocky hillside on the south side of the Stockholm inlet, the main shipping channel that has served the city since the thirteenth century. The shipyard's cranes were less than two miles from the Royal Palace, and from Finnboda's pier, it was easy to spy the church spires rising over the old city, Gamla Stan. Stockholm—so close at hand—was a growing and dynamic modern capital, with an expanding commercial sector and tourist trade. The musical group ABBA, by then a global sensation, had just opened a state-of-the-art recording studio in the city. Yet at Finnboda, life could seem as though it was out of a bygone age.

Finnboda was a long-established, creaking concern. It had been producing ships—old steamers, warships, ferries, and freighters—since the mid-nineteenth century. Since then, the shipyard had a series of private owners. The last of these, Götaverken, bought the yard in 1974. Götaverken was a storied Gothenburg-based shipbuilder, one of the largest in Sweden. But as the whole industry slowly collapsed in on itself, in 1977 the government combined Götaverken with three other major shipbuilders into Svenska Varv, a state-owned umbrella company.[21] Everyone understood that deep cuts were inevitable. Svenska Varv's task was simply to make them as minimal and painless as possible. In the meantime, as Finnboda's employees anxiously waited for the ax to fall, they drew their paychecks from the state.

Even after state takeover, the shipyard harked back to an older style of Swedish industry whose traces were fast disappearing. There were four separate company dining rooms at the yard: one for manual workers, one for white-collar workers, one for senior officials, and a final one for executives, featuring cigars and bowls of fresh fruit. At the same time, there was also a company sauna, which was open to all: a holdover perk from a more prosperous time.

The bustling Finnboda Varv in 1974, perched on the edge of the Stockholm Inlet in Nacka. The spires of central Stockholm are visible at the far right of the photograph.

Even during those prosperous times, Finnboda's workers faced dangerous jobs with serious risks. The bottoms of ships' hulls were covered with lead paint, and the shipyard made liberal use of asbestos as insulation. Hearing loss was a chronic problem, as were health issues related to inhalation of noxious fumes. In 1978, doctors at the shipyard's health center—opened three years before—dealt with 2,228 patient visits by employees, including 396 eye injuries.[22] As Mikael Josephson, a welder at Finnboda in the late 1970s, recalled,

> It was a work environment where accidents occurred. We had learned that if we worked at height and dropped a heavy object, we would not shout. In that case, the risk was that someone standing under would look up and get the object in the face. A lot could happen.[23]

Josephson himself acquired a collection of scars left by welding sparks and, like many of his colleagues, needed to have iron chips removed from his cornea. Despite strong health and safety advocacy by the shipyard's union, accidents were common and job conditions were unforgiving. Outdoor work stopped only if the weather fell below -20 degrees Celsius (-4 degrees Fahrenheit). Despite, or perhaps because of, these challenges, people working at Finnboda took real pride in what they did and in what they made. Josephson remembers that when the stern section of a large tanker that he had worked on was finally finished, "I considered it one of the most beautiful things ever created."[24] It would also be one of the last things ever built at Finnboda. The shipyard produced its final ship in 1981, a victim to the reorganization and downsizing overseen by Svenska Varv.

It was in these conditions, over the first half of 1979, that the Vessel was welded together. It was one of two identical barges, internally referred to as Nybyggen ("Newbuilds") 408 and 409, for which engineers had drawn up plans the previous year.[25] Despite its later designation, Nybygge 409 (the Vessel) was produced first. New ships built in the Finnboda yard at this time were constructed out of a combination of Swedish, Norwegian, Finnish, Belgian, and Japanese steel, stored in the shipyard's sheet metal yard. The plates were lifted from the yard to the plate hall, where workers marked them with chalk and cut them with torches into pieces. These pieces moved on to the next hall, where they were assembled into sections by teams of men wielding welding arcs, their faces covered by heavy masks, sparks flying from the end of their tools. Outside, large cranes lifted the welded sections into place while welders joined them together to form the hull of the ship. Once the hull was formed, more workers sandblasted and painted it.[26] In the case of the Vessel and its sister ship, however, the hulls came into the yard partially assembled. The initial hull work had been done in another struggling shipyard owned by Svenska Varv, Öresundsvarvet, in the southern Swedish city of Landskrona, which received just under half of the money that Finnboda charged for the Vessel.[27] Svenska Varv (and, behind it, the Swedish state) sought to spread out what scarce contracts it could get.

Nybygge 409 was a simple vessel: a shell with neither a propulsion system nor a cabin to furnish. But it was, nevertheless, a working ship, one that required a battery of controls and verifications. Finnboda's engineers painstakingly carried out stability tests on the hull, producing reams of schematics and reports.[28] Building even basic vessels like the two taking shape at Finnboda Varv required a tremendous amount of knowledge and labor, not to mention a host of component parts. In the plans for the Vessel, preserved among Finnboda's archives, there are hundreds of technical drawings, not just of the overall shape of the ship's hull but also of the rudder, the pump room, the pipes running around the ship, the ballast lines in the tanks. There are no fewer than twelve pages listing the different valves and fittings

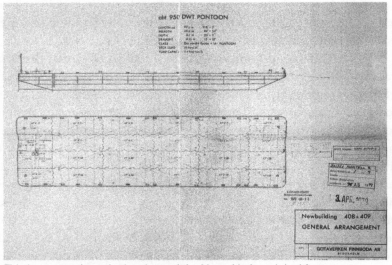

This is among the only drawings of the Vessel in its original form as a simple flat-bottomed barge. Copy of blueprints for the *Balder Scapa* and her sister ship, both simple pontoon barges, from Götaverken, August 16, 1978.

in the pump room, fifteen pages listing the various pipes in the pump room, and sixteen pages listing ballast lines in the tanks.[29] These pages of documentation—filed with the Swedish State's Ship Inspectorate (Sjöfartsverket)—are a remarkable historical archive. Not only do they demonstrate the capital and knowledge embodied in even a simple barge, they also reflect the scope of the state's involvement. They provide a vivid picture of how the Vessel came together, built by state employees at a state-owned facility, all under the watchful eye of state regulators.[30]

• • •

Yet if Nybygge 409 was a creature of the state, it was also a creature of international capitalism. Over 1978 and 1979, Finnboda set about procuring the many pieces of hardware necessary for outfitting an oceangoing craft. Doing so meant contracting with firms throughout Europe. It bought a 5,185-kilogram anchor from Schwermaschinenbau Ernst Thälmann, a manufacturer based in Magdeburg, East Germany.[31] The ship's winch, hydraulic pumps, and wire ropes each came from a different company in Norway. So too did its many lanterns. The paint used on the Vessel and its sister ship—costing nearly $100,000—was sourced from the Norwegian marine paint magnate Merethe Ring, who had started her career as a secretary in a paint factory.[32] Fixtures, including steel chains, rings, hocks, and swivels, came from Albrechtson-Hasse, a manufacturer in Gothenburg. Other chains came from a firm in Ljusne, 130 miles north of Stockholm on the Gulf of Bothnia. Finnboda bought a diesel motor for running the pumps and winches from R. A. Lister and Co., a machine works in Gloucestershire, England. It got bolt chain shackle from a Belgian subsidiary of N. V. Grosby, an American company headquartered in Woodbridge, New Jersey.[33]

In one of the most famous passages of *The Wealth of Nations*, first published in 1776, Adam Smith described the almost inconceivable magnitude of specialized labor that went into the manufacture of a simple woolen coat worn by a Scottish laborer. The coat was "the produce of the joint labor of a great multitude of workmen, [including] the shepherd, the sorter of the wool, the wool-comber or carder, the dyer, the scribbler, the spinner, the weaver, the fuller, the dresser."

But that was not all. To make the woolen coat, materials needed to be transported from some "workmen" to others. "How many ship-builders, sailors, sail-makers, rope-makers," Smith marveled, "must have been employed to bring together the different drugs made use of by the dyer, which often come from the remotest corners of the world!"[34] Smith's point was about the immense power of the division of labor to create the wealth of nations. Specialization was a funda-mental source of human progress and affluence. Only in a wealthy nation could a simple laborer afford something that required so much labor as a woolen coat.

What was true for the coat in the late eighteenth century was true for the barge two hundred years later, though on a much larger scale. The barge was the product of many specialized hands. There were welders and draftsmen, supervisors, and crane operators. There were also steelworkers, lantern makers, lightbulb manufacturers, wire pro-ducers, and mechanical engineers. The contract for the Nybygge 409 set in motion a wave of economic activity starting in the Nacka neigh-borhood of Stockholm that gradually rippled across interconnected markets: around Sweden, its neighbors in northern Europe, and over-seas. Building the barge depended on craftspeople, workers, traders, and seafarers. Like the woolen coat, the Vessel was a product of a set of interconnected markets; its existence depended on an integrated economy that spanned national borders.

If the production of the Vessel was connected to international capi-talism, its sale absolutely depended on it. The firm that commissioned the Vessel and its sister ship from Finnboda was a Norwegian shell company, Balder Barges I—or, in Norwegian, Balder Lekter I. The two contracts, each worth 11,200,000 Swedish kronor ($2.4 million at the time), were orchestrated and negotiated in April 1978 by Rutger Dehlin, a Swedish expat shipping agent based thousands of miles from the cold waters of Stockholm, amid the palm trees and pastel colors of Miami Beach. Dehlin had first connected Augustsson with Finn-boda's manager, and for his work as a middleman, Dehlin's fee came to 3 percent of the contract price: some 672,000 kronor (then about $160,000).[35]

Those funds came into Dehlin's account through a Miami bank. But Dehlin's company, Scandebo Shipping, was incorporated as a *sociedad anonima*—a limited liability company—not in the United

States but in Panama.[36] Setting up Scandebo Shipping as a Panamanian firm was an exercise in cost saving: a legal maneuver to avoid paying taxes in the United States. Businesspeople from anywhere in the world could set up a company in Panama without ever having to set foot in the country or conduct any business there. Because Panama only taxes income on a territorial basis, companies like Dehlin's that generated all their income outside the country paid no local taxes: no income tax, no capital gains tax, no stamp duties, no withholding taxes. As the leak of the so-called Panama Papers showed in 2016, this legal feature has long made the country a very attractive place to set up a shell company. Scandebo Shipping was just such a company. And so, to the extent that Dehlin's firm orchestrated its creation, the Vessel started out as a creature not just of international trade but of *offshore* international finance.

•   •   •

The company that purchased the *Balder Scapa*, Balder Barges I, belonged to the Balder Group (Baldergruppen), the commercial empire of one of Norway's highest-profile shipping magnates, Parley Augustsson. After growing up on a small farm on the coast of the North Sea, Augustsson made his way to the prestigious Norges Handelshøyskole—the Norwegian School of Economics. Upon graduation in 1962, he started work at Bergesen d.y., then one of the largest shipping companies in the world.[37] Augustsson's rise at Bergesen was vertiginous. Within five years, at the age of thirty, he became the company's director of shipping. As Augustsson tells it, six years later, the firm's head, Sigval Bergesen, agreed to appoint him as his successor. "We even had a glass of champagne on the deal," Augustsson recalls. Yet Bergesen was reluctant to finalize the deal, and in May 1974, Augustsson quit. With start-up capital of just 200,000 Norwegian kroner, (about $40,000 at the time) he hung out his own shingle.

The name he chose for his new company, Balder, was personal; it had been the name of a fishing boat worked (and partially owned) by his great-uncle.[38] At the same time, the name of Augustsson's company gestured toward sweeping ambitions. Balder (or Baldr) was a Norse god, son of Odin and Frigg, who was known both for having constructed a great ship, *Hringhorni*, and for being killed through the

sly scheming of the trickster god Loki. Like Balder, Parley Augustsson was responsible for building ships. Like Loki, he was a masterful
schemer. By the late 1970s, Augustsson's empire was rapidly expanding, thanks to a creative set of legal maneuvers. Augustsson was living
through an age of financial "innovation," in which financiers invented
new ways of creating wealth, largely without state oversight. And
Augustsson himself was a financial pioneer, specifically in the use of
limited liability, or K/S (*kommandittselskap* in Norwegian), partnerships. For each ship he acquired, the Balder Group would create a new
limited liability company to own it. Each company—of which Balder
Barges I was one—was owned in part by Balder, but typically by other
individual investors as well.

Augustsson's companies were attractive to investors because, under
Norwegian law, individuals could write off investments in Norwegian
shipping from their taxes. For the state, the policy was a way of sup-
porting Norway's own struggling shipbuilding and shipping industries,
akin to neighboring Sweden's industrial subsidies.[39] For taxpayers, it
presented a simple and entirely legal way to avoid paying taxes. Those
taxes were high: the marginal income tax for the top income bracket
in 1979 was 75.4 percent. Thanks to soaring oil prices and Norway's
booming offshore sector, money was surging into the country, transforming it into one of the richest in the world. Affluent Norwegians
like lawyers, doctors, and dentists (including one of Augustsson's best
friends) who were looking to circumvent the tax code understood
Augustsson's companies for what they were: shelters.[40] And though
many companies in Scandinavia and northern Europe offered limited liability investments in shipping, Balder became among the very
largest players in the field.[41] By the mid-1980s, the Balder group controlled seventy ships, collectively insured for nearly $450 million. It
did so through more than one hundred partnerships and subsidiaries,
with over fifteen hundred individual limited partners: dentists, doctors, and bankers who were happily investing in Norwegian shipping
and, in the process, paying less to the Norwegian state.[42]

The offshore oil and gas sector was a particular focus for Balder's
investments. Of the seventy ships that the group controlled, twenty-
six were oil field supply vessels operating in the United States, Canada,
the Netherlands, and the United Kingdom.[43] On top of that, Balder
entered into a joint venture with Chinese interests, involving the con-

struction of six offshore vessels in China.[44] The Vessel itself was commissioned from Finnboda with an eye toward North Sea oil.[45] These plans were reflected in the Vessel's first official name as a registered ship, the *Balder Scapa*. The first part of the name came, of course, from its parent company. The second referenced the Scapa Flow, a stretch of water in northern Scotland whose shores were fast becoming a hotspot for oil companies. As Parley Augustsson put it, the "*Balder Scapa* was a natural deal for us." Advised by the major shipbroker Furness, Augustsson had already ordered two similar barges to be built in Singapore, both to be used in "offshore oil exploration activities," and would commission another in Norway. For tax purposes, it didn't matter what kind of ship Balder invested in. But barges were particularly attractive; investing in them was a low-cost way of sidestepping into the offshore market, allowing the company to shift its holdings away from traditional shipping.[46]

The Vessel was thus officially designated as a transport barge, designed and earmarked for use in the offshore oil and gas industry. But by the time that Balder Barges I took possession of the ship, the market for offshore service vessels was slowing. Faced with a shortage of oil and gas contracts, the company began entertaining proposals from firms working in other sectors. In the late 1970s, Augustsson was approached by Scapa Flow Salvage, a Scottish company based in Perth, with a madcap idea to draw riches up from the depths of the North Sea. The riches in question were not oil or gas; they were, instead, tens of thousands of tons of high-quality steel.

*   *   *

More than six decades before, in late 1918, shortly after the end of World War I, the German fleet—some seventy warships strong—surrendered to the British Royal Navy in the Firth of Forth, near Edinburgh. Escorted north up to the Scapa Flow, the ships sat for month after month, still manned by their German crews, as peace negotiations slogged along in Paris. The German admiral in charge of the fleet, Ludwig von Reuter, knew that the talks were scheduled to conclude on June 21, 1919. Expecting that the Royal Navy would demand he turn over the entire German fleet as a war prize, the admiral prepared for the worst. When the twenty-first arrived, von Reuter

sent a message from his flagship, the cruiser SMS *Emden*, ordering
that the fleet be scuttled. Better the ships be at the bottom of the sea
than in the hands of the British, he thought. Out of contact with Berlin, he had not been notified that the talks in Paris had been officially
extended. The result was that on von Reuter's orders, German sailors
opened torpedo tubes and seacocks, quietly sending dozens of
warships—nearly the entirety of the country's modern fleet—to the
seafloor in just minutes. Von Reuter returned to Germany, where he
received a hero's welcome. His fleet stayed in Scotland, at the bottom
of the Scapa Flow. Most of the ships were salvaged over the next few
decades, but by the 1970s, some seven hulls still remained: a lure for
shipwreck hunters like those behind Scapa Flow Salvage and, by
extension, Parley Augustsson.

The Norwegian registration of the *Balder Scapa*, listing dimensions,
ownership, and place of construction. This is how the Vessel appeared in
the records of the Norwegian state. Note that Parley Augustsson's name is
associated with "Balder Lekter 1."

In the late spring of 1979, Balder took possession of the finished
barge in Stockholm and had it towed south, out of the Black Sea,
through the straits separating Sweden and Denmark, and up the western coast of Sweden to Norway.[47] Its first stop was Stavanger, a small
port city nestled on Norway's west coast, where it was officially registered as a Norwegian ship. There, in Stavanger, it was also fitted
with a custom-built wooden structure meant to provide shelter for
men working on the salvage operation.[48] Then, towed behind a tug,
it floated across the North Sea to Scotland. It arrived in Montrose, a
long-established trading center on the North Sea, in June. As the gate-

way to Britain's oil and gas fields, the small city of about ten thousand was the port of call for vessels servicing the industry's platforms off Britain's coast. Montrose was a boomtown and a waypoint. Within a week, the Vessel was back in motion, this time bound north for its namesake, the Scapa Flow in the Orkney Islands. Again hooked up to a tug, it made the nearly two-hundred-mile journey in thirty-three hours. The cost of moving the ship from Montrose up to the Orkneys was £8,200 (about $18,000). Added to the 215,000 Norwegian kroner (about $40,000) it took to tow the Vessel across the North Sea, the total expense involved in getting the *Balder Scapa* to the Scapa Flow was adding up. But for the Balder Group it was an investment. Balder's leadership expected to make real money off Scotland's coast, whether in the oil fields or off the long-lost remnants of the German warships.[49]

*   *   *

Augustsson and his Balder Group had agreed to partner with Scapa Flow Salvage to raise military-grade steel: that is, to undertake a very physical task. Yet from the very beginning, the Vessel at the heart of this story was equally a financial asset, one that allowed Augustsson and his partners to legally circumvent paying taxes.[50] For this purpose, it did not matter what the *Balder Scapa* contained, or what it did. The only thing that mattered was that it was a vessel registered in Norway. Arguably, it was worth more as a financial abstraction than as a concrete, working ship.

Lots of assets are worth more than their physical components. Money itself works on this premise. The value of a hundred-dollar bill obviously far exceeds that of the paper on which it is printed. The recent rise of cryptocurrencies and non-fungible tokens (NFTs) has provided even more extreme examples of assets that are inherently abstract, detached from the physical world. But there's another kind of financial asset: one whose financial value depends in some direct sense on an object's physical usability. Real estate is an example of this kind of asset. So too are commodity futures. The price of a future contract to deliver grain or soybeans or oil a year hence ultimately depends on the physical usefulness of grain, soybeans, or oil, even if it fluctuates because of speculation or risk. The Vessel was both kinds of assets.

In the first instance it had value because it was a working ship. But insofar as the barge was simply a mechanism for avoiding taxes, it was also an abstract object whose value had only a thin connection to its physical reality.

This dependence on abstraction would ultimately spell trouble for the Balder Group. Just a few years after taking possession of the Vessel, the company began a descent into spectacular collapse. Oil prices had stayed high for several years after the 1973 Yom Kippur War and were again boosted in 1979 by another political event in the Middle East, the Iranian Revolution. But as oil prices began to settle down after the 1979 shock, offshore activities all over the world fell off, and with them demand for service vessels. By 1984, it was becoming clear to investors that Balder's fleet was significantly overvalued, artificially inflated because of its status as a tax shelter. In 1985, Balder subsidiaries began to fold one by one. The next year, the key holding company in the Balder Group declared what continues to hold the record as the largest bankruptcy in Norwegian history. It was estimated that the whole group owed somewhere between $267 million and $400 million (in 1984 dollars, closer to $1 billion today), far more than the value of Balder's stake in its entire fleet of ships.[51] In the words of the receiver appointed by Norwegian authorities, "Parley Augustsson ran an extremely complicated organization." Though Augustsson took the collapse very hard, he was relatively insulated from its financial consequences. He had moved to London in 1983, claiming that Norway's regulations stifled the entrepreneurial spirit. But some observers came to believe that the move was a calculated step to protect his personal assets.[52] Auditors and, later, prosecutors would spend years conducting an investigation of Augustsson's alleged financial misdeeds. In 1990, they would indict Augustsson for, among other charges, "having willfully given incorrect or misleading information to investors." Found guilty on some charges and acquitted of others, Augustsson appealed all the way up to the European Commission for Human Rights.[53]

In 1979, when Augustsson acquired the Vessel, the most dramatic episodes in the unspooling of his Balder Group were still several years in the future, but there were already signs of instability. Balder Barges I was exactly the sort of limited liability company that was the basis of Augustsson's fortune. The firm emerged amid the wave of private "financial innovation" that swept through the late 1970s and early

1980s, crashing over state oversight and breaking down regulatory control of assets and markets. In this way, the Vessel's time as the Norwegian *Balder Scapa*—and concomitantly a shelter for Norwegian capital—portended later episodes in its life. Private-sector financial innovators were far from finished with the Vessel.

• • •

Back at Finnboda, managers were becoming increasingly concerned about when they were going to get their money from Balder Barges I. Already by November 1979, just months after Augustsson took possession of the Vessel, they worried that Balder Barges I was not in a financial position to pay what was owed for the second barge on order, the Vessel's sister ship, Nybygge 408. Augustsson reported that he was having difficulty securing a charter for the Vessel, either in Britain or in Norway. "The Situation regarding the BALDER SCAPA," one Finnboda report noted, "is gloomy to say the least."[54] Just weeks after Augustsson had the barge towed across the North Sea to Scotland, Scapa Flow Salvage declared bankruptcy. Its managers informed Augustsson that they were unable to pay a chartering fee. The company's divers had indeed located a wreck in the dark, frigid waters and pulled up some pieces of steel (one of which Augustsson kept on his deck as a memento), but hardly the quantities that had been imagined.[55]

Overall, the market for charters continued to weaken. In November, the local newspaper in Stavanger, Norway, reported that the Vessel had returned to the city from Montrose, towed back after an unpromising start.[56] It had cost Balder Barges I nearly $60,000 to get the barge to Scotland, but during its time there it was barely used. Because Augustsson's company did not collect its full fee from Scapa Flow Salvage before the British firm declared bankruptcy, the whole expedition had been a significant loss.

In short, Balder Barges I was in no position to take possession of the second barge it had ordered from Finnboda, even (or especially) after the delivery was slightly delayed.[57] In fact, almost immediately after signing a contract with Finnboda, Balder had run into difficulties meeting the payment schedule it had negotiated with Finnboda over the Vessel itself. By the terms of the contract, Augustsson's

company was to pay a lump sum of 3.36 million Swedish kronor
upon delivery of the Vessel and then an additional fourteen payments of 560,000 kronor every six months. Late payments were subject to interest charges: 4 percent over the Swedish Central Bank's
discount rate for the amortization, and 5 percent over the discount
rate for the initial 3.36 million Swedish kronor deposit.[58] According to Finnboda's accounts, by the end of 1979, Augustsson's company had not paid Finnboda *anything*: not the first of the fourteen
amortization payments, nor the lump sum that was originally owed
in cash. The interest charges were mounting. By December 1979,
seven months after the delivery of the Vessel, those charges came to
790,883 kronor.[59]

Augustsson's lawyers in the United Kingdom were (according to
Augustsson) busy trying to recover money from the bankrupt Scapa
Flow Salvage. If they could do so, Balder Barges I would at least be
able to cover interest payments on the 11,270,000 Swedish kronor
debt it owed Finnboda. If Augustsson could not pay, the struggling
Finnboda might have to repossess the barge at its own expense and
then look for another buyer. With everyone at Finnboda thinking of
layoffs and closures, the news landed particularly hard.

There were many advantages to Augustsson's strategy of arrang-
ing his business empire into discrete companies, one for each ship he
owned. His companies were shells, insulated both from one another
and from Augustsson himself. If one company defaulted on a debt,
the others would not be dragged down along with it. And indeed,
even as Balder Barges I teetered on the edge of default, Augustsson
himself was relatively protected. As an internal Finnboda document
almost ruefully put it, "Augustsson probably cannot be bound personally." It was his company Balder Barges I, not he, that was responsible
for debts to Finnboda. And "according to A[ugustsson]," as the Finnboda memo put it, "the company has no assets beyond the barge and
if it cannot be chartered, we cannot get any money."[60] Finnboda had
been, perhaps, a little too desperate for business, a little too cavalier
in its optimism. Its best hope now was for Balder to secure another
charter for the Vessel, which would at least cover the interest payments
on Balder's debt.

Late in 1979, Balder administrators reported the possibility of a three-month contract with Norwegian Petroleum Consultants (NPC), a consortium of oil companies, at a rate of 3,800 Norwegian kroner per day. Hoping for future payment, Finnboda's managers agreed not to repossesses the barge while it was chartered out, provided that Augustsson's company remit any profit it made (after insurance and operating costs), terms that Augustsson's representatives had proposed.[61] "This agreement," Finnboda's management stipulated to Augustsson, was "valid only if . . . [those] payments were punctually paid." And, as Finnboda's leaders underlined, they expected "full running information."[62]

As it happened, Finnboda received neither information nor payment, at least none that was preserved among Finnboda's papers. The contract with NPC did not pan out, but Finnboda executives did not learn that until later. In fact, it was not until March of the following year that executives at Finnboda learned that Balder had failed to make *any* money off of the Vessel.[63] By then, the barge was "in storage" along with two other ships owned by Augustsson's companies.[64] In May, Augustsson Telexed Finnboda communicating plans to charter out the Vessel in Høllen, on Norway's south coast, where it would be loaded with an oil derrick and then function as a "workdeck." The idea was to tow the barge the 130 miles (with the derrick on board) to Stavanger, in return for a fee of 2,000 Norwegian kroner ($450) per day.[65] At this point, Finnboda's leaders took a tougher line. They replied that "under the circumstances" and given the low daily rate, it was impossible to promise not "to make claims on the pontoon"— that is, to repossess it.[66] They were well aware that insurance alone on the barge ran to nearly 200,000 Swedish kronor ($45,000) per year, severely cutting into any profits Augustsson would remit to Finnboda.[67] It is not clear that Augustsson signed the contract. But in October, he once again wrote to Finnboda that there was another opportunity to charter the ship out, again at the rate of 2,000 Norwegian kroner per day.[68] Again, Finnboda's leaders replied that they could not "promise to refrain from legal actions during the period."[69] Shortly thereafter, Augustsson had the barge returned; it was simply costing too much to keep up and insure.[70] Augustsson had lost hundreds of thousands of dollars on the venture. But for Finnboda, the losses were arguably even greater. Finnboda had built two barges and lent one out for months on end, all without receiving payment. For a struggling shipyard on the verge of closure, the experience with Augustsson raised hopes but cost vast sums of money.

● ● ●

Augustsson's firm owned the barge for only a year and a half. In late February 1981, the *Balder Scapa* was back in Sweden exactly where it had started: at Finnboda Varv.[71] The return to the state-owned Finnboda and Swedish registry was perhaps a result of an overly optimistic public-private venture gone wrong, perhaps due to an overextension by the Balder Group, perhaps due to an unforeseen dip in the North Sea charter market.[72] One way or another, the Swedish state was the backstop for a set of risky private ventures. When financial innovation went wrong, it would be the state that picked up the pieces.

With the return of the Vessel to Finnboda's ownership in February 1981 came new monikers. The Vessel was renamed the *Finnboda 12*. Balder was out, Finnboda back in. Finnboda's managers had only recently given up hope of delivering the Vessel's identical sister ship to Balder Barges I.[73] Until then, it had been internally called the "Balder Floatell 1," but when officially registered in Sweden in 1981, it had the name *Finnboda 11*.[74] Well over a year after it was supposed to have been delivered, the Vessel's sister ship had not left the shipyard in the Stockholm inlet, costing both space and money. Now with the Vessel back from its abortive mission to Scotland, Finnboda was particularly eager to unload the barges. It ended up selling both at a substantial loss—some 4.3 million Swedish kronor (about $1 million at the time)—to a private Swedish company in March 1981. Another renaming soon followed.[75]

And so, after a flurry of name changes, transactions, and movements, the two barges were back together, this time under the ownership of a young Swedish company called Consafe Offshore.[76] Though Consafe was not owned by the state, like Finnboda it was a major beneficiary of state assistance aimed at propping up Sweden's struggling maritime industries. In the early 1980s, Consafe received hundreds of millions of dollars in low-interest loans from the Swedish government.[77] Certainly, its purchase of the Vessel entirely hinged on state support.[78] That support took several forms. The most obvious was that Consafe purchased the barges from a state-owned entity at an incredibly attractive price. When Finnboda sold the barge to Augustsson's Balder Barges I, the negotiated price had been 11.2 million Swedish kronor. According to papers filed with the Stockholm District Court, when Finnboda sold the Vessel and its sister ship to Consafe less than two years later, the price was just under 7 million Swedish kronor per barge: a 37.5 percent discount. A second way in which the state supported Consafe's purchase was through financing. Of the 7 million Swedish kronor that Consafe owed Finnboda for each barge, it only paid 1.4 million (20 percent of each ship's price) up front and then, just as Augustsson had done, negotiated a payment plan for the remaining 5.6 million.[79] And the Swedish state greased the wheels of these sales in a third way as well. Consafe took out a mortgage of 5.6 million Swedish kronor on each ship from Svenska Varv. But under a "credit guarantee" scheme meant to assist struggling shipbuilders, the Swedish government effectively assumed the risk of Consafe's default; it would guarantee the contract, providing Finnboda with the 5.6 million Swedish kronor in exchange for Consafe's debt.[80]

In the transaction with Consafe, the state was both the seller and the financier. Beyond that, it was the holder of all the risk. Consafe had borrowed from one arm of the state to buy ships from another. And if Consafe defaulted on its payments, a *third* arm of the state would step in to ensure that the repayments continued. The Vessel was back in private hands, but only because of the dedicated ministrations of the Swedish state.

. . .

As the Vessel took shape in Stockholm and plied the cold waters of northern Europe, it was embedded in a matrix of interactions between private and state actors. Though built with state assistance in a government-owned shipyard, its first owner, Parley Augustsson, was an archetypical international capitalist. But Augustsson's fortune—and the impetus to purchase the Vessel—in turn depended on a loophole in the Norwegian tax code. The business model of Parley Augustsson's empire of limited liability companies hinged as much on an arbitrary legal figment created by the Norwegian government as on the market for shipping.

At the same time, the Vessel also fell at the intersection of physical wealth and abstract finance. When Balder Barges I bought the Vessel from Finnboda, it did so with an understanding that the barge's value stemmed not from its status as a valuable object—a piece of tangible capital—but rather as an abstracted financial one. Yet the physicality of the Vessel turned out to be of vital importance. Balder bought the barge on credit. To service its debts, it needed cash. Unable to secure further loans to make its payments, Balder Barges needed to charter the Vessel out to operators in the North Sea. It needed, in short, to actually *use* the Vessel as a working ship. Its failure to do so spelled disaster. Notably, it resulted in the ship's returning to an arm of the Swedish state deeply concerned with materiality: Svenska Varv, the state-owned holding company established to protect the country's shipbuilders.

The tension between private financial abstraction and public material production served as a backdrop for the Vessel's peripatetic movement offshore between the Baltic and North Seas. In fact, its very existence depended on two key features of the late 1970s and early 1980s, which might be summarized as state-backed supply and private financialized demand. The Vessel was constructed, or supplied, by an interventionist state scrambling to address national industrial decline. At the same time, the demand for the barge—the reason that there was a contract for it in the first place—was driven by the sort of abstract "financial innovation" that underpinned the boom in global finance for the rest of the decade. Private and public, national and international, abstract and concrete: the Vessel was all of these at once from the moment an engineer first touched pen to paper to work on its blueprints.

CHAPTER 2

THE NORTH SEA

	The Vessel	The Sister Vessel
1981	The *Balder Scapa* is sold back to Finnboda and returns to Sweden, where it is reregistered. The Vessel is renamed the *Finnboda 12*. It is then sold to Consafe Offshore.	The Sister Vessel is renamed the *Finnboda 11* and is registered in Sweden. It is then sold along with the Vessel to Consafe Offshore.
1981–1983	Consafe renovates the barge in Gothenburg, Sweden, adding an accommodation block, and renames it the *Safe Esperia*.	Consafe renovates the barge in Gothenburg, Sweden (ending in 1982), adding an accommodation block, and renames it the *Safe Dominia*.

I n late 1978, several months before the last piece of the *Balder Scapa* was welded into place at Finnboda, Lorraine Henderson traveled from Britain to western Sweden. There, with great fanfare, she smashed a bottle of champagne against the hull of a brand-new vessel at a Götaverken shipyard in Gothenburg. The vessel that she christened, the *Safe Astoria*, was not really a ship but instead a floating platform: the first "accommodation platform" ever to be purpose-built. The idea behind the *Safe Astoria* was simple: to create a floating structure loaded with stacks of standardized shipping containers modified into living space. The *Astoria* was billed as a "floatel," a construction that could house hundreds of the oilmen who built, maintained, and worked on the offshore rigs floating on the North Sea.[1] Henderson came to the Götaverken yard because of the economic transformation of the North Sea. She was married to a senior construction manager at the British unit of Chevron, the American company that had already agreed to lease the new platform. Inviting her to do the honor of christening the *Astoria* was a nice gesture aimed at pleasing an important client. So too, perhaps, was the very name *Astoria*, a word that evoked both British and American grandeur.

The owner of the *Safe Astoria* was Consafe, a rising star of Swedish industry and the same company that would soon purchase the Vessel and its sister ship from Finnboda. Consafe's rapid growth and surging profits stemmed from its canny navigation of two developments that completely upended the global economy in the decades after the end of World War II—developments that were reflected in the *Safe Astoria* itself. The first was the containerization of global shipping. The second was the spectacular growth of offshore oil drilling. By the early 1980s, Consafe had become a major player in both container shipping and offshore oil. Its plans for the Vessel involved bringing the two sides of its business together. Under Consafe's ownership, the Vessel would become a very unusual container ship: one explicitly designed for service in the oil fields of the North Sea.

•   •   •

Shipping containerization was the brainchild of the self-made American trucking tycoon Malcolm McLean in the 1950s. Its real boom started after McLean convinced the U.S. military to use containerized shipping for its logistical operations in Vietnam, which entailed the shipment and handling of hundreds of millions of dollars of goods. The idea to transport the world's freight in standardized interlocking steel boxes revolutionized global trade.[2] Containers streamlined the processes of loading and unloading vessels at ports. Rather than having to handle irregularly shaped cargoes individually and by hand, by using containers, longshoremen could quickly and efficiently load goods and transfer them between vessels, trains, and trucks without ever unpacking them. Speed and efficiency depended on the proliferation of new physical objects: standardized boxes made from corrugated steel, huge cranes with booms that stretched a hundred feet from the dock, and purpose-built railcars and truck hookups. They also depended on massive new port facilities built around the world—from Long Beach to Busan, Port Elizabeth to Felixstowe. Together, this infrastructure shrank the costs of transporting goods to a fraction of their former size.

In this process, standardization and scale were vital. Standardization was—and is—what makes containerization work. Everywhere around the world, shipping containers are the same width, the same height, and one of two standard lengths. They are designed to stack one on top of another; they snugly fit together, secured with simple interlocking hardware located on each corner. Every shipping container will fit neatly on a container ship, on a truck made for containers, or on a train bed. A dockside crane will reliably fit every container that passes through a port, regardless of the cargo or the departure city.

Standardization is a marvel, but it is also a phenomenon that people take for granted until they feel its absence. During the world wars, the fact that British and American screws had slightly different threads caused untold headaches for Allied crews assembling and repairing all the goods that were built in the United States but deployed in Europe.[3] Trains across Europe used to run on different gauged tracks; when passengers crossed a national border, they were often obliged to transfer to an entirely different train carriage. In the 2020s, the lack of standardization in gauges between old Eastern Bloc and western European countries posed real difficulties for organizing freight rail shipments into and out of wartime Ukraine.[4] Shipping containers, by contrast, are remarkably standardized: not just in a country or region, but worldwide.

That global standardization, in turn, has enabled global scale. Trade—especially long-distance trade—rewards bigness. A shirt produced by low-paid factory workers in Bangladesh with Chinese equipment and American cotton will cost an American consumer much less than one specially woven by an artisan or even manufactured in a high-wage factory in the United States.[5] Long and integrated supply chains let producers take advantage of the lowest-cost materials and the lowest-cost labor. Put another way, globalization spawns ever larger and more integrated markets. Larger and more integrated markets in turn enable greater division of labor.

The division of labor is fundamentally related to market size.[6] When the production of a commodity is broken down into constituent parts, producers can specialize and thereby more efficiently produce each part, bringing down the cost of each finished unit. Large supply chains stretching over multiple continents allow businesses to divide labor and devote themselves to highly specialized work. In short, such long supply chains make shirts very cheap to produce. A long supply chain entails a lot of shipping. And here, too, scale matters immensely. Bigger shipments, bigger ships, bigger ports: all help lower the unit cost of commodities produced and consumed around the world. Containerization allowed for operating at unprecedented scales, massively expanded supply chains and ever larger and more integrated markets. In short, it facilitated and drove globalization. Today, nearly every consumer good in the world is transported or touched by the shipping container, from shirts to mugs, keychains to high-end perfume.

In the 1970s, as now, the economic logic of containerization hinged on reducing cost margins: the bigger the container ship, the lower the average cost of transporting each individual container. By the late 1970s, new ships had capacities of three thousand TEU, that is, three thousand "twenty-foot equivalent units," or twenty-foot containers. By today's standards, these ships were small—the largest container vessel operating in early 2023 had a capacity of more than twenty-four thousand TEU—but the container ships of the 1970s were still significantly larger than previous ocean freighters.[7] A bigger ship taking fewer trips meant savings on fuel, wages, and logistics. To maximize profits, shipping lines scrambled to acquire ever larger vessels; it was for this reason that shipyards flourished in the 1960s and 1970s, buoyed by a tide of new orders.

• • •

Christer Ericsson had ridden that surging tide. A former first mate in the Swedish merchant marine, in 1971 Ericsson pioneered a nylon strap to replace the unwieldy and dangerous chains that were used at the time for loading and unloading shipping containers and other cargo. The company he founded to promote it, Container Safe J C Ericsson (shortened to Consafe because of Telex abbreviations), was an immediate and spectacular success.[8] Containerization contributed hugely to the boom-to-bust swing in shipping that ultimately devastated Sweden's shipyards in the 1970s, but for Ericsson, containerization was simply the motor of fortune. In Sweden, as elsewhere around the world, global trends produced winners as well as losers. With his nylon straps, Ericsson literally undergirded the shipping container business. In the late 1970s, he began dealing in shipping containers themselves. Offering simple used and then increasingly specialized "furnished modules," Consafe became a major player in the world of maritime business. By the early 1980s, Ericsson was a major investor in shipping companies themselves.[9] By the middle of the decade, he was one of the richest people in Sweden.

Ericsson was a self-made man, and he actively projected his identity as a successful entrepreneur. The title of his 1987 memoir was *Head-on: My Enriching Life with Consafe*, with the word *rich* strategically underlined. Ericsson was also a loud critic of Sweden's big-state approach to governance: a defender of private enterprise and initiative. While at sea, he had met all sorts of people. And almost all of them—even the "passportless people who have nowhere to go," even the sailor who read Marx—shared the dream of becoming their own boss.[10] It was this dream that Ericsson himself acted on in founding Consafe and building it out from his dining room to ever larger offices, driving to meetings in an old Volkswagen. But though the dream of entrepreneurship was powerful, the big state was constantly getting in the way.

Ericsson's memoir is a book that drips with bile. Newspapers don't give him a fair shake. Bankers are duplicitous. Leaders at Svenska Varv are "rude" and "elusive." Volvo's management is underhanded. But Ericsson reserved his harshest words for politicians defending Sweden's socially progressive taxes. The memoir's epigraph is a blistering screed about Sweden's tax system. "I cannot understand," it reads, "why the Swedish tax system favors that which requires the least work effort and which is least useful to society." Income from tips, he points out, was not taxed; gains from stock market speculation were taxed at 40 percent, but "the person who starts a company, develops new products, exports and gives employment to thousands of people is of great benefit to society. If you earn a million kronor after this great effort, the tax will be over 100 percent."[11]

As in Parley Augustsson's Norway, in Sweden Ericsson faced a tax system that collected vast sums from top earners to fund an increasingly expensive welfare state. In addition to personal income taxes that topped out at 85 percent, Ericsson was responsible for taxes on his ownership of a highly profitable company. As Consafe grew, he often owed more in taxes than his take-home pay. This infuriated him. In fact, the whole idea of "tax planning" infuriated him: it was "a cancerous tumor on society" that inhibited the creation of economic value.[12] Ericsson campaigned for his beliefs, appearing on television and in newsprint. He was a high-profile organizer of the so-called October 4th movement, which saw more than one hundred thousand businesspeople march in protest around the country. The movement's 1983 and 1984 manifestations against the Social Democratic government's tax program amounted to the largest demonstrations in Sweden's history.[13] Ericsson well understood that he could offshore profits. Indeed, by registering some of his holding companies overseas, he did just that. But, at least in his own telling, Ericsson was committed to keeping his ships Swedish, hiring Swedish seafarers, and staying in Sweden himself. "If only I didn't think so damn much of my country," he declared, "I should have moved to London."[14]

And so, he paid Swedish taxes and built a fortune off the global offshore, all from his hometown of Gothenburg. Gothenburg had long been a center of overseas commerce. Founded by the Swedish King Gustavus Adolphus in the early seventeenth century as a fortified outpost for trading during the Thirty Years' War, the city was largely settled by merchants from the allied Dutch Republic. As Sweden's only major port on the North Sea, Gothenburg grew into a thriving mercantile hub; its quays and shipyards formed the beating heart of the city's commercial core. By the 1970s, it handled the bulk of Sweden's incoming shipping.

From his office in Gothenburg, Christer Ericsson was witness to the shifting winds of global commerce, but he also overlooked an emerging center of a second major economic transformation of the 1970s. For Gothenburg was a hub of the North Sea oil and gas sector: the same sector that had inspired Parley Augustsson's investment in the Finnboda barges.[15] While Sweden itself does not border the oil-producing regions of the North Sea, the country emerged as a center of offshore technology by servicing nearby oil producers whose output was booming. In neighboring Norway, oil production grew from virtually nothing in 1970 to more than 25 million cubic meters by the end of the decade. British oil production spiked from a few million cubic meters in 1975 to almost 150 million ten years later. By the mid-1980s, the UK was producing about as much oil as Iran or Kuwait does today. Sensing that North Sea oil could furnish enormous profits, Consafe's leaders changed the focus of their corporate strategy. As

Ericsson put it later, "We saw enormous possibilities for expansion when the industrialized countries began to discuss how they could become independent of the oil from the Arab states."[16]

• • •

The notion of drilling for oil and gas hundreds of feet below the sea was a wild idea, and one whose execution depended on a number of technological marvels. On land, the process for drilling for oil is simple enough. Crews bore into the earth's crust, taking care to line the resulting hole with new sections (or joints) of piping. To simplify matters, when the drill hits a deposit of oil, crews cap the well and install an electric or gas-powered pump that creates the suction needed to draw oil up the piping. The process is much more complicated and costly offshore. There is a perpetual risk of oil leaking out into the ocean, or water leaking into the drill hole. Pumping oil hundreds of extra meters up through the sea requires more energy. And, of course, the conditions of both drilling and extracting offshore are much more challenging. There is a major difference between trying to drill a hole into the Texas dirt and trying to drill a hole into an ocean floor through hundreds of feet of murky water, all while floating on the high seas, buffeted by gale force winds.

Those conditions meant that the cost of offshore extraction is (and was) very high compared to drilling in the California scrub or the deserts of the Middle East. But the oil shocks of the 1970s, all caused by political unrest and violence in the Middle East, made wells in the North Sea significantly more attractive to investors and Western oil companies. Thus, at the same time that the oil crises were wreaking havoc on shipbuilders across northern Europe, they were breathing vitality into the region's energy sector. State-led initiatives in Norway and Denmark suddenly became phenomenally lucrative, the basis for massive sovereign wealth funds. For the same reasons, major petroleum multinationals clamored to work in Danish, German, or British waters, despite the relatively high prices of local labor and of oceanic extraction.

The first oil well was drilled into the floor of the North Sea in 1964. Even in the 1950s, it was well understood that there were extensive petroleum reserves beneath the ocean, but extraction technology was not sufficiently advanced to make North Sea oil an attractive proposition. As importantly, the jurisdiction over deep-sea oil extraction was by no means clear. The legal murkiness had just begun to clear up in 1964. That year, the United Nations Convention on the Continental Shelf came into force, expressly stipulating rights of sovereign states over the continental shelves that lay adjacent to their coastlines. The convention defined the continental shelf, in the first instance, as "the seabed . . . adjacent to the coast . . . to a depth of 200 meters."[17] The North Sea is a relatively shallow body of water; the vast majority of it is well under two hundred meters in depth. Therefore, after the convention, the sea—along with all the oil and gas underneath it—was divided up among the countries that ringed it, the different national economic zones demarcated by straight lines on a map. That was in theory. In practice, partitioning the sea was not an easy task; the boundaries between national sectors were only resolved after a series of legal cases decided by the International Court of Justice in 1969.[18]

Still, well before those judgments came down from The Hague, it was clear that because of its geography the United Kingdom would come away with the largest sector of the North Sea's bed, ultimately figured at 95,300 square miles. And the British government wasted little time in issuing lucrative concessions for oil and gas extraction within its sector. It did so, first and foremost, to the state-controlled British Petroleum (BP) and the Anglo-Dutch conglomerate Shell. But it also issued concessions to major multinationals based outside of Britain, including Mobil and Chevron, the firm that agreed to lease Consafe's first offshore accommodation unit, the *Safe Astoria*.[19] From the get-go, Britain's offshore petroleum industry depended on partnerships between the state and (private) big oil and gas.

British oil production skyrocketed over the course of the 1970s, from virtually nothing at the beginning of the decade to more than 80 million tons in 1980. The year after that, Britain became a net exporter of oil for the first time in its history and a net energy exporter for the first time in decades, since its days as a coal-exporting giant decades before.[20] Though British heavy industry as a whole was struggling and unemployment was rising, thanks to the bounty under the North Sea the UK was once again becoming an energy powerhouse. But whereas the source of Britain's previous energy boom—coal—had been central to the country's popular identity, oil was not. Oil took far less labor to produce. By the 1980s, the country's oil and gas industries employed only about sixty thousand people, compared with hundreds of thousands of coal miners, who held very visible strikes throughout the 1970s and 1980s. Coal miners were unionized and politically organized, employed by a nationalized industry that had deep and evocative roots in British history. Oilmen were not. Because of the streamlined process for extracting oil, Britain's relatively few oilmen were contract workers employed far from population centers, largely by private multinationals like Shell and Exxon. They were not the stolid men who labored underground in the darkness of the pits. Instead, they were cowboys, roughnecks, and roustabouts accustomed "to the kind of icy winds that blow across the North Sea."[21] Although the lives of oilmen were dramatized as well paid and dangerous, the British oil and gas sector would never rival coal as a source of employment, nor figure so large in the national imagination.

As the journalist Tabitha Lasley has described them, the men of the oil industry were like detached and hard-living soldiers, or mercenaries, drawn from depressed parts of Britain by the lure of wealth.[22] Work was constant for two or three weeks at a time, with marathon shifts that lasted fifteen or more hours. Grime, dirt, sweat, and hair clogged the showers. After helicopters delivered them onto rigs, the men—and they were nearly all men—were surrounded by the sea.[23] "There was a tranquility," the longtime offshore electrician Bob Ballantyne noted. "But you could also look at the whole thing as a prison. You couldn't go anywhere. It was very regimented . . . you were not a human being. You were a 'bed.' "[24] It was, as he put it, "industrial apartheid."[25] Isolation was part of life. Dennis Krahn, an American transplant in Aberdeen, vividly recalled his first storm on a North Sea rig. "Just as far as you could see on a clear day, the wind blowing sixty miles an hour and rows and rows of forty-to-fifty-foot waves coming in. And that's when you suddenly say this is a really powerful place and it's not a place to trifle with because it's just waiting for you to make a mistake."[26]

Oilmen worked offshore. But they were also offshore workers. As veteran David Robertson recalled in a thick Scottish brogue, "We didn't come under the law." Health and safety was often a joke, administered by the same government department that was responsible for meeting production quotas; "it was a conflict of interest." The British Health and Safety at Work Act, which governed workplaces across the UK, did not apply to rigs more than twelve miles from land. As Robertson put it, "The protections under law that an ordinary worker had in a factory in Aberdeen did not apply to a guy who worked . . . on a semi-submersible offshore. That was a problem." It was also, per Robertson, an injustice. Because workers received their paychecks onshore, they were responsible for paying taxes. The law reached them; it just did not protect them.[27] Still, oil was lucrative; people working on offshore rigs could bring in double or even triple what they could make on land.

Oil was also a major source of capital for multinational corporations, especially in Britain. In Norway, the state nationalized the industry from the beginning of offshore extraction. In Britain, the state was also involved. The nationalized British National Oil Corporation (Britoil) had a statutory option to purchase half of newly discovered oil fields, and it exercised this right to great advantage. However, Britoil had to pay market rates. That is, even though it operated with an edge, it was still in competition with a host of private companies. And those companies were also given inducements to operate in the UK. Most importantly, they paid a petroleum revenue tax only after all their original investments had been recouped.[28] For energy multinationals, investing in the British sector of the North Sea was a safe bet.

Oil and gas were lucrative not just for big corporations but also for the British state and the British economy as a whole. For these reasons, the state actively promoted the production of oil through the nationalized and highly profitable Britoil. As importantly, in the 1970s, the government required that oil produced in the British sector of the North Sea be landed in Britain, and it pushed private firms to refine the oil within the country.[29] When Margaret Thatcher was elected in 1979, the UK's energy sector was flourishing. The contrast with the rest of the British economy was stark. The unemployment rate was well over 12 percent as old industries—steel, coal, and manufacturing—collapsed. The people who flocked to the difficult life of offshore oil work were often people who were wryly called "Thatcher's Children." They came largely from economically depressed areas like northeastern England, widely understood to be forgotten by the Conservative government in London. Offshore jobs did not come close to replacing those lost to deindustrialization. But the jobs that did exist were highly remunerated: nice work if you could get it.

• • •

As oil field after oil field was discovered, explored, and mapped in the North Sea, Consafe shifted the focus of its business away from nylon straps and toward offshore hydrocarbons. It was a move that mirrored a wider pivot in states bordering the North Sea, from heavy industry to oil. Working with state-owned shipbuilders in Gothenburg and financed by attractive loans from the Swedish state, Consafe began acquiring a small fleet of vessels meant to build, support, and service offshore oil extraction. Like Parley Augustsson's Balder Group, Consafe set up a host of shell companies to own its vessels, some of which were registered offshore. In this way, "each rig would be able to live its own legal life."[30] These ventures facilitated very rapid growth.[31] In 1980, Volvo, Gothenburg's largest employer, spent $1.5 million for a 30 percent stake in Consafe. It was a shrewd investment. When Volvo sold its stake four years later, it did so for forty-four times what it paid: some $66.4 million.[32] Consafe had taken off like a shot. By 1983, the company's fleet had grown to eighteen ships and it operated offices in more than a dozen countries. It would come to employ 610 people.[33]

In no small part, Consafe's story was that of Gothenburg itself. Certainly, the firm's rising oil-fueled fortunes buoyed those of the city as a whole. After the collapse of the container ship and tanker markets in the 1970s, Gothenburg's last remaining major shipyard, Arendal—owned by the state-run Svenska Varv—substantially shifted production to offshore platforms and support vessels. By the time Consafe acquired the Vessel and its sister ship in 1981, the shipyard was producing major oil rigs destined for British, Norwegian, and Mexican waters. As the *Financial Times* put it, "Arendal's breakthrough into the offshore market . . . is one of the factors currently generating renewed confidence in Gothenburg."[34] Consafe was a major client of Arendal's, having already placed six important orders with the shipyard. Indeed, Christer Ericsson himself enjoyed a heroic status in Gothenburg, a fact loudly acknowledged by the region's governor.[35] "To a large extent," the *Financial Times* pronounced at the time, "Gothenburg has to thank one man, Mr. Christer Ericsson, for the offshore breakthrough . . . he was the first to detect the market for offshore accommodation platforms."[36]

To open and operate offshore rigs, oil companies needed specialized equipment and the labor and expertise of thousands of oilmen. But they also required cheap, mobile, and temporary housing in which they could accommodate offshore workers: the tens of thousands of people who built and staffed rigs. Consafe set out to meet this demand with mobile floating hotels—also called "floatels" or "coastels"—to be leased by oil producers. Much like the technology behind Christer Ericsson's original nylon strap, the technology behind these new vessels in Consafe's fleet was not particularly sophisticated; they were effectively shipping containers mounted on some floating platform. Simple though they were, they had to be built somewhere, and demand for them kept shipbuilders employed.

The *Safe Astoria*—the craft Lorraine Henderson christened in 1978—was the first of a growing fleet of Consafe accommodation platforms and vessels built in Gothenburg. Their construction represented significant projects for failing Swedish yards—so significant that when the second one was completed at the Arendal yard, the queen of Sweden herself christened it.[37] These platforms were expensive to build—tens of millions of dollars apiece. As demand for offshore accommodation continued to surge in the early 1980s, Consafe's managers sought cheaper ways to provide offshore lodging.

This is how the Vessel and its sister ship became "accommodation vessels." Beginning in 1981 and lasting until 1983, the two barges would each be transformed—*obyggt* (rebuilt), in the language of the former's ship certificate—through substantial refits. The two ships were upgraded from humble barges to accommodation ships, floating hotels that could house hundreds of people.

Such retrofits had long been envisioned, if not actively planned. In late 1979, Parley Augustsson claimed that a "conversion was always in the picture," that there had been an informal understanding between him and Finnboda's leadership that the two ships might be converted to be "residential barges." On this, an internal Finnboda memorandum grudgingly noted that "one can perhaps admit that A[ugustsson] is partly right."[38] After all, when the Vessel's sister ship was under construction in dry dock, it had been known as the *Balder Floatell 1*. Certainly, after Augustsson took possession of the Vessel and experienced difficulty chartering it out, he called for Finnboda to refit the *Balder Scapa* and the *Finnboda 11* as residential barges as a way of tapping a new market. "In our opinion," he wrote, "this is the only possibility to be able to secure interest and repayment of the outstanding loans."[39] By that time, however, Finnboda's management was fed up with Augustsson. They dismissed his calls for refit at an *additional* cost of nearly 40 million Swedish kronor. "You have not fulfilled the contracts on either barge," they wrote. The answer was no.[40] Nevertheless, the notion of converting the barges into accommodation vessels still held appeal. In fact, Finnboda had already entered into negotiations with another potential partner over possible contracts to build "residential pontoons" (*bostadpontoner*).[41] That partner was Consafe.

· · ·

Ultimately, the renovations of the Vessel and its sister ship did not take place at Finnboda, but rather at the Von Tell Nico shipyard in Gothenburg, closer to Christer Ericsson's base of operations.[42] The refits amounted to total reinventions. Both ships entered the yard as simple barges and left as the next generation of coastels, equipped "for comfortably housing . . . 300 men."[43] There were generators and pumps added, improved safety measures, new electrical systems imported from Norway. Most strikingly, the two barges were each installed with multiple levels of modular accommodation units as well as units that housed galleys, gathering spaces, squash courts, and a swimming pool.[44]

The work in Gothenburg involved sourcing a wide range of "first class materials to be used by builder."[45] The fact that the barge would house *people*, as opposed to cargo, necessitated a raft of new improvements, starting with a new custom-designed aluminum gangplank (*Landgång*).[46] There would be a substantial new air-conditioning plant, freshwater generators, "hot dip galvanized" external stairs, a PA system, a telephone exchange with sixteen extensions, television and radio sockets. There were life buoys, new hydraulic mooring winches, a crane. Von Tell Nico ordered doors and ceiling boards made by a local company in Gothenburg.[47]

Much of this equipment needed certification to ensure that it was up to Swedish safety codes. Assuring the comfort and security of three

hundred "guests" in a coastel was an entirely different (and significantly more involved) matter than assuring the safety of a few crew
members or operators working on a cabin-less barge. Fire extinguish-
ers from the Swedish Foam Extinguishing Company had to be evaluated and tested, as did the steel used in new bulkheads and steel doors.
So too did the new "Halon 1301 Fire Extinguishing Total Flood System."[48] The three types of fire-resistant polyester used on the Vessel's
sofas and chairs had to be approved by the Swedish Textile Research
Institute.[49]

In reconstructing the Vessel and its sister ship in Gothenburg, Consafe brought together the two key components of its business: containerization and offshore oil. The refit turned two barges into container
ships, even if nontraditional ones, that would be deployed around
offshore rigs. In doing so, modularity was key. Nearly everything in
the deckhouse was to be standardized, in keeping with the logic of
containerization. Each "sleeping module" was to have:

> double bunk 2000 x 800 with 4 lockable drawers
>   (0.06 m3 each) and flame retardent [sic] spring mattresses.
> 2 lockable wardrobes 500 x 600 x 1900 mm . . . with shoe
>   shelf, hat shelf and coat hanger.
> 1 table 500 x 700 mm with 2 chairs.
> 1 bookshelf 600 x 250 mm.
> Newspaper net over each bunk.
> Bed curtains and window curtains (non combustible).

Each "toilet/shower module" would have a noncombustible shower
curtain, soap holder, toilet paper holder, coat hook, towel holder, mirror, and small cabinet.[50]

The accommodation decks themselves were constructed from pre-
fabricated units: what the plans for the refit referred to as "Type 1" and
"Type 2" modules. Type 1 modules were slightly modified standard
shipping containers: "Standard 20 ISO Cont[ainers]."[51] They were
used for the one-person cabins that would house the crew. Type 2
modules were a little larger. These were used for multi-person cabins,
showers and toilets, the galley and laundry area, as well as the store-
rooms. Like the Type 1 containers, they were interchangeable building
blocks. "The structural strength of the modules . . . [was] high"—

high enough for them to be approved for stacking by both Lloyd's Register and Norske Veritas.[52]

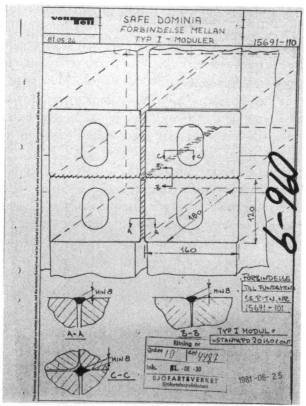

The superstructure of the Vessel and the Sister Vessel were converted shipping containers. Here, the modularity of the "accommodation units" is clearly visible.

•   •   •

That last clause was of vital importance, and a reminder that though the barges would be part of the offshore oil industry, they were inescapably creatures of international shipping. Det Norske Veritas (DNV) and Lloyd's Register were two of the world's preeminent classification societies: the private organizations that set international maritime standards and inspect and certify the world's shipping.[53] Without the signoff of a classification society like DNV or Lloyd's on almost every aspect of construction and outfitting, a ship is uninsurable. With-out insurance, a ship is functionally inoperable: the financial liability of an accident makes using an uninsured vessel prohibitively risky. Besides, certification is a prerequisite of registering a ship in any coun-try around the world, whether in Sweden, the United States, Liberia, or Panama. As a result, Consafe engineers were acutely alive to stan-dards set and administered by classification societies and were in con-stant contact with DNV agents. As the Vessel and its sister ship were refitted in Gothenburg as coastels, Consafe contracted with DNV to inspect and guarantee that the new equipment—the bulkheads, the modular units, the fire extinguishing systems—were up to interna-tional standards.[54]

The history of classification societies like DNV tracks the history of global trade itself. As overseas commerce picked up in the early mod-ern period, European shipowners sought to hedge their risks. Long voyages, whether to West Africa, North America, or the East Indies, were dangerous. Cargoes were lost, ships captured or destroyed. Early on—in the seventeenth century—spreading around the risk of such ventures happened fairly informally. In London, investors, merchants, and sailors would meet at Edward Lloyd's Coffee House in the heart of what is now the city's financial district to swap news, secure fund-ing, and negotiate insurance.[55] In 1760, a group of businessmen who frequented Lloyd's began collating information useful to insurers and underwriters, into a book that eventually became known as *Lloyd's Register*. The register graded ships. Hulls were evaluated on their soundness, using vowels in descending order from A through E and I to O. Equipment on board was judged to be of G[ood], M[iddling], or B[ad] in quality. Such information, standardized and accessible in a single collated resource, became vital for the insurance market; insur-ers simply would not underwrite voyages without consulting it.[56]

Lloyd's Register responded directly to the needs of the insurance market. It was not—nor has it ever been—an official government organ. Nor are any of the other major classification societies (includ-ing DNV) that popped up in trading centers around the world over the following decades; all have been private bodies. Collectively, clas-sification societies became a mechanism by which the market self-regulated. If ships were deemed unsafe, they simply became too risky to insure. If they were too risky to insure, they were too risky (and expensive) to operate.[57] Today, there are nearly seventy organizations claiming to be classification societies, though 90 percent of the world's shipping tonnage is classed by one of the eleven large societies that belong to the International Association of Classification Societies (IACS). By providing "a technical framework for safety" and providing inspection services, these private organizations effectively regulate the world's oceangoing vessels.[58]

In so doing, they perform roles traditionally reserved for states. There are compelling reasons for this. The government of a country might not be well positioned to guarantee a ship's seaworthiness. A single ship might be constructed in one country, sold to an owner in a second, registered in a port in a third, and insured by a company based in a fourth. In the shifting world of international shipping, it is useful to have an international standard, administered by a neutral arbiter. Classification societies are neutral, at least insofar as they are supranational. They are creatures not of one state or country but of international capital. They exist because of the economic incentive to insure shipping, the demand for maritime insurance translating to a market for professional evaluations of ships. Classification societies are integral to the modern maritime world. Even international standards negotiated and promulgated by the United Nations and its administrative bodies—the Safety of Life at Sea Convention of 1974 (SOLAS), for instance—rely on classification societies to act as inspectors and arbiters.[59] The product that classification societies offer is the strength of their guarantee, one that crosses borders and transcends national sovereignty. It is a guarantee that is founded on the universal power of the insurance market and of financial risk itself.

In the case of the Vessel, that guarantee had originally come from Det Norske Veritas, a 120-year-old classification society based just outside Oslo. As Finnboda's engineers designed the Vessel, they were in regular correspondence with DNV to ensure that plans and construction adhered to the society's standards.[60] DNV surveyors visited Finnboda Varv to inspect construction and installation. The certificates they issued—not only for the ship itself but also for its anchor, its lanterns, its winches, and many other pieces of equipment—were absolutely essential. Without them, the Vessel could be neither registered nor insured. And to keep hold of its certification, the Vessel would need to pass inspections every five years.[61]

• • •

As the Vessel and its sister ship were renovated into coastels in Gothenburg under the watchful eye of DNV observers, they grew in value. Consafe had purchased the Vessel from Finnboda for 7 million Swedish kronor. After the refit, Consafe took out a new mortgage on the Vessel for several times that: some 40 million Swedish kronor ($7 million).[62] Once transformed into coastels, the two barges were again renamed, rebranded with a reference to their new owner. As with all Consafe vessels, the first word of the names would be "Safe," part of the firm's own name and an evocative word in English, the lingua franca of global business. The Vessel itself became the *Safe Esperia* and its sister ship (formerly the *Finnboda 11*) became the *Safe Dominia*. During its time at the Von Tell Nico shipyard, the *Dominia* was fitted with a slightly smaller living area than the *Esperia*; it had four levels of containers to the *Esperia*'s five.[63] The two sister ships, originally identical, now had different profiles, different weights, and (slightly) different capacities.

For the five hundred or so people they were each intended to house, quarters on board both of the new accommodation vessels would be tight and spartan. The ships' sleeping modules were designed to lodge two men (women were not expected to work on oil rigs), who would sleep on bunk beds and share two chairs upholstered with the flame retardant fabric, as well as wardrobes, a desk, and a bookshelf—all "fabricated of PVC . . . coated steel plate." The barges were also equipped with some creature comforts. Each bedroom had its own bathroom and shower; there was a library and a dining room and several bars.[64] The Vessel, now the 327-foot *Safe Esperia*, had its own generators, air-conditioning units, freshwater production units, and an "incinerator system to take care of sewage and garbage." So too did the *Safe Dominia*.[65] The ships were thus outfitted to allow crews to operate autonomously, even when far offshore.

In Consafe founder Christer Ericsson's words, each vessel was "a big shoebox on a barge."[66] More precisely, they were *many* boxes on a barge. Like Ericsson's original innovation of the nylon strap, Consafe's accommodation vessels emerged directly from the containerization of global trade. As their blueprints make clear, they were simply standard shipping containers welded together into living units.[67] Those units

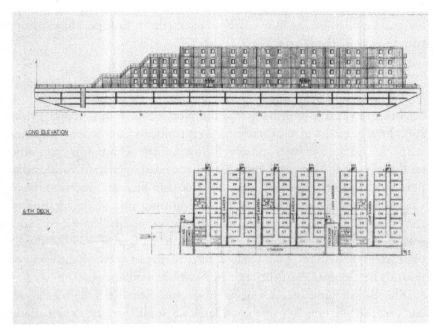

Architectural drawings of the *Safe Dominia*

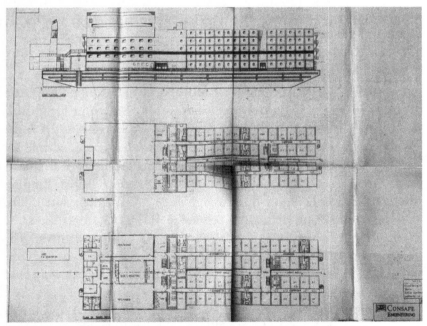

Architectural drawings of the Vessel as the *Safe Esperia*. Note the modular converted shipping containers that make up the Vessel's structure.

were to be filled by the new cowboys of northern Europe: the offshore roughnecks of the North Sea.

· · ·

Six hundred and fifty miles across the North Sea from Christer Ericsson's headquarters in Gothenburg, in an office in Liverpool, another corporate executive was closely following the changing economic landscape of offshore oil. Derek Bibby, the head of Britain's bulk shippers' association, knew all too well that his business interests were shaped by the river of hydrocarbons pumping out of the depths of the North Sea. Bibby's own family shipping company, the Bibby Line, was on the knife's edge of financial disaster. In fact, it was the threat of imminent disaster that pushed him to invest tens of millions of pounds in Consafe, and through it, North Sea oil and gas.

The Bibby Line was a storied Liverpool firm. It traced its roots back to 1805, when John Bibby, Derek's distant forebear, a self-made shipbroker in Liverpool, bought a share in four small sailing ships. One of them, the 186-ton *Eagle*, transported 237 enslaved Africans from present-day Cameroon to Jamaica.[68] The early Bibby was wildly successful. By 1821, John Bibby & Co. operated several vessels operating between Britain, the Mediterranean, and South America. In 1830, John Bibby himself was killed in suspicious circumstances. He was purportedly accosted by highway robbers on his way home from a board meeting, but his body was found miles away from his normal route and the cash he had been carrying was still on his body. Some devious scheme was long suspected, but the case has remained cold for nearly two hundred years. Despite his demise, the Bibby Line flourished, growing in Liverpool alongside the expanding British Empire. By 1865, its fleet had grown to twenty-three vessels. In the late 1880s, it began a passenger and cargo service to Burma. Around the same time, it landed the first in a series of contracts with the British army to transport British troops to postings overseas, a service that it continued until the 1960s.[69] By the 1980s, it was the oldest privately held shipping firm in Britain.

The Bibby Line's history tracked Britain's commercial and imperial fortunes, thriving and expanding in the long nineteenth century when Britannia ruled the waves. In the mid-twentieth century, it faced challenges along with the rest of the British merchant navy. Bibby had responded to containerization by investing in new massive ships, including both container vessels and supertankers. Under the helm of Derek Bibby, who in 1969 became the seventh man in his family to run the business, the firm's revenues grew dramatically, from an annual profit of about £5.5 million in 1971 to nearly £30 million in 1976.[70] Then came the collapse in freight charges in the late 1970s, which forced the company to sell six of its twenty vessels in 1978. That year, as the Iranian Revolution forced oil prices skyward and fuel shortages bedeviled drivers around the world, the company posted a pretax loss of over £13 million.[71]

Like Consafe's Christer Ericsson, Derek Bibby was a larger-than-life entrepreneur. Also like Ericsson, he sensed the importance of pivoting to oil and gas. In fact, he pivoted to Consafe itself. In 1982, the same year that the Vessel underwent renovation in a Gothenburg dry dock, the Bibby Group bought a Scottish oil engineering firm and a 20 percent stake in Consafe. Thanks to the acquisition of vessels like the *Safe Astoria*, *Safe Dominia*, and *Safe Esperia*, Consafe had rapidly become a major player in North Sea oil and gas. Investing in Consafe was a way for Bibby to diversify its portfolio. It was a wise move in the context of the debilitating shipping rate wars of the 1970s. By doing so, the line could still capitalize on its long-established maritime expertise, while pivoting away from its traditional shipping business and toward new global maritime services: accommodation, ship management, and consulting.[72] This was a different, new, and more abstract kind of British invisible export: not shipping, but shipping *services*. Through Consafe, Bibby would be especially able to provide such services to big oil.

Servicing offshore oil rigs was a profitable investment for British firms as much as it was for Swedish ones. Just as in Sweden, the decline of shipbuilding and the rise of offshore oil were changing the economic landscape in the United Kingdom. There, shipbuilders in once-bustling industrial cities like Liverpool, Newcastle, and Glasgow clamored for state protections akin to those furnished by Sweden.[73] Just as in Sweden, the shipbuilding trade in the United Kingdom had struggled in the 1950s and 1960s but was boosted by a surge of orders for container ships and tankers. Just like their Swedish counterparts, British shipbuilders gradually lost ground to Asian competitors that

drew on lower-wage labor forces and more modern shipbuilding technology. As in Sweden, the oil shock of 1973 brought the simmering
crisis to a boil. And just as in Sweden, Britain's left-leaning Labour
government intervened, bowing to pressure to save jobs in reliable
political strongholds in the industrial north. In 1977, it nationalized
thirty-two shipyards—97 percent of the country's shipbuilding capacity. Just five years later, half of those shipyards had shuttered. The
vacant lots became exemplars of Britain's declining industrial fortunes
and its struggle to adapt to a new global economic reality. The great
yards of Newcastle, Glasgow, Belfast: the producers of dreadnoughts,
the battleships of World War II, and even the RMS *Titanic* were
demolished or closed down. Many of the shipyards that remained
open did so by shifting their production toward offshore facilities to
be used in the North Sea.[74]

Historically, the interests of British shipbuilders neatly lined up
with those of British shipowners. What was good for one segment
of the maritime industry was often good for the other. But in the
mid-1970s, British shippers greeted state aid for the shipbuilders with
trepidation. The reason was, again, overcapacity. Derek Bibby, as the
head of a partnership comprising many of Britain's bulk shipping
companies, noted that the continued "intervention of governments
in their shipbuilding industries" would lead to overcapacity in their
merchant fleets.[75] Too many ships would chase too few shipments.
Bibby's was the basic insight offered by laissez-faire economic thinkers for hundreds of years: a state subsidy that helped one group might
wreak havoc on another. The danger was pronounced for all British
shippers, but especially for those that had invested in supertankers.
With the pricing shock caused by Middle Eastern oil suppliers, oil
shipments fell off and those tankers suddenly became extraneous. As
freight rates collapsed, many shipping firms were pushed to the brink
of bankruptcy.[76] Bibby sensed that it was time to pivot. He was right.

In the 1970s and 1980s, many British Conservatives looked back
fondly to a bygone imperial age before the cataclysm of World War II:
an age in which British shipping, British credit, and British capital
seemed to bind the world together. But it was becoming increasingly
clear that the golden age of the British merchant navy and the great
shipyards of northern England and Scotland had passed. The sun was
setting on the British Empire. As Derek Bibby understood, to turn a

profit in a new postcolonial world, British maritime prowess would need to find other outlets. For many observers, it was increasingly plausible that the North Sea oil boom could be just such an outlet. In fact, Britain's economic performance under Margaret Thatcher's Conservative government greatly depended on the increased extraction of fossil fuels from the bottom of the North Sea. State oil revenues—some £70 billion between 1979 and 1987—helped support unemployment payments and took the edge off a disintegrating manufacturing sector and rising joblessness.[77] At a time when public spending was consistently less than £50 billion per year, these sums were hugely significant. For the British state and the country as a whole, North Sea oil offered a much-needed economic lifeline.

· · ·

It was not just that Britain was in imperial decline, if not a postimperial slump. The whole global economic order was in flux. The same forces that were bearing down on Sweden's shipbuilders were squeezing American steelworkers and British coal miners. In wealthy countries around the world, industrial jobs were disappearing. Service-sector jobs—often less stable and less secure—were only fitfully emerging to replace them. From the perspective of Liverpool, Gothenburg, and countless other industrial cities in wealthy countries, it seemed as though physical, productive work was slipping away, moving offshore.

To a large degree, it was. Manufacturing and heavy engineering jobs were moving south and east, to parts of the world with much lower labor costs. In northern Europe, even the most successful new industry, oil, relied on the literal offshore. Old sources of stability were eroding and new opportunities arising. As the booming offshore oil sector set off a cascade of spending around the North Sea, established firms like the Bibby Line and new start-ups like Consafe alike maneuvered to get in on the action. With global shipping in a slump, both firms were eager to explore new opportunities, to pivot away from their traditional business models.

The rise of offshore oil and the decline in shipping: the Vessel was caught in the eddies produced between these two movements. But the Vessel was equally a *product* of both the global shipping business and the international oil industry, a barge meant to be modular and flexible and also entirely offshore. It was a container ship, but one designed to house humans in unforgiving conditions. In short, it could accommodate almost anyone almost anywhere.

But though Bibby invested in Consafe as a way of moving into the British energy sector, it would be years before an oilman would set a boot aboard either the newly refitted Vessel (now the *Safe Esperia*) or its sister ship, the *Safe Dominia*. The two ships would very soon become instruments of a British geopolitical resurgence, but not in the North Sea. They were instead destined for the South Atlantic.

CHAPTER 3

THE SOUTH ATLANTIC

	The Vessel	The Sister Vessel
1982		The *Safe Dominia* is reregistered in Jersey and then transported to Stanley in the Falkland Islands, where it serves as a barracks for British troops under the name COASTEL 1.
1983	The *Safe Esperia* is acquired by the Bibby Line and reregistered in the United Kingdom. It is transported to Stanley in the Falkland Islands, where it serves as a barracks for British troops under the name COASTEL 3.	
1985	The Vessel is renamed the *Bibby Resolution*.	The Bibby Line buys the Sister Vessel outright and renames it the *Bibby Venture*.

Late on May 20, 1982, under the cover of an overcast night, a fleet of ships carrying five thousand British commandos steamed toward four deserted beaches on a rocky island in the South Atlantic. The landing group approached slowly and under radio silence. The troops on board girded themselves for what was to come. Their commander, Brigadier Julian Thompson, predicted that the next few hours would "NOT be a picnic," but he had " 'absolute confidence' that the operation underway would succeed."[1] Thompson was right to be confident. In the early hours of the morning, British troops surged ashore with no resistance. Commandos skirmished with an enemy unit on a nearby hill, but by daybreak the unit had withdrawn, and the British had secured their beachheads. Supplies streamed in from ships anchored just offshore.

May 21, 1982, marked the beginning of the British land campaign to retake the Falkland Islands, an intense three-week fight between the United Kingdom and Argentina. When the British invasion force debarked near the remote settlement of San Carlos, the Falklands had been under Argentine control for seven weeks. Though the Argentine defenders expected a British assault, the landing took them by surprise. For days, the Royal Navy had bombarded positions sixty miles away, on the other side of the island, leaking false information about a "large combined operation" near the islands' chief settlement and administrative center, Stanley.[2] Still, just hours after the landing, Argentine forces counterattacked, breaking the typically quiet calm of East Falkland. That day, Argentine air force squadrons from the mainland destroyed the Royal Navy frigate HMS *Ardent*; over the next three days, the Argentines sank a second frigate and damaged six other British ships, losing forty-three aircraft in the process. On May 25, a patriotic holiday in Argentina, Argentine commanders intensified their attacks, sinking the destroyer HMS *Coventry* and a freighter carrying supplies.[3] But by then, British forces had secured a foothold on the islands. Two days later, they began their march to Stanley.

The next two weeks passed quickly. By June 11, the British force was nearing the city. After losing ground from two nighttime attacks on fortified hills around the city, beleaguered Argentine defenders called a ceasefire on June 14. Later that day, British troops entered Stanley and accepted the garrison's surrender; eleven thousand Argentine troops surrendered the day after that.[4] So ended the Falklands War. After two and a half months of fighting, 255 British and 649 Argentine servicemembers were dead. The episode was a brief but bloody encounter fought largely as an exercise in political theater. It was also the impetus that would bring the Vessel out of the North Sea and into the South Atlantic.

• • •

The story of the British recapture of the Falkland Islands, evocatively dubbed "Operation Corporate," was nothing if not dramatic.[5] Seized on at the time by a patriotic press in the United Kingdom, it filled the British news with jingoistic slogans and heroic images recalling military exploits of the past.[6] Yet as British forces cleared the islands

of Argentine soldiers, the drama of combat gave way to more pro-
saic questions about what would come next. There was widespread
agreement in London that a substantial British force had to remain
in the Falklands to guarantee that the Argentines would not simply
return. But garrisoning thousands of British soldiers and airmen on a
rocky island thousands of miles from the nearest friendly port posed
major logistical challenges. Near the top of the list was the issue of
where British servicemembers—some of whom had heroically "liber-
ated" the islands—would sleep. It was a real question. When the war
broke out, the Falklands were inhabited by fewer than two thousand
people. That number was dwarfed by the thousands of soldiers, sailors, marines, and airmen who would have to stay on the islands after
the war ended.[7]

Time was of the essence. Britain retook Stanley in June, in the
midst of the Southern Hemisphere's winter. Construction on permanent accommodations would have to wait for the warmer months and
even then would take considerable time and resources. But with tem-
peratures hovering just above freezing, there was tremendous pressure
to secure durable housing as quickly as possible. The army set about
erecting modified Portakabins—modular and portable buildings like
those used on construction sites—but living in such temporary accommodation was rough going.[8] What was needed was mobile, modular
housing that could be quickly transported across thousands of miles
of open ocean. To provide it, the British Ministry of Defence—like
the Thatcher government as a whole—turned to the private sector. It
turned, in particular, to a young Swedish company with strong British
connections: Consafe.

It was thus that just a few months after British troops raised the
Union Jack over Stanley, the Vessel and its sister ship—still called the
Safe Esperia and the *Safe Dominia*—came to be moored in Stanley
Harbour. For several years, the ships were key island landmarks, even
prominently featured on an official Falklands Islands postage stamp.
On the stamp, published as part of a 1987 set commemorating the
work of the Royal Engineers, the Vessel is pictured in the middle distance, third ship from the front; its sister ship sits more prominently
in the foreground. The two barges, along with another accommodation vessel seen just to the left of the *Safe Dominia*, were meant to be
temporary. But as the stamp makes clear, they dominated Stanley's

skyline. They were home to far more people than the permanent settlement just barely visible at the top left of the image. Liminal as it was, the Vessel became an imposing presence.

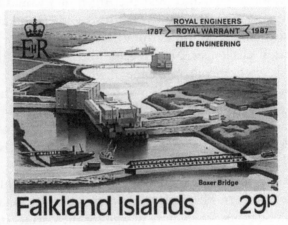

The three large vessels, from front to back, are the *Safe Dominia*, the British-built *Poursuivant*, and the *Safe Esperia*. The ships dwarf the small buildings of Stanley, clustered at the top left.

• • •

The Falkland Islands—Las Islas Malvinas, in Spanish—lie in the Atlantic about three hundred miles east of Argentina's Patagonian coast, about 750 miles north of Antarctica. The archipelago, some eight thousand miles from Britain, has been under British control since 1833: a strategically placed but far-flung imperial outpost. In 1832, Charles Darwin had stopped on the islands while sailing on *The Beagle* and commented on how barren and remote they were. Reflecting on the few settlers living there, he noted, "What a life of misery these men appear to us to lead!"[9]

By the 1970s, the Falklands had become a relic of the British Empire, home to about eighteen hundred islanders and six hundred thousand sheep. In London, the Foreign and Commonwealth Office was eager to wash its hands of the distant lands. There was a proposal circulating to formally cede the islands to Argentina, which claimed them, but to continue administering the archipelago on behalf of the residents. However, when the idea was pitched to the Falklanders themselves in 1980, it met with determined resistance. The islanders were fiercely patriotic and dead set on remaining British subjects.

The Falklands barely made it onto London's strategic radar before 1982. When they did receive consideration, in 1981, it was because the Ministry of Defence, struggling to meet the Thatcher government's goals of trimming expenditure, had announced that the HMS *Endurance*, a Royal Navy ice patrol vessel stationed in the Falklands and tasked with intercepting Argentine intelligence, was to be recalled to Britain and decommissioned.[10] It was a relatively minor announcement, though one that would prove to have major consequences. The military junta governing Argentina understood the decision to withdraw the ship—not entirely without reason—as a sign that British policy makers were no longer invested in controlling the Falklands. In January 1982, Argentina's leaders began planning an invasion.

For both the Argentines and the British, the Falklands War was a calculated exercise in rousing nationalist sentiment. The leaders of both countries were keen to shift attention away from disastrous economic conditions and political crises at home and toward what they imagined would be dramatic and stirring military victories. A short war and quick victory relatively far from home might not resolve basic economic problems, but a burst of patriotic flag-waving could do wonders for shaky political legitimacy.

Such was the calculus of Argentina's leaders, a group of generals who had been running the country since seizing power in a 1976 coup. By early 1982, Argentina was in serious economic trouble. Unemployment was climbing, and inflation hovered at nearly 200 percent.[11] Amid rising economic uncertainty and pain, the junta of generals in Buenos Aires faced increasing pressure to restore at least confidence in its leadership, if not economic prosperity. Whereas Ministry of Defence mandarins in 1980s London looked to slash budgets in the face of fiscal hardship, Argentina's leaders doubled down on military action as a powerful, if temporary, distraction from such difficulties.

Argentina's economic woes were not unique. Globally, the 1980s were a time of economic turmoil. In fact, Argentina was just one of many developing countries hit hard by the series of global economic shocks in the late 1970s and early 1980s that had so rocked the shipping industry. First came the "oil shock" of 1979—a contraction of global crude oil production due to the disruption of the Iranian Revolution and subsequent Iran-Iraq War. As during the oil crisis caused by the Yom Kippur War six years before, the so-called second oil crisis resulted in a sharp spike in energy prices, gasoline shortages, and rationing throughout the Global North. In the poorer Global South, the situation was more serious. As crude oil prices effectively doubled, prices for basic goods soared, squeezing household budgets to the breaking point.

To make matters worse, while the effects of the oil crisis were cascading around the world, the United States was tightening its monetary policy in an effort to face down mounting inflation. Under Paul Volcker, the Federal Reserve raised short-term interest rates to levels that today seem hard to believe. In May 1981, they topped out at over 16 percent. By comparison, when the Fed raised interest rates to fight inflation after the coronavirus pandemic, the short-term interest rate stayed well under 6 percent. For relatively poor and cash-strapped countries like Argentina—countries then commonly deemed "developing"—the one-two punch of skyrocketing oil prices and high global interest rates was devastating. Countries in eastern Europe and Latin America had little choice but to pay higher prices for imported oil, but they lacked the economic resources to do so. Desperate to maintain their energy imports, they turned to overseas lenders to secure the necessary capital. But to finance their dependence on foreign oil, they faced historically high interest rates. In short, policy makers in Latin America were squeezed between the oil and the Volcker shocks.

Since the 1976 coup, Argentina's Central Bank had (relatively successfully) tempered inflation by pegging the Argentine peso to the U.S. dollar and borrowing funds overseas to finance the country's large fiscal deficit. When the generals had taken power, inflation was over 1000 percent a year; by 1980, it had fallen below 100 percent— still a massive figure, but significantly lower. The problem was that the peg was artificial; the real value of the peso continued to fall against foreign currencies, a problem the Argentine government faced again in the early 2020s. And with rising foreign interest rates, the program of overseas borrowing that allowed the central bank to maintain the peg simply became too expensive. The central bank devalued the peso in 1981, and in order to meet its mounting debts, Argentine authorities turned to printing more money. A return to major inflation was the inevitable result.[12]

To a much greater extent than the United States and other wealthy Western countries, which also confronted rising prices during the period, Argentina faced devastating consequences from high inflation. Argentina had to import far more of its basic goods than large economies like the U.S., or even Britain. And a falling currency meant that all those goods became massively more expensive for Argentine consumers. Moreover, because Argentina's debts were denominated in dollars, as the peso lost value those debts only grew, scaring investors and prompting the state to print even more money, in a vicious and destabilizing cycle.

Caught in a global economic morass, Argentina's leaders desperately needed to change the narrative, to break the descent into uncertainty and panic. They needed a win. It was with this in mind that the generals in charge of the country fell back on their particular area of expertise: war. The Malvinas, long claimed by Argentina as part of the country's sovereign territory occupied by British imperialists, presented a tantalizing opportunity to shift attention away from domestic economic failures. The islands were so close, and so poorly defended. And after the British Ministry of Defence announced plans to withdraw the HMS *Endurance* from Stanley Harbour, it seemed highly unlikely that British policy makers valued the islands enough to stop Argentina from simply taking them. The result was Operation Rosario, a lightning strike meant to be painless and bloodless. It was an invasion designed for symbolic, rather than material, value. It was also a calculated risk: the islands were too remote and too economically unimportant for London to push back. Or so, at least, Argentine war planners thought.

• • •

Operation Rosario was a stunning success. Under the cover of darkness on the night of April 1, 1982, eighty Argentine commandos in rubber boats quietly paddled toward the coast of East Falkland. On a nearby beach, ten Argentine divers, dispatched from a submarine anchored offshore, were marking out a landing zone for amphibious vehicles.[13] By the early hours of the next day, the commandos had reached their objective: the single barracks for British marines stationed on the islands. They found it abandoned. The sixty-eight British men who were normally garrisoned there had all been pulled out, deployed to defend the airstrip and the islands' capital. The orders from the British marine commander were to inflict what limited damage they could to the overwhelming invasion force: to give the enemy "a bloody nose." Around 6:30 in the morning, the bulk of the Argentine assault troops began landing on the beach marked out by the divers. By 8:30, they had captured the islands' main airstrip with no casualties. Minutes later, seven Lockheed C-130 Hercules transports touched down from mainland Argentina, carrying the better part of an infantry regiment.

The seat of British authority in the Falklands was the so-called Government House, a tidy whitewashed stone building overlooking Stanley Harbour. It was here that the remaining British forces holed up, exchanging fire with the Argentine soldiers over the course of the morning. But when armored personnel carriers mounted with larger guns arrived from the landing zone, the British governor, Rex Hunt, had little choice but to surrender. At around 10 a.m. local time, the Union Jack was lowered over Government House. Argentina had captured the Falklands in a matter of hours, taking fewer than ten casualties and inflicting not a single casualty on the islands' residents or defenders.[14]

In London, the invasion of thousands of Argentine troops into British-controlled territory set up a high-stakes decision for British Prime Minister Margaret Thatcher. To retake the Falklands would entail a logistically difficult and costly military campaign, conducted in winter conditions, about two weeks' voyage from home. In addition to the thousands of lives it would put at risk, it would drive up government spending, rather than cut it back, as Thatcher had promised to do. And for what? In the early 1980s, the only real industry on the islands was sheep farming, and even this was barely profitable. On the other hand, for the so-called Iron Lady to bend the knee to a military dictatorship in South America was politically unthinkable. For most of its history as an independent state, Argentina had been at the edge of Britain's "informal empire"—a region in which Britain wielded outsized economic and political influence. For decades, Argentina was not a geopolitical rival, but rather simply where Britons got their beef. For many of Britain's conservative stalwarts, to turn the other cheek to Argentine aggression would have amounted not just to a public humiliation, but also to a formal admission that the sun had finally set on the British Empire. Even without the history of Anglo-Argentine relations, the invasion was an affront. As Thatcher announced to Parliament the day after the invasion, "For the first time for many years, British sovereign territory has been invaded by a foreign power."[15] There would be no negotiated peace. From a political standpoint, the decision to mount an expedition to retake the islands was simple.

Like the junta in Buenos Aires, the Thatcher government was in serious political trouble in the lead-up to the Falklands War. By the end of 1981, Thatcher's approval ratings among British voters hovered around 25 percent. She had become the least popular prime minister in the history of modern polling. Though inflation in Britain was down from where it had been a few years earlier, unemployment remained persistently high—well above 10 percent. Shortly before Argentina invaded the Falklands, the Conservatives, Labour, and the Liberal-SDP Alliance were essentially all neck and neck in national polling. It seemed as though Thatcher's days in Number 10 Downing Street were themselves numbered.

All that changed in the spring, when British forces triumphantly cleared the Argentine conscript army from the Falklands. In early May, a British nuclear submarine sank the Argentine ARA *General Belgrano*, a World War II–era cruiser, killing 323 people. The loss of the cruiser drove Argentine authorities to withdraw ships, including an aircraft carrier, operating around the Falklands, effectively forcing their aircraft to operate from mainland bases hundreds of miles from the islands. Still, shortly after the loss of the *General Belgrano*, Argentine fighters sank the HMS *Sheffield*, a British destroyer. But soon after that came the British landing at San Carlos, the dramatic march to Stanley, and the victorious re-hoisting of the Union Jack over Government House. Britain had successfully defended an outpost of its empire and had secured a striking victory, even if the gains were more symbolic than material, just as they had been for Argentina ten weeks before.

With triumph in the South Atlantic, Thatcher became, overnight, politically untouchable. The dramatic victory—which political commentators dubbed the "Falklands Factor" in British polling—doubled her approval rating to over 50 percent by the summer of 1982. Thatcher had delivered an emphatic victory, one that harked back to

imperial glories, and that Conservatives wasted little time in depict-
ing as a turning point in national decline.[16] "We have ceased to be a
nation in retreat," Thatcher jubilantly declared at a Conservative rally
at the Cheltenham Racecourse on July 3, 1982. Leading the crowd in
"rejoicing" at the success in the Falklands, she reminded Britons that
they did so "not as at some last flickering of a flame which must soon
be dead . . . Britain found herself again in the South Atlantic, and will
not look back from the victory she has won."[17]

The victory in the South Atlantic had little to do with the government's economic policies; if anything, thrift in national defense
spending had helped precipitate the crisis. But Thatcher was quick
to link decisive and brave action in one arena with decisiveness in
the other. In the speech at Cheltenham, Thatcher told the crowd that
striking railroad workers were being unpatriotic, that such action
"didn't match the spirit of these times." She also noted that the government had "abjured" printing money. The nation would not stand
for "that disreputable method" of "taking money from our people."
"That too," she noted, "is part of the Falklands Factor."[18] Thatcher
and her allies stretched the retaking of Stanley into a political platform
that somewhat incongruously linked imperialism in the South Atlantic with fiscal conservatism in Great Britain.

· · ·

The linkage was particularly tenuous because imperialism itself was
not cheap. By the middle of 1982, Britain had successfully reasserted
its imperial presence in the South Atlantic, but it faced the prospect
of garrisoning around four thousand British soldiers in inhospitable
circumstances eight thousand miles from home.[19] Doing so meant
signing a raft of new military contracts, including with the Vessel's
owner, Consafe. The British military was not a client that Consafe's
leaders had considered when they refitted the Vessel and its sister ship
as accommodation vessels in Gothenburg. But it was a client with a
problem that Consafe was uniquely qualified to solve. The logistics
required for delivering an accommodation unit from Europe to the
South Atlantic were quite similar to those required for delivering a
unit to an offshore oil rig in the North Sea or the Gulf of Mexico, tasks
with which Consafe had considerable experience. Defense of the old

British Empire would depend on the newly emergent international offshore energy sector.

In late October 1982, the Ministry of Defence finalized plans with Consafe and its British partner and part owner, the Bibby Line, to lease the Vessel's sister ship, the *Safe Dominia*, to house British soldiers.[20] North Sea oil—the sector for which the two barges had been built and outfitted—was booming, but so too was British defense spending, and the ministry made Consafe an offer it could not refuse. As part of its agreement with the British military, Consafe would make several further modifications to the *Safe Dominia*, which had just finished receiving its upgrades in Gothenburg. Most notably, it would add 400 beds to the 540 that had already been installed on board. Such refits were expensive, but the Ministry of Defence had few options when it came to securing ready-to-use accommodation that could be delivered an ocean away in just a matter of weeks.

Bibby, on behalf of Consafe, would arrange transport for the *Safe Dominia* to Stanley in the hold of a converted supertanker, called a "heavy-lift ship." As thousands of gallons of water filled ballast tanks on the lift ship, the ship would slowly settle further into the sea until its deck lay submerged below the *Safe Dominia*. The lift ship would then pump out its ballast tanks, loudly rising up to the surface so that the barge—water cascading off its hull—would be lodged in the tanker's specially designed hold. The use of these semisubmersible transporters is now common, but it was still relatively new in the early 1980s. As the *Financial Times* commented at the time, "The operation typifies the specialized operations which have developed in Sweden's offshore sector following the decline of its shipbuilding industry."[21]

Such foreign expertise had its price: £700,000 for the delivery, plus £3 million (about $6 million) per year to lease the *Safe Dominia* itself. These were hefty sums, considering that privates in the British army—hundreds of whom would be billeted in the *Dominia*—received somewhere between £11.34 and £18.60 per *day*.[22] But for a waning maritime and industrial power, contracting with a foreign firm was the simplest way of providing suitable housing to imperial forces in the South Atlantic. Despite her public patriotism and military boosterism, Margaret Thatcher proved quite comfortable with privatizing the housing of soldiers in the Falklands, even if it meant contracting with a foreign firm. Indeed, while her government was negotiating leases with Consafe, Thatcher was eagerly poised to privatize vast swaths of the British economy. She would start with one of Britain's most profitable and promising sectors: oil and gas.

• • •

Just as the Vessel's sister ship was arriving in Stanley, Thatcher began the program of privatization that would fully bloom during her second term. The number of unemployed in Britain had reached 3 million, with the rate at nearly 12 percent, but Thatcher was riding high on the wave of the Falklands Factor and fully anticipated electoral victory the next year, 1983. With political capital won in the South Atlantic, Thatcher pulled the state out of North Sea oil, one of the most lucrative parts of the British economy, leaving it to private industry. In particular, Thatcher sold off Britoil, Britain's state-owned oil company that had been set up to manage offshore oil reserves. The sale of Britoil, which oversaw a huge portion of oil extraction in the British-controlled sector of the North Sea, was momentous. Successfully raising £334 million for the state in a highly politicized effort to restore Britain's economic might, it became the first major state-owned industry to be privatized and set a precedent for future sell-offs that would come to define Thatcher's time in office.

The next year, the state sold some £500 million worth of shares of British Petroleum. The year after that, it raised a further £400 million from a spinoff of British Gas. In the latter part of the decade, the full privatization of British Gas and continued sell-off of the state's stake in BP would raise some £12.5 *billion*. These were mammoth sums; the entire British GDP in 1980 was around £235 billion. Indeed, the UK's oil and gas industry became a poster child for the economically liberal policies championed by Thatcher's government.[23] "Already," Thatcher told the Conservative Party Conference in 1982, "we have done more to roll back the frontiers of socialism than any previous Conservative government."[24] Further privatization would follow: British Airways, British Gas, British Steel, British Telecom, and British Shipbuilding— the public body formed to take over the country's shipyards—would all soon undergo sell-offs.

There was, thus, an irony in the political rewards from the Falklands War. Engagement in the South Atlantic furnished Thatcher with the political cover to launch dramatic economic agendas, even in the face of global dislocations. It was precisely this sort of cover that the Argentine junta had sought in invading the Malvinas in the first place. There was a second, double, irony as well. Argentina's leaders had turned to the Malvinas as a way to escape the political effects of a global economic blizzard. Thatcher, by contrast, used British success in the Falklands to push Britain further into the maelstrom of international capitalism. Britain's way out of the economic slump, Thatcher argued, was to actually reduce the state's role in the economy. Deregulation and privatization would better enable Britain to compete in a global marketplace.

The problem was that political triumphs had economic costs. Argentine leaders had (unsuccessfully) turned to the Falklands War as a distraction from a mountain of old debt. British leaders, having won the war, found themselves with a mountain of new debt. The Falklands War was a desperate response to grim economic realities, but at no point was it *economical*. As had been anticipated, the adventure in the Falklands came with a hefty price tag. The cost of replacing lost naval ships and armaments was significant. So was the newfound necessity of establishing and maintaining "Fortress Falklands," an endeavor that required a sizeable military presence. Altogether, the long-term bill for the war's aftermath would come to £3 billion.[25] In short, the episode in the Falklands enabled the Thatcher government not so much to *shrink* the British state as to shift its weight. For as it reduced social spending and privatized industries, it simultaneously committed to larger defense outlays: outlays that included leasing two offshore oil accommodation vessels from Consafe for tens of millions of pounds.

Thatcher's rhetoric of the small state was highly selective. While big government was to get out of the business of welfare provision and the regulation of private enterprise, it was to take an ever more prominent role in certain sectors of the economy. For all the noise over deregulation and privatization of the Reagan-Thatcher era, military spending increased substantially in both the United States and the United Kingdom in those years. In the 1980s, bristling national armories were the counterpoint to an increasingly integrated global economy. Between 1979, when Thatcher entered office, and 1984, British military spending doubled, from around £8.5 billion to £17 billion; it grew from 4.7 percent to 5.5 percent of British GDP (in 2020, it was 2.2 percent).[26] The volume and value of worldwide international trade was steadily increasing, yet the world was in the grip of the Cold War, organized into armed rival camps. The Falklands War was not, strictly speaking, a Cold War conflict. But it played out against fears of Soviet strength and of declining British stature as a world and imperial power. As a show of strength, Britain's defense of the islands was meant to have both domestic and international audiences.

· · ·

To some extent, British imperialism had always relied on a mix of public and private resources. Many of its early forays in overseas imperial expansion and colonization were entrusted to private corporations. In North America, British settlement was administered by the Virginia Company, the Roanoke Company, the Massachusetts Bay Company. These corporations were semi-sovereign instruments and projections of British power. In West Africa, Britain's hugely profitable forays into the slave trade came at the hands of the Royal African Company. Until 1858, the most powerful sovereign in the Indian subcontinent was (at least officially) not the British crown but the East India Company, a private corporation headquartered in the City of London, itself an independent corporate jurisdiction in the heart of the British capital. The Falkland Islands themselves had been developed, and in large part owned, by a private corporation set up with a royal charter. In 1846, Samuel Lafone, a merchant from Liverpool, bought eight hundred thousand acres in the Falklands from the British crown. Lafone, a wealthy beef trader based in Montevideo, Uruguay, hoped to bring the booming cattle industry to the islands. In 1852, after extensive lobbying, he secured a royal charter for a new corporation to do just that. That corporation, the Falkland Islands Company, was still in business 130 years later when the Vessel arrived. In fact, it had been among the most powerful and vocal opponents of Argentine administration before the start of the war.[27]

Throughout the nineteenth and twentieth centuries, British global power was a joint private-public project. British businessmen overseas doubled as official commercial attachés; private shipping companies, including the Bibby Line, functioned as informal arms of the military state, transporting commodities, the Royal Mail, and British soldiers to far-flung imperial outposts. Empire was always at once political and economic. Power overseas meant profits at home. In the heyday of the empire, when Britain "ruled the waves and waived the rules," global trade and the development of imperial markets enriched British traders, manufacturers, and financiers. British financial and mercantile dominance, in turn, redounded to geopolitical might. In short, as imperial boosters and critics alike noted, empire paid. And throughout the long eighteenth and nineteenth centuries, empire—especially the British Empire—was a prime driver of globalization and global capitalism.[28] Seen from a certain angle, the deployment of the *Safe Dominia* was continuous with the imperial British state's long history of marshaling private resources for imperial ends and making empire profitable for private corporations.

But the Ministry of Defence's turn to Consafe was different from traditional public-private entanglements in several key ways. Though the Bibby Line was an established fixture in Liverpool, Consafe was a Swedish company, not a British one. It was Consafe that officially owned the *Safe Dominia*, and Consafe's expertise that was instrumental in getting the barge all the way to Stanley in a reasonable amount of time. In the high years of British imperialism, maritime and naval power had been a primary bulwark of British supremacy. The fact that in the early 1980s the British state was contracting with a foreign maritime logistics firm to shelter its own soldiers on its own territory revealed how limited British might had become. After all, Britain had turned to a private multinational to perform what had previously been understood as an essential role for the military state itself. Securing Fortress Falklands was an (albeit somewhat atavistic) exercise in imperial defense. But unlike the muscular imperialism of the nineteenth century, British imperialism in the 1980s was, at least partially, outsourced. When confronted with a problem of military logistics, administrators at the Ministry of Defence turned to a foreign corporation to solve its problem. This move was straight out of the playbook of what the legal scholars Jody Freeman and Martha Minow have dubbed "government by contract."[29] It has become part of the standard tool kits of twenty-first-century states. In this way, the decision to hire Consafe and Bibby presaged the involvement of private military contracting firms like Halliburton and Blackwater in the wars in Afghanistan and Iraq, not to mention the Wagner Group's involvement in Syria and Ukraine.

• • •

In mid-1983, Britain's Ministry of Defence expanded its business with Bibby by leasing the Vessel, which had just been relaunched from the Von Tell Nico shipyard in Gothenburg and recently valued at $19,670,000.[30] It would be transported to the Falklands, via Tenerife, much the way the *Safe Dominia* had been, on the back of a converted supertanker.[31] Under the terms of the leases that the Ministry of Defence signed, the *Esperia* and *Dominia* would be registered as British ships and fly the Red Duster, the flag of the British merchant navy.[32] In both cases, the Ministry of Defence dealt with Consafe through the Liverpool-based Bibby Line, which was also responsible for staffing the ships.[33] To outside observers, it thus appeared as though the ministry was contracting with a British company for a British ship. Derek Bibby, Bibby's chairman, played up this point. In correspondence with Jerry Wiggin, the undersecretary of state for the armed

The then *Safe Esperia* (future *Bibby Resolution*) en route to the Falkland Islands in 1983

forces, he noted that the firm had decided to buy the *Safe Esperia*, and he pointedly reminded the staunch Tory Wiggin that the Bibbys were "long-standing supporters of the [Conservative] Party."[34] The reality was a little more nuanced. A Bibby Line subsidiary would indeed soon have title to the ship, which it was in the process of acquiring for almost $20 million, but the Vessel would still be heavily mortgaged with a Swedish bank.[35] And though the *Safe Esperia* was reregistered by a British agent in Liverpool, its sister vessel never fell within the formal jurisdiction of the British government at all. It was, instead, registered by a Consafe-controlled holding company in the tax haven of Jersey, an island in the English Channel technically outside the UK. The holding company itself did not even have an address in Jersey; it listed its address as a hotel on the neighboring Channel Island of Sark, officially part of the Bailiwick of Guernsey, an offshore tax haven in its own right.[36]

Worries about speed and cost drove the decision to contract out the housing of British soldiers. Undersecretary Jerry Wiggin, a former army officer from a military family, had personally resisted leasing a second Consafe coastel.[37] He was "concerned about the military risk of accommodating several hundred more troops in such large single structures . . . vulnerable to attack by Special Forces."[38] But in early 1983—some eight months after retaking Stanley—the Ministry of Defence was still facing an accommodation shortfall of some four hundred beds in the Falklands.[39] With a new winter bearing down on Stanley, time was of the essence. Another Consafe coastel offered a ready-made solution. There was internal discussion of buying the Vessel outright, but Ministry of Defence planners estimated that even with a very conservative estimate for inflation, leasing the barge for a term of three years at a rate of $16,000 per day would save the government nearly a million pounds. The Vessel was simply too convenient a solution to pass up.[40]

As before, with new context came new roles and new names. Once it arrived in the Falklands, the Vessel became known as Coastel 3. Its sister ship had already been dubbed Coastel 1 upon arrival (Coastel 2 was the *Poursuivant*, the British-built barge that appeared alongside the two Consafe vessels on the Falkland Islands postage stamp). Even if the ships were privately owned, military authorities saw no reason for their names to reflect that fact. Together, these Anglo-Swedish ships, intended to service the global hydrocarbon industry, would house thousands of British soldiers and airmen in a far-flung exercise in nationalist flag-waving that legitimized a shaky Thatcher ministry.[41] The empire might have won the war, but it would need private foreign assistance in guaranteeing the peace. Such was the uneasy bargain of Margaret Thatcher's government: globalism and nationalism, a growing state security apparatus, and a privatized economic sphere.

• • •

Soldiers living on the accommodation barges in Stanley shouldered the burden of that bargain. The barges were intended to improve the living conditions of troops in Stanley. Constantly billed as floating hotels, they were, at least according to Britain's defense minister, in part responsible for "the high morale of British forces there."[42] But morale was, in fact, not high at all. The Ministry of Defence had already reduced tour lengths for personnel stationed on the islands from five to four months "for reasons of morale and the poor overall living conditions."[43] In the words of one report, "The feeling of remoteness is a major factor in serving in the Falklands." Largely without trees and beset by howling winds, the islands were inhospitable. There was a single radio station, and service personnel were granted just one free telephone call per month back to Britain.[44] As Foreign Secretary Francis Pym noted, "Thank God for the Japanese . . . without the video revolution, our people out there would have virtually nothing to do."[45] Like the barges, the VHS tapes themselves had taken on new meanings. They had certainly not been designed to be instruments of war, but in the same strange and contingent way that the coastels had been transformed into barracks, the tapes became military morale boosters.

VHS tapes notwithstanding, life on board the two Swedish barges was difficult. In the memory of one RAF pilot billeted on the Vessel, "luxurious they were not. Sordid they could be."[46] There was, as reported to Parliament, "a tremendous sewerage problem."[47] Argyll and Sutherland Highlanders stationed on Coastel 2 composed their plaints into a short song, sung to the tune of "My Bonnie Lies Over the Ocean":

A two-person cabin aboard the Sister Vessel, *The Safe Dominia,* while stationed in Port Stanley

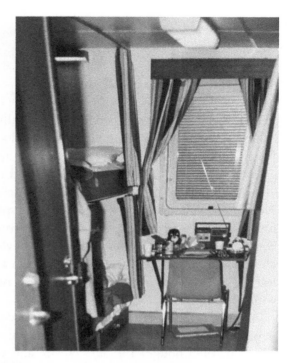

The mess aboard the Sister Vessel while in Stanley

When the wind blows here in Stanley
Our Coastel she rocks to and fro
The soldiers can't stand all this rocking
So they empty their stomachs below.[48]

Veterans who stayed on the vessels still ruefully recall their time there. "The Coastel was a dreadful place—lower floors freezing cold, upper floors baking hot!"[49] As another veteran put it, "The toilet in my bungalow is bigger than the 3 man room I had to share on co[a]stel 1." "Harry Potter had more room under the stairs," one man recalled.[50] Nevertheless, many also fondly remember a spirit of camaraderie. And for many of the first occupants, the accommodation provided a welcome change. For one veteran who had previously been billeted in a church hall in Stanley, the coastel "was like a 5-star hotel to us after leaving a dark cold overcrowded hall with no heating and smashed windows."[51]

Although the coastels were hardly ideal accommodations, they were nevertheless profitable for their owners, Consafe and the Bibby Line, which in 1983 bought the *Safe Esperia* and took a 50 percent stake in the *Safe Dominia*. Through its part ownership of the vessels, the Bibby Line reprised its longtime association with the British military. But instead of transporting troops to far-flung corners of the empire, as it had during the nineteenth and early twentieth centuries, it simply housed the soldiers when they got there.[52] Though the British government did not release any of the costs of leasing the barges after 1982, at that point it was costing the crown £7.5 million per year.[53] The barges stayed in Stanley until 1987, becoming fixtures of the local landscape, as the Falklands continued to bristle with British military might. Children from the islands even learned to swim in the Vessel's indoor pool.[54] All the while, the barges provided Bibby and Consafe millions in revenue.[55]

• • •

Yet despite the profits flowing northward from the South Atlantic in the mid-1980s, trouble was brewing in Sweden for Consafe. Oil prices—volatile, but generally high since the crises of the 1970s—were finally coming down. In the 1980s, the global economy ran on oil. It still does. For the past six decades, oil has been the world's single-largest source of energy, year in, year out.[56] In 1984, it was even more important than it is now—providing over 40 percent of the world's energy, compared to around 30 percent today. It heated homes, fed electric generators, and powered cars. It also turned the great propellers of the cargo ships that carried global trade. Oil was involved in the production and sale of just about everything. As a result, its price affected just about everything. This is why oil shocks—like those caused by the Yom Kippur War embargo and the Iranian Revolution—were such important and dramatic events for the global economy.

The price of oil was especially important for a company like Consafe, which dealt directly with the oil industry. While the oil market boomed, so too did the market for offshore exploration and development. But as the market cooled and big oil stopped expanding its capacity, so too did the market for offshore rigs. In early 1985, Consafe had a 55 percent market share of offshore accommodation platforms, but the market was, in words of the company's chairman, Christer Ericsson, "dipping." In April, Ericsson admitted that "we've had a lot of disappointed shareholders in Sweden and it's very embarrassing."[57] In July, Consafe announced that it was having difficulty servicing the interest on $265 million in Swedish state-guaranteed debt, the state assistance that had been so integral to the company's meteoric growth. Ericsson told reporters that the company's liquidity was in doubt; the $60 million in cash reserves it had held at the beginning of the year had dwindled to $25 million. If the slide continued, Ericsson said, "we are in trouble."[58]

It did continue. In September, Svenska Varv, the administrator of that debt (and onetime owner of Finnboda Varv), refused Consafe's request to modify its plan for financial restructuring, leading Consafe to declare bankruptcy. Shortly thereafter, in the lead-up to a national election, Sweden's Social Democratic government pushed Consafe into liquidation.[59] Almost 90 percent of Consafe's borrowed capital had come from the Swedish state. This arrangement had made sense because of the incredibly favorable terms on which the capital had been offered. But, as Ericsson put it, the problem with borrowing from the state was that the state was a political creature and politicians could "be guilty of just about any betrayal." He claimed that it would have been possible to save Consafe and avoid a "completely unnecessary" "capital destruction," if administrators and politicians had simply acted with more business sense and less prejudice. Consafe, according to Ericsson, was a victim of politics; the state had only withdrawn support because of his outspoken criticism of the government's tax policy. Could it be, he suggestively asked, that "the state wanted to stop a person who criticized our tax system too harshly?"[60]

•   •   •

Debt had pushed Argentina to invade the Falklands. Debt had brought the vessels to Stanley. Debt would also push them away from their Swedish owners. As the Vessel and its sister ship remained moored in Port Stanley with their complement of housed soldiers and airmen, the Bibby Line quietly acquired Consafe's remaining stake in the *Safe Dominia* from the state-appointed receiver. Shortly thereafter, the two barges—now the sole property of the Bibby Line—were officially renamed again. The Vessel became the *Bibby Resolution*, and its sister ship became the *Bibby Venture*, new names perhaps meant to evoke the patriotic service both ships were rendering in the Falklands.[61]

And so, after nearly three years of accommodating British soldiers and Royal Air Force personnel, the Vessel and its sister ship were both finally fully British owned. It is worth underscoring that the *reason* they became British owned had little to do with the British state. It was not because the Thatcher government decided to take more active and direct responsibility for housing hundreds of servicemembers moored at a rocky outcropping in the South Atlantic, eight thousand miles away from loved ones. Nor was it because the Ministry of Defence decided that it should improve its independent capacity to operate in far-flung theaters of war. Instead, the Vessel became British because of a simple economic calculation made in light of global economic changes. A private firm sensed an economic opportunity: a chance to pick up a valuable international asset at a good price.

Private enterprise, not the state, was responsible for the acquisition of new British assets and the growth of an old British company. But the sale of the Vessel and its sister ship took place against the backdrop of lucrative state contracts, contracts that were part of the billions of pounds that the Thatcher government spent on securing a remote corner of a fading empire. The barge's time in Stanley captured the subtle friction between two twinned political objectives of the Thatcher and Reagan era: an emphasis on privatization and a commitment to patriotic flag-waving backed up by military spending. For years, it was a foreign-owned barracks, housing for hundreds of British servicemembers, floating just off the coast of a sovereign British territory. It was a hulking instantiation of outsourcing and literally offshoring war and imperial defense to private companies. In this way, the Vessel's time in Stanley spoke to a fundamental feature of the 1980s political economy. Facing worldwide inflation and slowing growth, leaders in London, Buenos Aires, and Washington turned to distractions, deregulation, and privatization. In short, they turned to competition in the global economy.

CHAPTER 4

THE CARIBBEAN SEA

	The Vessel	The Sister Vessel
1987		The *Bibby Venture* leaves Stanley and is reregistered in The Bahamas. It is refurbished outside of London and then delivered to the New York City Department of Correction. It is moored at Pier 36 in the East River and called the Maritime Facility I.
1988	The *Bibby Resolution* leaves Stanley and is reregistered in The Bahamas. It is refurbished outside of London and then delivered to Volkswagen in Emden, West Germany.	

J ust around Easter in 1984, Britain lost four ships. The ships, all operating outside of British waters at the time, were not destroyed or damaged; their loss was not the result of negligence or physical violence. It came at the stroke of a pen. At the beginning of May, the four ships were registered in the United Kingdom. By the end of the month, they were registered in Hong Kong, then still a British crown colony.

The four vessels were all large liquified petroleum gas tankers, plying the world's seas, delivering energy from oil producers in the Global South to consumers in Europe, North America, and Asia. All four were owned by the Bibby Line, the same British firm that was operating the Vessel and its sister ship in Port Stanley. Together, they constituted the majority of Bibby's shrinking fleet, down from twenty ships in the mid-1970s to just six (not including the two accommodation vessels).[1]

By officially designating Hong Kong—rather than Liverpool—as the ships' home port, the Bibby Line made the ships Hong Kongese. They would no longer be able to hoist the Red Duster. Instead, they would fly the flag of Hong Kong. This "reflagging" was far more than a symbolic gesture. A change in registration, though somewhat abstract, had very real and very dramatic consequences. Those consequences came immediately. The moment that the Bibby Line's ships were no longer British, they ceased to be regulated by UK law. Gone were British workplace safety protections. Gone were British minimum-wage floors. Gone—in large measure—was the recourse to British courts. And for seafarers, gone was the weight of politically powerful British unions. Hong Kongese vessels did not have to play by British rules.

For the hundreds of seamen and officers serving on the four LPG tankers, the reflagging came as a particularly nasty surprise. The Merchant Navy and Airline Officers' Association (MNAOA), the British union that represented the maritime officers employed by Bibby, expressed outrage over the move. "It was done arbitrarily and secretively over Easter," a regional secretary noted. "The company didn't consult us . . . even though we had an MNAOA company committee meeting with management at the end of March." Bibby had written a letter to union officials indicating that reflagging was an option, "but by the time we had responded to their letter, it was a fait accompli." "Every member I've spoken to is appalled and dismayed at the way Bibby has handled this."[2]

For the officers represented by the MNAOA, Bibby's decision to reflag in Hong Kong was part of a deeply concerning trend. Through the flagging-out process, Bibby would lay off the entirety of its British-based officers and then rehire them through a Bermuda-based staffing agency owned by the British logistics firm Denholm's. Although members did not immediately stand to lose their jobs, because they would be employed not by a British firm but by a Bermudian one, they did stand to lose a raft of protections guaranteed by British law and the power of their Britain-based union.

For seafarers who were not commissioned officers—"ratings," in the parlance of the British merchant navy—the situation was considerably worse. Because of the transfer in registration, about eighty seafarers would lose their jobs immediately, to be replaced by lower-wage workers from elsewhere.[3] As one newspaper report at the time noted, these ratings had no chance to re-up with service on a Bibby Line ship. "They were sacked at the end of their last voyage and instantly replaced with Chinese crews."[4] The fact that these sailors were likely subjects of the British crown, holding Hong Kong passports, was irrelevant. For British unions and British sailors, the point was that they were not *British*, a key subtext being that they were not white. And the prospect of these losses prompted the ratings' union, the traditionalist National Union of Seafarers, to stage a sit-in in Bibby's offices in Liverpool. The demonstration achieved little, though NUS seamen "threatened to 'black' Bibby ships in all the world's ports!"[5] Bibby's actions were part of a wave. The writing was on the wall for Britain's merchant navy, with its (comparatively) high wages and workplace protections. Indeed, the writing was on the wall for the entire old order of the British economy, with ominous implications for the power of organized labor itself.

By the 1980s, it was clear that a major secular shift was underway. Across much of the industrialized world, manufacturing was being eclipsed in importance by the service sector. In Britain, the transformation was particularly profound. In the twenty years before Bibby reregistered its ships in 1984, Britain's manufacturing job base had shrunk by about 4 million jobs, contracting by over a third.[6] As in Sweden and elsewhere in western Europe, in Britain wages were simply too high to maintain global competitiveness, in the face of increasingly developed manufacturing sectors in Asia. As supply chains grew longer and the global economy more integrated, there were ever greater incentives for capital owners and corporate managers to outsource relatively high-cost labor.

Though shipping did not technically belong to the manufacturing sector, it was buffeted by the same winds. According to a 1986 estimate, crew costs for a thirty-thousand-deadweight-ton tanker registered in Bermuda with a Filipino crew was just 53 percent of the analogous costs of hiring an all-British crew on a British-registered vessel. A Hong Kong–registered vessel with a Hong Kongese crew was estimated to be even less: 44 percent of the British costs.[7] Why should a shipowner register a vessel in the United Kingdom and pay prevailing British wages with British benefits packages subject to suit in British courts, when it could register the ship elsewhere and take on cheap foreign labor?

These questions had haunted Britain's merchant navy for some

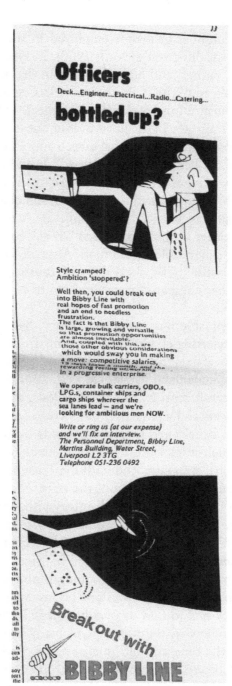

An advertisement recruiting offers for the Bibby Line, which appeared in the newsletter of the Merchant Navy and Airline Officers' Association in 1973

time. The total number of people employed in the merchant navy
had been falling steadily from the early 1960s. In 1962 there had been
146,710 seamen, ratings, and officers. By 1980, that figure had fallen
by more than half, to 69,160.[8] By the mid-1980s, gloomy comments
and bitter prognostications proliferated in the MNAOA's monthly
newspaper, *The Telegraph*. In the hot words of one member, "Between
Achilles and Hector there might have been more honour than this
sneak murder of the British merchant navy."[9] Even in the 1970s, *The
Telegraph* had been full of recruitment advertisements. One recurring
ad from the Bibby Line featured a stylized cartoon of an officer breaking out of a small glass bottle. "Style cramped?" it asked. "Ambition,
'stoppered'?" A career at Bibby promised "an end to needless frustration" and "almost inevitable" promotion. After all, Bibby was "large,
growing and versatile."[10] By the 1980s, of course, those ads (from
Bibby or any other company) were nowhere to be seen. An end to
frustration indeed.

As an imperial shipping company, Bibby had long employed
lascars—a term referring to any seaman hailing from east of the Cape
of Good Hope. Seafarers from South and Southeast Asia, the Middle
East, and British Somaliland had served in the British merchant navy
since the seventeenth century. But by the 1980s, the majority of the
Bibby Line's officers and a large part of its crews (mostly white men)
were recruited in Britain and employed directly by Bibby's Liverpool
office.[11] Such a high-wage labor force was a luxury at a time of belt-
tightening in global shipping. And with the Thatcher government in
power, there would be no relief from the state. Nicholas Ridley, the
president of the Board of Trade (the ministry responsible for Britain's
merchant navy), declared that he "would rather see it disappear than
offer it a subsidy."[12] Britain's shippers would be left to the tempests of
the global market. Those tempests showed few signs of subsiding.

But for Bibby to remain in the shipping business, it would need
to compete with foreign firms that drew on low-wage labor supplies.
To do that, Bibby had to find its own low-wage labor. To do *that*, it
would need to follow in the footsteps of many other international
corporations of the time and offshore its assets. Reflagging its ships
in Hong Kong allowed the company to recruit labor in Hong Kong
(or anywhere else), freeing it from expensive contracts with unionized
British seafarers.[13]

While workers objected to the "flagging out," for Derek Bibby the move was "an economic necessity." It was, of course, "very sad" to move away from all-British crews, he declared, "but we must not let our feelings govern our activities."[14] Bibby was a businessman, and offshoring was a matter of rational business decision-making. As the company put it in a 1984 statement, "Necessity has forced us . . . We have fought a long battle to resist this, but the appalling state of the LPG freight market and the adverse terms of this year's Budget left us no alternative." Costs had to be cut. Otherwise, according to Bibby, "it would only have been a short matter of time before the Bibby name disappeared from the shipping scene."[15] Over the next few years, the company began to shift its other ships into other registries, from Britain to territories and foreign countries with looser regulations and lower taxes.[16]

Bibby was hardly alone in registering its ships into overseas ports. The 1970s and 1980s saw a surge of the use of flags of convenience— that is, sailing a ship under a national flag other than that of the nation to which the shipowner belongs. In the early 1980s, the very word *reflag* came to refer to just this practice.[17] Flags of convenience were largely responsible for a worldwide decline of seafarers' wages; one study found that wages fell off by about a quarter between 1992 and 1999.[18] British shipowners were particularly eager to reflag. Between 1958 and 1982, world shipping tonnage increased 359 percent, but tonnage registered in the UK was effectively flat: 20,286,000 gross tons in 1958 and 22,505,000 gross tons two and a half decades later in 1982. It wasn't that British shipowners like Bibby were not investing in new vessels; they were. It was that they were not registering their ships in Britain, but rather in more permissive registries like Hong Kong, Liberia, Panama, or the Bahamas. The share of world tonnage flying a flag of convenience grew steadily, from 13 percent in 1958 to 24 percent in 1982 and 42 percent in 1990. By 2020, the number was at nearly 73 percent.[19]

. . .

By the mid-1980s, Derek Bibby had shepherded the struggling Bibby Line into the black. The company cleared more than £13 million in pretax profits in 1984, the same year that it reflagged its tankers.[20]

Derek Bibby had managed this feat by new measures like reflagging. But he had also done it by shifting the business from conventional trade to specialized maritime services, a strategy undertaken by several major British shipping companies. The move to invest in offshore accommodation units like the Vessel was part of that transition. It was a canny business decision that would pay major dividends. A picture in a brochure produced by the Bibby Group to promote its accommodation vessels shows the thrumming coastel department at the company's Liverpool headquarters, with office workers beavering away at their typewriters drumming up customers and producing profit. But investing in coastels meant steering the firm away from its long-established identity as an imperial shipping line toward a new one as a global diversified corporation. To some extent, decolonization and imperial decline necessitated this transformation. Shrinking military budgets led the British government to terminate lucrative contracts for Bibby ships to transport troops around the world in the early 1960s. On top of that, the rise of new national shipping services—including the Ceylonese National Line and Burma's Five Star Line—pushed Bibby out of the profitable shipping service connecting Ceylon and Burma with Britain.[21] Bibby's time-honored strategy of serving as a British imperial carrier simply would not be enough to survive in the

Coastel Department at Bibby Line Liverpool

The Bibby Line's thrumming and modern coastel department in the office in Liverpool, clustered around a model of a tanker owned by the line

1980s. Turning to new ventures like coastels was integral to the company's survival.

In its advertising, Bibby tried to highlight both its new logistical capabilities and its storied history. The company could deliver a "Coastel on site, even half a world away." It boasted of excellent "technical support" and an "unrivaled reputation for seamanship and efficiency."[22] This reputation was instrumental in landing the firm a contract to manage two ships for the Shipping Corporation of Trinidad and Tobago, a public enterprise owned by the relatively new postcolonial Caribbean state. It also made it an attractive partner for the British Ministry of Defence and other clients seeking to lease Bibby's new coastels.

Like Bibby's cargo ships and tankers, its coastels were offshored. The *Bibby Venture*—the Vessel's sister ship—had been registered in Jersey, a rocky ten-mile-long island in the English Channel, just off the coast of Normandy, since 1983. Because Jersey is formally a Crown Dependency, legally outside the United Kingdom, Bibby could avoid paying British taxes on the ship, while still guaranteeing it a British flag. In 1987, the Bibby Line shifted the *Bibby Venture*'s registry to Nassau, the capital of the Bahamas. The Vessel, by now called the *Bibby Resolution*, was reregistered from Liverpool to Nassau the next year.[23] When that happened, both barges became officially Bahamian ships. Because the Bahamas was part of the British Commonwealth, the barges and their owner continued to enjoy the protection of British-inspired common law. But they had never been further from British regulatory control. By reregistering the ships in Nassau, the Bibby Line substantively reduced its regulatory oversight. The ships would no longer fly the Red Duster; they would instead hoist the jack of a recently independent postcolonial state: a flag of convenience.

•   •   •

Although modern flags of convenience had existed for several decades by the 1980s, their popularity was in the midst of a surge. In the early twentieth century, ships generally flew the flag of the country with which they were most closely associated. In practice, this meant that shipowners typically registered their vessels in the country where they lived. Under international law, countries had broad discretion in

regulating (or not regulating) their own registries. As the Permanent
Court of Arbitration at The Hague put it in the Muscat Dhows case,
a landmark ruling in 1905, the ability of "every sovereign to decide
to wh[ich ships] he will accord the rights to fly his flag and . . . to
prescribe the rules governing such grants" was well established in cus-
tomary law.[24] Though shipping might be carried out in international
waters, the ships themselves were subject to the jurisdiction of landed
states. Shipping registries were, in this sense, projections of terrestrial
sovereignty on the high seas.

With every state able to set the rules by which its ships were registered, shipowners and operators were afforded considerable flexibility.
Indian traders operating in the Persian Gulf in the late nineteenth
and early twentieth centuries selectively transported goods under the
British flag for protection. Conversely, in the early nineteenth century, ships owned by the British East India Company sometimes flew
the red Arab flag to avoid privateers. European imperial powers effectively leased out the use of their flags to local craft as part of a strategy
to compete with their rivals. In short, in many parts of the world,
as the historian Fahad Bishara put it, "ships raised and lowered different colors with relative ease."[25] Such a fluid system was open to
coercion and abuse. European states used their ability to issue flags as
tools of imperial control and suasion, particularly in the Middle East.
And as early as the late nineteenth century, shipowners realized that
there were advantages to registering their ships overseas. Early flagging out depended on both push and pull factors. British shipowners,
for instance, began registering fleets in Hong Kong in the nineteenth
century to take advantage of low taxes and a large pool of cheap and
experienced merchant marine labor.[26] In the early twentieth century,
progressive legislation meant to protect merchant seamen with significant new rights pushed more shipowners to flag out. In the United
States, in particular, the passage of the La Follette Seaman's Act in
1915 induced shippers to register their vessels in Panama to sidestep
regulatory oversight.[27]

Foreign ship registration really took off in the late 1920s. It was
then that poor countries under U.S. political sway—first Panama,
then later Honduras and Liberia—launched so-called open registries,
in which ships were not required to have any meaningful connection
to the country.[28] For shipowners, the appeal of these open registries

was manifest. In addition to low taxes, as one shipping company official noted in 1922, "the chief advantage of Panamanian registry is that the owner is relieved of the continual . . . boiler and hull inspections and the regulations as to crew's quarters and subsistence."[29] By simply filing some papers, shipowners could opt out of onerous regulations, taxes, and standards. And so they did. At first, there was just a trickle of registrations in Panama. But after John D. Rockefeller's behemoth Standard Oil transferred much of its fleet of transport ships there in the 1930s, the popularity of the Panamanian registry exploded.[30]

Open registries severed the "genuine link" that had historically connected a ship and the state whose flag it flew.[31] In essence, such registries allowed savvy shipowners to leverage the formal sovereignty of poor states with "neither the power nor the administrative machinery effectively to impose any government or international regulations."[32] For a small fee paid to a poor country, shipowners could purchase sovereignty itself. As definitively described in 1970 by the British government's Rochdale Committee, which investigated the matter, states offering flags of convenience allowed anyone, citizen or not, to register a ship. Registration was easily done at a consul's office overseas and just as easily transferred. Taxes were "not levied locally" or were very low, and there were no restrictions on manning ships with foreign labor. The result, in short, made ships citizens of everywhere and nowhere.[33]

In the 1980s, when the Bibby Line registered the *Bibby Resolution* and the *Bibby Venture* in the Bahamas, flags of convenience had become markers of globalization par excellence.[34] They represented a race to the bottom, in which small, usually poor, countries competed to offer shipowners ever less onerous tax and regulatory burdens. Leveraging international maritime treaties, flags of convenience allowed states to rent out their sovereignty, if not sell it outright. Large companies were eager clients, seeking to buy their way out of local jurisdictions and regulations.[35]

• • •

Though flags of convenience depended, and continue to depend, on independent sovereignty, they were and are also unequivocally legacies of empire. The registry of Honduras was set up for the benefit of the United Fruit Company, the rapacious Boston-based firm responsible for establishing "banana republics" in Central America.[36] The fact that American shipowners flocked to the Panamanian registry reflected the long-standing American interest and power in the country. American troops were stationed in the zone around the Panama Canal, and the country was constitutionally dependent on the United States for military protection.[37] In fact, Panama's shipping registry was itself administered by the American state. By the late 1920s, American consuls in port cities around the world were able to legally record ships in the Panamanian register when a bona fide Panamanian consul was not available.[38]

American empire was even more clearly responsible for the development of Liberia's open registry, which became the blueprint for the modern flag of convenience. Liberia's flag of convenience owes its existence to a quirk of history. In February 1945, U.S. Secretary of State Edward Stettinius was on his way back to Washington from Crimea after having attended the Yalta Conference, the event at which Winston Churchill, Franklin Delano Roosevelt, and Joseph Stalin planned the fate of a defeated Nazi Germany. En route, Stettinius stopped in Liberia's capital, Monrovia, where he ceremonially opened new port facilities and an airstrip built with U.S. funding and meant to facilitate the Allied war effort.

Stettinius was a businessman, a twentieth-century American aristocrat. The son of a partner of J. P. Morgan, he had dropped out of college and gone to work for General Motors, where he rose up the corporate ladder. In 1938, just before war broke out in Europe, Stettinius became the chairman of U.S. Steel, the great corporate conglomerate founded by Andrew Carnegie. During his brief visit to Liberia, flying over the landscape, Stettinius was struck by the county's plentiful iron deposits. After the war ended, he formed a new company, Stettinius Associates-Liberia Inc., with the idea of mining iron there. But though Stettinius had initially been attracted by the prospect of mineral riches, he would make much more money by selling off a less tangible Liberian resource: sovereignty.[39] It was a bitterly ironic move, given Liberia's history. The country was founded by free African Americans on the coast of West Africa in the early nineteenth century. And though it relied largely on American funds and American investments—particularly rubber plantations owned by Firestone—Liberia was proudly independent. Leveraging its own sovereignty back to wealthy American businessmen was a new and symbolically laden step.

In late 1947, a group of American shipowners approached Stettinius with "a willingness to obtain registration under the Liberian flag."[40] Stettinius Associates was full of men who had worked under him in the American diplomatic corps—they belonged to the cohort of young officials who had helped redraw the lines and rewrite the laws of postwar Europe—and they quickly set about drafting a new maritime code for Liberia. In so doing, Stettinius Associates closely consulted on the wording of the code with American shippers and tanker owners, particularly executives at Standard Oil, the firm that had helped popularize the Panamanian registry just a couple decades before. With the help of former colleagues in the U.S. government and the sympathetic Liberian president, William Tubman, Stettinius pushed the new legislation through the Liberian legislature, waiting only for a green light on the wording from Standard Oil. The result was a shipping registry open to anyone in the world, administered through a shell company controlled by Stettinius Associates from New York. It was an offshore registry, not only from the perspective of U.S. or European shipowners but also from the perspective of Liberia itself. The registry, run by Americans, was Liberian in name only. It was a global creature whose structure has been copied by states offering open registries the world over.

The Liberian registry was a tool of American business and geopolitical interests. It was informal empire by any other name: a system engineered to serve American economic interests. Though Liberia was founded by free African Americans as a refuge *away* from the United States, Stettinius understood it as a continuous imperial extension of the U.S., its "sole beachhead in Africa" during a period of intensifying Cold War tensions.[41] As he put it in a press release, American ships registered in Liberia might seriously cut costs in getting Liberian iron to American markets, especially if the ships were manned by foreign officers and crewed by "native Liberian boys, who would receive in the neighborhood of a dollar a day."[42] The arrangement would allow American shipowners to circumvent American regulations and taxes. It would also furnish Stettinius's company with a tidy profit.[43] In fact, just 25 percent of profits from the registration fees would go to the Liberian government. The vast majority—65 percent—would flow to

Stettinius and his American partners (not even counting the operating costs charged by the firm). The remaining 10 percent went to a private fund for health and welfare programs in Liberia.[44] Even today, though a different U.S. firm manages the Liberian registry (now from just outside Washington, D.C.), the administrators of the Liberian registry are required by Liberian law to be American citizens, a fact that the registry uses as a selling point to potential foreign clients concerned about the country's political instability and corruption.[45]

• • •

What Panama and Liberia were for the United States, Jersey, Hong Kong, and, increasingly, a clutch of Caribbean imperial outposts were for Britain. For decades, British officials denied that these territories ran flags of convenience for British shipowners. Regardless of how permissive their regulations were, they were still subject to British control. As such, there was a "genuine link" between them and any British (or even Commonwealth) shipowner.[46] This claim was, at best, tenuous, but the logic of empire died hard.

In fact, the whole modern world of offshore tax havens and flags of convenience—what the historian Vanessa Ogle has termed "archipelago capitalism"—emerged largely out of the British Empire. This world grew in power, prestige, and political acceptance with decolonization, as the nation-state replaced the empire as the world's dominant geopolitical unit.[47] But it depended both on the formal independent sovereignty of postcolonial states and on their institutional connections with old imperial powers. Many of the world's foremost tax havens were forged over the mid-twentieth century in British colonial outposts under the protective umbrella of British common law and the stability of imperial protection.[48] Moreover, offshore havens were often set up with the active support of the British government, in the interest of trade, tourism, and development. The Bahamas, where the Bibby Line would ultimately register the Vessel and its sister ship as the *Bibby Resolution* and the *Bibby Venture* in the late 1980s, serves as a textbook example.

The Bahamas took off as an offshore site largely because of a 1955 deal cut between London and a somewhat suspect American lawyer, Wallace Groves. Colonial authorities gave Groves essentially free rein to develop a tax-free zone called "Freeport" on a barren stretch of sand eighty-five miles east of Palm Beach, Florida, including the right to enforce his own immigration policy. The transaction was legendarily shady: *The Times* of London would label it "one of the most one-sided agreements ever signed by the British Crown."[49] As Groves developed Freeport into a destination for both tourists and capital over the next two decades, the Bahamas as a whole became an ever more important center for so-called funk money.

Even before Groves arrived, the Bahamas had long been an offshore center. Just ninety miles from the coast of Florida, it had been used by gunrunners as a base to smuggle weapons to the Confederacy during the Civil War. In the mid-twentieth century, Meyer Lansky, the "Mob's Accountant," began parking millions in dirty money in the islands. Lansky had started offshoring funds in Cuba in the 1930s, but Fidel Castro's 1959 takeover pushed Lansky to find another jurisdiction that could offer him secret banking facilities. The Bahamas—a sleepy Caribbean outpost of empire—became just that. Incentivized by millions of dollars in bribes, local officials strengthened bank secrecy laws, even as British authorities in London fretted over angering officials in the United States seeking to crack down on the mob.[50]

Lansky was not alone in turning to the Bahamas. Decolonization, especially in Africa, pushed repatriated British colonial "settlers" to find shelters for their assets somewhere outside Britain's extractive tax regime. Increasingly, they turned to the Caribbean.[51] Especially for former colonials, the Bahamas' status as a continued part of the empire and the fact that its currency was linked to the pound and the Bank of England were major points of attraction, and played up by local officials. The Bahamas, the Cayman Islands, the Virgin Islands, and St. Vincent and the Grenadines were safe harbors for colonial assets. With permissive banking and tax laws, protected by strict privacy shields and governed by common law, the islands were simultaneously distant and familiar. They were English speaking with well-established communities of white expats.[52] They were also pleasant places to visit, should the need arise. And they still are. It is no coincidence that the now-jailed FTX founder Sam Bankman-Fried holed up in the Bahamas in 2022 as his empire crumbled. His plans to build a massive new office complex in the country's capital, Nassau, had been welcomed with open arms by then Prime Minister Philip Davis.[53]

For the same reasons, the Caribbean was an attractive place to move shipping assets. The Rochdale Report on shipping noted that by 1970, about 8 percent of the British-registered shipping fleet was owned by companies "set up in Bermuda and the Bahamas in order to obtain virtual immunity from company taxation." This meant that, "to the extent that the UK register covers such ships, it might well be regarded as offering a flag of convenience."[54]

When the Bahamas gained its independence, in 1973, its status as a safe place to park assets came into question; the stream of revenue generated from its status as a tax haven slowed, diverted to new centers like the Caymans. The Bahamas were a majority-Black country; under Prime Minister Lynden Pindling and the Progressive Liberal Party, the government stressed Black empowerment and banned the sale of land to foreigners, moves that (mostly white) American investors regarded with trepidation.[55] The decision to open its shipping registry four years later, in 1977, was seen as a step that would help the country recover lost income and reassure nervous internationals that the country was still very much open for business, despite the change in its leadership. It also helped further cement the status of the Bahamas as an offshore haven, one that would soon be exploited by drug cartels involved in the spectacularly profitable Colombian cocaine trade.

When it launched, the Bahamian registry boasted offices not just in Nassau but in central London as well, making it particularly easy for British and other European shipowners to flag out. By the time the Bahamas opened a third registry office in New York, in 1983, the global registry business was booming; about a quarter of the world's shipping, by tonnage, belonged to an open registry.[56]

The growth of these registries took place against the backdrop of an increasingly widespread commitment to the ideal of democratic internationalism. Flags of convenience most benefited shipowners who lived and worked in wealthy, industrialized countries. But open registries themselves fundamentally depended on the logic of egalitarian sovereignty that undergirded the charter of the United Nations.[57] According to the international legal framework of the mid-twentieth century, the sovereignty of every nation, no matter how small, was understood and forcefully asserted to be formally equal. Bahamian sovereignty was sacrosanct, equal to and equally worthy as British or American sovereignty.

This logic certainly undergirded the International Maritime Organization, the UN agency responsible for drafting and circulating regulations governing seagoing vessels. The IMO was meant to be neutral and supernational: a body that would protect the rights of all. Yet even the IMO—with its expert technocratic administration based on the river Thames in London—was poorly insulated from the political economy of the global shipping industry. The IMO derives its funding from membership fees paid by member states. Vitally, the relative size of those fees is determined by the size of the shipping fleet registered in each member country. The result is that countries with open registries like the Bahamas, Panama, and Liberia are largely responsible for funding the IMO. This gave them enough leverage in the 1980s to force their representatives onto the technical committees that determined international standards. The result was regulatory capture pure and simple, enabled and propagated by the shared value of democratic internationalism.[58] But unlike the UN's Security Council, dominated by traditional Great Powers, the IMO fell under the sway of small, relatively poor states: the states with open registries. States like the Bahamas.

• • •

Since 1982, both the Vessel and its sister ship had been docked in Stanley, each housing hundreds of British service personnel. The leasing agreement between Bibby and the British Ministry of Defence prevented the firm from reregistering the *Bibby Resolution* and *Bibby Venture* outside of British jurisdiction, which is why the ships were listed in Liverpool and Jersey. But when the contracts ended, so too did the impediments to reregistry in a Caribbean tax haven.

The contracts expired in 1987 and 1988. Five years after the liberation of the Falklands, the UK's Ministry of Defense finished construction of a barracks on the outskirts of Stanley to house the hundreds of military personnel needed to secure Fortress Falklands. With a replacement finally in place for the coastels still sitting in the harbor, the British government terminated its contract with the Bibby Line.[59] Bibby, with its ongoing strategy to offshore and diversify its assets, wasted little time in registering both of its coastels in the Bahamas. Doing so was hardly onerous. The switch did not require a flight to

the Caribbean but, instead, only a short visit to the Bahamian Registry Office in Britain's financial district, the City of London, literally a
block away from the Bank of England.

The City of London is itself a tax haven, an enclave of the offshore
world wedged deep within Britain's capital city. The City is a physical
place: a tract of just over a square mile comprising some of the most
expensive real estate in the world: St. Paul's Cathedral, Fleet Street,
and the gleaming glass towers of financial headquarters. As importantly, it is also an independent corporation with jurisdictional sovereignty. It has been for the better part of a thousand years, predating
Parliament and the Magna Carta by centuries. It maintains its own
police force, its own bylaws, and its own finances, including a fund
worth billions of pounds. When the king of England visits the City,
he is met by the lord mayor at the boundary and escorted in, touching
the lord mayor's sword as an acknowledgment of the City's ancient
rights and privileges.

The City of London is a city within a city, a state within a state.
And it is a state run largely by capital. In City elections, businesses get
votes just like human beings. And businesses in the City outnumber
humans three to one. The City has all sorts of carve-outs in British
law. It has a different, more permissive tax structure for corporations.
It is exempt from certain Freedom of Information requests. It shields
financial institutions from disclosures and transparency requirements
that pertain to the rest of the country.[60] In the 1980s, the City had a
reputation, if not for regulatory laxity, then at least for a permissiveness not matched by Wall Street. Finance was booming and London
was benefiting. In the words of one Bank of England official, "We,
at the Bank, have never seen any reason to place any obstacles in the
way of London taking its full and increasing share." As Robin Leigh-
Pemberton, the governor of the Bank of England from 1983 to 1993,
put it, "If we closed down a bank every time we found an incidence of
fraud, we would have rather fewer banks than we do at the moment."[61]

In a way, the City of London is finance's natural habitat: a key site
of the Financial Revolution of the seventeenth century and the nerve
center of global banking for hundreds of years. By the 1980s, it had
lost some of its prominence to New York, but it remained among
the most important enclaves of financial capitalism in the world. And
with its human and historical links to havens like Jersey, Hong Kong,

the Caymans, and the Bahamas, it remained the undisputed center of *offshore* finance: the hub from which offshore financial activities in crown dependencies and Caribbean outposts were coordinated.[62] It was hardly coincidental that the Bahamian government decided to place a maritime registry office in the City.

The ease of transferring registration underscored the sticky legacies of empire, but it also exposed the brittle bounds of territorial sovereignty and British national power. While the British government was sitting in Westminster spending millions of pounds defending a sparsely populated set of rocks in the South Atlantic, British ships were becoming Bahamian, not two miles away. Every month, more and more papers were being signed at the Bahamian Registry located in an elegant Edwardian stone building at 120 Old Broad Street, once the home to the Midland Bank, a pioneer of London's eurodollar market. This, as much as anything else, was Margaret Thatcher's Britain.

120 Old Bank Street, at right

At the time the Bibby Line registered the Vessel and its sister ship in the Bahamas, the country was one of the fastest-growing centers of maritime registration in the world. In 1980, there was a coup in Liberia, which made foreign shipowners wary of registering assets there. Then, in late 1984, British and Chinese authorities agreed on terms under which Hong Kong would revert to Chinese control in

1997. Uncertainty about the future of assets in Hong Kong—home to another major open registry especially popular among owners of British vessels—drove shipowners to look for new home ports.[63]

Nassau was a particularly attractive option. A ship registered in the Bahamas was not subject to any taxes on operation, income, or capital gains. Foreign-owned ships did not pay customs or stamp duties.[64] In fact, when the Bibby Line registered its vessels in the Bahamas, the country was one of the world's most unregulated open registries. Then, as now, newly formed open registries tended to adhere to very few international agreements, whether on environmental, safety, or labor standards. It is only over time, as a registry grows, that international pressure pushes it into compliance with regulatory norms.[65] This was exactly the pattern followed by the Bahamas when it created its registry in the 1970s. Even today, though the Bahamian registry has become less permissive than it once was, the Bahamas is still relatively free of regulations, and thus is the preferred flag for the oil-drilling vessels now developing the Caribbean's burgeoning offshore oil and gas industry.

In an era of ever-mounting awareness of human-caused climate change, it is becoming clear that the Bahamas is, in fact, paying a great price for the system to which its open registry belongs, and its acceptance of oil and gas ships. The globalized, deregulated world that open registries helped create has, in turn, spawned its own global weather patterns. Over the past two decades, the Caribbean hurricane season has become longer, and its storms—including the Category 5 Dorian, which hit the Bahamas in 2019—have grown more devastating. The Bahamas' attempt to attract money through an open registry is just a minor component of the larger overall system that is driving and enabling climate change. Yet in the context of more frequent catastrophic weather events, its open registry is becoming more costly for the country's residents as well as those of its neighbors.

Moreover, the benefits of open registration have hardly been spectacular. In 2019, a report submitted to the Bahamian parliament determined that the revenues from the privately administered open registry contributed less than $100 million over the past twenty-five years.[66] That is because registration is so cheap. Today, for a *maximum* registration charge of $22,500 and a modest annual fee, shipowners can purchase a wide degree of latitude. For a ship the size of the Vessel, the annual charge would come to around $4,000.[67]

• • •

Cost concerns and regulatory laxity were the principal draws when Derek Bibby reregistered the *Bibby Resolution* and the *Bibby Venture* as Bahamian ships. The worldwide contractions of the 1970s that pushed shipowners to diversify away from container ships also pushed them toward flagging out.[68] Flags of convenience offered a way out of high labor costs in northern Europe and the United States, a way to avoid taxes, and the possibility of sidestepping onerous safety regulations and costly inspections.[69] In short, open registries allowed shipowners like Bibby to circumvent national regulation. While the sea floor was being divided up into national jurisdictions through UN conventions, the surface of the ocean was increasingly populated by vessels functionally unregulated by national bodies. In this way, by the late 1980s, the Vessel and its sister ship had already borne witness to a simultaneous expansion and contraction of national sovereignty.

By the time the two vessels were registered in the Bahamas, Bibby had already found new clients eager to lease them. One was a major West German multinational company with an internationally renowned product: Volkswagen Aktiengesellschaft. The other was the operator of one of the world's largest carceral systems: the City of New York. Neither New York (the global center of increasingly deregulated capital) nor VW (a corporation in the process of outsourcing labor to factories in poor countries) had any problem with the ships flying the Bahamian flag. And so, in 1987 and 1988, the two barges owned by Bibby departed the Falkland Islands, their home for the previous five years. Both were bound for England for refitting. The *Bibby Venture* would turn around and again traverse the Atlantic, destined for New York. The Vessel itself would stay in Europe, towed across the North Sea to a small port city in Germany, minutes from the Dutch border. The sister ships were parting ways, with each one destined for a different corner of the same offshore world.

CHAPTER 5

THE RIVER EMS

	The Vessel	The Sister Vessel
1988	The *Bibby Resolution* leaves Stanley and is reregistered in the Bahamas. It is refurbished outside of London and then delivered to Volkswagen in Emden, West Germany.	The *Bibby Venture* is moved to Pier 1 in Brooklyn.

One morning in 1988, lights flickered on in a newly refurbished factory measuring 1.5 million square feet in Emden, West Germany. Sparkling new assembly lines hummed into life for the first time, heavy metal parts clanking as workers carefully fitted them together to create new machines. At the end of the line, the finished products rolled out of the plant into vast parking lots. Eventually each would be driven onto waiting cargo ships moored at a nearby dock. There they sat: rows upon rows of Volkswagen Passats, destined for dealerships across the United States and Canada. As shifts at the factory ended, workers began to clock out and make their way home. Many headed to homes in and around Emden, a clean and tidy small city of about fifty thousand people. But hundreds of others boarded corporate shuttle buses bound for a nondescript "hotel ship" floating in the harbor, very close to where the Passats were loaded onto freighters. That hotel ship was the Vessel—the *Bibby Resolution*—freshly arrived from the Falkland Islands via Britain. The Vessel had traded its cargo of soldiers for a load of factory workers.

• • •

When Volkswagen opened its sprawling production plant in Emden in December 1964, the company was the number one global car exporter. Its signature product—the Type 1, or Beetle—was soaring in popularity. Nowhere was this more the case than in the United States, the world's largest auto market. American consumers, according to a 1963 *Sports Illustrated* article, were in the midst of "a romance with a plain Jane": the Beetle.[1] In the Beetle, VW offered Americans a product entirely different from the massive four-door sedans being hawked by the Big Three automakers in Detroit. It was small—cute, even—and fuel efficient. As a result, VW's U.S. sales had grown by 20 percent each year from 1960 to 1963.[2] In the boom years of the 1960s, Volkswagen was one of West Germany's most important industrial exporters: 55 percent of its output left the country in 1963, and 70 percent in 1968. By comparison, the engineering conglomerate Krupp sold less than 20 percent of its output outside of Germany.[3]

The Emden assembly plant, located just across the muddy and brackish river Ems from the Netherlands, was constructed specifically to serve the growing export market. Volkswagenwerk Emden was built to be the last stop for cars leaving West Germany, the assembly site for a production process carried out across the country. As a VW publication put it, it received "bodies from Wolfsburg [site of VW's headquarters], engines from Hanover, gearboxes and frames from Kassel and axles from Braunschweig." Only the seats and the wiring harnesses were produced in Emden itself.[4] When it opened, the plant produced five hundred cars per day. Within two years, that number had more than doubled. The finished vehicles rolled off the assembly line and directly into a company port facility on the Ems, where they were loaded onto freighters for shipment to ports in the United States and Canada.[5] Few places embodied the export orientation of West German industry more than Emden.

Emden is the largest city in East Frisia, a region tucked away in Germany's northwest corner. It is a bucolic, pastoral place, a region stereotyped within Germany for its somewhat provincial attitudes. Emden is surrounded by miles of pancake-flat fields, with dikes and levees holding the North Sea at bay. Huge windmills dot the landscape, descendants of the great powerhouses of the past that helped drain the land. The city itself is a neat collection of brick, peaked roofs with cobblestone streets clustered around an old harbor near the mouth of the Ems. Four centuries ago, Emders diverted part of the river, drawing it into a moat around the town's defensive wall like a protective blanket. Like so many other places the Vessel had stayed, Emden is oriented toward water.

Standing in the center of the town, the salt air mingling with the aromas of nearby cows, it is easy to forget that one is in the midst of an industrial center. But Emden is industrial; out of its fifty thousand residents, a full eight thousand work at the VW plant. Volkswagen is far and away the largest employer, not just in the city but in the region, as well. Without it, the people of East Frisia would be considerably less comfortable. As it is, Emden is affluent. With a per capita GDP of well over €70,000, it is significantly wealthier than the German average.

Emden had been an important trading center for hundreds of years before VW arrived. In the seventeenth century, as Gustavus Adolphus was founding Gothenburg on Sweden's west coast, Emden prospered as a free city under the protection of the Dutch Republic. When it was annexed by the Prussian King Frederick the Great in 1744, it became Prussia's first port on the North Sea. As such, it was the home port of a short-lived state-supported trading company—the Emden Company—founded to foster Prussian trade with China.[6] At the end of the nineteenth century, thanks to a new canal network, Emden became the principal seaport for the Ruhr River valley: the heartland of Germany's coal and iron industries. Heavy industry came to Emden itself around the same time; in 1903, a major shipyard—the Nordseewerke—opened just south of the city center.[7] The city's industrial and military importance led to it becoming the namesake of Admiral Ludwig von Reuter's flagship, the SMS *Emden*, from which he orchestrated the scuttling of the German fleet in the Scapa Flow in 1919. Volkswagen, which opened its own plant in the city in the boom years of the 1960s, built on Emden's combined industrial and commercial legacy.

Over the 1970s and 1980s, Emden grew into an ever more important linchpin of Volkswagen's export-oriented corporate strategy because of its convenient access to a deepwater port, able to accommodate ships with ten-meter drafts.[8] Emden's port is not dominated by the great cranes that tower over other harbors. The reason is that its principal cargo—VW cars—are not lifted, but rather driven onto waiting ships, one unit at a time. Emden is not a container port. The overwhelming majority of its surface area is given over to vast parking lots. There, tens of thousands of sedans, sports cars, and SUVs coming from the nearby plant and from a constant flow of arriving trains are parked in orderly rows, grouped according to their destination. The parking lots do not so much culminate as simply end at the water, where land meets riverine coast in a reinforced concrete edge. The port is a liminal space. It is German territory, but still retains a British military presence: an enduring legacy of World War II. The quays are technically owned by the local state, Lower Saxony, but they are incredibly narrow strips. All the land around them has been owned by Volkswagen since the plant's beginnings.

•　•　•

In 1973, with manufacturing just beginning to cool in western Europe, Volkswagen converted its Emden plant to a more efficient, state-of-the-art hanging assembly line and installed new computer systems to rationalize workflow. After the final Beetle built in Germany rolled off the line at Emden in 1978, the plant shifted to assembling the make's new flagship car, the Passat, a large sedan designed especially

The Emden VW plant and port facilities in 2010. The port is visible in the top left of the image, surrounded by sprawling parking lots. Note the windmills in the top right of the frame and the rail links at the bottom left.

for the U.S. market.[9] As before, the units produced in Emden were all destined for foreign buyers. Exports drove Volkswagen's impressive growth in the 1980s. In 1978, the VW Group sold about 900,000 vehicles in Germany and 1.5 million abroad. A decade later, it was selling slightly fewer vehicles in Germany, but significantly more—well over 2 million units—abroad. North America continued to be important for VW, but new developing markets in other parts of Europe and in East Asia were fast becoming central to the company's business.[10] Growing wealth in the Global South was shaping corporate strategy.

It was the importance of the changing global export market that brought the Vessel to the river Ems. More markets meant more demand. And in 1988, Volkswagen again began refitting the Emden factory floor in order to fully automate production of its export-destined Passats. To bring production up to speed, workers—not just from Emden but also from facilities across West Germany—had to be trained on the new factory floor. As part of that training process, VW relocated nearly five hundred employees who worked at plants around the country to Emden to learn the ropes. Most came from the company's Hanover plant, a three-hour drive away. This meant that while the workers were in Emden, they would need somewhere to stay.

The Vessel aboard the *Goliath Atlantic* on the way to Emden, 1988

From June to September 1988, the Vessel—the *Bibby Resolution*—
was that place. Aggressively marketed by the Bibby Line as a flexible
solution for temporary housing, the Vessel was a quick and relatively
cheap fix for Volkswagen planners who needed to provide temporary
housing in a small (and relatively expensive) German city. The Vessel had arrived in Emden from the Falklands, carried back to Europe
aboard the *Goliath Atlantic*, another heavy-lift ship. In late spring of
that year, it was slowly lowered into the Ems. As the deck of the *Goliath
Atlantic* dropped below the waterline, the Vessel itself began to float
free, creaking as it debarked. As the *Goliath Atlantic* slowly moved
back out to the North Sea, the Vessel was towed to shore. At its new
berth, the Vessel sat just down from VW's own port and production
facilities, and the factory's managers set up a regular shuttle bus service
between the ship and the plant, a couple of kilometers away.[11] The
location was convenient for workers, but as in the Falklands, the ship
itself did not develop a good reputation. Its quarters were cramped
and stuffy. Even if the ship did offer resident factory workers indoor
squash courts, conditions were hardly opulent.[12]

●　　●　　●

Volkswagen's decision to automate its production lines responded
to the changing ecology of global manufacturing in the late twentieth century. VW had been a key contributor to West Germany's
Wirtschaftswunder—economic miracle—of industrial recovery after
World War II. The German experience of economic growth was dramatic, but not unique. The mid-twentieth century saw a golden age
of manufacturing in the industrialized "West": the *Wirtschaftswunder* in Germany; the "economic miracle" in Japan; the *trente glorieuses*
("glorious thirty years") in France; the *boom economico* in Italy. As
economies and consumption patterns recovered from the war, unemployment virtually disappeared and living standards surged. Thirty
years after the end of World War II, western European GDP per capita
nearly tripled. In West Germany, per capita GDP more than quadrupled. Everywhere, there were signs of prosperity: new appliances,
new houses, new cars.

German industrial growth, especially in export goods, kept German unemployment low—well under 4 percent—even in the face of

rising wages. Volkswagen itself was a poster child of the *Wirtschafts-wunder*. Between 1960 and 1970, the company nearly doubled the number of "wage earners" it employed, from 58,475 to 110,968. Over the same period, its global sales revenue grew more than threefold, from 4.6 billion to 15.7 billion Deutschmarks ($1.1 billion to $4.3 billion). But VW faced challenges in the 1970s and 1980s, especially in the key North American market, as the postwar boom slowed. Starting in the 1970s, the consumer advocate Ralph Nadar attacked the Beetle as "the most hazardous car currently in use." In the 1980s, the firm faced increasingly stiff competition in the small car market from Japanese automakers, which managed to chip away at VW's market share.[13] And then, there were the global oil shocks, which hit the automotive industry with almost the same force as they hit maritime shippers and shipbuilders. To compound the woes of German exporters, the West German Deutschmark gained considerably on the dollar throughout this period. By the mid-1970s, VW was losing money on every car it sold in the United States.[14]

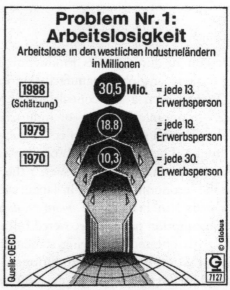

This image, which appeared in the *Nordwest-Zeitung* in 1988 next to an article about VW's automation program, gives the mounting losses in terms of the total number of people in the labor force. The text reads: "Problem No. 1: Unemployment—Job losses in Western industrialized countries in millions." It notes that the 1988 figures are estimates.

Closer to home, VW was confronting a final, even more obstinate, obstacle to profit. Persistently high wages in West Germany, a result both of the widespread prosperity of the preceding decades and strong industrial unions, cut deeply into VW's profit margins. After three decades of extraordinary prosperity, German industrial growth began to lag behind wage growth. As the *Wirtschaftswunder* ended, VW's leadership focused on streamlining inefficient production routines. It also cut back. In 1975 alone, it laid off thirty-two thousand workers.[15] These layoffs were part of a larger trend. Throughout the West German economy, job losses mounted, with unemployment creeping up from around 3 percent in 1980 to over 8 percent by 1988.[16] An article appearing that year in the *Nordwest-Zeitung,* the daily paper for Emden's region, proclaimed unemployment "Problem No. 1" facing Western industrialized countries.[17]

As with layoffs in other parts of western Europe—including those at the Finnboda shipyard in Stockholm—the majority of those who left Volkswagen were not unionized. They were, instead, mostly Italian *Gastarbeiter*—literally "guest workers"—who had been recruited during the boom years of German growth and were employed through temporary contracts. Across German heavy industry, when layoffs came, *Gastarbeiter,* whether from Italy, Turkey, or Eastern Europe, were the first to go.[18] With the writing on the wall indicating that their contracts would not be renewed, tens of thousands of *Gastarbeiter* left the country, induced by severance packages. Volkswagen's unionized workers, who were represented by one of the country's largest and most powerful trade unions, IG Metall, were better protected. But though the union was generally able to spare its members from layoffs, it was forced to accept the introduction of new labor-saving technologies that would limit job growth in the future.[19] These technologies were understood, at least by executives, as vital for the company to stay competitive. This was the era of the so-called Car Wars, in which large and established American and European firms were pitted against Honda, Toyota, and Nissan, Japanese manufacturers that were increasingly ascendant, not just in Asia and the United States but in markets around the world.[20] And to many, it seemed like the Japanese companies were winning. The oil shocks of the 1970s turbocharged the market for smaller, more efficient Japanese cars, backed up with new technology. In 1975, Toyota outsold Volkswagen for the first time in the United States, the world's most lucrative auto market.[21] Not to wonder: the Beetle, VW's signature small car, was by then almost forty years old.

VW Beetles waiting to be shipped overseas at the VW dock in Emden

Not coincidentally, throughout the 1980s, Volkswagen sought to expand its production capacity in regions with lower prevailing wages. Starting in 1977, its iconic Beetles—even those sold inside Germany—were all produced in a plant in Puebla, Mexico. As Beetles were unloaded for German consumption at the dock in Emden that VW had previously used for export, one reporter commented that "it was as if a movie was running backward."[22] For years, Germany had exported the Beetle. Now, the tide had turned. Starting in 1982, VW entered into a series of partnerships with state-run companies in communist China to produce cars there. In 1986, it took over the Spanish automaker SEAT, and in 1988, it closed its one assembly plant in the United States.[23] VW also looked east. By the late 1980s, the Cold War was thawing. In June 1987, Ronald Reagan, addressing a crowd in front of both Berlin's Brandenburg Gate and the concrete wall dividing the city in two, famously called on Soviet Premier Mikhail Gorbachev to "tear down this wall." Immediately after the fall of the wall two years later, VW worked to take over facilities in the former

East Germany, working with factories in Chemnitz and Eisenach, and buying out Škoda, the communist state–owned Czech carmaker, in 1991.[24] The logic of offshoring that had motivated the Bibby Line to reflag its ships in Hong Kong and the Bahamas similarly motivated VW to move production abroad. A global strategy that took advantage of laxer regulatory regimes and looser labor markets meant, quite simply, lower costs.

Locked in competition with Japanese rivals, VW's corporate thinking in the 1970s and 1980s was fixated on reducing labor costs and streamlining labor management. The company's increasingly global footprint lessened the impact of high wages in Germany, but VW was inescapably a German concern; its workers, factories, and infrastructure in West Germany remained central to the company's operations.[25] So, in those factories, VW upgraded, streamlined, and automated, squeezing the most productivity it could out of its expensive domestic labor force. The self-proclaimed focus of the company's leadership in the 1980s was the so-called technology strategy, which prioritized process automation.[26]

There is a long history of corporations and factory owners turning to machines as a way of saving on labor costs. One of the most influential accounts of why the Industrial Revolution took off in Britain (as opposed to elsewhere) was that Britain had comparatively high prevailing wages.[27] High wages, the story goes, created an incentive for technological innovation. The resulting machines—like James Hargreaves's spinning jenny, James Watt's steam engine, and Richard Arkwright's water frame—were catalysts for spectacular industrial growth. At the same time, for as long as factory owners turned to machines to save on labor, workers have resisted such movements. In the 1810s, facing the introduction of new industrial machinery and the inevitable loss of employment, textile workers across the English north and midlands began campaigns of machine breaking. Bands of men—followers of the fictional hero General Ned Ludd—would sneak into factories to destroy new technology. These "Luddites" were hardly alone. Twenty years later, when the mechanized threshing machine was introduced into English fields, agricultural workers—following the equally mythical "Captain Swing," reacted similarly.[28]

New technology has the potential to disrupt existing employment patterns and to put the squeeze on low- and middle-wage workers.

The current fears over what artificial intelligence will do to labor markets is a case in point. But fortunately for VW's employees working in Emden in the 1980s, the introduction of new technology was relatively smooth. The *Gastarbeiter* had few protections, but full-time employees were shielded by the powerful IG Metall, and VW itself expressed a commitment to employee welfare. The technology strategy depended on a softer kind of capitalist labor relation: a social partnership between management and well-cared-for, high-wage, skilled workers that sociologists at the time dubbed the "German model."[29] Compared to offshoring and wage cuts elsewhere, the German model seemed to blunt global capitalism with a dose of European welfare.

● ● ●

Immediately to the left of the grim graphic on unemployment as "Problem No. 1" that ran in the *Nordwest-Zeitung* in May 1988 appeared a flashy paid feature that sprawled over two pages. It lauded the new "JUST IN TIME" system that a German contractor had recently installed in the VW Emden plant as part of the major refit. A system of "remote data transmission" (*Datenfernübertragung*) connected the assembly line in Emden with a different facility that manufactured bumpers in Oldenburg, an hour and a half away.[30] An automated system run by computers would coordinate the needs of the factory in Emden with its supplier in Oldenburg so that no more than five and a half hours would elapse between the order being placed for the bumper and the installation of the bumper on the assembly line. The article reported that a "special technology of remote data transmission enables that bumper after bumper get to the line in Emden in exactly the right order." This was no mean feat; there were 240 possible bumper variants.[31] Today, such a system might be taken for granted, but in the late 1980s, it represented the bleeding edge of computerization and industrial technology.

This system was part of the major renovations that Volkswagen undertook in Emden—the renovations that pushed VW to lease an accommodation barge from the Bibby Line. The refit not only fully automated Emden's assembly line into a marvel of smoothly moving parts, it also linked the plant with another automated line sixty kilometers away. In fact, this computerized network would reach far

beyond East Frisia. After all, Emden was the German port of departure for Volkswagen Passats destined for global supply chains. Today,
the whole world depends on "just-in-time" manufacturing, in which
highly integrated supply chains allow factories to create products
essentially as they are demanded, rather than in advance. Doing so
avoids the costs of having to store surplus material or finished products; it allows the most efficient use of labor and capital. It also lowers
interest costs by reducing short-term debt used to purchase inven-
tory supplies. As the world's consumers discovered during the early
months of the COVID-19 pandemic, just-in-time manufacturing also
can result in supply chains collapsing when one supplier hits a snag. A
chain is only as strong as its weakest link. Without surplus products,
even a small disruption can snowball into a large one.

For Volkswagen in the late 1980s, however, the just-in-time system
was both a technological marvel and an integral part of the process
that launched Passats into overseas markets. And the Passat's trajectory
was indeed impressive: as the *Nordwest-Zeitung* put it, the new generation of Passat produced in Emden "started out with a bang."[32] In 1987,
VW sold 211,936 Passats worldwide; the next year, it sold 280,571. The
figures kept rising, year after year, to 427,395 in 1991. These healthy
worldwide sales figures were the reason that Volkswagen was able to
keep jobs in Germany: the payoff of the technology strategy. For even
as it outsourced more and more of its labor-intensive production to
Mexico, Brazil, Spain, and eastern Europe, booming global sales kept
jobs in Emden and elsewhere in the Federal Republic.[33] The Germans
who held these jobs were the people who stayed on the *Bibby Resolution* in Emden's harbor, helping bring the newly reorganized production facility online.

For technology—whether computerization, integrated just-in-time
systems, or automated factory floors—still depended on human labor.
Workers had to install the new equipment. Workers had to learn how
to use it. Those workers were human. They required infrastructure of
their own for education, transportation, and housing. The standard
story of Volkswagen's renewed prosperity in the 1980s invokes a set of
abstract transformations. It involved "market-making" in new regions
in Europe and overseas. It was enabled by outsourcing abroad and
by "automating" and "streamlining" labor at home in Germany. That
streamlining—"rationalization," in the parlance of the official com-

pany history—required new technology. It required digitized machinery and abstract systems of production. But it also required equipment that was much less cutting edge and much more concretely physical. It required objects like the Vessel.

• • •

The Vessel—still named the *Bibby Resolution* and still registered in the Bahamas—was moored in Germany for less than two years. While there, it left few traces in the historical record. The only time it was mentioned by name in the *Nordwest-Zeitung* was shortly before it departed, in a brief news item in early 1989, when it had already been vacated by Volkswagen employees. The article noted that the Vessel was undergoing renovations for a new purpose in New York.[34]

In the local article about the *Bibby Resolution*, the Vessel was described as "the former VW hotel ship [*Hotelschiff*]." Internal VW publications similarly referred to it as a "floating hotel." This moniker was noteworthy and significant.[35] The Vessel had been brought to West Germany in order to help streamline the production of a global commodity; while in Emden, it was to temporarily accommodate well-paid unionized workers employed in a newly automated VW plant. In this way, designating the *Bibby Resolution* a "hotel ship" was apt. Importantly, though the accommodated workers were temporary, they were not foreign. Volkswagen had already laid off the vast majority of its *Gastarbeiter*.[36] When the economy slowed down, the guest workers had been the first to feel the pinch. Therefore, the people who would stay in the so-called hotel ship were white northern European men; just as the people who had stayed in Bibby's "floating hotels" in the Falkland Islands had been white northern European men; just as the people who were anticipated to stay in Consafe's "coastels" in the North Sea were to be white northern European men. These were people who stayed in "hotels."

In this way, the Vessel's designation in the German press as the "former VW hotel ship" is a subtle but revealing marker. It is particularly striking when compared to the descriptions of other Bibby barges that were deployed in northern West Germany shortly after the Vessel departed the country. In 1989, the city of Hamburg, perhaps inspired by Volkswagen's experience with Bibby, chartered another Bibby barge—the *Casa Marina*—to house refugees from East Germany.[37] This began a long tradition of housing refugees on barges in the city. As Bibby phrased it in promotional materials, the " 'floating option' has provided Hamburg with a cost-effective, efficient and fast solution to a critical housing problem."[38] The advertisement found receptive audiences. More barges arrived in Hamburg as the number of refugees surged. In the early 1990s, Hamburg leased further barges from Bibby—the *Bibby Altona*, the *Bibby Challenge*, and the *Bibby Kalmar*—to accommodate a rising number of refugees fleeing war in the Balkans. Contracts from Dutch and British governments followed—including one for the *Bibby Stockholm*, which housed asylum seekers in southern England in 2023 and 2024. In 1992, there were around 19,700 asylum seekers in Hamburg alone; the next year, that number had more than doubled, to forty-two thousand.[39] By the early 2000s, the population housed on the barges had shifted to include more arrivals from Africa and Turkey, in addition to those from southeastern Europe. When described in the German press, these vessels were never "hotel ships," but instead "accommodation ships" (*Wohnschiffe*) or, occasionally, "container ships" (*Containerschiffe*), though they were built to essentially the same specifications as the Vessel.[40]

According to a *New York Times* article from 1995, the conditions on board the refugee barges in Hamburg amounted to "little more than squalor."[41] As the leader of a refugee rights group commented at the time, "These are not concentration camps. They are not prisons. But there are security guards. And you are floating in the water, isolated from normal city life. They are distinctly unfriendly places."[42] Conditions on the "container ships" in Hamburg were certainly worse than they were aboard the "hotel ship" in Emden. In this context, to liken the vessels in Hamburg to hotels would have been misleading, if not grossly euphemistic. But what really differentiated a hotel ship from a container ship was the sort of person it housed. German workers stayed on the former; refugees from poorer countries belonged to the latter. The *Bibby Resolution*, like other Bibby-owned barges, was an empty vessel; it took on meaning from what, or whom, it contained.

• • •

Whether in Hamburg or in Emden, the barges were "unfriendly places." For workers in Emden, the Vessel was unfriendly because it was meant to be transitory: it was cold and impersonal, even though it was moored in a city where residents hail total strangers with the jovial local greeting, "*Moin!*" But it was also unfriendly because of what it represented. The age of the *Wirtschaftswunder* was over, and with it, the age of relatively easy access to good, high-paying manufacturing jobs. VW's "German model" might have been considerably less brutal than the offshoring regimes of many of its competitors and analogs. Yet the company's emphasis on technological innovation did not change the basic reality that it was under great pressure to trim labor costs.

As high wages drove companies like VW to streamline, computerize, and automate, workers had to become more efficient. They themselves had to become better cogs in a global, multinational machine. And, whatever label it was given, the Vessel was a billet for productive cogs as much as it was lodging for people. Its architecture was utilitarian and modular because its *use* was utilitarian and modular. For the refugees and migrants in a Germany reluctant to welcome them in, the barges were made to be even more inhospitable. They too were treated as modular units to be fit into standardized housing. But even these refugee centers were not nearly as unfriendly as what the *Bibby Resolution* would become after it left Emden. For although in Germany Bibby's barges were becoming increasingly hostile places, in the United States they would become actual jails.

CHAPTER 6

THE EAST RIVER

	The Vessel	The Sister Vessel
1987		The *Bibby Venture* leaves Stanley and is reregistered in the Bahamas. It is refurbished outside of London and then delivered to the New York City Department of Correction. It is moored at Pier 36 in the East River and called the Maritime Facility I.
1988	The *Bibby Resolution* leaves Stanley and is reregistered in the Bahamas. It is refurbished outside of London and then delivered to Volkswagen in Emden, West Germany.	The *Bibby Venture* is moved to Pier 1 in Brooklyn.
1989	The *Bibby Resolution* is transported to New York, where it is leased by the New York Department of Correction. It opens as a jail at Pier 36 off Manhattan, officially called the Maritime Facility II.	The *Bibby Venture* is moved to Pier 40 in Manhattan, on the Hudson River.
1994	The *Bibby Resolution* ceases operation as a detention facility and is moved to Brooklyn. New York City buys the Vessel.	The *Bibby Venture* ceases operation as a detention facility. New York City buys the Sister Vessel.

On a mid-August day in 1990, U.S. Representative Chuck Schumer opened the proceedings of a special hearing of the House Subcommittee on Criminal Justice in an unusual location: the gymnasium of a New York City jail. Schumer had called the hearing to draw attention to new programs in jails that provided treatment for drug addiction. New York was in the midst of the war on

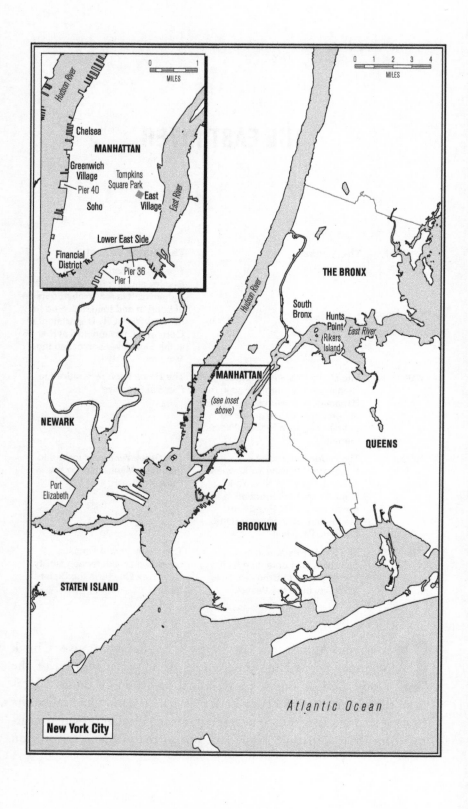

0 1
MILES

Hudson River

Chelsea

MANHATTAN

Greenwich
Village

Pier 40

Tompkins
Square Park

East
Village

East River

Soho

Lower East Side

Financial
District

Pier 36
Pier 1

0 1 2 3 4
MILES

THE BRONX

Hudson River

South
Bronx

Hunts
Point

Rikers
Island

East River

MANHATTAN

(see inset
above)

QUEENS

NEWARK

Port
Elizabeth

BROOKLYN

STATEN ISLAND

Atlantic Ocean

New York City

drugs, and the jail in which Schumer was speaking was a new weapon in the city's arsenal: a whole facility devoted to drug rehabilitation. In this, the jail was one of a kind. It was unusual in another way as well. Moored off Lower Manhattan in the East River, the "Maritime Facility II" was a floating penitentiary. In fact, it was none other than the Vessel: the British-owned *Bibby Resolution*. The barge—still registered offshore in the Bahamas—allowed the city to literally offshore its prisoners. With its Bahamian flag and its signage still in Swedish, the Vessel brought the offshore world to New York, and global capitalism to local mass incarceration.

To get to his congressional hearing on the Vessel, Chuck Schumer traveled through a troubled area. Driving through the Lower East Side, Schumer would have passed acres of public housing, testaments to the decades-long struggle to house New York's poor. There were the sprawling low-rises of the Vladeck Houses, built back before America had entered World War II; the squat brick towers of the Fiorello LaGuardia Houses, shaped like plus signs, which opened in the mid-1950s. There were the twenty-story Rutgers Houses, which opened in 1965 after being the site of ongoing civil rights protests, and the twenty-six-floor Two Bridges Urban Renewal Area, completed in 1975. Eventually, Schumer would have crossed under the six-lane FDR Drive and arrived at the East River, with the Williamsburg Bridge off to the left, the Manhattan and Brooklyn Bridges stretching across the water to the right. There, he would have found Pier 36 and, beside it, the *Bibby Resolution*.

• • •

Apart from the Vessel, Pier 36 was vacant. This fact was a direct manifestation of New York's rapid evolution from an economic center dealing in physical objects to one that traded in services and financial abstractions. Someone standing on Pier 36 looking south would have a sweeping view of the East River. In the foreground was a blighted waterfront: a relic of a once-thriving port that had atrophied into industrial decay. But immediately behind the lanes of FDR Drive rose the spires of New York's glittering financial district, dominated by the twin glass towers of the World Trade Center.

Pier 36 itself was less than twenty-five years old, its story one of international aspiration and untimely obsolescence. Designated as the new passenger and freight terminal for the Belgian Line, the facility had been constructed by the city for $7.5 million, with considerable investment from New York State. In the heady days of the early 1960s, city planners anticipated that it would link the city more directly with Belgium itself and with the Belgian Line's other destinations: the Congo and Angola. The pier was inaugurated in 1965 with great fanfare in a ceremony attended by a host of American and Belgian dignitaries, including the Belgian ambassador and the heir to the Belgian throne, Prince Albert.[1] In his remarks at the ceremony, New York's Republican governor Nelson Rockefeller hailed Pier 36's construction as signaling the "rebirth of this section of New York City waterfront once historically the center of New York's waterfront activities."[2] Rockefeller's optimism would prove to be significantly too rosy.

Pier 36's decline directly resulted from the advent of the shipping container. New York's leaders envisioned the pier competing with the massive new facilities that the state of New Jersey (working with the independent Port of New York Authority) was erecting just across the Hudson River in Newark and Port Elizabeth.[3] But unlike those facilities—located on hundreds of acres of cheap land near rail links—Pier 36 would never be able to accommodate container ships: its plot size was simply too small.[4] The result was that it became obsolete as a cargo facility almost as soon as it was built. By the mid-1970s, New York's harbor boasted the largest container port in the world, but none of that traffic went through Manhattan; nearly all of it went through New Jersey. After the Belgian Line's fifteen-year lease ran out, it did not re-up its contract, and the city struggled to find a new tenant. By the mid-1980s, Pier 36 was vacant, awaiting the Vessel and its sister ship.

The relentless efficiency of containers and container ports was devastating for longshoring employment around the world, but New York City was especially hard hit. Because of space constraints, it was impossible to convert existing port facilities in Manhattan and Brooklyn into container ship terminals. The result was that the city hemorrhaged jobs: the number of people employed at marine cargo handling companies in Manhattan fell from 19,007 in 1964 to 7,934 in 1976. In 1963–64, Manhattan businesses had employed 1.4 million days of longshore labor. That figure had fallen to just 127,000 twelve years later. An analogous story—only slightly less dramatic—had unfolded across the East River in Brooklyn.[5]

By the time the barges arrived in New York, Lower Manhattan— once home to a thriving port and small-scale manufacturing facilities—had lost much of the buzzing economic vibrancy it had enjoyed two decades before. Just as in Sweden and Britain, in New York, globalization and the transition to the service economy took its toll. Lower Manhattan's homeless population was among the largest and most visible in the city. The loss of industry had hollowed out the area. Its piers were empty; its streets full of litter; its arrest rate surging.

And then, in the late 1980s, the neighborhood was visited by something of a cruel joke. With the arrival of the Vessel and its sister ship, the area, bypassed and gutted by containerization, would end up playing host to two container ships. But these were container ships that were not meant to contain cargo. They were meant to house human beings.

• • •

The *Bibby Venture* arrived first. In 1988, two years before Chuck Schumer's hearing, as the *Bibby Resolution* made its way to Germany to house Volkswagen workers, its sister ship was transported to New York. It had been leased by desperate administrators at the city's Department of Correction (DOC) to serve as a floating jail. Space in New York's jails was at a premium; the jail population had crested above 106 percent of its system's designated capacity.[6] As the New York Police Department arrested more and more people, the pressure to find space to detain them mounted. That pressure motivated the decision to lease the barge, which could provide expanded capacity with minimal lead time. As a DOC spokesperson explained, the *Bibby Venture* "was made ready in three months from the time the Department started negotiating"—an astounding turnaround time.[7] The timetable was so short because the Bibby Line did not need to do much to the *Venture* to refit it as a prison. As Bibby's managing director put it at the time, "We have been asked to put bars on the windows, and to put locks on the doors."[8]

And so, for $19 million, the city secured a five-year lease on the 379-bed *Venture*, with the option to buy the barge for a nominal fee at the end of the term.[9] Compared with the costs of building a permanent prison, the choice seemed reasonable; when the city opened the Rose M. Singer Center, an eight-hundred-bed facility on Rikers Island, the next year, the up-front cost ran to $100 million. But there were lower long-term costs and other advantages to investing in a permanent, purpose-built structure. Few if any in city hall considered the barge a great bargain. The city was in an emergency and was willing to pay dearly to get out of it.

The "emergency" was very much of the city's own making. Space in New York's jails was scarce because of aggressive policing that overwhelmingly targeted young men of color. After years of "war on crime" and "war on drugs" tactics pushed and funded by federal policies, incarceration was at an all-time high. Over the previous decade and a half, the country had turned away from positive antipoverty efforts, abandoning faith in the possibility of rehabilitation to embrace an increasingly punitive approach to social disorder.[10]

An inflection point had come in 1973 when, just eight years after opening Pier 36 with the Belgian prince, New York governor Nelson Rockefeller pushed through a particularly tough crime bill aimed at prosecuting drug offenders. Dubbed the "Attila the Hun Law" for its severity by legislators in Albany, its aggressiveness tapped into a public concern about what Rockefeller called "an invading army" of drug addicts. The legislation, which inspired similar laws in other states, set the stage for an escalating regime of broken-windows policing, arrests, and imprisonment.[11]

These trends intensified under the Reagan administration's war on drugs, itself pitched as a moral battle for American values, fought on the streets of American cities with surplus military equipment. As the global economy slowed after the thirty-year postwar boom and old industries like ship handling fell away, guns replaced butter. When Reagan slashed social welfare programs in the name of individual responsibility and small government, he oversaw a major expansion of federal funding for law enforcement. The result was a rapid rise in mass incarceration. America's prison population grew fivefold between 1965 and 1988. Over the same period, the proportion of those incarcerated who were Black or Latino expanded from about a third to a half.[12] In New York City jails, the disparity was particularly dramatic. In 1990, New York was a city with a significant white plurality. Yet the Black population of city jails far exceeded the white. At any given moment in 1990, New York was incarcerating about 8,500 Black and 6,300 Latino people, compared to just around 1,500 white people.[13]

In fact, New York City was at the forefront of the trend toward punitiveness in the American judicial system, a place where growing doubts about the police's ability to maintain order became a hot-button political issue.[14] In the 1980s, the mayoral administration of Ed Koch (1978–89) launched a campaign to improve the city's "quality of life," an effort that included major crackdowns on people experiencing homelessness and addiction. Koch was elected in the aftermath of New York's fiscal crisis in the 1970s, an episode during which the city made massive and painful cuts to social services like hospitals and schools in order to stave off bankruptcy. As in Margaret Thatcher's Britain, in Koch's New York the welfare state was deemed too expensive to maintain in the face of tough economic realities. Drawing on fears of a repeat crisis, Koch positioned himself as a new kind of Democrat, one willing to slash antipoverty programs and take on powerful public-sector unions. But most of all, Koch foregrounded his tough-on-crime stance, promising to crack down on protesters and widely proclaiming his support of capital punishment.[15] During his tenure, the mayor steadily moved from urban liberalism toward a harsher approach to crime and disorder.[16] As the president of the local police union would recall, "In any police audience when the mayor was introduced, he literally got a rollicking standing ovation."[17] While Koch's policies won him ardent loyalty from the NYPD, his efforts to shore up political support among middle-class New Yorkers—both white and Black—led to more stops, arrests, and jail time, especially for Black and brown men.[18]

• • •

The 1980s was a time of mounting malaise over the perceived disorder of urban life. Consider the raft of blockbuster films set in dystopian near futures in which law had given way to chaos: *The Warriors* (1979), *Mad Max* (1979, 1985), *The Road Warrior* (1981), *Blade Runner* (1982), *RoboCop* (1987). In *Escape from New York* (1981), the director, John Carpenter, imagined a 1997 in which the entirety of Manhattan had been turned into a walled maximum-security prison. Real-life conditions in New York at the time were not quite so dystopian, but they were nevertheless grim. As arrests surged, conditions in city jails deteriorated. In 1983, overcrowding led to the court-mandated release of six hundred people from city custody. The release galvanized the mayor. Stanley Brezenoff recalled that when he became deputy mayor several months later, "Koch only raised one or two things with me." The jail release was one of them. Koch "mandated, appealed to me not to allow that to happen" again.[19]

Law and order depended on keeping criminals locked up. But keeping the prisons from overflowing was a Herculean task. The year of Brezenoff's appointment, inmates at the Correctional Institution for Men (CIFM), a city facility on Rikers Island, filed a class-action lawsuit against the city's Department of Correction. They alleged that overcrowding, inadequate staff, and violent conditions amounted to cruel and unusual punishment. The case would drag on for six years, ending in a stinging rebuke of the department.[20] But in the meantime, the number of people locked up by the city continued to surge. In early 1986, New York's jail population was 11,500. By the fall of the next year, it was pushing 16,000.[21] By comparison, in early 2022, the average daily population in New York City jails was around 5,700.[22] In the 1980s, holding cells were bursting; at one point, 30 women were packed into each cell, forced to share a single, only partially obscured toilet.[23] At another, the DOC loaded inmates onto city buses and drove them around at night, just to free up space in jails.[24] As lawsuits made clear, jails were dangerous places. In 1986, at the CIFM alone, there were six hundred recorded incidents of "inmate-inmate violence" involving weapons, including shanks, shivs, razors, ammonia, or bleach. Prisoners and expert witnesses testified to a culture of excessive force by corrections officers, recounting beating after beating. DOC officials admitted to twenty-two instances in which "force was misused" from 1985 to 1987 at the CIFM alone; by comparison, the entire Los Angeles County jail system, with almost ten times the population of the CIFM, reported twenty-five such instances over the same time.[25] City jails were full of noise, odors, violence. Most of all, they were full of people.

Time and again, the Board of Correction, the official oversight group tasked with monitoring and regulating the city's Department of Correction, found the incarcerated population "unacceptably high." The department was chronically understaffed, with more than four hundred vacant positions.[26] Even after a major riot at the CIFM, in October 1986, authorities kept the facility at 120 percent of its capacity, with plans to push the population to 140 percent. As BOC Chair Robert Kasanof objected, "The jails are not infinitely elastic." In the late 1980s, they were stretched to the breaking point.[27]

There was, of course, a simple way of reducing overcrowding: for the NYPD to make fewer arrests. Michael Jacobson, then the city's deputy budget director, recalls repeated efforts at the Office of Management and Budget (OMB) to find any way to bring the jail population down. But the mayor would not have it. It was simply politically impossible for him to direct the police to ease up.[28] The politics of law and order demanded more visible and more aggressive action.

Those politics were pervasive. They had even permeated the Board of Correction (BOC), the watchdog organization made up of reformers that oversaw the DOC. BOC members were generally progressives. Its chairman, Robert Kasanof, had previously directed the Legal Aid Society, a nonprofit that provided most of New York City's public defender services.[29] Rose Singer, another BOC member, had founded Friendly Visitors, an organization that helped women in prisons. Barbara Margolis was a volunteer prison advocate. David Schulte was the chairman of the New York Anti-Defamation League. William Booth had led the New York NAACP.[30] These were people who cared deeply about marginalized New Yorkers. But they confronted some stark political realities. Margolis, who was a personal friend of (and donor to) Ed Koch ruefully recalled Koch's attitude toward prison reform to an oral historian in 1994. "Ed to this day thinks I'm crazy," she said. "If Ed had his way, we [New York City] would buy a huge piece of acreage in northern Nevada and send most of our inmates there and let them do what they want for the rest of their lives." Koch, Margolis noted, "absolutely doesn't believe in . . . rehabilitation. But, he's a wonderful friend."[31]

Whatever their intentions, Board of Correction members helped oversee and signed off on the city's unprecedented program of mass incarceration. A broad coalition of political actors stood behind the policies that forged racist mass surveillance and mass incarceration in the United States. As James Forman and Michael Javen Fortner have shown, many Black leaders were powerful advocates for tougher approaches to drugs and guns in the 1970s and 1980s as ways to protect Black communities and Black lives.[32] The BOC was hardly responsible for the war on drugs, but against this political backdrop, it was quietist in the face of surging arrest rates. In fact, the board was a keen supporter of a new approach to crime management that emerged in the 1980s: a movement with well-meaning liberal origins that would exacerbate the crowding crisis even further. That approach was broken-windows policing.[33]

• • •

The theory of broken windows, first articulated by the sociologists George L. Kelling and James Q. Wilson in *The Atlantic Monthly* in 1982, was that visible signs of disorder—whether public drunkenness, graffiti, or broken windows—fostered a general urban environment of lawlessness, which in turn spawned more serious crime.[34] The upshot, according to Kelling and Wilson, was that to prevent that serious crime, it was important to police "disreputable or obstreperous or unpredictable people: panhandlers, drunks, addicts, rowdy teenagers, prostitutes, loiterers, the mentally disturbed." Public order was paramount, even if it meant prosecuting people at society's margins. As Kelling and Wilson put it, the

> wish to "decriminalize" disreputable behavior that "harms no one" . . . [is] a mistake. Arresting a single drunk or a single vagrant who has harmed no identifiable person seems unjust, and in a sense it is. But failing to do anything about a score of drunks or a hundred vagrants may destroy an entire community.[35]

In New York, by the mid-1980s, it was clear to city leadership that whole neighborhoods—the Lower East Side, for example—had fallen into the sort of disorder so deprecated by Kelling and Wilson. The liberals who made up the Board of Correction were powerfully taken with the broken-windows theory and with James Q. Wilson himself, a distinguished professor of government at Harvard University. Building on racist conceptions of Black communities and Black families, Wilson argued that rehabilitation was an empty promise; only enforcement and deterrence would curb antisocial behavior.[36] In 1987, the board received VHS tapes narrated by Wilson and purchased "a television and a VCR so that it can watch these and other recordings about the prison system."[37] In the fall of 1986, the board's chair asked Wilson, then perhaps the most famous criminologist in the country, to recommend someone that the board could hire as a consultant. Wilson suggested his former graduate student and frequent collaborator, John DiIulio, then at Princeton University. DiIulio, who became the board's official consultant and would go on to coin the term *superpredator*, was an advocate of managing prisons with a very firm hand. Order, rather than assistance, was necessary. For DiIulio, the goal of incarceration was not "rehabilitation," as had been accepted by liberals for decades. Rather, the goal was "management," to be undertaken with new administrative and scientific techniques.[38]

Such views were generally shared by the board's members. Robert Kasanof, the former head of the Legal Aid Society, saw the board as "primarily concerned with the protection of public safety" and he "asserted that, to a certain extent, the use of force is inevitable when managing a largely antisocial population."[39] At a board meeting after a violent jail "uprising" over prison conditions in 1988, David Schulte asked department officials whether guards had been armed with Uzi machine guns and whether they were authorized to use deadly force. No one in the room seemed surprised that the answer to both questions was yes, even though a department spokesperson had described the disturbance as "minor" to the press.[40] Inmates were simply to be managed. Richard Wolf, the board's executive director, spoke of an "inordinate number of the most incorrigible inmates, including the most notorious alleged drug dealers."[41]

All this is to say that when the Board of Correction objected to overcrowding in the city's jails, its primary concern was not prisoner comfort but rather "public safety," particularly the fear of riots. Technically, the board mandated that prisoners held in city jails have an average of sixty square feet of living space, though by the mid-1980s, this requirement was rarely met.[42] Still, each time the Department of Correction deviated from the sixty-square-foot minimum, it legally needed an "emergency" variance, which the board duly issued each month. By the summer of 1987, board members were reaching the limits of their patience. "The City," board chair Robert Kasanof noted, "agreed to the standard of 60 square feet for each inmate, and . . . the Board cannot continually grant 'emergency' variances without effectively abandoning the standards."[43] In response, DOC Commissioner Richard J. Koehler promised that the department would add new beds to the jail system—a total of additional 3,627 beds by the end of the next fiscal year.

But finding the space for those beds was not a trivial task, for doing so involved clearing a daunting hurdle: zoning. The Uniform Land Use Review Procedure (ULURP) had recently been mandated by a 1975 change to the city charter. It was, and continues to be, an unavoidable step in constructing or repurposing buildings, a process that could take months if not years. There were only a few ways of getting around land use review. One way was to build on Rikers Island, the 413-acre patch of land that New York has used as a jail site since 1932. Rikers is itself an offshore space, a massive fortified penal colony that is difficult to access from the mainland and where land use rules do not apply.[44] But constructing a brand-new facility on the island would take years. Another way to avoid ULURP was to move off *land* altogether. And this is what Koehler, in his desperation to find more beds, chose to do. Hundreds of new spaces could be provided by "floating facilities," which Koehler claimed could "be made ready in record time to serve a real need for inmate beds."[45] Because "floating facilities" were offshore—literally not on land—they did not require land use review. This is why they had such appeal. And one particular floating facility was especially attractive: a ship referred to as "the Falklands vessel."[46]

• • •

As city officials began to consider holding prisoners on ships, law enforcement in New York was becoming an ever more violent business. As the historian Elizabeth Hinton has put it, the city—like the rest of the country—was increasingly turning to "crime control as urban policy."[47] New York was a major beneficiary of federal programs meant to militarize police forces.[48] In fact, by the time the city considered leasing the "coastels" used in the Falklands, New York had a well-established military-carceral complex. That complex was deeply intertwined with maritime power. The Anglo-Swedish barges were hardly the first ships to serve as floating jails in New York. Even during the American Revolution, British authorities housed American prisoners of war on naval hulks, whose horrific conditions claimed thousands of lives.[49] In the 1980s, one of the first ways that New York sought to expand its jail capacity was to acquire a former naval prison in Brooklyn.[50] And throughout the decade, city officials enthusiastically sought to repurpose military facilities for carceral use. Mayor Koch proposed sending first-time drug offenders to Army boot camps.[51] In 1990, the department began recruiting jail officers from military discharge centers.[52] There were, therefore, some precedents when city officials began negotiations with the Bibby Line to lease the *Bibby Venture*, the Vessel's sister ship. After all, it was one of many decommissioned military facilities used by the growing carceral state. But though it had been recently occupied by soldiers, the barge was not American military surplus. It belonged instead to the world of global capitalism, a creature of offshore oil rigs and shipping containers. That world looked only a little less dystopian than a return to prison hulks.

After its third transatlantic journey, the *Bibby Venture* arrived in New York harbor on October 26, 1987. That day, the city's prison population reached 15,444, up nearly 75 percent from four years before.[53] When the New York City Department of Correction took possession of its new "maritime facility," it hailed the barge as a panacea. It was more than just a quick and temporary fix. It was, instead, a real, thoughtful answer to the scourge of regular seasonal overcrowding: a modular complex that could be towed anywhere along the coast of the city and brought in and out of service relatively quickly. This, at least, was how city officials pitched the barge publicly, giving the ship the new official-sounding name of "Maritime Facility I." Behind closed doors, however, there was considerable agreement that shunting prisoners onto barges was ridiculous: an expedient made necessary by a set of emergency circumstances.[54]

Almost as soon as the *Bibby Venture* arrived in New York, it became clear that a barge was, at best, an imperfect solution to the Department of Correction's problems. By law, the DOC needed to provide inmates with the opportunity for outdoor recreation. This the ship lacked, though its top deck was eventually converted to a basketball court. The ship also legally needed to be furnished with a law library and a space for receiving visitors. These requirements necessitated new facilities that would have to be constructed on the pier linking the barge to the mainland, negating some of the anticipated advantages of a temporary barge.

More importantly, the architecture of the barge itself—designed in Sweden for privately employed offshore oil workers—posed issues for penal administrators. After inspecting the *Bibby Venture* upon its arrival, one official noted that the barge's comfort made it "unsatisfactory as housing for inmates."[55] The accommodation units might have been too austere or uncomfortable for oilmen, soldiers, or factory workers, but they were considered far too *comfortable* for people who had been recently arrested. The privacy the barge's layout afforded its residents meant that patrolling officers would be "cut off by sight and sound" from each other. Each room had its own shower, with "dangerous" electrical fixtures and a "removable European-style shower[head]." Because of these issues, the Department of Correction pledged to take measures to avoid incidents on the ship. At considerable expense, it would post more guards to patrol the outside perimeter. It would, as a matter of policy, not house "known homosexuals" on the barge, and it took the extraordinary step of locking fire doors to better control the space. It promised to use the *Bibby Venture* to house only "low risk detainees."[56]

"Low risk" was an official designation. The department used a numerical scale to evaluate prisoners according to their riskiness, though the scale itself was often in flux. When its leaders promised the Board of Correction in late 1987 to house only "low risk" detainees on board the barge, they meant "inmates with ratings of 12 or less," even though the DOC's own most recent classification scheme qualified "low risk inmates" as "those defined with ratings between 1 and 5."[57] From the beginning, standards had to be lowered, corners cut.

Still, the very fact that the DOC was numerically rating the people it incarcerated showed the degree to which DiIulio's managerial ideal had permeated the department's thinking. The system for rating prisoners according to riskiness was itself a hallmark of what in the early 1990s the criminologists Malcolm Feeley and Jonathan Simon termed the "new penology."[58] The new penology was a reaction against the rehabilitative ideal. It was "markedly less concerned with responsibility, fault, moral sensibility, diagnosis, or intervention and treatment of the individual offender" than the rehabilitative ideal that it replaced. Instead, it was "concerned with techniques to identify, classify, and manage groupings sorted by dangerousness." The task, Feeley and Simon noted, was "managerial, not transformative."[59]

• • •

Even with "low risk," ostensibly easy-to-manage prisoners, using the barge as a jail faced further, geographic obstacles. The DOC planned to permanently moor the barge at a pier to be specially constructed on its offshore penal facility, Rikers Island (thus avoiding ULURP requirements). In the meantime, while the pier was being built, the department parked the barge alongside Manhattan's Pier 36 in the East River. But there was a catch. The Army Corps of Engineers approved its berth at that location only until August 1988, just ten months from the time the *Bibby Venture* first arrived in New York City.[60] And there was intense neighborhood opposition to a floating jail being moored off the Lower East Side, with its powerful Democratic political appa-

The Vessel's sister ship off Pier 36 in August 1988. Note the barred windows and the fenced area on the roof.

ratus keenly attuned to local resistance to more shelters or jails.[61] Just
three days after the barge arrived at its temporary mooring, a group
of residents, led by the future Democratic Speaker of the New York
State Assembly Sheldon Silver, secured a temporary restraining order
preventing the jail's operation on the grounds that the ship violated
land use regulations. Even though the jail was offshore, Silver argued,
it would still require changes in land use because of construction and
traffic.[62] Though the barge was ultimately ruled to be outside ULURP
oversight, the legal proceedings meant delays to the DOC's timetable.
Ultimately, it was not until February 26, 1988, some four months after
its arrival, that the *Bibby Venture* opened to prisoners.[63]

The irony was that by the time the ship was ready, the most acute
phase of the city's carceral crisis seemed to be over. By November 1987,
the city had a surplus of more than nine hundred beds in its jail system.[64] As the barge began receiving prisoners in early 1988, the DOC
still had vacant beds and there were proposals to use it as a homeless
shelter instead.[65] Part of the reason was the fact that, in 1988, the city
took the unprecedented and extreme step of opening two new seven-
hundred-bed jails in economically depressed areas far upstate near the
Canadian border, where labor costs were low and land use was not an
issue. Whereas prison barges represented an inexpensive way of bringing jails into the city, the two facilities along the St. Lawrence River,
built at a cost of $90 million, involved flying prisoners out; the city
actually spent $2 million a year to charter four weekly flights upstate
from LaGuardia airport.[66]

Even as summertime arrests again drove the city's jail population over
100 percent capacity, the *Bibby Venture* remained largely empty, due
to lingering safety concerns over its architecture.[67] These concerns—
widely shared by corrections officers—were exacerbated shortly after
the facility opened to prisoners, when one inmate, Paul Buttafuoco,
"escaped through an opening in the wall of the Venture . . . created by
mechanics installing an air conditioning system." The escape—one
of fifteen from New York jails over the previous year—exposed problems, not just of architecture but also of staffing. The *Bibby Venture*'s
warden, Eric Taylor, stated that he "should not be expected to know
everything done to [the] physical . . . [structure of the ship] by the
construction crew." But the problems went beyond mere miscommu-
nication. There was only a "skeletal staff" working at the facility, and

despite the DOC's promises to keep only low-risk inmates on board, Buttafuoco himself had a relatively high-risk rating.[68]

Buttafuoco's escape was, perhaps, the low point for administrators in a difficult first few months for the *Bibby Venture*. By the time the Army Corps of Engineers' approval for the ship ran out in August, and the ship had to leave the Lower East Side for Brooklyn's Pier 1, just across the East River (where it would sit idly for a year), it had only been open for six months. The neighborhood was up in arms, there had been an escape, and work had not even begun on the promised new pier at Rikers Island, a project that would be delayed indefinitely.

However, in spite of all of these facts, DOC officials deemed the experiment with the *Venture* a great success, so much so that the department sought two additional barges. The reason was simple: department officials expected that the prison population would rise by 1,500 by the middle of 1989, as the Koch administration rolled out its new "tactical narcotics teams"—a war on drugs initiative meant to disrupt street-level crack sales.[69]

One of the additional barges was to be a custom-built vessel that could house eight hundred inmates. City planners hoped to have this facility delivered and ready to use by 1990. To speed up the design process, New York planned on granting three or four $50,000 awards to competing contractors, one of whom was George Steinbrenner, then the owner of the New York Yankees and the chairman of the American Shipbuilding Company in Tampa.[70] The other barge was the Vessel, the *Bibby Resolution*, which had recently completed its service as a hotel ship for Volkswagen in Emden. The Department of Correction was "determined to acquire the Resolution" and the city's Board of Estimate quickly approved spending $17 million toward leasing it on similar terms to the *Venture* (the actual cost would turn out to be $21 million).[71] The only member of the eleven-person board to vote against it was David Dinkins, the Manhattan borough president and future mayor, who called the use of the barges "a Band-Aid solution" that was "antithetical to public use." Dinkins favored more proactive, positive solutions to New York's perceived crime problem: housing assistance and social services.[72] But he was out of step with the prevailing attitudes in city government; there would be more barges and more beds in the city's jails before Ed Koch was voted out of office.

And so, in early 1989, the *Bibby Resolution* was towed from Emden

across the river Ems to the larger port of Eemshaven in the Netherlands. There, in deeper waters, it was loaded aboard another semi-
submersible ship for transport to New York, where it would, once
again, join its sister ship.[73] The circumstances of the reunion were not
happy. When the Vessel arrived from West Germany in April 1989,
New York's jail population was again spiking, cresting above eighteen
thousand for the first time.[74]

• • •

Unlike the *Venture*, the *Resolution* was not intended to be a conventional New York City jail. Rather, it was planned to be a center to treat
incarcerated men addicted to crack, the vast majority of whom were
Black. Cratering cocaine prices in the mid-1980s had led to the widespread proliferation of the solid, smokable form called crack, which
devastated inner cities. As the sociologist David Kennedy put it,
"Crack blew through America's poor black neighborhoods" as though
"the Four Horsemen of the Apocalypse had traded their steeds for
supercharged bulldozers."[75]

Crack is the most addictive form of cocaine. Releasing a dump of
dopamine into the brain, it produces an almost immediate sense of
euphoria and confidence. But deep, grinding lows follow the highs.
Crack causes delusions, paranoia, and a desperate physiological need
for more. In the 1980s, that desperation cascaded over already marginalized communities in New York. As it did so, it often led to extreme
violence. In 1990, there were 2,245 reported homicides in New York
City, more than five times the number reported in 2022.[76] By the
time the Vessel arrived in New York, the city was in the midst of the
crack epidemic, whose violence ricocheted around poor communities
of color.[77] The extent of that violence goes a long way to explaining
why American drug policies became so punitive and why sentencing guidelines for crack possession were a hundred times harsher than
those for powder cocaine.[78]

Certainly, in New York, crack lay behind the surging arrest and
incarceration rates. As Deputy Mayor Stanley Brezenoff put it, crack
and crime, with all their pernicious consequences, were "at the top
of the political list."[79] Targeted and picked up by police on drug and

The Vessel moored at Pier 36 off the Lower East Side of Manhattan

vagrancy charges, people with addictions to crack flooded into New York's jails and courtrooms. The Department of Correction estimated that at least 60 percent of the inmates in its custody were "addicted to drugs and/or alcohol," many of whom posed little danger to themselves or others. By keeping them in a drug treatment facility rather than a higher-security jail, the DOC anticipated that it would save money. The idea was that the *Bibby Resolution* would require substantially less security than typical jails, even with its unconventional architecture and fancy European showerheads.[80]

There was another reason DOC leadership found opening the drug treatment facility on the Vessel attractive. The department was confronting an ongoing image problem of being too rough, too violent, too uncaring. It sought to use the *Bibby Resolution* as a prominently located example of a new, revamped rehabilitative model in corrections. According to the Board of Correction minutes:

Commissioner Koehler said that he wanted to moor the Bibby Resolution in lower Manhattan because it is in the center of the City of New York. The facility will be a visible example of drug treatment operation, a place where the Department of Correc-

tion can show that drug treatment can be effective and that an
inmate in drug treatment can change.[81]

The Bibby Line whistled the same tune. In the words of its promotional materials, the *Resolution* was effective "because the configura-
tion of the facility allows groups of about 40 inmates to work, eat and
sleep in a 'family' environment." There was good reason for Bibby to
put the word *family* in scare quotes. The ship was still a jail and an
instrument of violence. As Bibby itself claimed, it was "proving to be
a powerful weapon in the war on drug use."[82]

The DOC settled on a familiar site to moor the *Bibby Resolution*:
Pier 36 off the Lower East Side, much to the fury of local state Representative Sheldon Silver, who accused Commissioner Koehler of "bad
faith" for the decision to locate yet another jail barge in his neighborhood. Silver and his supporters had sued to block the *Bibby Venture*
from being moored in the East River but had dropped the case after
the city towed the ship to Brooklyn and announced that its future
mooring site would be on the Hudson. Now, the *Resolution* was moving into the same location. Because of the emergency of overcrowding, the city was able to disregard many requirements for review and
permits. Just like the *Venture* before it, because the *Resolution* was a
ship—literally offshore—it avoided the lengthy ULURP. The new
facility aboard the Vessel opened in May.[83]

On the *Bibby Resolution*, the DOC offered a three-tiered program
of therapeutic services for up to 384 people addicted to drugs. The
program was greeted with loud praise. *The New York Times* painted a
redemptive picture of addicts. It quoted the "hulking and imposing"
John Lowe, with "scars from a stabbing and two shootings." Lowe
recounted his time on the barge in "his surprisingly boyish voice." *The
Times* continued,

> "We are all part of a single family," he said . . . "I've seen these
> brothers open up their hearts, admit things that made them cry.
> I've cried myself," he said without shame.[84]

The *Times* article reflected the old liberal impulse to rehabilitate. But
though the program on the *Bibby Resolution* was high profile even
before Chuck Schumer's visit, it was extremely unusual: the excep-

tion that proved the new penal rule. The vast majority of those in New York's jail system—even in its floating jails—were receiving not treatment but punishment. It is important to remember that even the people undergoing drug rehabilitation on the Vessel were still sent there by a court as part of sentencing. Moreover, as a New York State Commission of Correction Report noted in 1990, the rate at which people incarcerated on the Vessel filed official grievances to the DOC was higher than at most other New York City correctional facilities. In December 1989, there were twelve grievances per hundred inmates on board the *Resolution*: the second-highest rate out of the fifteen facilities in the city.[85] Today, it is impossible to determine the nature of these grievances; the New York Department of Correction destroys grievance records after ten years.[86]

In any case, the grievances did not stop many from across the political spectrum from praising the impulse to treat rather than to punish that defined the purpose of the *Bibby Resolution*. This was certainly the message of Chuck Schumer, then the chairman of the House Subcommittee on Criminal Justice, during his 1990 visit to the Vessel. In fact, he was especially lavish in his praise during the hearing on board. "Drug treatment for drug-dependent offenders" like that offered on the *Resolution*, he held, "is the best chance we have for keeping them out of the criminal justice system."[87]

In fact, punishment did seem less cruel on the prison ships than in land-based jails. The health services, provided under contract by St. Vincent's Hospital in Greenwich Village, were comprehensive and sophisticated, and included drug treatment and HIV screening. "There were quite a few positive people," Maureen Powell, a counselor who worked on the two vessels in the early 1990s, recalled. Both "Bibbies," as they were called, were certified by the National Commission on Correctional Health Care and the Joint Commission on Accreditation of Healthcare Organizations, a rarity for jails in New York State.[88]

Some of the people incarcerated and serving on the *Bibby Venture* jokingly dubbed it "the Love Boat."[89] As one inmate, Angel Velazquez, told reporters, "We live large on the barge." "Here it is not all tense," noted another person staying on the ship. "There is less static flowing through the air." For Bruce Wilson, a man incarcerated on the *Bibby Venture* who had also spent a month in a jail on Rikers Island, the difference was stark. "The system is working here. Here we get our meals hot."[90] As Wilson's comment suggests, the facilities on Rikers Island set the bar very low. As a Department of Correction spokesperson later summed up: "We regard it as one of the more humane options in housing."[91] British newspapers were quick to note that the DOC was accommodating far fewer people on the Vessel than the nine hundred servicemembers the Ministry of Defense had billeted on it in Port Stanley.[92] Humane indeed.

• • •

Offshoring prisoners was a move consistent with a primary goal of Ed Koch's administration: to promote New York as a "global city," an attractive place for corporate headquarters and the middle- and upper-class people who worked in them.[93] New Yorkers had long seen their city as a refuge for, as the poet Emma Lazarus had written, the "poor . . . huddled masses yearning to be free." The words, after all, were inscribed at the base of the Statue of Liberty in New York's harbor. But by the late 1970s, as Felix Rohatyn, a former investment banker helping to administer the city's finances, put it, New York needed to look abroad and say, "Give me your rich."[94] Even as a fiscal crisis pushed the city to radically cut back social services—shrinking its budget by 20 percent between 1975 and 1981—city administrators prioritized retaining services that would attract tourists and please the wealthy. New York's status as a capital of global finance and business would depend on "cleaning up" its streets and displacing people who impinged on wealthy residents' "quality of life." In the midst of a collapse of federal funding for low-income housing, the city created massive tax incentives for new luxury housing and high-end commercial development. From 1974 to 1994, the city actually cut corporate taxes, from 10.1 percent to 8.85 percent. In Deputy Mayor Brezenoff's words, "We were very pro-development in the [Koch] administration."[95]

During the 1980s, the fortunes of New York's rich and poor diverged radically. Nowhere was this divergence more evident than in Lower Manhattan. Though unemployment in New York gradually decreased from a peak of 9.3 percent in early 1983, homelessness continued to soar, as did the rates of drug addiction. Both were on full display in the East Village's Tompkins Square Park, which became the most

visible center of homelessness in New York and the site of successive
violent clearances carried out at baton-point by the NYPD.[96] Meanwhile, New York's financial services industry boomed. While in New
York, the Vessel and its sister ship were at the very heart of the gilded
world of global finance.

Just two miles from Pier 36 on the East River, in New York's financial district, the same globalizing forces that hollowed out the Lower
East Side had driven a very different transformation built not on physical goods but on financial abstraction. The year that the first prison
barge opened in the city, 1987, was when Gordon Gekko, the corporate raider villain of the Hollywood blockbuster *Wall Street* played by
Michael Douglas, famously declared greed to be good. The film's plot
revolved around insider trading and skullduggery; Gekko's plan was
to buy a productive airline and then gut it, firing all its employees, in
a play to access its pension fund. *Wall Street* was a morality tale about
the dangers of financial abstraction; in its final scene, its hero, played
by Charlie Sheen, is urged to "create, instead of living off the buying
and selling of others." This was a time of financial "innovation" that
went far beyond Parley Augustsson's work with limited liability. It was
a time during which American finance experienced a full-scale cultural transformation that reshaped the entire global economy.

Wall Street's booming success was enabled, in no small part, through
purposeful deregulation by the U.S. government. In 1980, the Treasury repealed Regulation Q, a New Deal–era measure that capped
the interest rates banks could pay out for time and savings deposits.
When it was enacted in the middle of the Depression-rocked 1930s,
Regulation Q (and the low interest rates it guaranteed) was meant to
curtail reckless lending, a source of financial instability. Over time, the
regulation came to function as an automatic check on the overheat-
ing of the economy. When economic growth gave way to inflation,
interest rates on corporate bonds and Treasury bills would rise. If the
economy became too exuberant and interest rates crested above the
ceilings imposed by Regulation Q, investors would take their money
out of safe commercial banks and thrifts and put it into stocks and
other investments in the capital market, where they could earn a much
higher return. With less money under their control, Main Street banks
and thrifts would then be forced to restrict their lending for business loans and mortgages. Fewer mortgages meant the housing market

would contract. A slowdown in the U.S.'s massive housing market would then act as a brake on the whole economy.[97]

This sort of economic thermostat system worked for more than three decades, but it began to break down in the 1970s. The problem was that as the long postwar boom finally ended, inflation was high and durable. In fact, inflation kept capital market interest rates persistently above the Regulation Q ceiling, pushing investors to take their money out of Main Street banks and put it into the capital market. At first, banks restricted lending, as they had done before in similar situations. But the economy did not cool down; interest rates stayed stubbornly high—well over the Regulation Q ceiling. After months and then years of losing deposits to the capital market, Main Street banks found their business under tremendous pressure. Without deposits, they could not make loans. Without loans, they made no money. In short, prolonged inflation left banks desperate to attract funds. Many would have been glad to offer high interest rates, but they were blocked from doing so by Regulation Q. What they needed was a source of money that was not covered by the regulation's restrictions.[98] They found what they were searching for in Europe, specifically in the rapidly expanding eurodollar market.

Eurodollars were a niche bit of financial engineering, created by bankers for other bankers. They had been around since the 1950s, when European banks on both sides of the Iron Curtain began holding large quantities of U.S. dollars.[99] Because these accounts were not in the United States, they were effectively offshore. Many of them, legally based out of branches in tax havens like the Cayman Islands, were functionally unregulated.[100] Certainly, the European banks controlling them were free to push interest rates on lending (in U.S. dollars) well over the Regulation Q ceilings that prevailed within the United States. Such expensive rates did not discourage American banks desperate for capital. In the 1970s, big American banks entered into the euromarket in record numbers, borrowing dollars in Europe through their local branches there and then sending the money back to the United States.[101] But small banks and savings and loan associations could only access the euromarket indirectly. Because the large players were better able to circumvent regulations than the small ones, Regulation Q came to apply unevenly across the American financial landscape. While mortgages (typically offered by small banks and thrifts) became increasingly difficult to obtain, big banks had practically unlimited access to credit. For many observers—especially those sympathetic to the small banks—Regulation Q looked grossly unfair. In this context, as the historical sociologist Greta Krippner has argued, doing away with the regulation became an attractive political option.[102] And so the state deregulated, scrapping Regulation Q entirely in 1980.

Deregulation had the effect of globalizing New York even further, fusing the offshore with the onshore, in much the same way the Vessel itself did. Combined with decisive action by the Federal Reserve under Chair Paul Volcker to curb inflation, the abandonment of Regulation Q resulted in a rapid spike in U.S. interest rates, which reached 20 percent in the early years of the decade. Policy makers anticipated that the high rates would act as a brake on the U.S. economy, raising the cost of borrowing and investing. But though the so-called Volcker Shock did result in a spike in unemployment in 1981 and 1982, high interest rates did not provoke nearly as sharp an economic contraction as policy makers had imagined. Instead, they attracted foreign capital to the United States: $221 billion in 1986 alone, a figure larger than the federal budget deficit that year. Rather than stifling the inflation or growth in the American economy, high interest rates in the 1980s turned the U.S. into a center for foreign capital, especially from Japan and elsewhere in Asia. These massive capital inflows forestalled an American fiscal crisis and the tough political choices that would have accompanied it. At the same time, however, they pushed up the value of the dollar, which rose some 63 percent from 1980 to 1985, with disastrous results for American manufacturing.[103]

Though much of the basis of postwar American prosperity was eroded in the 1970s and 1980s, the financial sector was ascendant, in terms of both profits and political capital.[104] Nowhere was this more obvious than in Lower Manhattan, the site of the old port facilities that hosted the Vessel and its sister ship. After all, when capital flowed into the United States, it did so through New York.[105] All the while, in Albany and Washington, New York–based banks lobbied hard (and successfully) for deregulation, contending that looser restrictions and lower taxes would better position American finance to attract international business. In 1981, after several years of seeking international regulation of the eurodollar market, the Federal Reserve essentially gave up and began allowing New York banks to create special accounts to

conduct business with foreign customers "as if they were 'offshore.' "[106]
This change of policy allowed American banks to fully participate in
the eurodollar market alongside their foreign competitors.[107] In 1985,
the Treasury allowed foreign nationals to buy government bonds anon-
ymously.[108] National sovereignty relaxed; global finance moved in.

These measures served, in the historian Vanessa Ogle's description,
to "lure some of the offshore business from the Bahamas, the Cayman
Islands, London, Panama, and Singapore back onshore." In essence,
New York banks offered "to do, in a limited and circumscribed way,
what they had been doing 'offshore' for decades." New York, formerly
the global center of "onshore" banking, quietly became a deregulated
free port—the kind of place in which the privately owned, Bahamian-
registered Vessel could become a city jail. As *The New York Times* commented at the time, the "opening of New York as a free banking zone
will not be an event that will involve laying cornerstones or stringing
up bunting . . . the banks, for the most part, will only change some
signs on office doors to read, 'International Banking Facility.' " The
creation of these "IBFs" inside existing New York banks would not
result in job growth or even the construction of new buildings. But
the banks themselves saw "a rich opportunity in having won the right
to cast their lines in a long forbidden stream," a market worth $1.34
trillion (several times that in today's dollars).[109] They had successfully
established a free banking zone inside Lower Manhattan, one exempt
from state and local taxes on profits and in which regulations governing reserve ratios and state and city taxes simply did not pertain.
Within half a year, there were three hundred IBFs in New York.[110]

In the 1980s, then, the shadowy offshore world came to New York
and embedded itself within the onshore system of American finance.
Championed and lauded by that finance industry, the IBF was, from
the beginning, an expediency for federal and state policy makers. With
all the money they brought into the United States, IBFs were a way of
providing short-term capital relief in the face of a fiscal crisis. Debt,
in essence, delivered a way of avoiding politically difficult decisions.
The parallels between the IBF and the two Bibby barges are striking.
They too were imported from abroad. They too were artifacts of a
shadowy offshore world; registered in the Bahamas, the vessels were
foreign assets outside the control of local authorities. They too were
short-term fixes, justified by their champions as solutions to a fiscal

crisis. They were even products of the same macro political economy: a trend toward globalized trade and globalized finance that sacrificed factories and conventional ports.

Moreover, there was a direct and intimate connection between the boom in New York's financial sector and the boom in its incarceration rate. New York's efforts to court the world's rich through its "global city" strategy involved jailing its poor at record numbers.[111] It was only in this context that barges made sense as prison ships. With jail space perennially at a premium, barges could be used as temporary housing, towed where they were needed. This was exactly what happened. In August 1989, after a year sitting idle in Brooklyn, the *Bibby Venture*, the Vessel's sister ship, was towed back into service as a jail: this time to Pier 40, at the end of Houston Street on the Hudson River.[112]

• • •

Pier 40 was within view of the skyscrapers of Wall Street, a quick taxi ride up the West Side Highway. But it might have been a world away. The pier was constructed between 1958 and 1962 as the grand new terminal for the Holland America Line. In many ways, its story mirrored that of Pier 36, across Manhattan. Built by the city at a cost of nearly $20 million (well over $150 million today), it was part of a bid made by city officials to lure ship traffic away from New Jersey. Since the nineteenth century, Holland America had operated both its passenger and cargo service out of Hoboken. In the 1950s, New York's planners were eager for both services to relocate across the Hudson River. Doing so would, they hoped, put a stop to a decades-long trend of port facilities expanding in New Jersey, at the expense of those in New York. When it was built, Pier 40 was a state-of-the-art facility: a looming square, multilevel pier sticking four hundred feet into the Hudson. But by the late 1970s, its scale—once a point of pride—had turned from impressive to trivial, dwarfed by the new container ports of Elizabeth and Newark. Even Holland America moved its passenger service to the New York Passenger Ship Terminal in midtown in 1974. By the early 1980s, Pier 40 stood vacant, a memorial to a more ambitious vision for New York's waterfront. It was to that memorial that the Vessel's sister ship was tied.

Though Pier 40 was vacant, the *Bibby Venture* was never really welcome there. Even as the ship was towed into the Hudson, it was understood that the mooring at Pier 40 would be temporary; the Army Corps of Engineers had approved the location only for a year. Permanently keeping a floating jail there, the Corps noted, "would be inconsistent with the protection and use of that public space." The problem was that even after nearly two years of deploying prison accommodation barges, with another on order, the city did not yet have "a master plan for the location of its barges."[113] There was real, and well-justified, worry among residents in the West Village that the short-term permit would quietly calcify into a permanent fixture. "This is the opening of the floodgates," one community leader told *The New York Times*.[114]

The Vessel and its sister ship were modular, flexible, and offshore. Even now, when remembering his three years working as a rookie corrections officer on the two barges, Rob Peaco recalls having to walk up and down the aluminum gangplank—designed in Gothenburg just eight years before—that separated the vessels from the pier each time he went to work. Maureen Powell, an HIV counselor who worked on the ships, recalls them rocking back and forth at moorage.[115] The barges were afloat, not rooted in a community or even a particular jurisdiction.

That the barges were adrift inside a legal loophole infuriated their critics. The nonprofit Federation to Preserve the Greenwich Village Waterfront called the plan to moor the *Bibby Venture* at Pier 40 "clearly illegal." Ted Weiss, the Manhattan state representative, noted that even if it were legal, "it was certainly inappropriate."[116] There were vociferous objections to the barges in Manhattan, but the jails' status as ships allowed the DOC to effectively bypass local planning and zoning restrictions. That status was the very reason the ships were so attractive to city administrators.

The vessels' transience served as a justification for the Department of Correction and the Koch administration's continued disregard of community preferences.[117] "No one wants [jails] anywhere," a Koch spokesperson told reporters in 1989. But the city needed to expand its prison capacity, and floating jails provided the "quickest and safest" way to do it. The DOC claimed that the *Bibby Venture* needed only a permit from the Coast Guard, as it would be moored only temporarily off Greenwich Village. But what "temporarily" meant was by no means clear. According to a deputy commissioner in the DOC, though the *mooring* would be deemed "temporary," the *Bibby Venture* was to "permanently" be a jail. Then again, the same official claimed that the department "intend[ed] this as a permanent location of the Maritime Facility for the extent of its useful life." That meant twenty-five years. "This is the most confusing situation I've ever seen," noted the state senator Manfred Ohrenstein, "and I think it's deliberate."[118] As it turned out, the barge would remain in place for three years: far fewer than twenty-five, but still significantly more than the original one year that had been approved.

The Bibby barges were not just vessels, but *foreign* and *private* vessels, registered in the Bahamas and owned by a British company. Both had British barge masters—employees of the Bibby Line who piloted the vessels when they moved.[119] The barge master responsible for the Vessel in New York, a British man named Connell, had been with the barge since its time in the Falklands.[120] In corridors, the Swedish words *utgang* and *nodutgang* appeared alongside their English translations, "exit" and "emergency exit."

The foreign ownership of the ships gave them a special legal status. When the DOC wanted to lock fire doors, it appealed to the Bibby Line for permission, not to the New York Fire Department. Indeed, fire department approval was not required at all, "because as an international vessel the Bibby Venture was approved pursuant to the Safety of Lives at Sea (SOLAS) agreement."[121] SOLAS was an international treaty that came into effect in 1980 and set minimum standards for the equipment and maintenance of international ships; fire protection, detection, and extinction were covered in Chapter II of the agreement. In the United States, the terms of the agreement were enforced not by local authorities but by the Coast Guard, which was responsible for quarterly inspections.[122] Just like New York's financial services industry, the barges were simultaneously on- and offshore, both foreign and domestic.

For David Dinkins, by then running for mayor, the transient and flexible status of the barges was not an asset, it was a liability. "Utilization of barges," he declared, "has turned planning for jail expansion into an ad hoc process. I am concerned that we are headed down an expensive and unproductive road with no end in sight."[123] Dinkins was steadfastly opposed to the continued growth of jails in New York. Upon becoming mayor in 1990, he appointed a new DOC commissioner, Allyn Sielaff, who promoted alternatives to incarceration. As Sielaff wrote in his first report to corrections staff, his appointment signaled "a new direction"; he was at pains to stress "alternatives to incarceration and detention."[124] One of his first acts was to appoint a new assistant commissioner to specifically handle alternatives to jail.

Nevertheless, the barges remained. And despite Dinkins's and Sielaff's aspirations, New York's jail population kept climbing, surpassing twenty thousand in 1990. Homicides within jails spiked, and more than five hundred cells had to be removed from use due to disrepair. Crowding in the jails continued to be terrible. The crisis was not subsiding; if anything, it was getting worse. Sielaff was found in contempt of court for his department continuing to detain prisoners in unsanitary holding pens in gymnasiums, and a federal judge, Morris Lasker, ordered the city to pay each of the thousands of prisoners held in improper conditions $150 per day.[125] Such costly penalties for continued overcrowding meant that city authorities were eagerly anticipating arrival of the new custom-built eight-hundred-bed barge—to be named the *Vernon C. Bain*, after a jail warden who had recently died in a car crash.[126]

But the *Vernon C. Bain* was a colossal boondoggle. The city had ordered the ship from Avondale Industries, a Louisiana shipbuilder that typically filled military contracts.[127] The cost was significant: some $125 million (not counting more than $10 million for a new dock in the Bronx and consultants' fees). This meant that it would cost $171,000 per bed, triple what the city had paid for the two vessels from the Bibby Line and about the same as what it had paid per bed for each of the last three brick-and-mortar jails that had been built within the city. The only real advantage of the ship relative to new construction on Rikers was that it was expected to be ready in a third of the time.[128] Even here, expectations fell short of reality. When it finally arrived in February 1992, the new barge was a year and a half behind schedule and $35 million over budget. And because of understaffing at the DOC, many of the barge's features would be rendered useless; its large dining room would remain closed, as would several classrooms.[129]

By then, the rationale for barges was a thing of the past. The longtime barge critic David Dinkins was living in Gracie Mansion as mayor. In part because of Dinkins's emphasis on decarceration, the jail population had finally fallen under the system's capacity. The Board of Correction had also come out against barges; its new chair, William Booth, contended that the *Vernon C. Bain* should be the last of its kind: "They're too expensive and too uncertain."[130] The truth of those words was borne out daily. The *Bain*, moored off Hunts Point in the Bronx, directly across from Rikers Island, continued to be beset by further delays and would not open until November 1992. While it closed in November 2023, it was still in the harbor as of early 2024.

In any case, when the city announced in March 1992 that the two barges leased from the Bibby Line would close as penal facilities, few people were surprised. In the early 1990s, Greenwich Village was gentrifying quickly and home prices were skyrocketing.[131] Pier 40, where the *Bibby Venture* was moored, was being considered for a major redevelopment: a park that would, according to a contemporary planning study, "make residential Chelsea a more attractive place to live, would boost residential values and could contribute toward accelerating displacement pressures."[132] A Greenwich Village newspaper noted that the barge's (mostly Black) "occupants had concerned and alarmed Village and Soho residents," who were increasingly white and middle class. Though there had been "no incidents," "the general feeling in the neighborhood is that the barge belongs at Rikers Island, not in downtown Manhattan." The *Venture*'s residents themselves might not have been walking through Manhattan's streets, but their visiting friends and relatives certainly were.[133] As in other American cities, the segregationist rhetoric of "not in my neighborhood" was alive and well in New York, even before the full-scale gentrification of Greenwich Village.[134]

• • •

Plans to develop New York as a "global city" had, in the mid-1980s, involved the expansion of jails, including docking the two Bibby barges in Lower Manhattan. In an important way, the logic of the global city strategy was also responsible for forcing the barges out of their moorings. The redevelopment and renewal of Chelsea and Greenwich Village left no space for prison hulks. There was a reason that the *Vernon C. Bain* was to be moored off an industrial area of the South Bronx and not Lower Manhattan. In short, the very success of the global city strategy drove the closure of the prison barges.

The proximate cause of the closures, however, was not gentrification and the growth of white-collar jobs, but the threat of a federal
lawsuit. The Army Corps of Engineers had never granted permanent
approval for the barges to be moored in Lower Manhattan, and for the
better part of two years the Corps had been pressing the Department
of Correction to move the ships. Noting "broken commitments," on
February 7, 1992, the Corps commander responsible for New York
informed Dinkins that he would press the Justice Department to file
a lawsuit against the city unless the vessels were removed.[135] Even the
barges' liminality had its limits; the two jails closed within a matter of
months.

At the end of the five-year leases from Bibby, the city exercised
its rights to formally acquire the barges in order to resell them. And
so, for the first time in their lives, the barges became public property. At the time, there were few worries about finding buyers; prison
systems across the United States were still strained, and the Federal
Bureau of Prisons had even expressed interest in leasing one of the
ships from New York.[136] For several years, the Bibby Line had sent
representatives to the American Correctional Association conferences
"with a model of one of the detention centres, 'Bibby Venture,'" to
drum up business. It had encountered "a lot of interest from many
Correction Departments."[137] Bibby even drew up schematics showing how another barge—then used as a floating hotel—could be easily converted into a corrections facility.[138] But for New York, selling
the ships proved harder than anticipated. Within months, the city
received several bids, the highest of which was $3.25 million. How-
ever, the city's Office of Management and Budget rejected the offer;
it had anticipated selling the barges for $20 million.[139] And so, the
Bibby Venture and *Bibby Resolution* sat empty for two years, costing
the city $1.6 million per year to maintain. There was a thought to
turn one of them into a hotel, as a money-making venture, but the
idea went nowhere.[140] Increasingly desperate, the Department of Correction "offered the two barges to every agency that may have had a
conceivable interest in them. Not one agency was interested." Officials
from Norfolk, Virginia, under court orders to rapidly expand their
own jail system because of overcrowding, toured New York's prison
barges, but concluded that they were examples "of how not to build

one."[141] Finally, in the middle of 1994, the barges were again put up for sale, this time at bargain-basement prices. The high bidder—offering a paltry $1.8 million—was reported to be an undisclosed European company acting through an American agent, A. L. Burbank.[142] But though the City of New York sold the barges in 1994, it would be three years before the Vessel or its sister ship was moved out of the harbor.

• • •

At a distance, the Vessel's time in New York might be understood as a simple story of supply and demand. When the tough-on-crime "new penology" ran up against the grim realities of the crack epidemic, arrests surged. As the city's jail population swelled, the available supply of jail space became scarce. Demand for more space rose. By the late 1980s, it had become so acute that city administrators were willing to spend tens of millions of dollars on stopgap measures. The Vessel and its sister ship were just that: temporary quick fixes for which increasingly desperate municipal administrators were willing to pay top dollar.

There is nothing striking in the story of a city overpaying to address an acute crisis. What *is* striking, and revealing, is that city leaders turned to the global offshore to solve their problems, just as British Ministry of Defence and Volkswagen officials had done before them. It is worth pausing to marvel at the simple fact that New York City administrators were able to do this.

The city's ability to offshore its carceral problem depended first and foremost on the legal line that existed between on- and offshore. Land use law applied on land, but not off it. Walking up a short gangplank meant crossing into an entirely different legal world. Next, the possibility of leasing the barges depended on the existence of the barges themselves: ships built to serve multinational big oil companies operating miles offshore. Third, it depended on a foreign firm whose business model was to furnish generic accommodation, not for a particular industry or for a particular country but for anyone, anywhere. It mattered that Bibby was foreign because foreign ships were treated differently under the law. Thanks to a legal carve-out for international ships, city administrators could ignore regulations and local democratic resistance to the barges. And finally, New York's ability to operate offshore jails depended on the fact that the city's waterfront was largely abandoned. Because of the rise of containerization and the subsequent collapse of New York's ship-handling industry, the city had its pick of any number of underused piers at which to moor the Vessel and its sister ship.

With all this in mind, the fact that New York's administrators were able and inclined to offshore two of its jails might seem like a serendipitous coincidence. But it wasn't. It was the product of a set of interrelated global transformations. These were the same transformations that were making New York into an onshore center of offshore finance, a global city that targeted "quality of life" goals. And they were unfolding all over the world: both in the city that never sleeps and in a sleepy town on the English coast.

CHAPTER 7

THE ENGLISH CHANNEL

	The Vessel	The Sister Vessel
1997	The Vessel is acquired by the British government and transported to Portland, England, where it begins service as a prison under the new name HMP *The Weare*.	
2005	HMP *The Weare* closes. The Vessel is renamed *The Weare*.	

E ngland in 1997. The Manchester United star David Beckham meets Victoria Adams, then better known as Posh Spice, for the first time. *Teletubbies* first airs on the BBC. Harry Potter is introduced to the world. Princess Diana dies. The year sees Britain in flux. The final stretch of nationalized railways in the country is privatized, a delayed postscript of one of Margaret Thatcher's marquee policies. Hong Kong is ceded to China, marking (at least for some) the definitive end of the British Empire. And after eighteen years of Conservative rule, a new, center-left Labour government under Tony Blair is swept into power in a landslide election. Though the country is hardly abandoning its recent history, it is in the midst of a pivot.

In early 1997, the Vessel turned back to Britain. Loaded on a heavy-lift ship in New York, its destination was the picturesque seaside town of Portland, perched on a limestone outcropping connected to the south coast of England via a long causeway. There, it would reprise its role as a prison. As *The Independent* newspaper put it, the "floating prison . . . from America" received an unfriendly berth. It was "not pretty and . . . not welcome."[1] There was fierce opposition in Portland at the prospect of a floating prison moored in the harbor. And, as the local paper, the *Dorset Echo*, would recount, "Opposition fires were stoked to new heights when it was revealed that the . . . arrival, far from being a state-of-the-art craft, would in fact be a rusting barge."[2]

Importing a prison from the United States was a powerful symbol in 1990s Britain. It was a physical instantiation of the British government's acceptance of the massive carceral state and tough-on-crime attitude endemic across the Atlantic.[3] The barge would also come to represent a globalized American emphasis on systematized box checking: on businesslike managerial practices that met "benchmarks" and hit "key performance indicators." For within a few years of its arrival in Britain, the Vessel would become firmly embedded in a new kind of supranational order: the "knowledge economy." The foot soldiers of this order were global consultants and international businesspeople. Its apostles were "Third Way" politicians, most notably Bill Clinton in the United States and Blair in the United Kingdom. In Portland, the barge would be both a witness to and a participant in the global Third Way movement. Its story would expose the uneasy relationship between globalization and liberal democracy.

• • •

But all that lay in the Vessel's future. In 1997, the Vessel was delivered to Portland for the same simple reason that it came to New York: prison overcrowding. Britain's incarceration rate had surged during the 1990s under the government of Conservative prime minister John Major, Margaret Thatcher's successor. In 1990, the prison population of England and Wales hovered around forty-five thousand; by the new millennium, it was nearly sixty-five thousand.[4] In the early 1990s, Blair, then Labour's shadow home secretary, played on public fears, championing the slogan "Tough on crime and on the causes of crime."[5] The Conservatives responded in kind. With the appointment of Michael Howard as home secretary in 1993, Britain followed the United States in taking a sharp punitive turn in its approach to criminal justice. Howard ushered in a new politics of law and order; at the Conservative Party conference in 1993, he bluntly asserted that "prison works," and proceeded to outline twenty-seven new anti-crime measures, most of which became law through crime bills enacted over the next two years. Just as in New York, the new legislation was aimed at improving "quality of life"; it targeted ravers, squatters, and travelers, people who lived in ways outside the social norm. It also chipped away at the principle of proportional sentencing, replacing it with mandatory minimum sentences and judicial attention to criminal records.[6] The impact was especially dramatic in southeast London, where major public infrastructure projects—including the Millennium Dome, now the O2—were meant to spur economic growth and draw in wealthier residents. What was good for one "global city" was good for another.

Yet Britain's prison policy stretched far beyond London. British prisons, at least in England and Wales, are administered nationally. Those sentenced in London might be sent hours away. And across Britain, public opinion was seized by a tougher, punitive outlook. As the Thatcher and Major governments steadily shrank the proactive assistance provided by the postwar welfare state, they turned to punishment as a way of providing security and order.[7] Just as in the United States, this meant embracing privately financed and privately managed prisons.[8] And just as in the United States, it meant tougher sentencing. In 1997, the government introduced a three-strikes law, enacting stringent minimum sentences for several classes of third offenses. In the decade between 1997 and 2007, the British state created 446 new imprisonable offenses.[9] The result was entirely unsurprising: Britain's incarceration rate rose precipitously.

For Ann Widdecombe, the Conservative prisons minister, the rising rate was totally necessary. Widdecombe would become a prominent Brexiteer, but even twenty-five years before the 2016 Referendum, she was a conservative hard-liner. In the 1990s, she opposed the legality of abortion and converted to Catholicism after the Church of England began to ordain women as priests.[10] She later supported reintroducing the death penalty. As the Conservative minister in charge of prisons, Widdecombe championed the mantra that "prison works."[11] But though Widdecombe was sanguine about Britain's rapidly filling prisons, others were not. In fact, her views considerably outstripped those of the Prison Governors' Association, which was "deeply disturbed by her belief that a rising prison population is a factor in reducing crime rates." "Hers," the PGA asserted, "is a simplistic and potentially damaging approach to the management of criminal justice."[12]

Indeed, despite Widdecombe's public stance, overcrowding was an

increasingly worrisome issue to the Prison Service she oversaw. Like
their New York counterparts, British penal administrators understood
barges as quick fixes for the acute effects of a chronic problem. Barges
could be acquired simply, and more or less ready to use, and could be
situated almost anywhere along Britain's thousands of miles of coast.
They also made for flashy headlines. Though civil servants were hesi-
tant about acquiring barges, ministers appreciated the public visibility
of quickly adding beds.[13] Towing in a barge was a dramatic and, arguably, decisive action. Towing in a barge from *New York* made the move
feel even bolder still.

In 1993, the Home Office had considered mooring two barges leased
from Bibby in Barrow-in-Furness, a town in Cumbria, in northwestern
England. Like other shipbuilding centers, Barrow had fallen on tough
times, especially as the end of the Cold War reduced demand for warships. With the city's unemployment rate above 10 percent, the Home
Office deemed Barrow an especially good candidate for a new prison
and for the hundreds of jobs that would come with it. Administrators
even dispatched officials to the *Bibby Venture* and *Bibby Resolution* in
New York to evaluate conditions on board.[14]

Thus, when the Home Office ultimately acquired the Vessel three
years later in 1996, Britain's Prison Service had been contemplating a
barge for several years. At the time, the price certainly seemed right. At
£3.5 million (about $5.8 million), the sticker price for purchasing the
barges outright was far lower than what the New York City Department of Correction had paid, even if it was significantly more than the
$1.8 million the DOC had received for the sale of the two barges. As
had been the case throughout its history, the *Bibby Resolution* made
private brokers a tidy profit. And as in the past, the actual cost of
maintaining a floating jail turned out to be far higher than anticipated. The Prison Service would invest £11 million in improvements
in the first few months of its use and pay out another £10 million over
the next ten years to maintain it.[15]

Nevertheless, as a stopgap, a floating prison was useful, at least for
the purposes of government ministers bent on immediately and vis-
ibly increasing the prison system's capacity. The Vessel's nearly 500
minimum-security beds (some 120 more than in New York) would
help reduce growing pains in Britain's prison system; indeed, the
Prison Service described the *Bibby Resolution* as "emergency accom-

modation" introduced "in response to increasing population pressures."[16] Those pressures were most severe in London, due to the rapid gentrification of the capital, but it was neither politically practicable nor cost effective to place a new prison in the city. Though it was inefficient to transport prisoners the three and a half hours to Portland, the ship's location could also be excused as an emergency measure. After all, it was never intended to be permanent; the very fact that it was a transient ship broadcasted to the public that it was addressing an acute crisis. As her counterparts in New York had done, Ann Widdecombe underscored that the Vessel would be temporary: it would only stay in Portland for three years, until further, more permanent accommodation could be constructed.[17] Widdecombe was closely following Ed Koch's playbook.

• • •

Britain had its own long and entangled history of turning to the offshore as a solution to its carceral problems. By the signing of the American Declaration of Independence in 1776, the British government had already dispatched tens of thousands of political prisoners and people convicted of various, often petty, crimes to its thirteen North American colonies.[18] Georgia was organized in the 1730s expressly as a way of managing the movement of people recently released from London's squalid jails. It was run by a royally backed corporation established to help settle the "miserable wretches . . . together by way of colony."[19] Australia too was populated by offshored prisoners. When the "First Fleet" delivered the earliest British settlers to Australia in 1788, more than half of the 1,373 arrivals were convicts: the first of some 168,000 to arrive on the continent over the next eight decades.[20] Offshoring, or "transportation" of prisoners to far-off penal colonies in America, New South Wales, or Tasmania, was big business. Merchants were paid handsomely for taking prisoners off the state's hands, and prisoners themselves provided a source of cheap, even unpaid, labor. Transportation was also a way for authorities in Britain to manage unruly populations. It was with public order in mind that the British government exiled hundreds of machine-breaking Luddites to Australia, where they could cause little harm.

Throughout the eighteenth and nineteenth centuries, British officials sentenced criminals to service in the Royal Navy and deployed retired naval vessels as squalid overflow spaces to alleviate crowding in English prisons on land. Pip, the hero of Charles Dickens's *Great Expectations*, encountered a "black Hulk" by torchlight, "like a wicked Noah's ark . . . cribbed and barred and moored by massive rusty chains."[21] That history seemed to come alive when the barge was towed into the harbor in March 1997. *The Times* noted that when the barge arrived in Dorset, "the shadow of Victorian England fell over Portland Harbour . . . not since the 19th century have criminals been housed in 'hulks' moored off the coast of Britain."[22]

The barge thus represented a return to a violent carceral past.[23] Convict labor had shaped the English south coast; the long breakwaters that protected Portland's harbor were quarried by Victorian prisoners. The whole town is overlooked by a nineteenth-century citadel that was repurposed as a prison following World War II.

• • •

Portland itself lies off the coast of Britain. It is a "tied island" of four and a half square miles linked to the Dorset coast by a single road. With fewer than fourteen thousand inhabitants, it is a close-knit place. It is also a place apart: a fortified island that commands among the largest harbors in Europe. Like many great fortresses—Gibraltar, Malta, or Alcatraz—Portland is a rock. Its pale limestone interior has been quarried for centuries. Many of the residences forming central London's stately squares were made from Portland stone; Buckingham Palace was built from the stuff. The houses on Portland are less grand. Those in the cluster of villages at the island's northern end are oriented toward the sea. Victorian terraced houses and postwar semi-detacheds (duplexes) wrap around the central hill. Most look out onto Chesil Beach, a vast expanse of stone shingles that extends unbroken for nearly twenty miles along the Dorset coast. Some look down on the harbor, on the other side of the beach. There, the views are no less sweeping: rolling hills ending in white cliffs that rise up out of the sea. But here, the views also feature the business end of Britain's south coast: a harbor with piers, warehouses, and freighters, all protected by a series of breakwaters and coastal forts.

Portland in 2019. The causeway onto the island hugs the beach to the left. The harbor is in the middle of the frame. The Vessel was moored just behind the hill on the right, which is topped by the old citadel.

Because of Portland's geographic features, it had been a military site for centuries. The village at the northern end of the island (where the Vessel was sited) is called Castletown. Anyone who drives the one road onto the isle is faced with an old nineteenth-century citadel that looms over both the town and a Royal Navy cemetery. Other monuments to military activity are nearby. Close to shore sits a restored artillery fort constructed under Henry VIII, just blocks from a museum dedicated to D-Day. Portland was the staging ground for American forces landing on Omaha Beach during Operation Overlord, and some 418,000 American troops passed through the town between June 1944 and May 1945. Two giant concrete modular "Mulberry Caissons," built in England and towed to France to form temporary harbors to support the landings, still sit just off Portland Port.

At the time the Vessel arrived, the military presence in the town was even stronger than it is today. For more than a century, the Royal Navy maintained a base on the island, but in 1995, with the Cold War won, the military shuttered the facility, which had brought an estimated £7 million per year into the community.[24] When the Vessel arrived two years after the closure, a vast swath of Portland's harbor, formerly occupied by the base, still lay vacant, a gaping reminder of the navy's absence. As a plaque in Portland's harbor now euphemistically puts it, the departure of the Royal Navy left "a vast area ripe for civilian development."[25] To locals, authorities in London tried to stress aspects of continuity when opening the Vessel as a prison, emphasizing how it would replace jobs lost when the navy left. What more appropriate place was there to house a prison ship than in an old navy town? Perhaps to give it a greater sense of place, the barge was again renamed, this time after a local river. The Vessel would thus become Her Majesty's Prison *The Weare*.[26]

•   •   •

But despite the best efforts of authorities to highlight how the Vessel fit with Portland's own history, when the Vessel was towed into the harbor in March 1997, locals immediately understood it as an American import, an imposition of a violent, almost dystopian, carceral future. The ship was, as one put it, "our own little Alcatraz."[27] The recreation yard on the roof was particularly striking. In the words of one of the locals who redecorated the Vessel's interior, "We'd never seen anything like that before . . . [except in] American TV programmes."[28]

The *Bibby Resolution* arriving in Portland aboard a heavy-lift ship in 1997

The Vessel was an incongruous presence. Aside from being an island port, Portland was nothing like New York. An offshore prison might have been unusual in the urban jungle; it was downright incongruous in a quiet seaside town. But for the ocean of difference separating New York City from Portland, local reactions played out similarly in the two places. Much like the residents of Lower Manhattan had done, concerned Portland locals bitterly contested the Vessel mooring in their town. And like her counterparts in New York, prisons minister

Ann Widdecombe was dismissive of local resistance. "I do understand why it is that people sometimes get concerned about having prisons permanently near them, though oddly enough when we then try to close down the prison, they always resist it." The citizens of Portland who opposed mooring the floating prison, Widdecombe predicted, "will resist it [leaving] when we say we don't need it any more."[29] Widdecombe's statements did not stop the Weymouth and Portland District Council from denying the ship planning permission. But pressure in London to increase imprisonment was too great; even the shadow home secretary, Labour's Jack Straw, backed the plan to moor *The Weare* at Portland after he was warned by the Prison Service about a potential "loss of control" if prison populations continued to grow. In fact, New Labour was generally supportive of increased incarceration and broken-windows policing. As Straw himself put it, "If crime is rising, the prison population is bound to rise."[30] It was a line straight out of the repertoire of Nelson Rockefeller or Ed Koch. Mass incarceration was a simple and universal matter of cause and effect: criminality drove punishment. The *causes* of criminality were immaterial, whether in the United States or Britain.

The result was that Portland's many local objections were swept aside by Conservative environment secretary John Gummer.[31] As in New York, the local government—in this case the District Council—had very limited authority over a ship moored in its harbor. Legally, the barge was outside its control; the council's appeal was technically based on its authority to prevent construction of a five-meter-high fence adjacent to the barge on land.[32] But even this objection had little sticking power. The port facilities themselves were privately controlled by Langham Industries, a marine engineering firm that purchased Portland Port from the Royal Navy earlier that year in 1997.[33]

Meanwhile, slowly but surely, the Vessel was prepared for its new role. A "gang of local lads" was hired to renovate and repaint the interior, which had fallen into disrepair. One of the redecorators particularly remembers "three inches of green water" sitting in the long-disused indoor swimming pool: a breeding ground for untold bacteria. The pool was drained and subsequently converted to storage space.[34]

The first twenty-one prisoners boarded the Vessel—now HMP *The Weare*—on June 11, 1997. Only two weeks later, they had to be temporarily removed after the ship's fire safety sprinkler system was found to be defective and began an extensive leak. Local fire officials had warned earlier that the Vessel posed fire risks but had been summarily ignored. As had been the case in New York, they had no authority over an international vessel. And *The Weare* was still an international ship. Though now owned by the British state, it continued to be registered offshore in the Bahamas.[35]

There were other lingering connections to the ship's past. Several of the prison officers working on board had lived on the Vessel while serving in the Falklands. The ship's metal bunk beds still had words engraved by former residents in the 1980s, memorializing their regiments and their time in Port Stanley.[36] Two civilian engineers rotated on and off *The Weare*, staying in a small flat aboard the ship throughout its time as a British prison. They worked twelve-hour shifts to service the toilets, generators, and hot water system. Both were employed by Denholm's, the firm specializing in marine services for the "international energy sector" that had been responsible for restaffing Bibby ships when they were reflagged in the 1980s.[37] Even though the Vessel had finally become public property, its maintenance still required private expertise.

• • •

Despite the parallels between the barge's reception in New York and Dorset, there was an important difference. Unlike in New York, and true to Widdecombe's prediction, *The Weare* quickly became enmeshed in local Portland life. Even with its temporary status and its austere facade, the barge was accepted as part of the local furniture of the town.[38] One reason for this was that the Prison Service launched major local recruiting drives for the new prison, yielding several dozen new employees, a practice that has since stopped systemwide.[39] By late 2001, the Vessel had also won over local elected officials, who granted planning permission for the barge to stay until March 2003, with the possibility of extension. Many in town—especially the 250 people employed by the prison—were eager to see it remain where it was. As the *Echo* put it,

> Reality proved less damaging than some people had feared, with sightseers and tourists keen to view the new ship . . . Time

passed and HMP Weare became part of the local scene. It even won awards for its catering skills, together with a glowing report on the ship as a whole from prison inspectors.[40]

Tourist boats would come and "hover nearby"; there was a steady local trade in souvenirs and commemorative T-shirts, not to mention contracts with news agents, taxi services, catering suppliers, and local contractors.[41] The ship was even the setting for a surreal scene in which Ukrainian children visiting Dorset on an arranged trip from an area near Chernobyl "took part in a hectic afternoon of fun and games under the watchful eye of prison staff." The visit to the prison was, according to one news report, the "highlight" of the month the children spent in England.[42]

Just as in the United States, in England, many of HMP *The Weare's* residents understood the Vessel to offer certain advantages over conventional prisons. The very fact that it was a ship held some appeal. When Ray Bishop was contemplating transfer to HMP *The Weare* from HMP Belmarsh in southeast London, he thought the move "sounded like a change and great fun." Many of the transferred Londoners were excited to move down to the sea, even if the cells themselves were "claustrophobic."[43] The Vessel's carpeted cells had televisions and stereos, and though the Prison Service had intended to house up to five hundred people on it, by 2001 there were only around 360. "It's a good prison, it's alright," one claimed in 2001. "I've served time in a London prison and I tell you I'd rather see the sea than tower blocks any day."[44] One told an inspection team that the food served on board was the "best he ever had"; others praised the provision of fresh food during Ramadan.[45]

Early inspections revealed "a surprisingly well-run and positive regime."[46] The prison's governor was a highly respected administrator, Susan McCormick. A champion of prison theater groups who had spent time working for a social justice nonprofit, McCormick was also a longtime veteran of the Prison Service. In 1973, at the age of twenty-eight, she had become the youngest woman to assume the governorship of a prison.[47] Under McCormick and her successors, the *Weare* continued to garner praise. In 2006, a former inmate—the post-punk rocker Daniel Treacy—recalled that being transferred from a facility in Brixton (in south London) to what he called "the

Inside a cell aboard HMP *The Weare*. Conditions on board were not luxurious, but generally more comfortable than they had been for people incarcerated on the Vessel in New York. Beyond the bars on the window, there was a view of the sea.

The visitor room at HMP *The Weare*. Note the chairs and tables bolted to the ground, the security cameras, and the claustrophobic low ceilings.

A prison officer watches prisoners play volleyball in the Vessel's onboard gym

Good Ship Lollipop . . . was the best thing that could have happened. I was not in a cell but a cabin and could look out of the window over Weymouth Bay. The prison warders were pretty cool and there were computers."[48] Another resident deemed HMP *The Weare* "one of the best" prisons in the UK, with an "absolutely fantastic" drug treatment program.[49] Official evaluations generally praised the ship's conditions. The most serious failing highlighted by a report on the ship from the chief inspector of prisons in December 2001 was that the dental waiting list was too high.[50]

At one point, the relatively comfortable conditions on board led to grumbling among prison staff. In 2002, several officers protested the prison's decision to give small Christmas gifts to children visiting their fathers incarcerated on *The Weare*. The Prison Officers Association (POA) deemed the gifts "quite sick," "a huge security risk," and "a ludicrous idea." The POA's chairman claimed that such gestures made it feel like officers were "working in a hotel rather than a prison." The particular wording of the claim highlights how remarkably flexible the Vessel's status was. When the barge was billed as a hotel, it was criticized as being too much like a prison; when it was a prison, some deemed it too much like a hotel.

But in general, staff morale was high. Portland was a desirable posting for prison officers. Because many of the people who worked on the ship were hired locally, there was a strong esprit de corps and a shared commitment to a new project. Many had worked through the summer of 1997 to prepare the ship for the arrival of prisoners. One officer recalled, "We had a really good camaraderie on *The Weare* and most of my colleagues . . . have never experienced anything like it since." Staff met to fish and golf. They went out together on the weekends. For several years, a group of prison officers maintained a dragon boat team. At the same time, those who worked at the prison understood that, at least early on, the *prison's* position was tenuous. Officers were given "a talking to" that emphasized "how politically sensitive *The Weare* was and how we had to make sure that we represented it correctly."[51]

●   ●   ●

By the early 2000s, relations between the Portland community and the prison had warmed considerably. Yet there was lingering hesitation about extending the barge's time in the town; one district councilor noted that the 2001 proposal to extend the Vessel's stay for several years "underlined" fears of permanency.[52] And the ship was by no means a purely positive presence. In 2001, there was a serious allegation of abuse by staff against an inmate. A report by the prison's Board of Visitors noted nine cases of prisoners injuring themselves, including attempted suicides and two instances when inmates poured "boiling water containing high concentrations of sugar over other inmates." There had been an attempted escape and tension after Afro-Caribbean inmates were dismissed from employment in the kitchen for "not conforming to hygiene regulations."[53] The prison barge's population was majority white—69 percent, according to a 2004 report—but, as in the United States, Black Britons were dramatically overrepresented in the prison's population. Twenty-two percent of HMP *The Weare*'s residents were identified as Black, whereas in Britain as a whole that figure was 3 percent.[54]

And as time wore on, *The Weare*'s facilities suffered from increasing wear and tear. The air-conditioning system often needed repair. Even when it was working, the ventilation was poor. In the summer, it was "like a sweatbox; you literally dripped with sweat." Moreover, "if someone got ill with a cold or the flu . . . the whole wing went down. You did feel like you were suffocating."[55] At one point, all the toilets failed. At another, a large piece of the gym's roof blew away. An officer remembers looking out the window and seeing part of the roof flying down the jetty.[56]

These physical issues contributed to a damning review of HMP *The Weare* in a 2004 inspection report. The new, independent chief inspector of prisons, Ann Owers, held that the ship was "literally and metaphorically a container . . . Prisoners' living accommodation has no access to fresh air, and in some cases little natural light."[57] The upshot was that authorities made something of an about-face in their evaluation of the barge in seven years, deeming the Vessel "entirely unsuitable for use in its present function as a 21st century . . . training prison."[58] Unless the British government was prepared to sink millions of pounds into updating the ship, Owers concluded, the prison should be shuttered.

Why the change of policy? The increased pressure to shutter *The*

HMP *The Weare* in Portland Port in 2008. As of 2024, another barge owned by the Bibby Line, the *Bibby Stockholm*, sits in the same location.

Weare did not come from a shrinking British prison population. By 2005, the national prisoner level had reached a record number of seventy-six thousand. Due to quality-of-life policing inspired by American cities including New York, London's jails were crowded enough for the Metropolitan Police to consider buying *The Weare* from the Prison Service outright for short-term detention in the capital. In fact, there was plenty of demand for accommodation barges; drawing on the example of Hamburg's use of the vessels to house refugees, the British government considered mooring one or more of the Bibby Line's barges in Essex, northeast of London, for the same purpose.[59] In 2023, another Bibby barge, the *Bibby Stockholm*, arrived in Portland for just this job, to widespread public outcry.

In short, the reason that the Vessel had to go had nothing to do with the demand for beds in the UK. Rather, it was simply that the conditions on *The Weare* were out of step with the image of reform that officials in Tony Blair's New Labour government wanted to project. A hulk was, in the words of the new prisons minister, Paul Goggins, "not suitable." It offered "very little scope for activities which might reduce re-offending."[60] "Activities" meant work and classes. The ship was too small to house many of the workshops and facilities that would typically employ prisoners at other sites.[61] For the same reason, it lacked classroom and exercise space; even in New York, there had been consistent concerns about the small size of the onboard law library.

Such concerns reflected a central principle of New Labour's shifting criminal justice policy in the 2000s: to back up punishment with rehabilitation and threaten punishment for reoffending. New Labour's platform stressed individual responsibility: of minors who committed offenses, of drug addicts, and, of course, of prisoners. In this world, rehabilitation and punishment were two sides of the same coin; welfare programs were an extension of the carceral state.[62] Compliance with the strict terms of state-provided welfare was backed up with harsh criminal penalties; time in prison was to set the groundwork for future gainful employment. If British penal policy had followed that of the United States in taking a punitive turn toward the "new penology" in the early 1990s, New Labour sought to soften its edges in the new millennium.

In keeping with its focus on individual responsibility, the government invested hundreds of millions of pounds in "a strong programme to improve offenders' education attainment, raise skill levels and secure better employment outcomes."[63] This initiative was why *The Weare* was "entirely unsuitable for use in its present function as a 21st century . . . training prison."[64] New Labour represented the new caring face of individualist capitalist growth. The barge was neither individualist nor caring enough to survive. The Vessel was an empty, interchangeable artifact of global capitalism: a relic of America's violent war on drugs. It simply did not fit with the redemptive vision being outlined by policy makers in London.

• • •

When he was elected in 1997, Tony Blair surged into power on a wave of what was called "the Third Way," a synthesis of social democracy and market liberalism. It was a center-left position, one that (depending on perspective) either mellowed out Thatcher's laissez-faire orthodoxy or loosened the collectivism of mid-twentieth-century socialism. The collapse of the Soviet Union, in 1991, ushered in a moment of international optimism about the future of liberal democratic society. The end of the Cold War, the American political scientist Francis Fukuyama declared, marked the definitive and permanent ascendancy of Western liberal democracy as a universal democratic system: the end of history itself.[65] Market-based capitalism had triumphed on a global scale, and that triumph opened political possibilities for new left-leaning social programs grounded in the transformative power of education. Blair belonged to a cohort of political leaders—including Bill Clinton in the United States, Romano Prodi in Italy, and Gerhard Schröder in Germany—who paired faith in the market and individualism with commitment to positive social engagement.

The Third Way emerged out of the end of the Cold War, when the long-standing global dichotomy of left and right began to break down. Without the Soviet Union, Western powers like the United States and the United Kingdom no longer had an enemy. And, as Anthony Giddens, the most prominent theorist of the Third Way, put it in 1998, "to regain legitimacy, states without enemies have to elevate their administrative efficiency."[66] Doing so meant borrowing from the business world: governments still had "a good deal to learn from business best practice," Giddens noted. A strong, legitimate state was to be efficient and productive like the best businesses. Like the best businesses, a strong state would act nimbly in an increasingly globalized world. Vitally, a strong nation was "a nation sure enough of itself to accept the new limits of sovereignty."[67]

In certain ways, the Vessel fit in with a Third Way approach to the world. It was, after all, an artifact of offshore capitalism, built on the principles of profit maximization and efficiency. The whole point of the Vessel had been to check as many boxes as possible, as cheaply as possible. It was a product of globalization, just like Third Way politics itself. In a jointly written Third Way manifesto, Blair and Schröder declared that "adaptability and flexibility are at an increasing premium in the knowledge-based service economy of the future . . . we need to become more flexible, not less."[68] The barge was nothing if not adaptable and flexible.

Yet the key words in Blair and Schröder's sentence were not "adaptable" or "flexible," but rather "knowledge-based service economy." Blair and Schröder, like Clinton and Al Gore in the United States, were committed to a vision of a highly skilled, highly paid workforce. They dreamed of an economy in which growth would be driven by knowledge-intensive industries: biotech, IT, advanced manufacturing, telecommunications.[69] This was the age of the personal computer and the ascendant Steve Jobs and Bill Gates, a golden era of possibility and global integration opened up by the burgeoning World Wide Web.[70]

The ideal of the knowledge economy offered a potential way out of industrial decline in the Global North: a way for countries like Britain and Germany to compete with lower-wage rivals through efficiency and "high performance."[71] In essence, the idea was that rich countries would be able to *think* their way out of industrial stagnation. In this vision, humans came to be figured as vital reservoirs of skills and ideas. The more skills they had, the better. For this reason, education was at the center of Third Way agendas. In a famous 1996 speech, Blair declared that the three main priorities for government were "education, education and education."[72]

Ultimately, the Vessel, with its limited space for workshops and classrooms, did not accord with New Labour's commitment to the knowledge economy. This is why HMP *The Weare* had to close.

When the time came, the Vessel was condemned in the language of global business-speak, the favored dialect of Third Way devotees. For government administrators, being an effective modern prison meant meeting benchmarks, like the Prison Service's publicized goal to ensure 80 percent classroom attendance in its facilities. Whether those benchmarks actually translated to meaningful rehabilitation was dubious. The 80 percent attendance goal, for instance, resulted in the service stacking classrooms with those most likely to attend classes rather than those who needed the most help.[73]

Criminologists have shown that in the late twentieth and early twenty-first centuries, prisons became less about real rehabilitation than about managing populations (as John DiIulio had advocated). To this end, penal administrators grew ever more focused on meeting certain "objectives" borrowed from the world of global business. The yearly reports from the UK's Prison Service read like corporate shareholder reports, highlighting "performance against performance indicators" (see figure below).[74] As one criminologist noted in 2000, prison governors were "becoming increasingly concerned with process issues, 'box ticking', efficiency and economy. The approach becomes one of ensuring through administrative and bureaucratic mechanisms that the establishment runs as smoothly and cost effectively as possible."[75]

As HMP *The Weare*, the Vessel did not tick enough boxes. In par-

PERFORMANCE AGAINST KEY PERFORMANCE

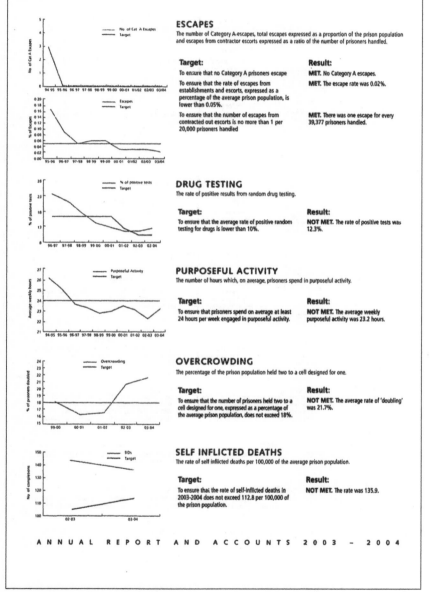

ESCAPES

The number of Category A escapes, total escapes expressed as a proportion of the prison population and escapes from contractor escorts expressed as a ratio of the number of prisoners handled.

Target:

To ensure that no Category A prisoners escape

To ensure that the rate of escapes from establishments and escorts, expressed as a percentage of the average prison population, is lower than 0.05%.

To ensure that the number of escapes from contracted out escorts is no more than 1 per 20,000 prisoners handled

Result:

MET. No Category A escapes.

MET. The escape rate was 0.02%.

MET. There was one escape for every 39,377 prisoners handled.

DRUG TESTING

The rate of positive results from random drug testing.

Target:

To ensure that the average rate of positive random testing for drugs is lower than 10%.

Result:

NOT MET. The rate of positive tests was 12.3%.

PURPOSEFUL ACTIVITY

The number of hours which, on average, prisoners spend in purposeful activity.

Target:

To ensure that prisoners spend on average at least 24 hours per week engaged in purposeful activity.

Result:

NOT MET. The average weekly purposeful activity was 23.2 hours.

OVERCROWDING

The percentage of the prison population held two to a cell designed for one.

Target:

To ensure that the number of prisoners held two to a cell designed for one, expressed as a percentage of the average prison population, does not exceed 18%.

Result:

NOT MET. The average rate of 'doubling' was 21.7%.

SELF INFLICTED DEATHS

The rate of self inflicted deaths per 100,000 of the average prison population.

Target:

To ensure that the rate of self-inflicted deaths in 2003-2004 does not exceed 112.8 per 100,000 of the prison population.

Result:

NOT MET. The rate was 135.9.

Metrics and "box ticking" of "performance indicators" became increasingly important in evaluating prisons.

INDICATORS DURING 2003-2004

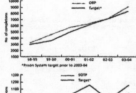

OFFENDING BEHAVIOUR PROGRAMMES
The number of prisoners completing programmes accredited as effective in reducing re-offending.

OBP Target:
To ensure that 8,444 prisoners complete programmes accredited as being effective in reducing re-offending.

Result:
MET. 9,169 OBPs completed.

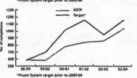

SOTP Target:
To ensure that at least 1,168 prisoners complete the Sex Offender Treatment Programme.

Result:
NOT MET. 1,046 SOTPs completed.

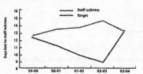

STAFF SICKNESS
The average number of working days lost through sickness absence.

Target:
To ensure that the average rate of staff sickness does not exceed 13.5 days per person.

Result:
MET. The average rate of staff sickness was 13.3 days per person.

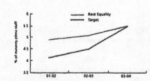

RACE EQUALITY
The proportion of minority ethnic staff.

Target:
To ensure that the number of minority ethnic staff in the prison service, expressed as a proportion of the total workforce, is at least 5.5% by April 2004.

Result:
MET. 5.5% of staff were from minority ethnic groups.

SERIOUS ASSAULTS
The number of serious assaults on staff, prisoners and others, which result in a positive disciplinary adjudication, expressed as a percentage of the average prison population.

Target:
To ensure that the number of serious assaults, expressed as a proportion of the average prison population, does not exceed the level recorded in 2002-2003.

Result:
NOT MET. The total rate of serious assaults was 1.54%.

EDUCATION
The number of awards achieved by prisoners including basic skills and key work skills.

Target:
To achieve 7,174 awards at Basic Skills Entry Level.
To achieve 13,660 awards at Basic Skills Level 1.
To achieve 13,648 awards at Basic Skills Level 2.
To achieve 52,672 Key Work Skills awards.

Result:
MET. Prisoners achieved 12,529 Entry Level awards.
MET. Prisoners achieved 17,864 Level 1 awards.
MET. Prisoners achieved 13,338 Level 2 awards.
MET. Prisoners achieved 103,583 Key Work Skills awards.

RESETTLEMENT
Prisoners discharged with a job, training or education place, including FRESHSTART job outcomes.

Target:
To ensure that 29,044 sentenced prisoners in 2003-2004 have a job, education or training outcome within one month of release.

Result:
MET. There were 32,592 ETE outcomes.

PRISONER ESCORTS

Target:
To improve the proportion of prisoners escorted within the contracted area that arrives before the court sitting time.

Result:
MET. 82% of prisoner escorts arrived on time against an overall target of 81%.

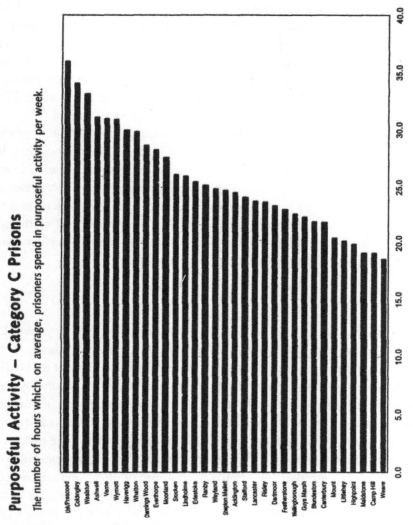

Purposeful Activity – Category C Prisons

The number of hours which, on average, prisoners spend in purposeful activity per week.

Note HMP *The Weare*'s position in this ranking of how well minimum-security prisons offered "purposeful activity": last.

ticular, it ranked dead last among Category C (low security) prisons in number of hours of "purposeful activity," which included job training.[76] Such a marker put the *Weare* in grave danger. Education and upskilling were integral not only to the rehabilitative ideal, but also to New Labour's vision of the knowledge economy itself.

Education—human capital, as it was increasingly articulated—was at the center of Third Way liberals' commitment to "positive social investment."[77] In fact, it was a key feature that purportedly distinguished Third Way liberals from the enthusiastic deregulators and privatizers who preceded them. As Blair and Schröder put it, "Modern social democrats are not laissez-faire neo-liberals. Flexible markets must be combined with a newly defined role for an active state. The top priority must be investment in human and social capital."[78]

According to the Prison Service's metrics, the Vessel was not set up to properly augment the requirements of human and social capital. It is worth considering what that meant. It is true that the Vessel did not have space for the sort of job training that was offered at other prisons; this was the *Weare*'s main shortcoming, in the eyes of its official evaluators. But it also received glowing reviews by members of staff and people incarcerated there. These suggest a rosier picture of a place that might well have been generating "social capital."

• • •

In March 2005, the Prison Service announced that the prison would close by the end of the year. As the news dawned on Portland, Ann Widdecombe's prediction came true. Local grumbling about HMP *The Weare* was largely drowned out by hearty denunciations of the possible closure. Although Portland's mayor was ambivalent about the departure—"I wouldn't be able to say whether I was either sad or glad to see it go"—many others were deeply concerned about the prospect of the Vessel's removal.[79] The Conservative Party spokesperson for South Dorset stressed the negative economic implications and noted that "a rash decision to close the ship will have a big impact on local jobs and an already fragile economy." So too did a local councilor who taught classes on *The Weare*. The director of Portland's port noted that "there is no reason why the vessel cannot stay beyond 2006."[80] As soon as the ship left, the port would lose £250,000 a year in moorage fees and the town would lose 250 jobs.[81] The economic life of the dockyard was beginning to recover due, in no small part, to the traffic drawn by the Vessel. Certainly, the prison officers themselves wanted *The Weare* to stay.[82]

Local efforts to keep the ship as a prison turned out to be just as futile as those to keep it away had been eight years before. The Vessel had been meant to be temporary. It would only stay off Portland's coast as long as its political benefits exceeded its economic costs. By 2005, the costs—millions of pounds a year in maintenance and staffing—outstripped its benefits. The facility closed in August 2005 as the last prison ship in Europe. As Portland's mayor put it, "It's the end of an era."[83] But even for Portland itself, that era was short and transitional. The *Weare* was a temporary stopgap, not just for Britain's Prison Service but also for Portland itself. When it opened, it filled a hole in the economy left by the shuttered naval base; Britain's shrinking military presence was replaced by its growing carceral one. Yet by the late 2000s, Dorset's economy was growing, driven largely by tourism.[84] With this in mind, there were briefly plans to sink the barge near Portland to encourage recreational diving in the area.[85]

However, the Vessel was not destined to sink and become a reef. It was, finally, after nearly three decades, to be used for its intended purpose: as accommodation for workers in the offshore oil industry. To take up this role, it would have to leave Portland harbor on another long journey, towed thousands of miles southward to the oil-rich Niger River delta. But before it budged from the harbor, it would become the subject of intense litigation in London, between two off-shored corporations.

CHAPTER 8

THE RIVER THAMES

	The Vessel	The Sister Vessel
2005	HMP *The Weare* closes. The Vessel is renamed *The Weare*.	
2006	*The Weare* is acquired by Pacific Maritime (Asia) Ltd. and then by Holystone Overseas Ltd. The two firms dispute their contract in English court.	
2008	The Vessel, still in Portland, is renamed the *Jascon 27* and registered in St. Vincent and the Grenadines, by Sea Trucks Group, the parent company of Holystone.	

The London Court of International Arbitration is one of the busiest and best regarded in the world. Offering strict confidentiality about its proceedings, every year it quietly settles thousands of cases, involving major companies headquartered across the globe. But in 2007, several lawyers representing a company based in Hong Kong entered the Royal Courts of Justice on the Strand in central London and proceeded to very publicly narrate how arbitration proceedings would be totally unfair for their client. They did so in a location that was steeped in history and tradition; even in 2007, when appearing in the great Gothic revival law courts, some lawyers and judges still wore wigs and gowns. At the same time, the courts stood almost in the shadow of gleaming new glass towers of the City of London, the hypermodern heart of international trade and finance, just a few blocks away. The location was fitting for a case that was to test the boundaries between traditional British commercial law and the international arbitration favored by global firms of the twenty-first century.

In court, the lawyers for the Hong Kong company were persuasive. Not only did their client ultimately win a tidy settlement, but the English court also set a precedent that would limit the power of London's commercial arbitrators. The 2007 court case—*Pacific Maritime (Asia) Ltd. v. Holystone Overseas Ltd.*—was about the Vessel. Its outcome would demonstrate the limits both of the barge's fungibility and of global capitalism detached from national sovereignty.

The Royal Courts of Justice, an imposing neo-Gothic building on the Strand in London where the fate of the Vessel was determined

The Vessel had always been an internationalized financial asset, but the legal proceedings that unfolded in 2006 and 2007 showed just how global it really was. Two firms, based on different sides of the world, haggled over the barge in London, citing commercial valuations from China and Scotland as part of their arguments. Perhaps the most confusing and contentious part of the disputed contract involved the guaranteed delivery of the barge's modular accommodation blocks (or a substitute for them) thousands of miles away from both the barge and the proceedings, in Batam, Indonesia.

The complicated details of the contract and the circuitous course of the dispute are publicly available only because Pacific Maritime took Holystone to (English) court. If the two companies had settled the matter through commercial arbitration—as the contract between them had stipulated and as thousands of these matters are settled every year—this chapter of the Vessel's story would have remained private, sealed by the confidentiality of the London Court of International Arbitration. As it turns out, then, the English Commercial Court case helps shed light on what happened to the Vessel and offers a rare window onto the shadowy world of arbitration and international business in the heady months just before the 2008 financial crisis.

•   •   •

The lead-up to *Pacific Maritime v. Holystone* started in early 2006, when the British government contracted with a British shipbroker, Babcock Disposal Services, to sell off the Vessel, still sitting in Portland harbor. Babcock quickly worked out the details of a contract with Pacific Maritime, a company incorporated in Hong Kong, to buy the ship for £1.5 million (about $2.8 million), some $3 million less than what the British government had originally spent. Pacific Maritime paid the British government a 10 percent deposit of £150,000 and agreed to pay the full amount by the end of July.[1]

In late July, just before it was to settle up with the British authorities, Pacific Maritime agreed to resell the Vessel—now *The Weare*—to Holystone Overseas Ltd., a shell company that had been set up in the offshore tax haven of the British Virgin Islands specifically for the deal.[2] Even in 2006, this sort of offshore registration was a common enough practice, though it has become even more regular over the past decade and a half. The sale price of the Vessel was, again, £1.5 million. The two firms signed a memorandum of agreement—a contract—setting out the terms of sale. If there was any dispute, the contract stipulated, both companies would have recourse to arbitration in London subject to English law. At this point, Holystone assumed possession of the ship in Portland harbor.

Holystone may have been registered in the British Virgin Islands, with a distinctly British-sounding name, but it was entirely owned by the Sea Trucks Group, a Nigerian company whose primary business involved servicing offshore oil facilities. Holystone's president, Jacques Roomans, was also the president of Sea Trucks. *The Weare* was Holystone's only asset. In this way, Holystone was much like the very first owner of the Vessel: Balder Barges I, the limited liability company set up by the Norwegian tycoon Parley Augustsson in 1979. It was a holding company, part of a larger group, created as a shell to manage a single ship, a single asset. But it was also different: set up in a tax haven offshore, Holystone limited liability and responsibility in a much more profound way than Balder Barges I had. Even Augustsson, the "limited liability king," contends that this sort of offshoring is "a rotten business."[3]

After three decades of service as a troop ship and prison barge, after having been named and renamed, bought and sold, mortgaged and leveraged, the Vessel was coming full circle. It was again owned by a shell company, and it was being slowly converted back to serve its original intended purpose as a service vessel for offshore oil and gas workers. In 2007, Sea Trucks began refitting the Vessel in Portland Port, adding beds and kitchens and tearing down security barriers. Since the Home Office had taken over the Vessel, the IMO certification issued by Det Norske Veritas had lapsed; if the Vessel was again to go to sea, it would need a substantial renovation.

And so, over the better part of the next two years, Hampshire-based contractors transformed the prison back into an oceangoing ship and two hundred cells back into cabins: restoring ventilation panels where the Prison Service had filled them in, fitting fire safety equipment, and repairing damaged ceilings. They upgraded game rooms and toilets. The former visitors' area was transformed into a new mess with a serving area.[4] One striking feature that the contractors did not touch were the bars on the windows; wherever the barge was going, security would remain an issue. The renovations were significant—almost £2 million worth of work—but there was only so much that could be done. "It was an old ship," the project manager recalls: "a bit rough and tatty."[5]

These changes to living space were just the tip of the iceberg. The biggest planned alteration was to remove fifty cabins from the front of the ship and replace them with a large crane.[6] The intent of the new owners was to refit the Vessel so it would be able to operate not just in coastal waters but also far offshore in service of the global oil and gas industry. Preliminary estimates put the costs of such a transformation at $7.76 million, several times more than the purchase price.[7]

The Vessel was again being emptied, to be filled with a new role, new inhabitants, and new meanings.

The deal between Pacific Maritime and Holystone was an exemplar of the globalized, financialized, and increasingly abstracted world of the early twenty-first century. The British state sold off a physical asset to a holding company in Hong Kong (Pacific Maritime), which almost simultaneously resold it to a holding company in the British Virgin Islands (Holystone), for use in Nigeria. The agreement governing this second sale was somewhat complicated. Most saliently, it stipulated that Holystone would provide the forward block of modular accommodation units—consisting of twenty-five "accommodation modules (resembling in appearance five portakabins stacked upon each other with 5 windows in each)"—back to Pacific Maritime at no cost.[8] This is why Pacific Maritime was willing to sell the Vessel for the exact price that it *paid* for the Vessel. Holystone was buying the Vessel, but it was on the hook for providing Pacific Maritime *back* with modular accom-

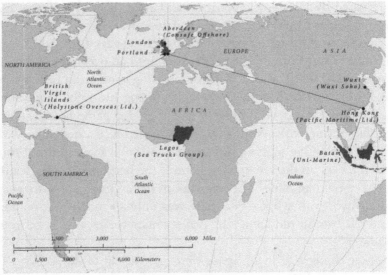

The dispute in London between Pacific Maritime Ltd. and Holystone Overseas Ltd. featured a host of global players. The barge was bought by a company based in Hong Kong, which then sold it to a company headquartered in Nigeria but incorporated in the British Virgin Islands. The Vessel—or at least part of it—was to be delivered to Indonesia. In considering the value of the Vessel, a court in London considered estimates from Scotland, Indonesia, and China.

modation units: the key element that Consafe had added to the simple barge in Gothenburg more than twenty-five years before. In particular, Holystone had to send the accommodation modules to Pacific Maritime at a specified location.

That location was the rub. It was literally on the other side of the world, in Batam (or Batan), Indonesia. The island was a boomtown and a designated free trade zone less than ten miles from the bustling financial and commercial hub of Singapore. Like Jersey, the Bahamas, and Singapore, Batam was an island tax haven, a node in the archipelago of offshore capitalism.[9] It was also a node in the highly connected world of petro-capitalism. Working with American and Japanese engineering firms in the 1970s, Indonesia's state-owned oil and gas company, Pertamina, had developed the city as a key center for oil exploration. In the late 1990s, the unelected development authority tasked with managing the city shifted its focus, and the area began to attract manufacturing facilities, particularly shipbuilders, with foreign-owned yards springing up along its coastline facing the Singapore Strait.[10] By the 2000s, Batam's growth rate was over 15 percent a year, and the population of its metropolitan area was approaching a million. It was here, in loosely regulated Batam, that one of Pacific Maritime's sister companies—Uni-Marine—was prepared to carry out the conversion work involved in physically removing the accommodation block from the barge. According to the agreement between Holystone and Pacific Maritime, if Holystone was to move the barge anywhere *other* than Batam, it would have to provide Pacific Maritime with "an accommodation unit of similar size and volume as the Accommodation Modules."[11]

The latest sale of *The Weare* absolutely depended, therefore, on the modularity of the Vessel—on the ability of its physical space to be described and understood as "blocks" and "modules" that could be disassembled and sold off. The Vessel was physical but at the same time able to be abstracted. Its blocks were easily conceptualized as abstract space: standardized and fungible like capital itself.

• • •

Like the Vessel, modern capitalism depends on a signature blend of abstraction and physicality. Since at least the time of Aristotle, economic thinkers have drawn a distinction between the value of *using* an object and the value of *trading* an object. A shoe has value, Aristotle claimed, because it serves a physical purpose by protecting a foot. But it also has a more abstract value: that someone somewhere might be willing to buy it. The shoe was both a shoe and a tradable good.[12]

Over time, the relationship between physical and abstract value became more and more complicated. By the late nineteenth century, traders and financiers had constructed vast new apparatuses of abstraction. A grain trader in Chicago, for instance, could buy a physical bushel of wheat from a farmer. But he—almost all traders were men— could also sight unseen buy a standardized bushel, stored in some massive silo in Chicago's hinterlands. Without ever seeing the wheat or taking physical possession of it, the trader could sell it off again, hopefully at a profit. More than that, the trader could buy an option to purchase the wheat at some future date for a set price, or enter into a contract to sell wheat at some future point at some other price. That is, the trader could bet or speculate on the rise and fall in the price of wheat. On the futures market, wheat was not just a foodstuff that could be consumed. It was the basis of a whole variety of tradable assets, whose prices depended on expectations about the future: whether there would be a good harvest or a bad one; whether demand for bread across the country would rise or fall. By the turn of the twentieth century, wheat had become an abstracted asset. And much to the consternation of farmers, consumers, and politicians, speculation in wheat could cause the price of real wheat to fluctuate wildly.[13]

An equally dramatic abstraction was taking place in New York and London just as Pacific Maritime and Holystone were squabbling over the Vessel. In the decade leading up to 2007, the average price of a new home sold in the United States almost doubled. Fueled by low interest rates and easy financing, bankers issued a wave of new mortgages in the 2000s. Mortgages are loans. They are debt obligations from homebuyers to banks and thrifts: abstract financial assets whose value depends on the physical value of a house. By owning a mortgage, a bank effectively owns the right to collect interest on a debt. By 2007, banks had turned mortgages into the basis of new, more complicated derivative assets. There were insurance policies on mortgages; new financial instruments that bundled thousands of mortgages together and then split them into risky and less risky tranches;

insurance policies on each those tranches. On the foundation of real, physical American houses that provided shelter to tens of millions of real people teetered a massive scaffolding of financial products, each more abstract than the last.

In certain ways, the Vessel was a physical object like a house or a bushel of wheat. It was, after all, a ship made out of steel. On the most basic level, its value depended on its ability to accommodate people offshore. This everyone knew. From the memorandum of agreement between Pacific Maritime and Holystone, it seems that Pacific Maritime intended (or at least was very much prepared) to physically remove the forward accommodation block at its facility in Indonesia. As per the agreement, Holystone bought a physical barge in England and promised to deliver a physical accommodation block in Indonesia. Yet at the same time, the basic premise of the memorandum of agreement signed between the two firms was that the block itself was fungible; that it could be replaced with a "unit of similar size and volume." This was, after all, the essence of containerization, and the Vessel was, as much as anything else, a container ship. In short, the contract was premised on an understanding of the Vessel as an abstract, or abstracted, asset: a commodity that had substitutes. It was an asset that could be replaced or revalued depending on changing circumstances.

• • •

Relations between Pacific Maritime and Holystone began to fray shortly after Holystone took possession of the barge in Portland. The agreement stipulated that "On delivery of the Vessel" from Pacific Maritime to Holystone, Holystone would "take the Vessel to a destination" of their choice. If Holystone took the ship to Batam, Pacific Maritime would be responsible for removing the accommodation modules at their own expense. However, if Holystone took the ship "to a destination other than Batam, Indonesia, the Buyers hereby agree to construct for and deliver in Batam, Indonesia, to the Sellers at the Buyer's cost an accommodation unit of similar size and volume as the Accommodation Modules."[14] When it moved the Vessel, Holystone would have a choice: either get it to Indonesia, or deliver a substitute.

What happened was that, for months after delivery in July 2006,

Holystone did not take the Vessel anywhere. As the court ruling narrated, in August, Holystone president Jacques Roomans "reconfirmed
that he would build for Pacific an accommodation block of the same
dimensions either in China or Batan." But by that autumn, "it became
increasingly apparent that Holystone was not minded to take the vessel to Batan and that Pacific wanted a cash settlement."[15] Roomans
agreed in theory to a payment, and he set about "establish[ing] the
cost with our outfitters in China." Without waiting for that estimate,
in early October, Pacific Maritime's managing director, Robert Vogel,
delivered a quote from Uni-Marine for $4.08 million to build "a new
forward accommodation block."[16] In short, Pacific Maritime wanted
cash, and quite a bit of it. "The block on its own is of no use to Uni-
Marine," and though Pacific Maritime did (apparently) have designs
to acquire an accommodation block, time was money; it was better to
get hard cash than to wait for the construction of a brand-new block.

Roomans and the team at Holystone were, seemingly, prepared to
pay cash, but balked at the quoted figure of $4 million. Instead, sev-
eral months later, Roomans offered $1 million, which Pacific Mari-
time rejected as inadequate. By the spring of 2007, Pacific Maritime
was getting nervous about the negotiations. In particular, there were
fears that Holystone would take the Vessel out of British waters. Holystone was a company registered in the British Virgin Islands "believed
to be without assets other than the vessel," and "it was anticipated"
that the Vessel would "leave [British] jurisdiction at the end of May or
early June in order to be employed for a period of five years in West
Africa."[17] If it did so, it would be unclear if Pacific Maritime would be
able to enforce its claim against Holystone at all.

● ● ●

The memorandum of agreement between the two companies had
specified that any dispute over the terms or fulfillment of the sale could
be handled through the London Court of International Arbitration—
that is, outside of the official British legal system. Such an arrangement
promoted both privacy and efficiency. The understanding was that, in
the case of a disagreement, the two companies would turn to what
amounted to a huge, privatized court system that operates parallel to
the traditional state-based judicial systems, and has done for well over

a century. The companies would hire international arbitration lawyers who specialized in this sort of work, based in London, Paris, New York, or some other global center. They would make their cases to an independent arbitrator (typically a former arbitration lawyer), who would weigh the case and determine a binding settlement. Though arbitration is a private process, the vast majority of the world's states have signed on to international agreements to enforce their rulings. Though data on such rulings are not publicly available, it is safe to say that most companies comply with them, without the matter ever involving state authorities.

In the case of the sale of the Vessel, international arbitration would have permitted the two companies to conduct their business effectively offshore: without state oversight and without the risk of a very lengthy and very costly legal battle waged in public. Going private was, in general, more efficient and less damaging. Yet in early 2007, Pacific Maritime chose the public option, filing for an injunction in an English court, and thus bringing its dispute with Holystone into the public record and opening a window into an otherwise closed world. Taking such a costly step was a difficult but strategic decision. Until that point, the dispute between Pacific Maritime and Holystone had been conducted directly between the two companies; an official arbitrator had not yet been appointed by the London Court of International Arbitration. As Pacific Maritime's leaders became increasingly concerned that Holystone would simply move the barge out of Britain to Nigeria without settling the matter, they turned to the English courts to ensure that the barge stayed in Portland harbor. Only an English court—not an arbitrator—would have the power to compel immediate police action. Only official authorities could directly leverage the threat of state violence to compel Holystone to keep the barge where it was. In April 2007, with the barge still undergoing refurbishment in Portland and no settlement reached, Pacific Maritime secured a freezing injunction from an English court, blocking Holystone from removing the Vessel from its current location.[18] The authorities at Portland Port seized on this opportunity. According to the Vessel's barge master, the port almost tripled its daily moorage fees. Holystone had little choice but to pay.[19]

But Holystone quickly applied to the court to dismiss, or at least alter, the impound order. According to court records, Roomans "expressed the belief that Pacific was not acting in good faith in putting forward an inflated figure of $4,080,000 for the provision of a small part of a vessel sold for £1.5 million." The figure Uni-Marine quoted was simply, "a poor and transparent scam driven by greed aimed at getting a lot of money for doing nothing and bearing no risk." One of the Chinese companies with which Roomans had worked—Wuxi Soho—had provided him a quote of only $405,650 for a block "built to a higher standard than the existing block."[20] Moreover, Roomans asserted that the worth of the forward accommodation block only amounted to its value as scrap. The major international oil and gas consultancy Noble Denton had estimated the scrap value of the ship itself at only £69,750, less than 2 percent of what Pacific Maritime was asking Holystone to pay.

In short, the case that made its way to the Queen's Bench of the Commercial Court of the High Court of England and Wales in 2007 was about the valuation of the barge. Pacific Maritime argued for a high valuation, one that would be tied to a freezing order that kept the barge in Portland until Holystone paid up. Holystone, on the other hand, held out for a lower valuation and petitioned the court to dismiss the order altogether. By this time, an arbitrator from the London Court of International Arbitration had finally been appointed, and Holystone argued that the freezing order should be changed; "the question of relief should be remitted to him."[21]

Whether or not the matter was left in the hands of an arbitrator, Holystone's lawyers contended that Holystone was responsible only for the cost of fulfilling its agreement in the cheapest possible way. They argued that under the agreement, Holystone had a choice: it could either take the vessel to Batam or take it somewhere else. If it did the latter, it was responsible for constructing and delivering to Pacific Maritime "an accommodation unit of similar size and volume to the forward block." But, according to Holystone's legal team, "in fact, Holystone has taken the vessel nowhere."[22] In short, Holystone had been given the option to honor the agreement in one of two ways, but had done neither. In this situation, the company argued, Holystone was only responsible for damages based on the assumption that it would have chosen to fulfill the contract in the least costly way available to it.

• • •

In making this argument, Holystone's lawyers deployed a legal strategy that would have been unavailable to them if the matter had been decided by an arbitrator: arguing from precedent. Precedent is a fundamental part of the common law systems used in most parts of the English-speaking world. Under the doctrine of *stare decisis* (literally, "stand by things decided"), courts are obliged to apply the law in the same way as in other cases with the same facts. That is, one court decision creates binding or decisive guidelines for subsequent decisions. International arbitration does not have a doctrine of precedent. Arbitrators are not bound by decisions that other arbitrators have made in the past.[23] Indeed, because of the confidential nature of many arbitral proceedings, a full doctrine of precedence would be difficult to maintain (much less enforce) in practice. But when Pacific Maritime brought its dispute with Holystone to English courts, it opened the door to arguments from precedent. Holystone's legal team exploited that opening. In fact, in its legal argument, Holystone relied on a ruling that was more than 150 years old, one set out in *Robinson v. Robinson*, an English case decided in 1851. In an onshore English court, the two sparring companies would have to reckon with the messy baggage of history.

Just like *Pacific Maritime v. Holystone Overseas*, *Robinson v. Robinson* concerned the value of tradable assets over time. Both cases were argued against the backdrop of rapid financial innovation and abstraction away from physical assets and tangible measures of value. When Matthew Robinson died in 1837, his will instructed his executors to convert his sizable personal estate either to government bonds or "real securities." The executors were then to act as trustees, paying Robinson's son, Augustin, the dividends and interest from the estate for the rest of Augustin's life. The problem was that the trustees had not immediately converted certain assets—nearly £11,000 of Bank of England and London Dock stock—into either real securities or government bonds. In fact, they waited eight years to convert these stocks into "3 per cents"—bonds that paid out 3 percent of their issue price every year in perpetuity. Over those eight years, the price of those bonds had risen considerably. If the executors had done their duty and *immediately* converted the entirety of Matthew Robinson's estate into "3 per cents" rather than waiting eight years, the estate would have been much larger than it was.

The reason for this was that the 1840s—like the 2000s—had been a particularly volatile time for British financial markets. Much of the decade had seen an economic recovery and market boom, fueled by a mania for railroad investment. It was during this time that the price of 3 percent bonds had surged. But in 1847, the speculative bubble popped. Financial panic ensued. The stock market crashed, and many people were ruined.[24] Matthew Robinson's executors had bought financial assets at precisely the wrong time: at the height of the market, right before everything collapsed.

Once this fact became clear, attorneys acting on behalf of Augustin's "three infant children," who would inherit their grandfather's estate after their father's death, filed suit against the executors.[25] The grandchildren's lawyers asserted that the trustees owed the infants the current value of all the 3 percent bonds that *might have* been purchased at the time of Robinson's death. In 1849, the judge presiding over the case agreed. But on appeal in late 1851, the court ruled that though the trustees had failed in their duty by not immediately buying government securities after Robinson died, they could not be held responsible for a particular market outcome. They clearly owed the heirs something, but the heirs could not "say to the trustee, If you had done your duty . . . the trust fund would now consist of a certain amount of £3 per cents" since the trustees might have fulfilled their duty by buying different kinds of eligible securities.[26] The key point was that financial markets were complicated, consisting of a whole host of different assets. Capital itself was a fungible, fluid abstraction. It was not tied to the value of any particular asset, even any particular *financial* asset.

Therefore, the court ruled in 1851 that the beneficiaries of the trust were entitled to the dividends they would have received had the trustees purchased the bonds when Matthew Robinson died in 1837, but not the gains in value that the trust fund would have seen had the trustees purchased government bonds at the low price in 1837 rather than the higher price in 1845.

Robinson v. Robinson emerged from a period of profound financial turmoil and equally profound financial innovation: a time that necessitated increasingly complex legal rules for the management of financial assets. *Robinson* produced one such rule. In his ruling, the presiding judge, Lord Cranworth, summarized a new principle:

> Where a man is bound by covenants to do one of two things, and does neither, there in an action by the covenantee, the measure of damage is in general the loss arising by reason of the covenentor having failed to do that which is least, not that which is most, beneficial to the covenantee.[27]

To summarize, the executors had had a choice when Matthew Robinson died: they could buy either real securities or government bonds. But they did neither. The court ruled that the executors were only liable for the *minimum* amount that would have accrued to Robinson's estate had they chosen an option.

This was the principle that Holystone invoked in arguing its case in 2007, in the midst of another period of profound financial volatility, innovation, and abstraction. *The Weare* was a financial object. The contract to deliver it—or a part of it—actually was a contract to deliver its financial value. And that value was contested. Using the principle set out in *Robinson*, Holystone contended that if its dispute with Pacific Maritime were to be settled in the form of a cash payment, Holystone was responsible only for the value of the accommodation block itself, not for the actual cost of constructing and delivering a new accommodation block of the same size. At this point, the logic of Holystone's case took a curious turn. Holystone's lawyers argued that the value of the accommodation block was simply its value as *physical* scrap: the small figure of £69,750.

· · ·

In the rendering of Pacific Maritime's lawyers, the matter was very different. Holystone had an obligation to deliver the barge to Batam. Failing that, it had to deliver a newly constructed accommodation block. Since Holystone did not take the barge to Indonesia, it was obliged to deliver a new block. Holystone did not do that either. Therefore: "The Claimant is entitled to claim damages in respect of the Defendant's failure to construct and deliver the new accommodation block—i.e., the market value of what it ought to have received at the time that it ought to have received it."[28] Whereas Holystone contended that the value of the accommodation block was simply the value of the physical materials that went into it—its value as scrap—Pacific Maritime contended that the value of the accommodation block was, in essence, the value of its use: the value of securing an accommodation block in Batam, Indonesia. Its abstract rather than its physical value was what mattered.

This latter understanding was consistent with the Vessel being both a container and also a product of containerization. The ship had been constructed by Consafe out of shipping containers. The virtue of shipping containers whose virtue was the promise of standardization: that twenty- or forty-foot containers were interchangeable and fungible units.[29] They allowed differentiated goods to be abstracted into unitary volume; they allowed previously hard-to-move and hard-to-store physical commodities to flow through time and space.[30] The containers themselves were incredibly cheap to produce, costing little more than their weight in steel. But their *worth* went well beyond their production costs. It was their contents and their very ability to contain that gave them value and meaning. By extension, it was the Vessel's status as a container—as an empty vessel—that defined it and shaped the ways in which people engaged with it. The only part of the Vessel that was entirely *non*-fungible was its status as a container.

The dispute between Pacific Maritime and Holystone exposed the multiple ways in which the value of containers might be assessed. On the one hand, they were made from very inexpensive materials. On the other, they enabled incredibly valuable and lucrative economic activity. The cost of *not having* an accommodation block in Batam was well over ten times the value of the steel used in the block. And with this in mind, the judge presiding in the case, Christopher Clarke, was skeptical about Holystone's low estimates. "It seems to me," he wrote in his ruling, "that I should look with some circumspection at Mr Roomans' assertions about the value of the forward block or an equivalent."[31]

In fact, the judge "was persuaded" by Pacific Maritime that the company was "in principle entitled to a freezing order for the highest amount in respect of which it has a good arguable case."[32] He accepted Pacific's argument that the contract fell "into the same category as a

simple contract to supply A or B": either the actual forward accommodation block of *The Weare* delivered to Batam or, failing that, a
new accommodation block. Having failed to deliver A, Holystone was
obligated to deliver B. Option B, it turned out, was quite expensive.

London Offshore Consultants, a firm hired by Pacific Maritime
shortly before the barge's sale, had collected a number of quotes for
"similar 96 cabin accommodation blocks." The lowest of these ran
upward of $4.7 million. One quote, offered by the Aberdeen office
of Consafe Offshore—a successor to the Swedish company that had
owned the Vessel in the early 1980s—was significantly higher: some
$7.5 million.[33] In light of these figures, Clarke rejected Holystone's
assertion that *The Weare*'s facilities were "old and tired and very obviously of limited value." The actual worth of the forward block was
surely more than its scrap value.[34]

Instead, the real value of the forward block was in its ability to be
used—"in the rental income that can be earned from it." That is, the
value of the block was to be determined by the market for its use.
And the market for accommodation blocks had boomed during the
previous two years. It was widely understood that the sale price of £1.5
million that the British government had realized for selling HMP *The
Weare* had been very low indeed: a fire sale bargain for the buyers.
As Christopher Clarke noted, "Disquiet has already been expressed
as to whether the Government obtained a fair price." Soon after the
British state had sold the Vessel in 2006, it proposed to "charter her
back at £10,000 per day, a sum which was rejected by Mr Roomans as
inadequate." Holystone offered to charter the Vessel back to the British state at a rate of some £25,000 per day. At that rate, the British
government would have paid back the £1.5 million it gained from the
sale of the Vessel in a mere two months.[35]

Having concluded that the value of the accommodation block was
better determined by the cost of a working substitute rather than
from its worth as physical scrap, the court set about determining a
valuation. Based on market prices for leasing similarly sized modular
accommodation, the judge settled on a figure of $2,750,000 for the
block. Clarke then used this figure to determine the amount of money
that would be tied to the freezing order. He started with the base sum
of $2,750,000 and then added 10 percent for interest and $180,000
for costs, among them legal fees.[36] On top of this, he added Pacific

Maritime's claim for loss of use. Again, using a quote from Consafe in Aberdeen, Pacific calculated that the rental value of the forward accommodation block was about $5 million per year. Clarke deemed a year to be a "modest estimate of the time lost during which the vessel could have been hired out." Though Roomans protested that the estimate of $5 million was too high, as the court noted, Roomans's own refusal to accept £10,000 (over $20,000) per day from the British government for the barge made the $5 million figure seem reasonable.[37]

Pacific Maritime had brought Holystone to court simply to prevent it from taking the Vessel out of Portland before settling the matter of compensation for the accommodation unit. Pacific Maritime won. What that meant in practice was that the court continued a freezing order on the barge. The freezing order would only be lifted once Holystone reached an agreement with Pacific Maritime or (failing that) coughed up the sum of $8.2 million (3.2 million for the accommodation block plus 5 million in lost revenues). The ruling was a setback for Holystone and its parent, the Sea Trucks Group, though not a catastrophic one. The company had already invested somewhere between £10 and £15 million in renovating the Vessel, and Sea Trucks "had proved able to provide sizable sums at short notice in the past."[38] And besides, it was by no means clear that Holystone would have to pay that full amount; Pacific Maritime had previously asked for just over $4 million.

The subsequent negotiations over appropriate compensation for the accommodation unit would not be settled in public court, but rather through commercial arbitration as originally stipulated in the contract. The English courts had intervened, but the Vessel's fate was still subject to arbitration, another impersonal offshore system, like flags of convenience, overseas tax sheltering, or the law of the sea itself. "The appropriate course for all concerned," the judge ruled, "is to apply to the arbitrator for a speedy determination."[39] So ended the case in the Royal Courts of Justice. The sovereign state had weighed in; the ball was now back in an offshore court.

• • •

But though the case may have ended, *Pacific Maritime (Asia) Ltd. v. Holystone Overseas Ltd.* was to have an ongoing legacy. In fact, it would prove important in staking out the limits of commercial arbitrators' power and legal authority. Under English law—specifically the Arbitration Act of 1996—courts could intervene "only if or to the extent that the arbitral tribunal . . . has no power or is unable for the time being to act effectively."[40] When Pacific Maritime applied to the English courts for a freezing order to prevent the removal of the Vessel, an arbitrator had not yet been appointed to adjudicate the matter. At that point, in the absence of an arbitrator, the national courts were clearly able to step in to adjudicate the claim. However, by the time that the judge, Christopher Clarke, was making his ruling, an arbitrator *had* been secured and approved by both companies. And a key part of Holystone's argument for the court to dismiss or vary the freezing order was that by the time the matter was being heard in London, an arbitrator had been appointed. In short, the English court no longer had jurisdiction and could kindly step aside.

According to Holystone, once an arbitrator was in place, it was the arbitrator who could and, indeed, should, be the authority responsible for detaining the Vessel in port. The dispute, after all, was between two companies over the interpretation of a memorandum of agreement that clearly stipulated that disputes should be handled by arbitration rather than by the English courts. And, Holystone's lawyers argued, the arbitrator was quite able to issue orders that were, in essence, replacements for the freezing order. UK law set out these powers quite explicitly.[41]

The problem with Holystone's argument was that though the arbitrator would certainly be able to *rule* that Holystone should keep the Vessel in Portland harbor, the arbitrator would be hard pressed to enforce that ruling. As Christopher Clarke put it, the "arbitrator tribunal lacks the power . . . to act *effectively* in relation to the preservation of assets." In other words, whatever the arbitrator ruled, there would be little to stop Holystone from simply hiring someone to tow the Vessel out of Portland and British jurisdiction. Clarke noted, with more than a hint of frustration, that the dispute was "not one between two large and reputable corporations whose likely compliance with any order of the arbitrator can be taken for granted." This certainly applied to Holystone. "The Court has already been persuaded that there is a risk of dissipation by Holystone . . . a corporation in the BVI [British Virgin Islands] with no other apparent assets."[42] That's why an official court order was important. An order from the English High Court would prevent third parties (like port authorities in Portland) from assisting with the removal of the Vessel. The English court, therefore "declined" "to leave the matter to the determination of the arbitrator."[43] Put more bluntly, it actively intervened to keep the Vessel in Portland.

This final part of the ruling, concerning the power of the arbitrator, was the most legally significant part of Christopher Clarke's judgment. In fact, it is the reason that *Pacific v. Holystone* continues to be cited as a case in setting out the limits of an arbitral tribunal's scope.[44] After all, it outlined a condition under which a national court might intervene in enforcing a memorandum of agreement. As summarized in the *Arbitration Law Reports and Review*, the case was significant because it held that the "Arbitrator lacked power to act effectively to preserve assets."[45] In this situation, the English commercial court could well step in.

Pacific Maritime v. Holystone was an expression of the simple fact that, even in the history of a ship like the Vessel, physical place and national sovereignty mattered. Ultimately, the judge in the case ruled that the British state was responsible for the enforcement of the contract between the two companies with interest in the barge. The global world of shipping deals was opaque or invisible, populated by shell companies registered in tax havens. To a large extent, these shadowy players settled disputes among themselves quietly through arbitration. The judgment in *Pacific Maritime v. Holystone* was premised on the fact that arbitration—though long established in England, since the Arbitration Act of 1889—was often hard to enforce.[46] And when the arbitrator lacked effective power, it fell to the state to step in and ensure that a contract signed under English law, concerning a ship in an English harbor, was carried out.

Yet at the same time, the evidence provided in *Pacific Maritime v. Holystone* speaks to the degree to which the Vessel was always embedded in an international world of trade and global big business, far outside the control of any one national jurisdiction. Even after having served as a prison in the United Kingdom, owned by the British government, *The Weare* was still flying a Bahamian flag of convenience. The barge was bought by a company based in Hong Kong, which then sold it to a company headquartered in Nigeria but incorporated in the British Virgin Islands. The Vessel—or at least part of it—was to be delivered to Indonesia; the freezing order blocking its movement came out of fears that it would be towed to West Africa. In considering the value of the Vessel and its forward accommodation block, a court in London considered estimates for modular housing blocks that came from Scotland, Indonesia, and China.

The whole case depended on the fact that the Vessel was modular: that the forward accommodation block could be removed from the rest of the vessel at minimal cost and that it could be used equally well in Southeast Asia as in Great Britain. The case, in short, depended on *The Weare*'s heritage as an actual container ship, built out of standardized, comparable, and movable building blocks. The value of those blocks was precisely in their fungibility. The value of the blocks reflected far more than the raw materials that went into them. The price reflected, instead, the block's usage as a container for human beings, anywhere in the world. When the Queen's Bench Division of the Commercial Court used the cost of an accommodation block in Batam as a benchmark for the value of the block sitting on *The Weare* in Portland harbor, it reaffirmed the barge itself as a fungible container of standardized space. In this way, the court ruling echoed the original memorandum of agreement between Holystone and Pacific Maritime. The Vessel was a physical object, but it could equally be understood and rendered as an abstract financial asset. Its value depended less on what it did than on what it would cost to replace it.

· · ·

The timing of *Pacific Maritime (Asia) Ltd. v. Holystone Overseas Ltd.* makes its ruling particularly striking, at least in historical retrospect. The year, 2007, was a high-water mark for creating financial abstractions from physical assets. Banks around the world—most notably in the United States—had leveraged themselves as never before, investing in new securities that had little relation to physical reality. Just as the barge became a financial figment, so too had physical houses all over the world. Mortgaged, packaged, insured, and securitized, homes became the basis for new financial derivatives: the abstract assets that

were at the heart of the 2008 crash. Houses are inescapably physical—
no less physical than a ninety-four-meter-long barge. Their primary
purpose is to shelter occupants from physical phenomena: the wind
and the rain, the cold and the heat. Yet in the hands of clever financiers working in Lower Manhattan just blocks from where the Vessel
had been moored, home mortgages were sold and resold, bundled
together into huge portfolios that were then sliced into "tranches,"
insured (and reinsured) against default. By 2007, houses were not just
houses, they had been turned into the bases of "mortgage-backed securities," themselves used as collateral.[47] The limits of abstract thinking
would become devastatingly clear the next year. When the market for
physical housing stumbled, the whole system of abstraction that had
been built on it came crashing down like a house of cards, leading to
the largest financial crisis since the Great Depression. Financial crises,
however abstract, have concrete and lasting consequences: millions of
foreclosures, tens of millions of workers thrown out of jobs around
the world, a noticeable uptick in the suicide rate. Abstraction does not
come without risk.

It is hard to say precisely what negotiations transpired between
Pacific Maritime and Holystone after the English Commercial Court
upheld the freezing order on the Vessel. At that point, the matter moved
to arbitration in London. The narrow window onto the obscure and
hidden world of commercial negotiation offered by the commercial
court case of *Pacific Maritime v. Holystone* slammed shut. One of the
"main advantages" for firms entering arbitration under the London
Court of International Arbitration [LCIA]—rather than, for instance,
arbitration in the United States or Australia—is that the "LCIA Rules
preserve the confidentiality of the proceedings and submissions."[48]

What is certain is that the Vessel was not moved out of Portland's
harbor until just before Christmas in 2009, nearly five years after the
closure of HMP *The Weare*. At that point, it no longer had its forward
accommodation block. The modular technology at the heart of the
dispute had been torn off to make room for a crane, and sold for scrap.
The Vessel was still owned by Holystone's parent company, the Sea
Trucks Group. The matter between Pacific Maritime and Holystone
was likely settled by means of a cash payment, though the precise
figure has never been made public. The Vessel never went to Batam.
Instead, it was towed to Onne, near Port Harcourt, in Nigeria. As

the *AHT Independence*, a tug owned by an Italian ship management company, slowly pulled the barge out of sight of the English coast, the "team at Portland Port were saddened to see the vessel depart after so many years." As the port's newsletter noted, "Long-established relationships had been made between the owners, crew and port."[49] Those relationships had come to an end.

CHAPTER 9

THE GULF OF GUINEA

	The Vessel	The Sister Vessel
2010	The *Jascon 27* is towed to Onne, Nigeria, where it begins service as an accommodation vessel for offshore oil workers.	
by 2013		The Sister Vessel is renamed the *Venture* and is registered in St. Vincent and the Grenadines. It is owned by the British shipowner Intership, and is used as an accommodation vessel off the Nigerian coast.
2016		The *Venture* is purchased by an Indian shipping group, Halani.
2018	The Sea Truck Group's leadership splits. One faction, operating under the name West African Ventures, takes possession of the *Jascon 27*.	The *Venture* is operating off the coast of Namibia when its crew is abandoned by Halani, prompting intervention by the International Maritime Organization and the International Labour Organization. It is deregistered from the shipping registry of St. Vincent and the Grenadines.

I n late 2009, the Vessel was slowly towed out of Portland harbor. As the English coast gradually receded, *The Weare* was trading one offshore world for another. Behind it lay the world of carceral capitalism; ahead lay that of petro-capitalism.[1] It was on its way to Nigeria, where after three decades' delay it would take on the role for which it had been originally intended: as housing for offshore oil workers. In more than one way, the journey to West Africa brought the Vessel full circle, back to its origins.

Its new owner was the Sea Trucks Group (STG), the Nigerian parent company of Holystone Overseas Ltd. Sea Trucks bore some important similarities to Consafe, the Swedish company that had refurbished the Vessel as an accommodation ship in Gothenburg nearly three decades before. STG had been founded in 1977 in Nigeria by the Dutch expatriate Jacques Roomans. Like Christer Ericsson in Sweden, Roomans had started his career in the world of global shipping, in his case as an insurance broker. Like Ericsson, Roomans launched his company in the 1970s just as offshore oil exploration was taking off.[2] As the West African offshore oil industry—dominated by major multinational oil and gas companies—flourished, so did STG.[3] The company's success was reflected in the new name that the Vessel received upon entering into Sea Trucks' fleet. Like those of Consafe and Bibby, ships belonging to STG all had a common word in their names—Jascon—followed by a number. The Vessel became the *Jascon 27*. This new official name would be the Vessel's seventh.

As Roomans expanded his company, oil was becoming ever more central to the Nigerian economy and the Nigerian state. Nigeria is the tenth most oil-rich country in the world. Over the course of the 1990s, and much of the 2000s, Nigerian oil production—especially offshore production—rose. Output surged from around 1.8 million barrels a day to more than 2.4 million barrels a day, about what Britain was producing at the height of its oil boom in the 1980s. Then, as now, the Nigerian oil business functioned through public-private cooperation. Technically, only the state-owned Nigerian National Petroleum Company (NNPC) is licensed to operate in the industry. But since its formation in the late 1970s, NNPC has partnered with huge American and European multinationals, particularly Shell, Mobil, and Chevron.[4] In short, though Nigeria's oil production is officially nationalized (a condition of joining OPEC in 1971), the country has largely privatized and outsourced its operation.

Who controls Nigeria's oil and who profits from it are questions of critical importance, not least because of oil's centrality to Nigerian economic and political life. These questions have divided stakeholders, regions, and ethnic groups in the country since independence, and they lay behind the deadly Biafran War, which claimed well over half a million lives between 1967 and 1970.[5] Since then, oil has only become more important to the national economy. By the turn of the twenty-first century, Nigeria was unambiguously an oil state; its

politics were petro-politics.[6] When STG purchased *The Weare* from
the British government in 2006, oil rents (the value crude oil produced minus the cost of its production) accounted for about a sixth
of the country's GDP.[7] As importantly, oil sales accounted for almost
the entirety of Nigeria's exports. And despite rampant corruption—
estimated in 2004 to eat up some 40 percent of oil revenues—sales
from oil made up the overwhelming majority of the federal budget:
nearly 90 percent in 2006.[8] *Offshore* oil was of special importance for
the Nigerian federal government. Under Nigerian law, individual state
governments had claim to a portion of the revenue derived from oil
produced within their territory.[9] But oil that was extracted tens, if not
hundreds, of miles off the Nigerian coast was different. Proceeds from
offshore oil were commonly understood to be the sole property of the
federal government.[10]

Offshore oil, then, undergirded the state. And for better or worse,
Nigeria had a lot of it, both close to shore and farther out. In early
1982, after a decade of debate and negotiation, the United Nations
promulgated a new convention on the law of the sea to update the

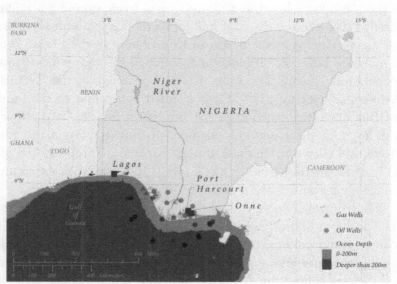

A map showing the existence of oil and gas wells in Nigeria. When the
definition of the continental shelf was expanded to cover sea depths
greater than two hundred meters, huge new oil and gas deposits fell under
Nigerian control.

terms decided at the 1964 convention, which had set off the scramble for North Sea oil and gas.[11] The changes made in 1982 proved particularly dramatic and portentous for coastal West African countries. Under the 1964 convention, states had clear jurisdiction over the ocean floor up to the edge of the continental shelf bordering their coast. The continental shelf, in turn, was defined geologically, by depth: it was the part of the ocean floor abutting a coastline less than two hundred meters below the surface. That changed in 1982. Instead of defining the continental shelf (and thereby national sovereignty) by ocean depth, the 1982 UN Convention on the Law of the Sea (UNCLOS) redefined it as the part of the seafloor that lay two hundred miles from the coast, regardless of how far beneath the waves the floor lay.

The change in the definition was driven by the geopolitics of international governance. Whereas northern Europe and the Atlantic Coast of North America have wide geological shelves, much of the rest of the world does not. When the first UN convention took place, European and North American states had enough votes and power to draft the international law of the sea to their own ends. Defining shelves by depth did just that. Countries including the United States, Britain, and Norway were granted rights to the ocean floor hundreds of miles from their coasts. Countries like Nigeria, by contrast, were accorded rights over only a relatively narrow shelf—in Nigeria's case, some fifty miles wide. Nigeria had joined the UN six days after gaining its independence in October 1960, which meant that it had been able to vote on the 1964 convention. But dozens of newly decolonized states in Africa and the Asia Pacific region had missed this opportunity. By the 1970s, when the UN began debate on the UNCLOS (1982), the organization contained far more postcolonial member states than it had two decades before. Many of these states were islands (Samoa, Nauru, Tonga, and Fiji, for example), and many others—especially in Latin America—had coastlines with very narrow geological continental shelves. For all these states, defining continental shelves in terms of the distance from the coast, rather than depth, was a matter of major importance. As in Caribbean tax havens, at the UN, decolonization would fundamentally shape the growth of the offshore world.

In the United Nations, each country, regardless of size or military expenditure, wields a single vote. Today, this organizing feature of the UN has given low-lying island nations leverage in the global struggle against climate change. In the 1970s, the UN's voting rules gave many of the same nations the power to seize control over fossil fuels buried off their coastlines. In those years, states with geologically narrow continental shelves collectively exerted tremendous power in the UN—enough to change the very definition of the continental shelf. This change was hugely important for Nigeria, whose continental shelf almost quadrupled under the new definition. After 1982, Nigeria and other West African states suddenly found themselves with jurisdiction over vast new tracts of the ocean floor. As a result, they also found themselves in possession of much more offshore oil than they were short months before. Almost overnight, offshore exploration and extraction boomed; there were dizzying profits to be made far below the surface of the Bight of Biafra and the Gulf of Guinea.

· · ·

Since Nigeria's independence in 1960, policy makers had hoped that oil wealth would stimulate economic growth. After a century of British colonial rule, Nigeria was a poor country. The vast majority of its population lived below the poverty line. The oil industry, it was thought, could be a magic bullet for "solving" Nigeria's poverty. Yet despite such aspirations, oil failed to kickstart economic growth. For over three decades, oil has accounted for more than 80 percent of Nigeria's merchandise exports. One way of interpreting that statistic is that while oil itself has boomed, other industries have hot. Put in more technical, economic terms, there has not been a positive correlation between oil production and GDP growth.[12] In fact, Nigeria is an often-cited example of the so-called resource curse, or the paradox of plenty: the counterintuitive correlation between the abundance of valuable natural resources in a country and a low economic growth rate.[13]

There are several explanations for the paradox of plenty. When a country's economy is dependent on the prices of a single commodity—especially one as volatile as oil—growth itself can be unstable. Moreover, the immediate prospect of massive oil profits often has the effect of discouraging investment in more sustainable, labor-intensive economic activity like manufacturing. Whereas in the United Kingdom, oil wealth helped provide at least a modest cushion for a declining manufacturing sector in the 1970s and 1980s, in Nigeria it choked off development of manufacturing in the first place. Finally, many economists have argued that the immense boon of high-value commodities like oil or gold or diamonds may spawn the institutionalization of graft and corruption, which are major drags to economic growth. This was certainly the case in Nigeria when the Vessel arrived. The state-owned Nigerian National Petroleum Corporation, the clearinghouse for all oil and gas business in the country, has long been plagued by corruption. A 2011 study showed that the group received an astounding score of 9/100 for its transparency—dead last out of the forty-four major global oil and gas companies evaluated.[14]

Corruption and opacity grew up alongside the Nigerian oil industry, the product of strategic noncommunication and lobbying by foreign oil companies that wished to avoid regulatory or public scrutiny. From its beginnings in Nigeria, oil was a shadowy big business, from which major Western multinationals—Shell, Chevron, Mobil, and Gulf— garnered huge profits.[15] Because oil is so valuable and because its production depends on relatively few people (compared, for instance, to coal), the wealth and power of oil tends to be concentrated in the hands of a few corporate and state actors.[16]

In this way oil often intensifies existing inequalities. The vast majority of Nigeria's nearly 160 million people (the country's population in 2010) saw little if any benefit from their country's immense mineral wealth, a pattern common to many oil-producing countries with a history of imperial rule. As a carpenter and father of four from the oil-rich east of the country expressed it in 2008, "They celebrate oil exploration every day in Abuja [the national capital], but what do we have to show for it? Absolute neglect, environmental devastation, misery, poverty, unemployment, no roads, no hospitals, no schools."[17] A 2006 report concluded that 85 percent of oil revenues ended up in the hands of 1 percent of the country's population.[18] In the oil-rich Niger delta, life expectancy is just forty years, compared with fifty-five for Nigeria as a whole.[19] As the geographer Michael Watts put it, "From the vantage point of the Niger Delta . . . development and oil wealth is a cruel joke."

• • •

The small city of Onne is a place where that cruel joke plays out. It sits
in the midst of the Niger delta, surrounded by flat, fertile land and the
Bonny River, which empties into the Atlantic Ocean twenty miles
away. Just downstream from the bustling city of Port Harcourt, Onne
is a thrumming hub of West Africa's massive offshore sector; it boasts
shipyards, workshops, oil and gas terminals, and a polyglot international community that services the dozens of rigs perched offshore.

The Onne Oil and Gas Free Zone on the Bonny River, where the Vessel
arrived in 2010

When the Vessel arrived in Onne at the end of its long journey
from Portland in 2010, it was returning to the familiar world of petro-
capitalism.[20] Thirty-one years before, the same ship had been towed
from Norway across the North Sea to Montrose in Scotland. Montrose was different from Onne. It was cold and blustery, hilly rather
than flat, Scottish rather than Nigerian. Onne was certainly bigger
and newer. But both cities were oil boomtowns: international, newly
rich, and full of machismo. And both were gateways to the offshore.
The main feature of Onne is its massive port, the second largest in
Nigeria. Above all, the port services oil and gas exports. At its center,
set over a sprawling twenty square kilometers, lies the world's largest
free trade zone devoted to oil and gas. Established by national legislation in 1996, the zone's legal status allows oil companies operating
offshore platforms nearby to import supplies and export oil without
paying Nigerian customs duties. Additionally, foreign companies and

expatriate employees operating in the zone pay no value-added tax, no withholding tax, no corporate tax, and no capital gains tax.

This is where the Vessel ended up. When Sea Trucks, acting through Holystone, had purchased the Vessel, its managers had envisioned restoring it for use as a working offshore accommodation ship. It was with this goal in mind that they arranged for it to be refurnished in Portland and for the front accommodation block to be replaced with a hydraulic crane. But from the start, there were problems. The agents that had carried out the purchase on Sea Trucks' behalf had been sloppy in their investigations. In Onne, it was discovered that, at some point, structural supports had been removed from the part of the barge holding the swimming pool and squash courts. This was fine for a ship moored at a pier, but a problem for a ship operating miles from land.[21] To make matters worse, the barge had sustained considerable damage on its two-month journey to Africa. The modular accommodation units had all been designed to bend slightly with the torsion of heavy seas. But the sprinkler system had not. Jostled by the waves over the course of its five-thousand-mile trip, the converted shipping containers twisted back and forth in their rubberized mounts. The piping of the sprinkler system, however, remained rigid, and was ripped out of the walls. When the Vessel arrived in Nigeria, its pipes had burst and it had suffered considerable water damage.

And then there was the air-conditioning. Like the rest of Onne, the zone is hot and drippingly humid, low-lying in the midst of the Niger River delta. For centuries, the whole area was infamous for its mosquitoes and unforgiving climate. In New York and Portland, the barge had been hooked up to an onshore electrical system. But in Onne, it had to rely on its old Volvo generators for power. Those generators were simply not up to the task of powering the huge Carrier air conditioners needed to cool the barge in the African heat. Two full levels of accommodation units had to be closed off because of insufficient power; they were too hot to live in. The Vessel, designed to go anywhere and to fit any situation, still had to confront the physical reality of local conditions. It could not operate in Onne the same way it did in Portland.

In short, the Vessel was not leaving the shore, much to the frustration of Jacques Roomans and Sea Trucks' other managers. It would stay in the Oil and Gas Free Zone, providing temporary housing to about 120 Sea Trucks workers, principally from Indonesia, the Philippines, and Nigeria. Its crew was similarly diverse: eight Nigerian deckhands, two Filipino electricians, two Indonesian mechanics, and two British barge masters. One, James Wild, was a Portland native who had been a crew member of the barge since 2001.[22]

Life on board could be isolating. It took hours to get out of Onne and into other parts of Nigeria, even the nearby city of Port Harcourt. It took two days of travel to get to Europe and longer to reach East Asia. The quality of food was variable, even after Sea Trucks hired a caterer. At one point, the barge master discovered that a festive "fruit" display consisted largely of hard-boiled eggs that had been dyed bright colors. Alcohol was restricted. Sea Trucks was a dry company—it forbade the consumption of alcohol, despite its ready availability from local women who brought small boats up alongside the barge, peddling beer.

The Onne Oil and Gas Free Zone is an enclave. It is fenced off with barbed wire from the other parts of the Onne port complex. It needs to be. From a tax accounting and enforcement perspective, it is legally outside of Nigeria's boundaries—one of dozens of offshore "free trade" and "special economic" zones set up and cordoned off around the country.[23] It is as if the zone were not Nigeria at all, but rather an extension of the entirely international and multiethnic world of the offshore oil rig, where workers from dozens of countries—from China to Britain, Indonesia to the Philippines—live in claustrophobic proximity.[24] Nigerians live there too, though with a different status. In the zone, offshore workers are typically identified by their nationalities—American, or French, or Filipino—but Nigerians are often referred to simply as "nationals": an indication of how *international* the population of the zone is.

The zone itself is, at best, ambiguously national. Whereas the port in Onne is administered by the Nigerian state, the adjacent zone is managed by an independent semipublic, semiprivate organization, the Oil and Gas Free Zones Authority. The group was set up to minimize corruption, though it has met with only limited success on this front. In the zone, the authority, not the state, is in charge. It even has its own security apparatus. As the anthropologist Omolade Adunbi has written of another, similar zone, "The presence of . . . Nigerian officials is mainly symbolic because" such zones "have and do exercise their own regulatory practices."[25]

In this way, the Oil and Gas Free Zone was another outpost of the wider offshore world, like the Bahamas, the British Virgin Islands, or the City of London. But unlike those other places, the Onne zone was meant to attract industry as well as capital. The 1996 creation of the zone was a manifestation of Nigerian hopes that oil would kickstart the development of more durable export sectors. The theory was that it would attract investment from multinational behemoths including Shell, Chevron, and the French group Total, which would operate within the zone, insulated from compromised Nigerian institutions.[26] Indeed, the zone was established at a time when many African countries were widely pursuing what was known as "industrialization by invitation."[27] At the crest of a wave of privatization and deregulation in the 1980s and 1990s, the wisdom of the day held that African states were not up to the task of stimulating industrial development by themselves—that it was better for states to step aside and invite private initiative. These ideas were at the very center of the World Bank and IMF's policies of "structural adjustment" that prevailed throughout the 1990s and early 2000s. By making loans to African states contingent on liberalizing economies reducing barriers to foreign trade, international organizations hoped to promote economic growth.

By the mid-2000s, these policies were largely acknowledged to have failed in their mission to stimulate growth.[28] Yet the logic that oil zones might spawn wider economic development through investment in infrastructure continues. Over the past twenty-five years, the free zone in Onne has expanded from 220 to nearly 5,000 acres (nearly eight square miles). In 2020, the Oil and Gas Free Zones Authority boasted that there were "eight principal oil companies and more than 220 service companies in these terminals."[29] Industrial manufacturers were notable for their absence.

Certainly, when the Vessel arrived in Onne in 2010, there was little evidence that the zone was taking off as an industrial powerhouse. In 2007, there were 112 companies operating in the area, but as one economist noted, "with the exception of a cement factory, a pre-cast panel factory, and a pipe coating and machine shop, most of the activities are focused on warehousing for oil companies . . . The main beneficiaries are the oil companies that have a free and secure area with few

hindrances for storage."[30] And the establishment of free zones is not
without costs, including disease and death. As zones expand, longtime residents are displaced, ancestral practices cut off, and economies and ecologies disrupted. Dredging has destroyed fishing grounds
and maimed palm forests. The sulphur dioxide and other toxic fumes
released from refining crude oil cause vomiting, headaches, and nau-
sea. They hang in the air, provoking asthma and lung disease. They
come down on Nigeria in the form of acid rain.[31] The air smells toxic,
the muddy water of the river troubled by more than just silt.

Free zones exist everywhere. In 2022, the Kiel Institute for the
World Economy counted more than five thousand of them around
the world.[32] All of them function on the premise of exception; they
are legally, jurisdictionally, or culturally distinct from the country in
which they sit. But not all of them are economic powerhouses. And,
indeed, the scorecard of those in Nigeria is decidedly mixed. Yes,
many of them are bustling centers of economic activity. But like that
of the oil industry itself, the ability of Nigerian free zones to generate
new economic activity has been profoundly underwhelming. A 2011
study found that such zones had virtually no effect on Nigeria's export
composition. Oil—and oil alone—remains king.[33] A 2018 survey of
fifty-four enterprises operating in four free zones revealed a "very low"
"level of value addition in the Nigerian zones." The economic activity
that took place in the zones made extensive use of low-wage Nigerian
labor, but not Nigerian materials or technology.[34] The well-paid oil
workers were more likely to be British, French, American, Italian, or,
increasingly, Chinese. In the last decade, China and Chinese-backed
companies have been the primary drivers and financiers of new zones
in Nigeria, modeled loosely on the fabulously successful example of
Shenzhen, the "special economic zone" just north of Hong Kong that
reformist Chinese authorities set up in the 1980s.[35] Whatever the
nationality of foreign money and expertise, the development of the
offshore oil trade by big oil is just the latest chapter in a long and sordid history of exploitation in the region. After all, labor around Onne
has been commodified (and worse) at the behest of European and
American businesses for hundreds of years.[36]

Onne sits on a tributary of the Bonny River, just a few miles
north of Bonny Island, one of the largest historical slave entrepots in
West Africa. From the 1730s until the end of the slave trade nearly

a century later, Bonny Island was the principal port and point of African-European contact along the Bight of Biafra, a center where Aro traders, who controlled the riverine supply of captives, met Portuguese and then British slavers. Bonny was an island, an offshore enclave devoted to trade. Set amid mangrove swamps, the island had very little arable land and was infested by mosquitoes. Among Europeans, it was understood to be a "horrid hole." Among enslaved Africans, it was understood to be much worse.[37] As historians have shown, what distinguished Bonny from other slave ports was its ruthless efficiency. Bonny stood out for "its ability to keep loading times down."[38] Historians have estimated that, at Bonny, an average of five and a half captives embarked every day on each waiting slave ship in the late eighteenth century: a number up to three times that at other trading sites on what was horrifically labeled the "slave coast" on many European maps. [39] This fact drew money-minded European slave traders back to the port time and time again. In so doing, as one shipmaster wrote in 1790, they forged lasting business and credit relationships with "expert traders," including the rulers of Bonny itself. The result of efficient business was human misery. According to the Transatlantic Slave Trade Database, some 407,422 Africans embarked on slave ships at Bonny. Only 347,688 disembarked at the end of their voyages.[40]

As G. Ugo Nwokeji and other historians have pointed out, there are arresting continuities between the slave trade and the trade in Nigerian oil in the twentieth and twenty-first centuries. In both cases, benefits and profits "flowed almost wholly to the political classes." And both trades depended on an opaque network of commerce: "the often unaccountable operation of the world of joint ventures and business alliances," as Nwokeji put it.[41] There is another structural similarity between slavery and oil. Like special economic zones and the Vessel itself, slave ports were offshore spaces. They were set up on islands, or on so-called floating factories made from ships bound together and moored in the riparian harbors—places where rivers met the sea.[42] Like free trade or free enterprise zones, they were liminal spaces that existed on the literal margins of authority. Oil and slavery both depended on the offshore. Both depended on empty vessels.

• • •

Running empty vessels was lucrative. The new owner of the Vessel, the Sea Trucks Group (STG), had ridden the wave of surging petroleum production in the 1980s and 1990s. By the early 2000s, STG had grown from a relatively small Nigerian firm into a highly profitable global business. The group was headquartered in Lagos and operated mostly in West Africa. But starting in 2002, it began moving its assets to a new holding company—Sea Trucks Group Ltd.—which was incorporated in Road Town, the capital of the British Virgin Islands, another Caribbean tax haven.[43] Like many companies operating offshore, Sea Trucks had dealings with Mossack Fonseca, the storied Panamanian law firm whose leaked files came to be known as the "Panama Papers."[44] Sea Trucks grew to include subsidiaries such as Holystone—many of which were incorporated in the tax haven of Guernsey, an island in the English Channel. There were also subsidiaries incorporated in Ghana, Australia, the Netherlands, and the United Arab Emirates, where Sea Trucks came to own twenty acres of waterfront in the Hamriyah Free Zone in Sharjah.[45] Indeed, according to a 2012 audit by the global accounting firm PricewaterhouseCoopers (PwC), not one of the constituent companies of the Sea Trucks Group was incorporated in Nigeria itself. Firms based in the Global North were not the only ones taking advantage of offshoring.

Through the early 2010s, Sea Trucks thrived. It received major contracts from the French group Total, from the American firm Hess, and from British Petroleum, the once-nationalized company that Margaret Thatcher had privatized after success in the Falklands.[46] According to the PwC audit in 2012, Sea Trucks had more than $1.2 billion in assets and had posted post-tax profits of about $25 million the previous year. It was rapidly expanding, supplementing its fleet of ships to include larger and technologically advanced class 3 "dynamic positioning" (or DP3) ships. These vessels were equipped with computer systems that enabled them to automatically maintain their exact positions in the rough and shifting waters of the open ocean, well outside coastal waters. There, they could install pipelines and wells hundreds and even thousands of meters below the ocean's surface. "Four of our new vessels can work at those [deeper] depths," Roomans told *Foreign Affairs* in 2009; "something no one else in Africa can do."[47] The value of its fleet grew from $635 million in 2010 to more than $760 million the next year, with an additional three vessels worth $277 million under construction.[48] In 2012, the company opened a European office in Rotterdam with fifty employees and ordered a major new DP3 vessel to be constructed at a shipyard in Singapore.[49]

Sea Trucks' rapid expansion depended on financing. In 2007, the company took out a $20 million loan from the First Bank of Nigeria, which was paid off five years later. In 2010, it borrowed $311 million from the Bank of Scotland, which was serviced at a rate of $14.5 million per quarter.[50] More significantly, in 2012, Sea Trucks issued $575 million in bonds through Nordic Trustee ASA, a large Oslo-based bond and loan agency that did considerable business with the oil and gas industry.[51] It was a substantial amount of debt, but expansion made sense. Even as the financial markets were reeling in the wake of the 2008 crisis, oil was booming.

• • •

But then, in the mid-2010s, global oil prices collapsed and Sea Trucks faced the same difficulties that Consafe had three decades before. As in every chapter of the barge's life, its fortunes were at the whim of global markets, particularly the energy market. The principal reason for the drop in oil prices was the rapid expansion of American shale oil and gas production. In 2007, the United States produced 1.3 trillion cubic feet of shale gas. In 2015, it was producing more than ten times that amount. By 2020, U.S. shale production had crested above 26 trillion cubic feet.[52] Booming extraction sites in the continental United States, from Pennsylvania to North Dakota, fundamentally shifted the political economy of the world's energy sector. In a few short years, the United States drastically reduced its dependency on foreign oil (a key political talking point since the Iraq War) and turned into a major gas exporter.[53] The advent of plentiful American gas played havoc with oil markets. Over the course of 2014 and 2015, the average global price of crude oil dropped from $124 per barrel to a low of just over $42 per barrel. Suddenly, oil producers operating in other parts of the world confronted a buyer's market. The result was a loss of profit and power.

For Sea Trucks—just like for Consafe and the Balder Group before it—the collapse in oil prices was disastrous. Lower prices meant fewer wells. And fewer wells meant less business servicing wells. As contracts dried up, Sea Trucks struggled. To raise cash, in 2016, it sold off

a newly constructed DP3 pipe-laying vessel—the *Jascon 18*—to the
Russian state energy giant Gazprom, for an undisclosed price through
an intermediary. As it was reported in the foreign press, the purchase
made geopolitical sense for Gazprom. It allowed the state conglomerate to build undersea oil pipelines—especially the controversial Nord
Stream 2, connecting Russia to Germany under the Baltic Sea—
without "having to worry about international sanctions," a prescient
concern six years before the invasion of Ukraine.[54]

Even with the sale, which likely brought in tens of millions of
dollars, financial pressures were mounting for Sea Trucks. In late
2016, those pressures culminated in a dramatic leadership contest in
Sea Trucks Group's boardroom. As Sea Trucks had grown, Jacques
Roomans had recruited a set of European executives—all men, many
with backgrounds in oil and gas—both to manage the company in
Nigeria and to serve on its board from afar in Europe. By 2016, there
was brewing discontent among these executives over Roomans's continued leadership as president and CEO of the company. In October,
when Sea Trucks defaulted on its repayments to Nordic Trustee, the
agent of the bondholders, that discontent came to a head. Consequences came swiftly. In the corporate restructuring that followed
two months later, Roomans and other directors were replaced by a
new "independent" board of directors. To observers sympathetic to
Roomans, this was little more than a power grab orchestrated from
Europe; disgruntled board members worked with STG's bondholders
(affiliated with Nordic Trustee) and the Sea Trucks executives to oust
him from the company he had founded and overseen for four decades.
Revolt rumbled, at least seemingly, from many corners. The managers
of Sea Trucks, Roomans alleged, had organized against him "through a
complex business arrangement with other third parties," and "unlaw-
fully" forced him off the board.[55]

Roomans might have been out of the boardroom, but he was far
from out of the picture. According to a report to creditors issued on
behalf of Sea Trucks executives, Roomans was still the principal owner
of Sea Trucks through a trust, even if he was no longer its president.
In March 2017, he sought to remove the new board and reassert control.[56] Because of the claims of the bondholders, the effort failed. But
Roomans still had cards to play. Back in 1995, he had set up a separate
company called West African Ventures (WAV), which, among other

activities, leased ships from Sea Trucks and operated them. The precise nature of the relationship between the two companies was opaque and has been disputed, but what is clear is that after Roomans formally left Sea Trucks, he still was in control of WAV. And WAV seemed to be in physical possession of the majority of the STG fleet, some thirty-three vessels, including the *Jascon 27*. Importantly, whereas STG was a company registered in the British Virgin Islands, WAV was an independent company that was registered in Nigeria itself.[57]

Starting in 2017, the two formerly partnered companies descended into a bitter dispute, waged in legal battles and echoed in the pages of Nigerian newspapers. Several publications ran stories—all sharing similar nationalistic language—alleging dastardly behavior by Roomans's former partners. In these tellings, "expatriates" had "hijacked" a business from Roomans, its rightful "Nigerian owner," a pattern that evoked the long history of extractive imperialism in Nigeria.[58] The specter of imperial rapaciousness loomed large. As one sympathetic report put it, "WAV said the cabal which comprised some British expatriates cannot reap where it did not sow, by stealing the funds and assets of a company built by a Nigerian with Nigerian funds and catering for the welfare of [the] millions of Nigeria."[59] Several newspapers reported that Sea Trucks' Dutch and British managers hired "a retired naval admiral, who tried to forcefully take one of WAV's vessels, *Jascon 55*, out of Nigeria. The Nigerian navy, however, promptly intervened and stopped the attempted theft." The "cabal" also allegedly tried to "take out WAV vessel Jascon 30 . . . This time around, it got so violent that the Nigerian crew of WAV and STG were all locked up and their phones taken from them." Again, the situation was reportedly saved by the timely intervention of the Nigerian navy.[60] In the rendering of West African Ventures, Sea Trucks and its new management were trying to steal thirty-three vessels from the company and, even more seriously, from Nigeria.

• • •

Extralegal possession and intimidation were not uncommon in Nigeria's oil industry, especially in the eastern part of the country around the Niger River delta. Between corruption and outright theft, about a quarter of Nigerian oil revenues between 1970 and 2006 simply disappeared.[61] Oil might not require a great mass of workers to produce, but it does rely on vast and geographically expansive networks of wells, pipelines, refineries, and transit sites. Interrupting or siphoning off the flow of oil is relatively easy. As the political theorist Timothy Mitchell has pointed out, disruption and the profits that come with it are also a source of power, especially in places without intense state-backed security.[62] The Niger delta region was one of those places.

Security was a constant concern, even within the heavily guarded free zone. Foreign employees of Sea Trucks lived a cloistered life, confined to ships and compounds. They did not go anywhere without an armed escort, often provided by the Nigerian army. On board the Vessel itself, security was guaranteed by a detail from the Nigerian navy.[63] The threat posed by militant groups in the area led Shell to consider moving all of its operations offshore.[64] But even offshore rigs were not immune from armed violence, especially from Ijaw militants operating in eastern Nigeria. Rescue attempts could be particularly dangerous. In 2006, the Nigerian military launched an operation to free seven foreign workers taken hostage on an offshore oil rig operated by the Italian group Agip. One hostage died during the operation, as did two hostage takers and a member of the rescue team. The head of security for one of the major oil operators in the country later called the operation a "fiasco," not just because of how it was executed but because it took place at all. He sanguinely accepted that hostage taking was simply part of the landscape of Nigerian oil. "There's nothing wrong with negotiating with the hostage-takers like we have done in the past, and safely, with huge success," he was quoted as saying. "Any time strong-arm tactics are applied, this sort of thing [e.g., death] is bound to happen."[65] Sea Trucks too saw its share of kidnappings. James Wild, the Vessel's barge master, narrowly missed a pirate attack in 2012. After working for months repairing a generator for a different barge offshore, Wild flew back to the *Jascon 27* in Onne. Just days later, pirates raided the offshore ship, killing two Nigerian naval personnel and taking four men hostage, including Wild's replacement.[66]

Even under the best of circumstances, the offshore oil industry is a rough-and-tumble sector, full of machismo and casual violence. It attracts men from poor and neglected areas. And the specter of explosion and disaster hovers ominously over daily life. As the anthropologist Hannah Appel has explored, oil rigs are hermetic spaces, where the rituals of safety are held out as paramount.[67] Yet as one oil worker told a journalist, "The 's' in 'safety' is a dollar sign."[68] And in the Nigerian offshore, negotiating with hostage takers has simply been part of the cost of doing business. So too has a shocking degree of violence. In the late 2000s, it was estimated that more than a thousand people per year died in oil-related incidents, whether at the hands of individuals or corporate and state actors.[69]

The story of alleged theft of WAV ships promulgated by many Nigerian news outlets should be understood against this backdrop of regular violence. It rested on the all-too-common experience of violent seizure of oil and oil-related property. Moreover, the purported theft by Sea Trucks also evoked anti-colonial narratives of extralegal expropriation by foreign companies, which enacted a different, even more systematic kind of violence on the country. After all, Nigeria is a former British colony, with a dark and brutal history. Economic globalism, carried out at the hands of multinational corporations operating offshore in special tax-free enclaves, had a bad look. To many, it was simply an extension of European colonial rapaciousness, dressed up in new legal terminology and carried out under a different name. The attempts to seize ships like the Vessel and others from West African Ventures smacked of an older, long-standing extractive violence. WAV's story was, in short, a powerfully resonant narrative.

• • •

But seen from the perspective of WAV's critics, it was nonsense: little more than a set of fabulations cooked up by the company and spoon-fed to an uncritical nationalist press. In a press release, Sea Trucks Group and its UK-based consultants, FTI Consulting, asserted that it was "the registered legal owners of the 33 vessels . . . all of which are located in Nigeria. West African Ventures Limited ('WAV') has undertaken an untruthful press campaign to dispute this position."[70]

From London, the story looked markedly different than it did from Lagos, Port Harcourt, or the Onne Oil and Gas Free Zone. According to Sea Trucks' new leaders, while Roomans had still been in control of both STG and WAV, Sea Trucks had chartered most of the vessels to West African Ventures. But the chartering agreements did nothing to change the fact that the vessels were still owned by Sea Trucks.

What is more, the ships had been used as collateral for STG's $575 million bond issued by Nordic Trustee. According to the managers of STG, the story was very simple. After STG defaulted on its payments to Nordic Trustee, the latter demanded new oversight. Roomans was out. But he did not go quietly. In late 2016, his failed attempt to wrest control and reinsert himself into STG management prompted Nordic Trustee to call in the "full balance of approximately US$482m" owed to the bondholders.[71] The creditors sought to collect the ships, but the ships were in possession of the Roomans-controlled WAV, which refused to part with them. According to STG:

> The true story is that Sea Trucks, under the full control of Mr. Roomans, failed to pay its debts, and that WAV, also under the control of Mr. Roomans, failed to return the vessels that it had no rights to, which had been mortgaged to secure the loan.[72]

As a result, Sea Trucks "had no option but to take legal action to recover its vessels, including through arbitration in London.[73] One of those vessels, still in the possession of WAV, was the barge the *Jascon 27*.

In early May 2017, Sea Trucks entered liquidation under an order from the Eastern Caribbean Supreme Court in the British Virgin Islands, where Sea Trucks Group Ltd. was still incorporated. To some extent, the notion that Sea Trucks was a Nigerian company had long been a fiction. It was founded by a Dutch expat and, for at least the last several years, overseen largely by Europeans. Its major assets were officially owned by a company registered in the Virgin Islands. But it had still, largely, been administered from Nigeria. With liquidation, the firm's Nigerianness was revealed to be if not purely a facade then at least tenuous and complicated. From the perspective of international law and international finance, the firm was not Nigerian at all.

Sea Trucks' decision to liquidate in the British Virgin Islands was carefully calculated. STG's directors understood that with the company in liquidation, Roomans would be barred definitively from further influencing the company. The liquidators, approved by the court in the Virgin Islands, were principals of FTI Consulting, the London-based group hired by STG.[74] In short, this meant that the liquidators were working hand in hand with STG's European "management team to achieve a financial restructuring of the Group."[75] STG's executive chairman noted in a press release, "The appointment of Provisional Liquidators has no impact on the Group's operations; the management team remain at the helm and look forward to working with our loyal customers to continue to develop our successful trading relationships."[76] Choosing to undergo the liquidation process in the Virgin Islands was a strategic move to ensure that the European directors had full control. Presumably, it was a move that would reassure global bondholders.

Once liquidation was underway, FTI Consulting immediately set about evaluating STG's assets and liabilities. The company had just about $3 million in cash and available investments in subsidiaries. These resources would do little to repay the $481,727,037 it owed to the bondholders represented by Nordic Trustee. The only way STG was going to put itself on better financial footing was to leverage its most valuable assets: its ships, most of which were "mortgaged in favour of the Bond Trustee as collateral for the bonds."[77] The problem, however, was that most of the thirty-seven vessels that STG had on its books were in the physical possession of West African Ventures. They were situated in Nigeria, well outside the jurisdictional reach of the Supreme Court of the Eastern Caribbean in the British Virgin Islands. STG was only in full control of four vessels, which had been operating outside Nigerian waters at the time of the schism. Fortunately for those in charge of the company, these were four of the five dynamic positioning DP3 vessels, which were by far the most valuable ships in the fleet. The fifth DP3 was operating in Nigeria, and WAV claimed joint ownership of it, a claim that Nigerian courts effectively backed.[78]

Working with its liquidators, Sea Trucks transferred the ownership of the four ships to a newly established company, Telford Offshore, founded by Sea Trucks' managers and incorporated in the Cayman Islands.[79] The "sales" of the vessels from STG to Telford "reduced the debt owed by Sea Trucks group under its secured bonds by $215m." In essence, the restructuring allowed the new company, Telford Offshore (based in Dubai as of 2023), to take over and refinance the four DP3s.[80] But by October 2017, the remaining thirty-three ships, including the fifth DP3 and the *Jascon 27* (the Vessel), were still in Nigeria in the possession of West African Ventures, subject to ongoing arbitration—once again at the London Court of International Arbitration—between STG and WAV.[81] Physical possession, it turned out, might not have been a full nine-tenths of the law, but it mattered a great deal. So too did legal jurisdiction. Offshoring lent flexibility and financial advantages, but enforcement relied on a diffuse sort of power: the power of the marketplace rather than the concrete power of the state.

The Vessel in Onne, taken by James Wild, the Vessel's barge master, in 2017

•   •   •

Arbitration in London; registration in the Cayman Islands; court orders from the Virgin Islands: this was the administration of international law, par excellence. It was also global capitalism, par excellence. But international capital still had to contend with Nigerian national enforcement. As in Norway, New York, and Britain, as the *Jascon 27* the Vessel existed both as an abstracted artifact of global capitalism and also as a concrete object to be used for local ends. WAV was a Nigerian company with few international assets, and it refused to cede control of the thirty-three vessels that were claimed by Sea Trucks. From Sea

Trucks' perspective, WAV was simply breaking a contract and violating an international agreement. As a sympathetic Nigerian article from late 2017 put it, "There is a need for companies operating in Nigeria . . . to play by the book and respect agreements. This becomes more important when weighed against the backdrop of Nigeria's poor ranking on the global list on ease of doing business." The same article even hinted that WAV might be engaging in corrupt practices with the assistance of the Nigerian government.[82]

Sea Trucks and West African Ventures reached an agreement in November 2018 "after a period of extended negotiations" in Lagos brokered by Nigerian government officials. The resolution, which allocated vessels between the two feuding companies, was touted by a senior Nigerian official "as a win-win":

> The significance of the peace agreement and the decision to work together amicably . . . is to correct the impression outside the country where people believe that coming to invest in Nigeria as an international business will only leave you to lose your investment and assets.[83]

In the rendering of Nigerian authorities, Sea Trucks was "an international company" and WAV "a local company"; the resolution of the conflict was a testament to the neutrality of Nigerian authorities in resolving a commercial conflict between a Nigerian firm and a foreign firm. It was proof that the rule of law and the protection of private property rights were alive and well in the country that was notorious for sweetheart deals and corruption.[84]

In the division of the thirty-three contested ships, the Vessel stayed in the hands of West African Ventures as part of the negotiated settlement. In a sense, the ship was Nigerian; it was now owned by a Nigerian company and guaranteed by Nigerian state authorities. In a flier advertising the *Jascon 27* to potential clients, WAV billed itself as "your 100 percent Nigerian Partner."[85] Throughout its bitter contest with STG over physical assets, WAV had deployed (or at least benefited from) the powerful rhetoric of nationalism to combat that of STG's globalism. To that end, the empty Vessel had to take on a national identity to an extent that it never had before. Over the previous four decades, the Vessel had typically been understood as foreign. In New York, it had been the "Falklands Barge"; in England, a "little Alcatraz." When it was in Sweden, it had a Scottish name.

And even in Nigeria, the *Jascon 27* remained an artifact of global capitalism. The man at the helm of WAV was a Dutch expat, though also a Nigerian citizen.[86] At some point in the early 2000s, the ship had been reregistered, not in the Bahamas but in another Caribbean postcolonial tax haven, St. Vincent and the Grenadines, whose registry is administered in two other more venerable tax havens: Geneva and Monaco.[87]

So, too, coincidentally, had the Vessel's sister ship, the *Bibby Venture*, by then renamed simply the *Venture*. By the mid-2010s, the Vessel's longtime companion was owned by a London-based shipping group, Intership. The *Venture* was also involved in the West African offshore oil industry, operating nearby off the coast of Nigeria.[88] After years apart, the ships' journeys had again converged. Both were operating in Nigerian waters, and both were Vincentian vessels.

• • •

This last point is worth underscoring. After a long and costly fight to establish the Vessel's Nigerian bona fides, the ship was no less a global object than its long-lost sister ship. Indeed, for all the noise about its Nigerian identity, it was more *Vincentian* than ever before. Since its construction in 1979, the Vessel had always been an artifact of the offshore world. Yet after forty years, it had come a long way. Not only had it traveled tens of thousands of miles, it had moved further offshore in a metaphorical sense. The barge was built by people ultimately employed by the Swedish state. For a time, it flew a Swedish flag, was owned by a Swedish company. When it was in Nigeria, it flew a Vincentian flag, was owned by a company based in the Virgin Islands, and served as collateral to a group of international investors whose agent was based in Norway. It operated out of an offshore free trade zone—barely part of Nigerian sovereign territory—in the service of multinational corporations extracting oil miles offshore.

The Vessel had become more offshore because the world had become more offshore. The barge was constructed to ride the literal waves of the ocean, but it also was constructed to ride the wave of the booming offshore oil market. Perhaps unintentionally, it had been put together in a way that allowed it to ride the even larger wave of offshoring itself. As people, corporations, and even states have colonized and settled the global offshore space, they have required offshore technologies. The Vessel had become just that: a tool of multinational interests seeking to step outside the boundaries of national sovereignty and make a profit at a new, postimperial global frontier.

WALVIS BAY

	The Vessel	The Sister Vessel
by 2013		The Sister Vessel is renamed the *Venture* and is registered in St. Vincent and the Grenadines. It is owned by the British shipowner Intership, and is functioning as an accommodation vessel off the Nigerian coast.
2016	The *Jascon 27*'s status is "laid up."	The *Venture* is purchased by an Indian shipping group, Halani.
2018	Sea Truck Group's leadership splits. One faction, operating under the name West African Ventures, takes possession of the *Jascon 27*.	The *Venture* is operating off the coast of Namibia when its crew is abandoned by Halani, prompting intervention by the International Maritime Organization and the International Labour Organization. It is deregistered from the shipping registry of St. Vincent and the Grenadines.
2021		The Sister Vessel is renamed the *High Ocean IV* and reregistered in St. Kitts and Nevis. It is towed to Gujarat in India, via Port Louis, Mauritius.
2022		The *High Ocean IV* is scrapped in Alang, Gujarat.

The global offshore is built on jurisdictional ambiguity. The battle over the Sea Trucks Group was not simply between rival factions within a company, or between two successor firms. It was, rather, a contest between different legal authorities: the Nigerian state, a court in the British Virgin Islands, and arbitrators based in London.

The offshore lies beyond legal frontiers: a place with shadowy rules. It is a gray zone. And troubling things happen in gray zones.[1] Power comes with its own special kind of impunity. Possession is close to nine-tenths of the law. Might often makes right. With little oversight or recourse to the enforcement of international law, there is little to check theft or abuse.

The burden of the offshore falls on the most vulnerable. And off-shore laborers are far more vulnerable to exploitation than offshore financiers. They stand to lose not just property but their very freedom. This is what befell seafarers working on board the Vessel's sister ship, the *Venture*. For as the Vessel, along with the rest of the Sea Trucks fleet, was contested off the coast of Nigeria, the crew of its sister vessel confronted a far more dramatic fate two thousand miles southeast, in Walvis Bay, Namibia.

• • •

Walvis Bay is a small city of about sixty thousand inhabitants perched between the Atlantic Ocean and the edge of the Namib desert. The city is set amid a harsh landscape; dry and windy, its sulfurous air corrodes metal at a remarkably fast rate. The land around Walvis Bay has been inhabited by the Topnaar people and their ancestors for two millennia, but Walvis Bay itself dates only to the late eighteenth century, when it was founded as a stopover for Dutch East India Company ships traveling between the Netherlands and Cape Town. Since then, Walvis Bay has been a safe harbor, sheltered from the South Atlantic by a natural sandbar. Today it is the only deepwater port in Namibia and the country's second-largest city.

For most of the past 150 years, Walvis Bay has also been an off-shore enclave. During the so-called Scramble for Africa in the 1880s, the settlement fell under British control, while the land surrounding it for hundreds of miles in every direction became the German colony of Southwest Africa. In 1884, the enclaved city became administratively part of South Africa. Even after Namibia gained full independence from apartheid South Africa in 1990, Walvis Bay remained South African. The South African government was loath to give up the strategic advantage of controlling Namibia's only deepwater port.

Walvis Bay, dominated by its harbor, as seen from above in 2017. The Namib desert stretches out in the distance.

For some time, the city was represented in South Africa's parliament as part of a district in Cape Town, some eight hundred miles away. Only in 1994 did it formally join the rest of Namibia, and even then the city was only gradually decolonized and integrated into the rest of the country. For years, its harbor facilities continued to be controlled by Portnet, the South African state-owned port operator.[2] And the port is what defines Walvis Bay. The city is a gateway: an intermediary space between ocean and desert, between Namibia and the outside world.

The *Venture* arrived in Walvis Bay in early 2018. But though Walvis Bay provided a natural harbor for the vessel in early 2018, it was hardly a *safe* harbor. Since 2016, the *Venture* had been owned by Halani Shipping Private Ltd., an Indian company based in Mumbai that, like Sea Trucks, specialized in providing offshore service for oil and gas companies. As global energy prices fell in the mid-2010s, Halani struggled to find customers, just as Sea Trucks did. In early 2018, the *Venture* and three other ships owned by the firm—another accommodation barge, a tug, and the DP3 vessel called the *Halani 1*—were lying unused, at anchor about a mile or two offshore Walvis Bay.[3]

Halani Shipping was in trouble. Finances were so tight that the firm had begun withholding the wages it owed to the officers and crew of its four vessels in Namibia.[4] With no money coming in, by mid-

March 2018 crew members "were only eating dal with plain rice, without onions [or] tomatoes." Amarjit Singh Bajwa, the captain of the largest ship, *Halani 1*, alleged to the UK-based NGO Human Rights at Sea, "The intention of the owner was to starve and demoralize us, so we would return home without our salaries."[5]

In short, Halani Shipping had "abandoned" the crews of the four ships it owned. Abandonment, in the official International Maritime Organization (IMO) definition, "occurs when the shipowner fails to fulfil certain fundamental obligations to the seafarer relating to timely repatriation and payment of outstanding remuneration and to provision of the basic necessities of life."[6] Unfortunately, this practice is not rare and has intensified in frequency after the recent oil crisis during the COVID pandemic. According to Mission to Seafarers, a nonprofit headquartered in the United Kingdom, abandonment is "a surprisingly common event."[7] The *Halani 1* was one of thirty-four cases of abandonment reported to the International Labour Organization (ILO), one of the UN organizations that handles such matters, in 2018. That number has since skyrocketed. In 2023, the ILO recorded 132 abandoned vessels.[8]

Abandonment is a symptom of the loose regulatory order that pertains to international shipping and the offshore world in general.[9] Part of the attraction of open registries and flags of convenience is that they allow shipowners to sidestep legal protections for seafarers imposed by wealthy countries in the Global North. The only substantive bar that Halani had to clear in order to register the *Venture* and its other ships in St. Vincent and the Grenadines was to secure an insurance policy for its ships. And although insurance helped mitigate risk, it also created moral hazard. If Halani defaulted on its debts, it would ultimately be the insurance company that would have to pay seafarers' wages; Halani itself would face few short-term financial or legal consequences from abandoning the seafarers in its employ. In this way, the phenomenon of abandonment speaks to the unequal distribution of risks in the offshore world. When things go wrong, shipowners, often leveraged and protected by shell companies, have little to lose from simply walking away from their vessels. For abandoned crews, however, the losses are profound. Owners understand this dynamic. As Human Rights at Sea founder David Hammond has put it, "Every ship owner should have a separate fund to look after the crew, in case of financial difficulties. But unscrupulous owners know the limitations of the law and put profit before people."[10]

· · ·

After months of waiting in Walvis Bay's harbor alongside the *Venture*, the crew of the *Halani 1* contacted the International Transport Workers' Federation (ITWF), the global union federation representing seafarers, which had long campaigned against flags of convenience. But, in the words of Captain Bajwa, after trying "hard to get the owner to pay our wages and repatriate us . . . they also gave up." The ITWF contacted officials who managed the registry of St. Vincent and the Grenadines (SVG), the country in which the four abandoned ships were registered, but allegedly did not receive a response.[11]

Two months later, in May, members of the crew filed suit against Halani Shipping's owner. The goal was simple: to secure back payment and repatriation to India. But even as their case was presented in central Walvis Bay, it was unclear what Namibian courts would be able to do. One of the few things Namibian authorities *could* do was "arrest," or seize, the vessels abandoned in Walvis Bay. Having done so, Namibian officials at last began supplying the crew with provisions to supplement the rice and dal. Around the same time, the IMO intervened by pressing the government of St. Vincent and the Grenadines to dispatch an inspector to the abandoned vessels.[12] It seemed, finally, as though the international system was swinging into gear.

The inspector arrived in Walvis Bay on June 8 in the midst of the sub-Saharan winter. By that time, Halani Shipping had finally pledged to issue back pay to crew members and repatriate them to India. But as June slipped into July, these promises proved illusory. Finally, Halani announced that the ships' protection and indemnity (P&I) insurer, Navigators—a subsidiary of the Hartford, the American insurance behemoth—would provide four months of back wages and the costs of repatriation.[13] This sounded like a great win, but payment of four months' wages was the legal minimum required of insurers by an amendment to the Maritime Labor Convention that had recently come into force in 2017, to which St. Vincent and the Grenadines was a signatory.[14] And, in fact, most of the crew was owed far more than four months' wages; they had already been owed back wages when they were abandoned in Walvis Bay four months earlier. Still, to the administrators of St. Vincent and the Grenadines's registry, once Navigators agreed to cover the four months of back pay, it seemed as though the situation had reached a neat conclusion. This was, after all, what marine insurance was for. If the owner of a ship ran out of funds to pay the crew, the insurer had to pick up the tab. As a Geneva-based "technical manager" for the Vincentian registry wrote, "This Administration believes that the matter is clear now."[15]

The rusting *Venture* seen next to the *Halani I*, abandoned in Walvis Bay. The vessels were slowly becoming ghost ships.

To some degree, the matter *was* clear. Several crew members, including those who had manned the *Venture*, flew home to India. But a core group of eight seafarers was caught. Namibian port authorities prohibited them from leaving the vessels unattended in the harbor, and no one had arranged for replacements. As Bajwa put it, the ships' owner "kept giving me excuses as to why our repatriation was delayed, until the end of December when he went incommunicado."[16]

As 2018 ended, the eight crew members from the *Halani 1* overseeing the four vessels still floating in Walvis Bay had been stuck off Namibia without pay for over nine months, caught in an interstitial limbo between strict local regulations and the limits of international maritime law. They had been foresaken in a world of little oversight and even less responsibility. Both on paper and in reality, the four abandoned vessels were fast becoming ghost ships: eerie, creaking places without documentation, insurance, or legal protections. As the crew member Chandra Rakesh Singh Negi put it, "We have no safety on board and because of all this I am always under mental tension that in case if anything happens to me on board then who will be responsible. I come from a poor family, where along with my job I have to look after my family also." The cook, Santosh Singh Negi, noted that his passport would soon be expiring. "My mental state is not alright. I feel very stressed all the time." Another crew member pointed out, "There are no medicines on board. So I am very scared on board that I should fall sick."[17] Even then, in the midst of emotional crisis, the crew was polite and generous. John Guard, a ships' surveyor and chair of the local Walvis Bay chapter of Mission to Seafarers, recalls the crew being very welcoming, and that it was "quite a pleasure to go on board."[18]

By January 2019, according to the International Chamber of Shipping, the eight remaining seafarers were "facing extreme fatigue, stress, lack of wages and mental health issues." Spurred in part by the publicity that was generated by Human Rights at Sea, the International Chamber of Shipping and the IMO pressed "the Flag State [St. Vincent and the Grenadines] to resolve this case of abandonment urgently."[19] For their part, administrators at the Vincentian registry in Geneva were "astonished to learn that there [were] still eight seafarers on board the vessel." After the insurers promised to make repatriation arrangements back in October, officials at the Vincentian registry thought the case was closed.

But it was not closed, and now it was a real jurisdictional headache. Halani Shipping had declined to renew its insurance policies for the *Halani 1* and, presumably, also for the *Venture*. To register a ship—even in an open registry like the one maintained by St. Vincent and the Grenadines—the ship had to have an active insurance policy. When insurance lapsed, so too did registration. Even flags of convenience had limits to their permissiveness.

Without insurance, late in 2018, the *Halani 1* and the *Venture* were stricken from the St. Vincent and the Grenadines registry. If either ship had still been registered there, it would have legally fallen to the Vincentian state to arrange and fund the repatriation of the abandoned seafarers under the 2006 Maritime Labour Convention.[20] But as it was, with the vessels' lapsed registration, the seafarers were no longer the problem of the government of Saint Vincent and the Grenadines. With no legal responsibility to the crew, officials at the Vincentian registry simply pledged to "contact that relevant authorities in Namibia requesting Port State assistance for the repatriation of the crew."[21] The crew members had been doubly abandoned: first by their employer, and then by the country whose flag their ships had flown. That was the drawback to flags of convenience: there was, really, no meaningful connection between ship or sailor and nation, no "genuine link."

The action then shifted back to Namibia, where port officials were still preventing seafarers from returning to India if it meant leaving the four ships floating unattended in Walvis Bay. The simple solution would be to find a replacement crew, but the Namibian authorities—particularly at the Ministry of Works, long plagued by allegations of corruption—dragged their feet.[22] Fortunately for the seafarers, under international treaties, Namibia did have certain obligations to the abandoned crew. In late March, a senior legal officer at the IMO, Jan de Boer, addressed a letter to the permanent secretary of the Namibian Works Ministry, Willem Goeiemann, highlighting the enumerated responsibilities that Namibia bore under the 2006 Maritime Labour Convention:

7. Each Member shall facilitate the repatriation of seafarers serving on ships which call at its ports or pass through its territorial or internal waters, as well as their replacement on board.
8. In particular, a Member shall not refuse the right of repatriation to any seafarer because of the financial circumstances of a shipowner or because of the shipowner's inability or unwillingness to replace the seafarer.[23]

De Boer noted that, together, the two clauses made "it quite clear that the port authorities of Namibia cannot deny repatriation to the crew in the current circumstances." The ship was already arrested by the Namibian High Court; the costs of repatriation "could be settled by the eventual sale of the vessel."[24]

A representative from the seafarers' union ITWF, still in contact with Bajwa, was more dramatic in his own letter to Goeiemann:

> Please take the time to put yourself in the shoes of the crew. They do not want to be there. They are working on the vessel against their will . . . These seafarers are being abused and exploited. It is within the power of those reading this email to end that. I ask them to do so immediately.[25]

Yet for all their fervor, the letters were more requests than demands. International organizations that ostensibly regulated the world's shipping were dependent on the cooperation of local authorities for the enforcement or enactment of any policies. Again, physical sovereignty mattered. For months on end, Namibian and Vincentian authorities had disregarded or given cursory attention to IMO directives. And when officials at the St. Vincent and the Grenadines registry removed the vessels from their books after Halani's insurance policies lapsed, Vincentian responsibility for the well-being of the crew effectively evaporated. Though under international law the Namibian government was prohibited from blocking repatriation, it was by no means clear where the buck would stop, or whether it would stop at all.

· · ·

Such jurisdictional ambiguity is built into the architecture of the twenty-first-century maritime world. The proliferation of flags of convenience and open registries has largely been driven by the desire of shipowners to avoid responsibility: responsibility to pay taxes, to maintain costly maintenance standards, to ensure the well-being of officers and crew members. Shipowners and administrators of cooperative open registries have sought out the interstitial spaces of international legal regimes, the gray zones outside of established enforcement. Life for seafarers in these zones can be precarious. Crew members have always traveled through contested and marginal spaces, but today, they are particularly at risk of falling through jurisdictional cracks. This is what happened to the Indian crew of the *Halani I.*

Finally, in April 2019, six of the eight seafarers flew home to India, replaced by a local crew that Mission to Seafarers' John Guard helped assemble.[26] The remaining two, Bajwa and one other, stayed with the vessels—including the *Venture*—until May.[27] At that point, the local crew members took charge of the four ships still lashed together in Walvis Bay. The new staff would also be subjected to long delays in receiving payment.[28]

Halani's financial troubles continued, and it was not until the next year that the *Halani 1* and the tug, the *Ima Atisi*, were finally auctioned off by the Namibian state to cover staffing costs. As the world descended into pandemic lockdowns, the *Halani 1* left Namibia on a weeks-long journey to its final destination. In late 2020, it finally arrived in Alang on India's west coast, the site of the world's largest and most notorious shipbreaking center, as well as the world's largest ship graveyard.[29] There, it was slowly broken up into scrap, piece by piece. Laborers, working at barely subsistence wages, removed fixtures and cabinets, doors and lightbulbs, before rending apart the steel hull

Ships aground at Alang in Gujarat from a satellite, April 2017

of the ship for their employers to recycle and sell. Shipbreaking is
a tremendously hazardous and environmentally catastrophic process
that releases oil, mercury, and asbestos into the local landscape. It is
undertaken by migrants who "risk gas explosions, falling from heights,
being crushed by massive steel plates" for well less than ten dollars
per day. The conditions under which the world's shipping is disassembled and its scrap salvaged are horrific, carried out by precarious
populations at the margins of a tremendously profitable and important international system. According to a 2019 survey, more than half
of shipbreaking workers have been injured on the job.[30] Considering
that workers skew young—some barely more than children—the statistic is particularly alarming.

Meanwhile, the two accommodation barges—the *Venture* and the
DSH 1—remained in Walvis Bay, still owned by Halani Shipping
Ltd., lashed together under the supervision of a locally hired Namibian crew living on the *DSH 1*. Finding a buyer for the rusting and
unregistered vessels proved difficult. According to the ship surveyor
John Guard, "buyers came and buyers left."[31] Finally, in April, another
Indian company bought the two barges for scrap and brought in its
own crew. The new staff began a thorough cleaning of the vessels, as
they waited for a heavy-lift ship to arrive and transport them to India
for scrapping. Conditions on board the *Venture* had worsened considerably since the ship had arrived in Walvis Bay. Its facilities had not
been luxurious at the best of times, and after months of abandonment
they had degenerated considerably. In mid-2021, crew members were
using a portable generator for electricity and a strobe light to signal
other ships: in the understated words of John Guard, it was "not much
in the way of amenities."[32] The Vessel's sister ship was slowly disappearing into the abstract financial asset it had always been.

The *Venture* continued to float in limbo off Walvis Bay for several
months, awaiting its final voyage to a salvage yard in Gujarat, where it
would lose its physical form altogether.[33] At some point in 2021, the
Venture's new owners, operating out of Dubai, renamed the ship *High
Ocean IV* and reregistered it in St. Kitts and Nevis, another Caribbean
former British colony with an open registry that is often used by companies intending to scrap ships.[34]

Late that year, the *High Ocean IV* was lifted onto the deck of a
heavy-lift ship, as it had been so many times before. After it was

secured on board, the ship slowly moved south out of Namibian waters, then west around the Cape of Good Hope, up the east coast of South Africa, past Madagascar to the small island nation of Mauritius. According to ship-tracking websites, in January 2022, it left Port Louis, the Mauritian capital, on a monthlong journey northeast across the vastness of the Indian Ocean. In mid-February, it arrived at Alang on the Gujarati coast: the end of its 3,500-mile journey. The last information registered on the tracking websites was received on Valentine's Day, 2022. The ship is registered as "stopped." Its location is on land, its prow pointing inland.[35] Over the following weeks and months, the Vessel's sister ship was ripped apart, piece by piece. Gradually, it became a beached skeleton, incapable of holding anything at all.

· · ·

Perhaps a similar end awaits the Vessel itself. A 2019 advertisement produced by West African Ventures featuring the *Jascon 27* noted that the ship is "suitable to accommodate staff and workers for offshore / construction projects." It said the *Jascon 27* boasts a galley, a mess room, four game rooms, four recreation rooms, and a gymnasium. In the ad, there were few traces of the Vessel's former lives. The deck on top of the ship, where men played basketball overlooking the East River in New York, was still there, but the insides had been extensively renovated. The ship was advertised to accommodate 304 persons— far fewer than it held in Stanley, New York, or Portland. In a picture that later appeared on WAV's website, the Vessel was clearly visible. Located at the company's supply base in the Onne Oil and Gas Free Zone, the barge looked ready to accommodate.[36]

At the moment, however, the Vessel is out of action, and has been for some years. In 2016, it was "laid up," temporarily rendered idle in Onne, across the river from the free zone, without any maintenance program. Its cabins and communal spaces were stripped, and all but one of its doors welded shut. Two local men were hired to look after it, but conditions on board were so bad that they slept outside, under a tarpaulin. The next year there was some interest in converting it to a prison in Brazil—"something like the Vernon C. Bain Correctional Center." The plan was for it to accommodate eight hundred prisoners,

far more than had been held there in either New York or Portland. But
by then, mold had taken over, covering nearly every surface. Reha-
bilitating the barge would simply cost too much. At some point, the
Vessel was towed to a new location, but it remained nearby, close to
Onne.[37]

The ship now known as the *Jascon 27* left service because of the
sharp downturn in world oil prices in the mid-2010s. Booms and
busts have played key roles in the Vessel's story. The *Safe Esperia* was
launched in 1983 when the offshore oil industry in the North Sea
was booming and the global market for shipping was busting. There
would be an elegant bookending to the story if the Vessel finally fell
victim to a major downtown in the international oil market.

Yet given its history, there is still reason to doubt that the Vessel has
entered its final act. Time and again, it and the other barge built at
Finnboda for the Balder Group in 1979 have shifted form and taken
on new roles and meanings. With minimal adjustment, it could be
transformed from barracks to jail, from "hotel" to adjunct oil rig. The
Vessel took on new names, new monikers, new social meanings almost
as easily as taking on new passengers. Perhaps there is yet another role
for the Vessel still to come.

INTERNATIONAL WATERS

Throughout their lives, the Vessel and its sister ship were meant to be temporary, mobile, adaptable, fluid. It was their ability to take on new roles and meanings—to code-switch—that made them so valuable. They could be filled with almost anything; they could take on a dizzying array of roles and meanings. The barges were parties to dramatic events and moments, but they were rarely the focus of attention. They were almost always in the background, out of focus—creatures lurking in the shadows of the global offshore. Physically, the barges remained largely unchanged after their major refurbishment by Consafe in the early 1980s. They were constants as the world swirled around them, morphing into new and unrecognizable forms.

The onshore locations with which the barges were associated, however, have been subject to the neoliberal transformation of the world economy in the late twentieth century. The dockyard at which the vessels were constructed on the outskirts of Stockholm, Finnboda Varv, closed in 1991. Its welding hall was converted into a rave dance club in the 1990s. The wharf is now part of an upscale residential complex, whose construction began in 2004.[1] Teslas are parked amid walls of glass and polished concrete. The dance club is now a gleaming supermarket. The old Finnboda engine workshop is a showroom for a designer furniture company that sells $7,000 sofas.[2] Though there are many plaques highlighting the area's industrial roots, the remnants of industry itself have been turned into sleek design elements. On the other side of Sweden, in Gothenburg, the shipyard at which Consafe transformed the two ships from mere barges to "coastels" has undergone a similar redevelopment. Around Sannegårdshamnen, the harbor that once housed Von Tell Nico's working yard, are new luxury buildings and a sea walk. Where cranes once lifted modified shipping containers onto the barges' decks, now there are sailboats and speed-boats moored at private docks.

Finnboda welding hall in the Nacka neighborhood of Stockholm, now an upscale grocery store, with a wide selection of organic goods. It is surrounded by new apartment buildings.

The North Sea itself has been the site of a major transition in the world's energy market, with oil and gas production falling steadily over the past few years, replaced by American shale gas and renewable energy. And while Norway has grown the profits from its oil revenues into the world's largest sovereign wealth fund, worth some $1.2 trillion (holding 1.4 percent of all the world's listed companies), the end of Britain's oil-based prosperity is well in sight, if not already arrived.[3] After Margaret Thatcher's program of privatization, Britain did not save its oil wealth like Norway did. In recent years, layoffs have wracked the British oil and gas sector, as big multinationals replace British workers with foreign ones who are paid less. These transformations also reflect increasing anxiety about climate change. In late 2020, Denmark—the European Union's largest oil producer—brought an end to new oil and gas exploration in its sector of the North Sea, for just this reason.[4] Today, windfarms, rather than oil rigs, are rising from the waves.

On the other side of the world, the Falkland Islands' economy also has changed, though in a less encouraging direction. It still relies on

Finnboda Varv, now a gleaming new housing development, in 2019. The engine workshop is the long building between the two piers in the center of the picture. The welding hall turned grocery store is at the top of the hill from the shorter of the two piers.

fishing and agriculture, but tourism—particularly ecotourism—has become increasingly important. By 2009, it was receiving nearly seventy thousand visitors a year. But its recent prosperity also has stemmed from another, less forward-looking industry: oil was discovered off the coast of the islands in 2010.[5] As the North Sea moves toward renewables, the South Atlantic might be discovering hydrocarbons.

• • •

The VW works in Emden is still humming as an export-oriented factory, now for the ID.4 and ID.7 electric vehicles as well as for the Passat and the Arteon, another large gas-powered car.[6] The latest transformation in the way that cars are produced in Emden has been particularly dramatic. Renovating the facility so it could produce electric cars involved constructing huge new factory buildings, opened in 2022, and retraining thousands of workers, much like in the 1980s. And just as in the 1980s, the new changes provoked some grumbling, even as they enabled new growth. At the cost of around a billion euros, the Emden factory has become one of the marquee sites of VW's investment in a new generation of electric cars. The city is a striking setting for such an investment in a greener future: essentially at sea level, the VW plant there is surrounded by huge windmills that dominate the horizon. But nearby, a different story is unfolding. The Nordseewerke, the storied German shipyard near where the *Bibby Resolution* had been moored, became insolvent in the early 2010s. After restructuring, it began to specialize in manufacturing offshore oil equipment, an echo of the specialization of the shipbuilding industries in western Sweden and northern Britain decades ago.[7] Green energy might be on the rise, but the petro-economy is far from dead. There are still plenty of profits to be made from offshore oil and gas.

The author visited the VW plant and was shown around in this brand-new ID.4 electric car, fresh off the factory floor.

In 2019, Volkswagenwerk Emden again played host to a "hotel ship," which Volkswagen rented to accommodate about eighty visiting workers from Bratislava, Slovakia, employed by Škoda, the Czech carmaker that the VW Group bought shortly after the fall of the Berlin Wall. In Emden, the Škoda workers complained about the living conditions. A "hotel ship" was simply not a hotel, as they had been promised. When the plant hired more than a thousand temporary-contract workers some years later, as the new electric car lines began production, it chose to accommodate them on land.[8]

• • •

In New York, there are dramatic signs of change. The barge that replaced the Vessel and its sister ship, the *Vernon C. Bain*, has finally closed, the last prison ship in the United States. There are also plans to close Rikers Island itself, but those plans have been repeatedly delayed. The pandemic devastated New York's incarcerated population, COVID ripped through the city's jails, and the great resignation spawned a massive staffing shortfall. Every so often, there is talk of jail conditions getting so bad that the federal government will step in and assume management of the system. But Rikers remains open, and as of early 2024, the empty *Bain* continues to hulk off the South Bronx neighborhood of Hunts Point, at the end of a long service road flanked by barbed wire.

There, it is a neighbor to other elements in New York's hidden physical infrastructure: wholesale food markets, scrap shops, and a large Department of Sanitation facility. The roof of the jail offers a panorama onto the history of the city's relationship with offshoring. As is the case for so many offshore sites, the view is perversely beautiful: a waterfront window onto the onshore world.

Looking out directly across the East River is Rikers Island, which has housed city prisoners off the mainland since 1932. Turning right, a bit further to the east, sits North Brother Island, the site of a now-abandoned quarantine hospital, in which "Typhoid" Mary Mallon spent more than two decades in the early twentieth century. Further east, just along the coast of the Bronx, is a much newer addition to the offshore world: an incongruous beacon of crystal-clear blue water jutting out incongruously over the sludge of the East River. Just blocks from the *Vernon C. Bain* is a floating swimming pool installed in a retrofitted barge that has been operated by the Parks Department since 2008.[9] Behind each of the sites in this panorama soar the towers of Manhattan.

In Manhattan, the changes that pulled and pushed the *Bibby Resolution* and *Bibby Venture* around the harbor have continued at a dizzying pace. The Lower East Side has undergone a profound process of gentrification (before the pandemic, the average monthly cost of a one-bedroom rental in the neighborhood was over $4,500). So too has the West Village and the Brooklyn waterfront. Lower Manhattan is whiter and richer than it has been in living memory. After the Vessel relocated to Dorset, its former berth, Pier 36 on the East River, became the departure point for sightseeing cruises and potential mooring for mega yachts.[10] Now, it has been transformed into what's been called "NYC's premier event space," used for immersive art shows, sporting events, and concerts. In 2022, it hosted a major cryptocurrency conference.[11] Pier 40, where the *Bibby Resolution* was moored, is now a large recreational complex, run by the Hudson River Park Trust. The complex is a mix of new and old New York. It boasts a marine biology field station, a trapeze school, and a sprawling Astroturf sports field in its middle. But throughout, paint is peeling, sidings rusting. Much of the pier, once the gleaming pride of the neighborhood, has been converted to a parking garage.[12] Pier 1, in Brooklyn Heights, where the *Bibby Venture* was docked for a brief moment in 1988, is now part of Brooklyn Bridge Park, a development undertaken by Michael Bloomberg's mayoral administration to improve the quality of life in Brooklyn. Like Pier 40, the park is not run by the city but by a non-profit corporation.

• • •

The economic forces that facilitated the rise of the service sector also swept over England. In Liverpool, in 2019, the Bibby Line moved out of its historic offices near the waterfront to occupy a new, larger space in the commercial heart of the city.[13] By then, the Bibby Line was just a small part of the larger Bibby Line Group, a major conglomerate with vast real estate, financial services, and corporate holdings, including the UK discount supermarket chain Costcutter.[14] Derek Bibby's move toward diversification has completely transformed the company; it is now a far cry from an old imperial shipper.

In London, the Commercial Court no longer sits in the storied Royal Courts of Justice on the Strand, but rather a couple blocks away in a purpose-built building opened in 2011. With a facade made from blue glass and limestone quarried in Portland, the £300 million Rolls Building was built as part of a conscious effort by David Cameron's Conservative–Liberal Democrat government to attract high-profile business disputes from around the world. It would, according to then

Justice Secretary Kenneth Clarke, offer "the world's most modern and hi-tech courts complex built specifically to resolve financial, business and property disputes."[15] The Rolls Building was meant to entrench London's status as a global legal capital as well as a financial one.

Like New York and the Falklands, Dorset experienced a move toward tourism and recreation. New luxury vacation homes have sprung up on the site of the former naval base. Parts of Portland harbor have been redeveloped as a recreational boating center. It hosted sailing events for the London 2012 Olympics. But the small island of Portland is still the site of two British prisons, and the area continues to struggle economically. And the shadow of HMP *The Weare* continues to loom large. In April 2023, the British government announced plans to temporarily house asylum seekers on a five-hundred-bed accommodation barge in Portland's harbor, much to the consternation of many local residents.[16] The new barge bore a striking similarity to HMP *The Weare*. To "reduce the burden on local public services," the government announced, the ship would house only "single adult males." The Conservative government, alive to fears of crime, stressed that "all sites will have 24/7 security" and would be provided with a "security specialist."[17] They turned to none other than the Bibby Line to provide the barge, the *Bibby Stockholm*.

As in the past, the government stressed the costs of accommodating migrants on land—some £6 million per day—the temporary nature of the barge, and the employment it will bring to the area. As in the past, locals were resistant. Some were appalled at housing refugees like prisoners. Others were much more reluctant to see outsiders come to Portland; one of the major Facebook groups used to organize protests around the barge was littered with white nationalist rhetoric.[18] On the streets of Portland in July 2023, "fact sheets" and fliers exhorting protest were tacked up on bus shelters and disused phone booths.

The fact sheets highlighted a "secretive and lucrative" deal between the head of Portland Port and the Home Office, as well as the fact that migrants would be able to "come and go . . . on taxpayer funded buses" that would drop them off in the center of town. The presence of migrants was objectionable, especially given the costs of accommodating them. The barge would be expensive, and housing migrants would be a major drain on local services, especially the NHS and the police.[19] Just days after the barge opened in August 2023, it had to be

THE PEOPLE OF DORSET SAY

NO **TO THE BARGE**

SHAREABLE FACT SHEET *Campaign Group*

- **FACT (1)** - Portland Port Ltd and its CEO Bill Reeves made a secretive and lucrative deal with the Home Office (HO) - estimated to cost the taxpayer two million pounds plus per year - to house 500+ single men aged 18 to 65 from various countries on the Bibby Stockholm barge to be berthed in Portland, Dorset.
  Source: gov.uk/government/publications/asylum-accommodation-factsheets/factsheet-asylum-accommodation-on-a-vessel-in-portland-port-accessible

- **FACT (2)** - The Times reported the barge would cost £15,000 a day to charter, while berthing it in Portland would be £4,500+ a day. More would be required for services, including but not limited to waste, catering, transport, security and medical staff. How is this cost effective, as Mr Sunak claims, over the hotels?
  Source: thetimes.co.uk/article/home-office-faces-legal-action-over-20-000-a-day-migrant-barge-kzs920vq3

- **FACT (3)** - This doesn't include £1.6 billion divulged by The Independent that was quietly given to an Australian firm, Corporate Travel Management (CTM), criticised for their mismanagement of Covid quarantine hotels. This lucrative two-year contract was awarded directly to CTM without competition.
  Source: independent.co.uk/news/uk/home-news/barge-australia-asylum-contract-travel-b2354578.html

- **FACT (4)** - Dr Paul Johnson, NHS Dorset Chief Medical Officer, spoke at the only public meeting in Portland (06/06) to hear residents' concerns and alluded to a "minor illness type service" which will be onboard the barge for the 500+. The same authority closed the Minor Injury Unit in Portland that served 13,562 existing residents in January 2022.
  Source: facebook.com/772839031/videos/18487701855166391/

- **FACT (5)** - Weymouth Councillor David Harris shared that the 500+ barge residents will have free access to NHS Dorset without agreed additional funding, thereby, stretching an already underfunded service. Portland Port, however, is estimated to receive over two million pounds from the Home Office without contributing to local services.
  Source: dorsetecho.co.uk/news/23608543.councillor-letter-home-secretary-barge/

- **FACT (6)** - The Independent revealed the HO could be forced to pay police millions to cover security operations for future barges and military bases housing asylum seekers. Our own Dorset Police and Crime Commissioner, David Sidwick, is still waiting on extra resources and stated this will create extra demand for the force in its busiest period.
  Source: independent.co.uk/news/uk/home-news/asylum-barges-military-bases-cost-police-b2358970.html

- **FACT (7)** - Within the original HO Fact Sheet (05/04), a safety and welfare check call was to be made at 11PM for the asylum seekers, which was removed and it was made clear that they would be non-detained. Free to come and go on foot 24/7, and/or on taxpayer-funded buses from the port to drop off points in Portland and Weymouth.
  Source: web.archive.org/web/20230405001064t/https://www.gov.uk/government/publications/asylum-accommodation-factsheets/factsheet-asylum-accommodation-on-a-vessel-in-portland-port-accessible

- **FACT (8)** - Only CEO Bill Reeves of Portland Port Ltd, and the Langham family, said yes to a barge. Liverpool, Essex, and London, a city of 9 million plus, said NO TO THE BARGE due to infrastructure, consent, and inhumanity of the plan. How can a small seaside community of 13,562, already struggling with local services, be forced to support?
  Source: lbc.co.uk/news/sadiq-khan-asylum-seeker-barge-londons-royal-docks/

A poster protesting the arrival of the *Bibby Stockholm* on a bus shelter in Portland

evacuated because *Legionella* bacteria was found in its water supply. The thirty-nine asylum seekers on board were transferred to a local hotel on terra firma.[20] Just weeks later, they were back on board. But the *Bibby Stockholm* proved even more temporary than its predecessor. In July 2024, shortly after surging into power in a landslide election, Keir Starmer's Labour government announced the *Stockholm* would close.

• • •

The settings in which the Vessel existed were important, but the barge at the center of this story has always—at least partially—been between or outside formal jurisdictions. Local ordinances and zoning restrictions did not apply to it; safety standards that would have been enforced on more traditional facilities in Stanley, New York, or Portland went unheeded. In Nigeria, the dispute over the ownership of the Vessel ultimately came down to the degree to which Nigerian authorities would honor court orders issued in the British Virgin Islands or arbitration decisions made in London. It has been a creature of the offshore world itself—a fantasy world, as the anthropologist Hannah Appel has put it, "of capitalist desire."[21] Yet at the same time, the Vessel has been embedded in hyper-specific contexts. Throughout its existence, it has been a liminal object, caught between local and global systems, local and global power structures. It has belonged, in short, to the global offshore.

"Offshore" is a relational category. To some degree, its meaning is derived negatively, in opposition to the solid, dry "onshore." If the onshore world is established, safe, reputable, and secure—a place of strong states enforcing law and order—then the offshore world is risky, dangerous, lawless, and wild, a place where power is much more diffuse. There is an implicit hierarchy in the relationship between on- and offshore. When people refer to jobs or capital moving "offshore," they are using the word as an attribute to compare two different locations: one with more power and one with less.

But *the offshore* is also a very real place. It has its own norms and customs, its own languages, logics, and boundaries. It has its own history, rooted in European empire and the twentieth-century triumph of the nation-state.[22] It has institutions like arbitration tribunals and classification societies. It has a polyglot citizenry of expatriates and seafarers. And it has its own infrastructure, of which the Vessel has been a part. Understanding the offshore as a real, physical place is vital for understanding how the world works now and how it has worked over the past five decades. Not only has the offshore been tremendously important in facilitating globalization, it has also exerted an irresistible creeping influence on the onshore world. It has undermined labor

protections and completely revolutionized financial regulation. It has
knitted the world together through trade and money and energy. In
so doing, it has rendered the world more homogenous, modular, and
interchangeable. In short, the physical realities of the offshore world
have slowly eroded the very distinction between on- and offshore.

The Vessel and its sister vessel have been passive players in this
unfolding global drama. Although their design and very physicality
sometimes constrained action or resisted change, the ships themselves never had agency. In the foregoing pages, the two barges have
consistently been described in the passive, rather than active, voice.
They have been towed, lifted, refitted, repurposed. As vessels, they
have been filled. For this reason, their purpose and meaning changed
depending on what or who physically filled them. In some ways, too,
they were inanimate chameleons, fitting into local context and local
populations.

It is this passive receptiveness and mutability that is the barges'
defining characteristic. It is their emptiness—their ability to be
filled—that has made them vessels for the major social and economic
transformations of the late twentieth and early twenty-first centuries.
David Dinkins referred to them in disgust as a "Band-Aid solution."
But Band-Aids are useful and versatile devices. They cover all sorts of
scrapes, scratches, and gashes. They protect from frictions of all kinds.
And the world is full of frictions. Because every local context is different, every time people, goods, or ideas move between local contexts,
there are frictions of understanding, of travel, of use.

In fact, the vessels of this story have been valuable specifically
because such frictions exist. They were valuable, that is, because they
could function in a variety of local contexts and solve a variety of
highly specific problems in different places around the world. They
were adaptable Band-Aids, not bespoke, individualized treatments.
This is why the Vessel was especially valuable during crises. It almost
did not matter what the crisis was: oil shock or prison overcrowding,
war in the South Atlantic or fierce competition in the auto industry.
Seen over forty years, demand for the Vessel did not depend on one
market or one sector, but instead on the assumption that there would
always be some crisis somewhere in the world it could help address.

If there are always frictions between local contexts, then globalization might be understood as a gradual reduction of such frictions

around the world. Globalization makes speaking and bargaining, buying and selling, joking and mourning easier across distance and cultural divides. The Vessel has been a technology of globalization. It has moved between contexts around the world, used as a tool to circumvent or neutralize frictions. But more than that, it has been part of a vast system that has homogenized, standardized, and collapsed difference itself. The offshore world, accessible from Oslo, New York, Portland, Onne, and Nassau, has not just brought such disparate places closer together, it has made them fundamentally more alike, hollowing them out in the process.

In this way, the Vessel has also been an important player in installing and entrenching a new global order with a code and a logic of its own. Historians and commentators have a name for this complex of global economic and political entanglements: neoliberalism. Originally a way of describing a particular approach to economic theory, the term has come to encompass a wide array of forces or ideas. *Neoliberalism* is a term whose contemporary meaning is diffuse and opaque, a fact acknowledged even by its leading theorists and those who outline a relatively narrow definition of it. Popularly, it has come to be a catch-all umbrella category for a widespread array of forces or ideas that have disempowered or marginalized people to the benefit of a lucky few. Sometimes, it is used synonymously with twenty-first-century global capitalism, sometimes with the emergence of market-driven anomie or *homo economicus*.[23] It is a system with many faces—a hydra with many heads. Financialization, free trade, globalization, corporate sovereignty, economic inequality, gentrification, mass incarceration, conspicuous consumption, environmental degradation. It is easy to argue—even prove—that these abstract nouns are all related. But how exactly, and with what significance? After all, if one looks long enough or hard enough, it becomes clear that *everything* is related to everything else.

One common denominator of the "-isms" and "-ations" that fall under the popular category of neoliberalism is that they are all objects of condemnation. In particular, the thread linking them is the fact that they have been deemed disempowering, engines of inequality and domination. Perhaps the common denominator, then, is their negative effects on people. But even those negative effects take a multitude of different forms. The effects depend on which "isms" are at play, as well as on local contexts and the people themselves. All this is to say that the boundaries of neoliberalism are hard to positively define. As it is used, the term itself frequently gestures, however suggestively, to an incoherent category.[24]

But even if neoliberalism obscures as much as it clarifies, the trends and forces with which it is associated *are* themselves related, even interrelated. So too are the people they affect. The Vessel helps reveal the ties, not in theory, but in historical reality.[25] Its story is a material microhistory of an object that was involved in a set of overlapping macro transformations. The barge is a physical guide. It—like all of us—has been swept up in and by the swirling economic and political forces of the past half century. Its story is a red thread, connecting a host of abstract processes with physical places and real people around the world. The red thread history of the barge has been spun from the many fibers of the history of neoliberalism.

Throughout its existence, the Vessel has facilitated vital activity at the margins of social orders, industries, and jurisdictions. Workers, soldiers, prisoners—people rarely visible to the public eye—have stayed on and passed through the Vessel, enabling the state to run and the private economy to hum. At the same time, money and meaning have also filled the barge. Even when it lies empty, it continues to be a container for the economic forces and social systems that are shaping our world.

Those forces and systems are abstract and dynamic. Capitalism. Globalism. International law. Imperial decline. National sovereignty. Inflation. Sectoral stagnation. Gentrification. Mass incarceration. Booms. Busts. Racism. Greed. Like the winds or tides, their boundaries are shifting and penumbral, their power functionally ineffable. Acting sometimes individually, sometimes in concert, sometimes at cross-purposes, they determined the path and contents of the Vessel. The Vessel's course and manifest were haphazardly and contingently determined. The Vessel had no motor, no keel, no rudder. It was at the mercy of dynamics well beyond its control, much like Arthur Rimbaud's "drunken boat" featured in this book's epigraph.

The path of the Vessel could well be described as drunken. It crisscrossed the Atlantic, taking on a variety of odd jobs. It was constantly changing owners, flags, names, and cargoes. The people who stayed on the Vessel were diverse. From a bird's-eye view, it is easy to see how different they were: Nigerian oil workers, American prisoners, British soldiers.

From a barge's-eye view, the story is much bleaker. Imagine the Vessel's story if it were told using a frame of reference that focused solely on the barge itself. It would feature a ship at rest with the world spinning madly around it, with people rushing into the Vessel and out of it again. From this view, the Vessel itself is not fungible and modular; rather, the people who boarded it were. The Vessel looks even more like Rimbaud's drunken boat, caring "nothing for all my crews / carrying Flemish wheat or English cottons." The people the Vessel contained would simply be cargo, replaceable and movable, arranged in ordered units. They would be driven on board because of the same systems and forces that drove the barge around the world, whether capitalism, globalism, law, politics, or prejudice.

One of the conceits of this book is that its central character is uncharismatic: a dumb pontoon without voice, personality, or drive. This character—so unlike a living, breathing person—was defined by its status as an empty vessel. But the Vessel is also a metaphor for other vessels of meaning—people themselves. Its story suggests that the forces that have pushed this particular vessel around the world, that have filled it with meaning and value, are at work upon all of us.

ACKNOWLEDGMENTS

Like all histories, *Empty Vessel* is a product of many hands and many heads. I have been immensely fortunate in all the generous help in transforming just a glimmer of an idea into the book you are now reading. My agent, Katherine Flynn of Calligraph, has been the most steadfast and masterful advocate for this unconventional project. At every turn, Todd Portnowitz at Knopf offered incredible support and brilliant edits. So too did Joe Zigmond at John Murray, who, like Todd, understood the full potential of this book before I did. Amy Stackhouse and Kevin Bourke provided discerning copyedits. Najya Gause was an invaluable research assistant. Thanks also to Sarah Khalil at Calligraph, Sandy Violette at Abner Stein, Ben Shields, and Margot Lee at Knopf, and Siam Hatzaw at John Murray for shepherding the book (and me) over innumerable hurdles.

Friends, colleagues, and family members played a huge role in shaping the manuscript. Emma Rothschild, Maya Jasanoff, Charlie Maier, and Diana Kim read various versions and provided bracing encouragement and support along with their characteristically crystalline insight. Shane Bobrycki uncovered the narrative arc of the barge's story in an early draft. A great number of others read portions of the manuscript or discussed the ideas behind them with me. These included Wesley Antell, Matt Aucoin, Aditya Balasubramanian, Ian Beattie, Aaron Bekemeyer, Jon Booth, John Brewer, Judith Brunton, Angus Burgin, Asa Bush, Sannoy Das, Elsa Génard, Victoria Gray, Michael and Patsy Kumekawa, Sabrina Gharib Lee, Dylan Matthews, Salmaan Mirza, Surabhi Ranganathan, Travers Rhodes, Mikaël Schinazi, David Todd, and David Yang. All the faults are my own.

I wrote *Empty Vessel* at Harvard and MIT. The support and resources of both institutions were vital to its completion. At MIT, teaching and thinking with Anne McCants was a source of great inspiration. Two of the maps were designed by the crack cartographers Jeff Blossom and Gigi Sung at the Center for Geographic Analysis, and the Harvard University Digital Scholarship Support Group provided important input. Especially important was the Center for History and Economics at Harvard, the ideal academic home for the past few years. Lively conversations with EHP Fellows, including Mallory Hope, Jacob Moscona, Michael O'Sullivan, and Tara Suri, have been deeply stimulating and generative; the assistance of Emily Gauthier and Jennifer Nickerson has been vital. Thanks also to the Centre for History and Economics in Cambridge and to Inga Huld Markan in particular.

This is a book about one thing, but it is also a book about many different things. In writing it, I have relied on the advice, expertise, and memories of others living around the world. The people I formally interviewed, by Zoom or in person, are cited in the text—I am incredibly grateful for their help and participation. But there were many others who helped behind the scenes. Special thanks to, among many other, Mikael Josephson for sharing recollections about Finnboda; Tobias Bernander Silseth, Bob Rust, and Stig Tenold for explaining Norwegian shipping; Ashley Smith for providing a guide to Portland history; Hugo Manson for discussing stories of offshore oil; Sven van Krugten and Cilla Ingvarsson for helping me grasp the history of Swedish shipbuilding; Freunde der Schifffahrt-Emden and Johann Alberts for helping me track the barge in Emden; Mike Ricketts for sharing stories and insights about the Vessel; Howard Stein for tips on understanding Onne; and Jade McClune, Gail Wearne, and Mission to Seafarers for explaining what happened to the *Venture* in Walvis Bay. A chance encounter with Keith Davies at the MRC was both delightful and incredibly useful for grasping the decline of the British merchant navy. John Boston, Sandra Susan Smith, the Legal Aid Society of New York, and Tom McCarthy helped me connect with people in New York. Rachel Billington and *Inside Times* were instrumental in connecting me with people with experiences of HMP *The Weare*. Linda Halwaß was the most exceptional host at VW-Emden. Thanks to her and so many others at Volkswagen for showing me around and sharing the plant's history with me. I have been astounded, over and over again, at how generous people have been with their time, their stories, and their expertise.

Archives and libraries, both virtual and physical, stand at the heart of this project, and I'm immensely grateful for the help I received from archivists and staff members. Thanks to the British Library Sound Collection, the Columbia University Oral History Project, the Föreningen Centrum för Näringslivhistoria, the Harvard University Libraries, the Nacka Local Historical Archive, the National Archives of the United Kingdom, the National Library of Norway, the National Museums Liverpool, the *Nordwest Zeitung*, the Regionarkivet Västra Götalandregionen, the Riksarkivet–Göteborg, the Sjöfartsverket, the Stadtarchiv Emden, the *Stavanger Aftenblad*, VW Aktiengesellschaft, and the University of Warwick Modern Records Centre.

Empty Vessel was researched (largely) during a pandemic. At times when travel was impossible, I depended on the help of archivists and researchers to scan and collect documents unavailable to me. I want to thank especially Charlotte Murray at the National Museums Liverpool, Anna Bayard at the Sjöfartsverket, Helena Elisabeth Mattison at the Regionarkivet Västra Götalandregionen, Magnus Hansson at the Riksarkivet–Göteborg, and Ulrike Gutzmann and VW for going above and beyond. Thanks also to John Winrow for scanning additional documents in Liverpool and to Isobel Akerman for chasing down materials in London. Thanks also to Per Askergren, Rob Barnard, John Gale, and my dear friend Christian Hampel for use of their photographs.

I'd also like to thank the students of History 16B, a seminar I taught in 2024 at Harvard. Their insights, intuitions, and critical examinations of and about the offshore world helped me immensely in clarifying my thinking about the subject. Last but very much not least, thank you to the people who kept me grounded and supported and smiling through this adventure: particularly my folks in Vancouver, the "Quaranteam" in Milton, Woody Fan Club, the fortnightly TTR group, and of course, Sabrina.

NOTES

ARCHIVAL SOURCES AND ABBREVIATIONS

BL: British Library, London, United Kingdom
BOCM: New York City Board of Correction Minutes, New York, NY
CfN: Centrum för Naringslivhistoria, Stockholm, Sweden
LiG: Landarkivets i Göteborg (LiG), Gothenburg, Sweden
MAL: Archives Centre at the Maritime Museum, Liverpool, United Kingdom
MRCL: Modern Records Centre, University of Warwick, Coventry, United Kingdom
Norwegian National Archives, Oslo, Norway
OHA: Oral History Archives, Columbia University, New York, NY
RVG: Regionarkivet Västra Götalandsregionen och Göteborgs Stad, Gothenburg,
    Sweden
Sjöfartsverket—Swedish Maritime Administration, Norrkoping, Sweden
TNA: The National Archives, Kew, United Kingdom

INTRODUCTION

1. David Brown, "Falklands Deadline Draws Near for Swedes," *Financial Times*,
   November 2, 1982.
2. William Cronon, *Nature's Metropolis: Chicago and the Great West* (New York: W. W.
   Norton, 1991), part II; Jon Levy, *Freaks of Fortune: The Emerging World of Capitalism
   and Risk in America* (Cambridge: Harvard University Press, 2014), chapter 7.
3. See Quinn Slobodian, *Globalists: The End of Empire and the Birth of Neoliberalism*
   (Cambridge: Harvard University Press, 2018).
4. Karen Hao, "Training a Single AI Model Can Emit as Much Carbon as Five Cars in
   Their Lifetimes," *MIT Technology Review*, June 6, 2019.
5. It is an example of what James Vernon has called an "emplaced history," though one
   in which the place is itself transient. James Vernon, "Heathrow and the Making of
   Neoliberal Britain," *Past and Present* 252 (August 2021), 217.
6. In using this designation, this book follows the work of Mike Ricketts, who also
   focuses on the flexibility of the barge and its connection with modern capitalism. *The
   Vessel* is also the title of a short film about the barge by the Ricketts. Mike Ricketts,
   The Vessel (Film), 2013, available on YouTube. See also Mike Ricketts, "Encounters
   and Spatial Controversies," PhD thesis, University of the Arts, 2015.

7. Maya Jasanoff, *The Dawn Watch: Joseph Conrad in a Global World* (New York: Penguin, 2017).
8. Like other global microhistories, *Offshored* "follows" a thing. Romain Bertrand and Guillaume Calafat, "Global Microhistory: A Case to Follow," *Annales: Histoire, Sciences Sociales* (English ed.) 73, no. 1 (2018), 3–17. But rather than simply showing the "intersection of contexts," this book also attempts to develop a picture of a supernational, general offshore context. On global microhistory, see also John-Paul Ghobrial, ed., "Global History and Microhistory," *Past and Present* 14, supplement (2019), and Francesca Trivellato, "Is There a Future for Italian Microhistory in the Age of Global History?," *California Italian Studies* 2, no. 1 (2011).
9. Edoardo Grendi, "Micro-analisi e storia sociale," *Quaderni storici* 12, no. 35 (1977), 506–20. See also Francesca Trivellato, "Microstoria/Microhistoire/Microhistory," *French Politics, Culture & Society* 33, no. 1, special issue, "The Politics of Empire in Post-Revolutionary France" (Spring 2015), 122–34.

CHAPTER 1: THE BALTIC SEA

1. Parley Augustsson (Management) to Finnboda (G. Lind) (Telex), December 4, 1979, Contracts for 409, Finnboda Papers, Centrum för Naringslivhistoria, Stockholm, Sweden (hereafter CfN); Leif Kasteskog to Parley Augustsson, March 4, 1980, Contracts for 409, Finnboda Papers, CfN; Leif Kasteskog to Messrs Førsund, Knap, Rafen & Co., March 4, 1980, Contracts for 409, Finnboda Papers, CfN. See "Ny start for Parley Augustsson," *Dagens Naeringsliv*, March 23, 2004, www.dn.no.
2. Author's interview with Parley Augustsson, May 12, 2023.
3. Mike Ricketts, "Encounters and Spatial Controversies," PhD thesis, University of the Arts, 2015, 131; *Bibby Resolution* Registration, The National Archives, Kew, United Kingdom (hereafter TNA), BT 110/2075/32. The registration mistakenly identifies Finnboda Varv as being in Gothenburg, where Götaverken was based.
4. Leif Kasteskog to Parley Augustsson (Telex), December 5, 1979, Contracts for 409, Finnboda Papers, CfN.
5. "Employment by Economic Sector, Sweden," www.OurWorldInData.org.
6. Robert Rowthorn and Ramana Ramaswamy, *Deindustrialization: Its Causes and Implications* (Washington, DC: International Monetary Fund, 1997).
7. Marc Levinson, *The Box: How the Shipping Container Made the World Smaller and the World Economy Bigger* (Princeton: Princeton University Press, 2006), 14–15, 222.
8. The number of people employed in shipbuilding grew from 28,548 to 37,276. Rikard H. Eriksson, Martin Henning, and Anne Otto, "Industrial and Geographical Mobility of Workers During Industry Decline: The Swedish and German Shipbuilding Industries 1970–2000," *Geoforum* 75 (2016), 89.
9. On the use of oil as political tool, see Timothy Mitchell, *Carbon Democracy: Political Power in the Age of Oil* (London: Verso, 2011), chapter 7.
10. United Nations Conference on Trade and Development, *Handbook of International Trade and Development Statistics, 1981 Supplement* (New York: United Nations, 1982), 45.
11. Levinson, *The Box*, chapter 11.
12. The shipyard was Lindholmen. Carl Hamilton, "Public Subsidies to Industry: The

Case of Sweden and Its Shipbuilding Industry," Seminar Paper No. 174, Institute for International Economic Studies, Stockholm, Sweden, June 1981, 6.

13. "Offshore Orders Generating Confidence for Shipbuilders," *Financial Times*, March 24, 1982, 35.

14. "1981 Report on Swedish State-Owned Companies," October 8, 1981, 100, www .data.riksdagen.se; Mikael Josephson, *Finnboda varv och fartygen som byggdes där* (Stockholm: Trafik-Sostalgiska Förlaget, 2020), 89–90, 94.

15. Hamilton, "Public Subsidies to Industry." 4a.

16. Ibid., 8a.

17. In general, Swedish unemployment was very low, at less than 4 percent. See Anders Forslund, "Unemployment—Is Sweden Still Different?," *Swedish Economic Policy Review* 2 (1995), 15–58.

18. Lars Bruno and Stig Tenold, "The Basis for South Korea's Ascent in the Shipbuilding Industry, 1970–1990," *The Mariner's Mirror* 97, no. 3 (2011), 201-217; Gabriel Jonsson, *Shipbuilding in South Korea: A Comparative Study* (Stockholm: Institute of Oriental Languages, 1995). See also Peter Stokes, *Ship Finance: Credit Expansion and the Boom-Bust Cycle* (London: Lloyds of London Press, 1992), chapter 12.

19. Milton Friedman, "Nobel Lecture: Inflation and Unemployment," *Journal of Political Economy* 85, no. 3 (June 1977), 470. On Friedman and politics, see Angus Burgin, *The Great Persuasion: Reinventing Free Markets Since the Depression* (Cambridge: Harvard University Press, 2015).

20. Fartygbevis (Ship Certificate) for *Finnboda 12*, December 17, 1980, Sjöfartsverket, Norrkoping, Sweden, Safe Esperia SJZH.

21. See Gunnar Hedin, *Svenska Varv—Världsledande* (Göteborg: Tre Böcker, 1995); "Svenska Varv: From Rescuing Companies to Promoting Markets," *The Motor Ship* 68, no. 802 (May 1987), 39; Josephson, *Finnboda varv*, 89–90.

22. Josephson, *Finnboda varv*, 107–14.

23. Ibid., 111. Translated from the original Swedish.

24. Ibid., 108, 115.

25. Certificates for NYB 408 and 409, Finnboda Papers, CfN. The only difference between the two vessels discernable in the records of the Finnboda Yard is that NYB 408 was fitted with a 5,270-kilogram anchor, while NYB 409 carried a 5,185-kilogram anchor manufactured by the same firm.

26. Josephson, *Finnboda varv*, 94–98.

27. Invoice from Öresundsvarvet, February 7, 1980, Contracts for 409, Finnboda Papers, CfN.

28. Certificates for NYB 408 and 409, Finnboda Papers, CfN.

29. Loose drawings related to Finnboda Numbers 408 and 409, Finnboda Papers, CfN.

30. Certificates for NYB 409, Finnboda Papers, CfN; Certificates for *Safe Esperia*, Sjöfartsverket, Sjöfartsinspektionen, Stockholms Distrikt, Landarkivets i Göteborg (hereafter LiG), Gothenburg, Sweden, F2A:376.

31. Ernst Thälmann had been the leader of the German Communist Party until 1933.

32. Invoice from Transocean Marine Paint, September 10, 1979, Contracts for 409, Finnboda Papers, CfN. Tor Martin Lein, "Selger hytteperle," *Dagbladet*, July 18, 1999, www.dagbladet.no.

33. Certificates for NYB 409, Finnboda Papers, CfN.

34. Adam Smith, *An Inquiry into the Nature and Causes of the Wealth of Nations*, ed. Edwin Cannan (London: Methuen and Co., 1904), book I, chapter I.

35. Author's correspondence with Parley Augustsson, May 29, 2023.

36. Memorandum, November 5, 1979, Contracts for 409, Finnboda Papers, CfN. See also invoices from Scandebo Shipping Co. S. A. Panama, Contracts for 409, Finnboda Papers, CfN. Another company in which Dehlin was involved, Biscayne Shipping, this one incorporated in Florida, also received commissions for contracts related to the two barges.

37. Author's correspondence with Parley Augustsson, May 8, 2023.

38. Ibid.

39. Augustsson notes that his companies significantly helped Norwegian shipyards, with dozens of orders for new builds and equipment. Author's interview with Parley Augustsson, May 12, 2023.

40. "Top Marginal Personal Income Tax Rates, 1975–2013," Tax Policy Center, April 16, 2014, www.taxpolicycenter.org; author's correspondence with Parley Augustsson, May 8, 2023.

41. Peter Stokes cites estimates that suggest the K/S market raised $3 billion for shipping deals in the late 1980s. Stokes, *Ship Finance*, 102–3.

42. "Severe Criticism of Augusstson's Management," *Norway Times*, March 13, 1986, 1–3; "Parley Augustsson Faces Cliffhanger After Cliffhanger," *Norway Times*, April 25, 1985, 9.

43. "Parley Augustsson to US," *Norway Times*, March 28, 1985, 9; "Parley Augustsson Faces Cliffhanger."

44. Author's correspondence with Parley Augustsson, May 8, 2023.

45. Contract, dated in Oslo, April 6, 1978, Contracts for 409, Finnboda Papers, CfN.

46. Author's correspondence with Parley Augustsson, May 8, 2023; author's interview with Parley Augustsson, May 12, 2023.

47. *Bader Scapa* Registration, National Archives of Norway, Skipsregisterkort, Serie IV Fartøy, RA/S-1627/H/Hd/L0003, available online at www.media.digitalarkivet.no; Svenska Varv Annual Report, July 24, 1980, www.data.riksdagen.se.

48. Author's interview with Parley Augustsson, May 12, 2023. Augustsson recalls the structure costing nearly half a million Norwegian kroner. The structure was built by Moelven.

49. Invoice from Stad Seaforth Shipping, June 8, 1979, Contracts for 409, Finnboda Papers, CfN. See also Trond Presterud to Finnboda (Telex), June 8, 1979, Contracts for 409, Finnboda Papers, CfN. Invoice from Haaland & Sønn, June 1, 1979, Contracts for 409, Finnboda Papers, CfN.

50. Augustsson recalls that the *Balder Scapa* was owned entirely by the Balder Group, not outside partners. Author's correspondence with Parley Augustsson, May 8, 2023.

51. "Severe Criticism of Augusstson's Management"; "Augustsson Bankruptcy Largest in History," *Norway Times*, January 22, 1987, 1–2.

52. "Augustsson Sold Harkmark to His Children for 15 Cents," *Norway Times*, May 1, 1986; "Severe Criticism of Augusstson's Management"; Stokes, *Ship Finance*, 103.

53. "Augustsson Bankruptcy Largest in History"; *Augustsson v. Norway*, European Commission of Human Rights (Second Chamber), February 28, 1996.

54. Memorandum re: Sverker Albrektson, November 1, 1979, Contracts for 409, Finnboda Papers, CfN.
55. Author's interview with Parley Augustsson, May 12, 2023.
56. "Havnen," *Stavanger Aftenblad*, November 10, 1979, 4.
57. Augustsson notes that the contract was canceled because of the late delivery. Author's correspondence with Parley Augustsson, May 8, 2023.
58. Contract, dated in Oslo, April 6, 1978, Contracts for 409, Finnboda Papers, CfN.
59. Leif Kasteskog to Parley Augustsson, March 4, 1980, Contracts for 409, Finnboda Papers, CfN; Leif Kasteskog to Messrs Førsund, Knap, Rafen & Co., March 4, 1980, Contracts for 409, Finnboda Papers, CfN. See also Probate Debt (Skuldebrev), May 23, 1979, Contracts for 409, Finnboda Papers, CfN.
60. Memorandum re: Sverker Albrektson, November 1, 1979, Contracts for 409, Finnboda Papers, CfN.
61. Leif Kasteskog to Parley Augustsson (Telex), December 5, 1979, Contracts for 409, Finnboda Papers, CfN; Parley Augustsson (Management) to Finnboda (G. Lind) (Telex), December 4, 1979, Contracts for 409, Finnboda Papers, CfN. On Norwegian Petroleum Consultants (NPC), see Sachi Hatakenaka, Petter Westnes, Martin Gjelsvik, and Richard K. Lester, "From 'Black Gold' to 'Human Gold': A Comparative Case Study of the Transition from a Resource-Based to a Knowledge Economy in Stavanger and Aberdeen," Industrial Performance Center, MIT Working Paper Series, MIT-IPC-06-004, July 2006, 109, www.ipc.mit.edu; Parley Augustsson to Finnboda, November 15, 1980, Contracts for 409, Finnboda Papers, CfN.
62. Leif Kasteskog to Parley Augustsson (Telex), December 5, 1979, Contracts for 409, Finnboda Papers, CfN.
63. Leif Kasteskog to Parley Augustsson (Management), March 3, 1980, Contracts for 409, Finnboda Papers, CfN.
64. Sven Sejersted Bødtker to Finnboda Varv, March 10, 1980, Contracts for 409, Finnboda Papers, CfN.
65. Parley Augustsson to Finnboda (Telex), May 7, 1980, Contracts for 409, Finnboda Papers, CfN.
66. Leif Kasteskog to Parley Augustsson (Telex), May 7, 1980, Contracts for 409, Finnboda Papers, CfN.
67. See insurance policies for the *Balder Scapa* from Gjensidige Norsk Skadeforsikring, May 21, 1980, Contracts for 409, Finnboda Papers, CfN.
68. Parley Augustsson to Finnboda (Telex), October 23, 1980, Contracts for 409, Finnboda Papers, CfN.
69. "Under radande omständigheter kan vi med tanke på den låga dagsraten inte utlova att avstå från legal actions under perioden": Leif Kasteskog to Parley Augustsson (Telex), October 24, 1980, Contracts for 409, Finnboda Papers, CfN.
70. Author's interview with Parley Augustsson, May 12, 2023.
71. Finnboda registered the Vessel in Sweden in December 1980, but did not officially buy it from Balder Lekter I until February 25, 1981. See Deed, February 25, 1981, Sjöfartsverket, Safe Esperia SJZH.
72. Fartygbevis (Ship Certificate) for *Finnboda 12,*Sjöfartsverket, Safe Esperia SJZH.
73. Gösta Lind to Sjöfartsreistret, December 9, 1980, Sjöfartsverket, Safe Dominia SJZA.

74. *Bader Scapa* Registration, National Archives of Norway, Skipsregisterkort, Serie IV Fartøy, RA/S-1627/H/Hd/L0003; Fartygbevis (Ship Certificate) for *Finnboda 12*, Sjöfartsverket, Safe Esperia SJZH; Eric Hallberg, "Finnbodas historia i korthet," *Länspumpen* 34, no. 139 (2007), 18.

75. Purchase Deed (Köpebrev), March 2, 1981, Sjöfartsverket, Safe Esperia SJZH.

76. Consafe took out a mortgage of 5.6 million Swedish kronor on the *Safe Esperia* and used the mortgage as collateral.

77. "Consafe AB of Sweden Seeks Bankruptcy Protection," *Wall Street Journal*, September 1985, 1

78. Such loans were administered by Svenska Varv. *Bibby Venture* Registration, BT 110/2088, TNA; "Venture," www.marinetraffic.com.

79. See Statement from Finnboda Varv, March 2, 1981, and Registerutdrag of *Safe Esperia*, March 2, 1981, Sjöfartsverket, Safe Esperia SJZH. See Statement from Swedyards, March 25, 1981, Sjöfartsverket, Safe Esperia SJZH. Bill of Sale, Contract File for Nyb. 409, Finnboda Papers, CfN.

80. Köpebrev (Deed) for *Finnboda 11*, January 30, 1981, Sjöfartsverket, Safe Dominia SJZA. Agreement between Finnboda Varv and Svenksa Varv, March 2, 1981, Contracts for 408, Finnboda Papers, CfN.

CHAPTER 2: THE NORTH SEA

1. "Offshore Floatel to Accommodate 600 Workers," *Maritime Reporter* (September 1978), 58. "Offshore Orders Generating Confidence for Shipbuilders," *Financial Times*, March 24, 1982, 35. J. Christer Ericsson, *Utan omsvep: Mitt berikande liv med Consafe* (Stockholm: Timbro, 1987), chapter 4.

2. Marc Levinson, *The Box: How the Shipping Container Made the World Smaller and the World Economy Bigger* (Princeton: Princeton University Press, 2006).

3. James Surowiecki, "Turn of the Century," *Wired*, January 1, 2002.

4. "How to Get 20 Million Tons of Grain Out of Ukraine," *The Indicator from Planet Money*, NPR, June 1, 2022.

5. See "Planet Money Makes a T-Shirt: The World Behind a Simple Shirt, in Five Chapters," *Planet Money*, NPR, 2013.

6. Adam Smith, *An Inquiry into the Nature and Causes of the Wealth of Nations*, ed. Edwin Cannan (London: Methuen and Co., 1904), book I, chapter I.

7. See Theo Notteboom, Athanasios Pallis, and Jean-Paul Rodrigue, *Port Economics, Management and Policy* (New York: Routledge, 2021), chapter 1.

8. Stefan Nilsson and Linette Israelsson, "Så blev Christer Ericsson miljardär," *Expressen*, June 28, 2016, www.expressen.se.

9. Ericsson, *Utan omsvep*, chapter 3, 151. Consafe took a 17 percent stake in Transatlantic and a 10 percent stake in Broström, both Swedish shipping companies, in 1981. Westerley Christner, "Consafe Buys Stake in Transatlantic," *Financial Times*, September 24, 1981, 30.

10. Ericsson, *Utan omsvep*, 55.

11. Ibid., 5.

12. Ibid., 73.

13. A. Craig Copetas, "The Revolt of the Capitalists," *Inc.* (September 1985), 92-95. In

particular, the business leaders objected to proposed "wage earners funds," which would require companies to put aside 20 percent of their annual profits to buy new stock for employees.

14. Ericsson, *Utan omsvep*, 239.

15. Robert Mabro et al., *The Market for North Sea Crude Oil* (Oxford: Oxford University Press, 1986); Alexander Kemp, *The Official History of North Sea Oil and Gas*, vol. I: *The Growing Dominance of the State* (London: Routledge, 2011).

16. Ericsson, *Utan omsvep*, 157. Translated from the original Swedish.

17. Convention on the Continental Shelf, 499 UNTS 311, Article 1, quoted in Surabhi Ranganathan, "Ocean Floor Grab: International Law and the Making of an Extractive Imaginary," *European Journal of Law* 30, no. 2 (2019), 581.

18. Ronald W. Ferrier and J. H. Bamberg, *The History of the British Petroleum Company* (Cambridge: Cambridge University Press, 1982), 201–3. On jurisdictions in the North Sea, see Alex G. Oude Elferink, *The Delimitation of the Continental Shelf Between Denmark, Germany and the Netherlands: Arguing Law, Practicing Politics?* (Cambridge: Cambridge University Press, 2013).

19. Svein S. Andersen, *The Struggle over North Sea Oil and Gas: Government Strategies in Denmark, Britain, and Norway* (Oslo: Scandinavian University Press, 1993), 41–53. The *Safe Astoria* ultimately would not be operated by Chevron, but rather by ConocoPhillips in the Norwegian sector. It was purchased from Consafe by the Mexican firm Cotemar in 1984. Ericsson, *Utan omsvep*, 127–33.

20. Department for Business, Energy and Industrial Strategy, "Crude Oil and Petroleum Products: Production, Imports and Exports 1890–2019," 2020, www.gov.uk.

21. Bryan Cooper and T. F. Gaskell, *The Adventure of North Sea Oil* (London: Heinemann, 1976), 1. On Britain as a coal-powered power, see David Edgerton, *The Rise and Fall of the British Nation: A Twentieth-Century History* (London: Penguin, 2019), 80–86, 295–98. On the differences between oil and coal production, as related to democratic politics and identity, see Timothy Mitchell, *Carbon Democracy: Political Power in the Age of Oil* (London: Verso, 2011), 36–40.

22. Tabitha Lasley, *Sea State* (New York: Ecco, 2021), 110. "They were in the business of maintaining civilization, and this work had a paradoxically coarsening effect on their behavior."

23. Hugo Manson, interview with Alexa Reid, 2000, Aberdeen, Lives in the Oil Industry Oil History Project, The British Library, London, United Kingdom (hereafter BL), C963/47.

24. Terry Brotherstone and Hugo Manson, "From *The Little House on the Prairie* to the 'King Eddie Suite': Life-Stories from North Sea Oil," *History Scotland* 2, no. 1 (2002), 42.

25. Hugo Manson, interview with Robert Ballantyne, 2000–2002, Aberdeen, Lives in the Oil Industry History Project, BL, C963/53.

26. Brotherstone and Manson, "Life-Stories from North Sea Oil."

27. Hugo Manson, interview with David Robertson, 2000–2001, Aberdeen, Lives in the Oil Industry Oil History Project, BL, C963/61.

28. Juan Carlos Boué, "The UK North Sea as a Global Experiment in Neoliberal Resource Extraction: The British Model of Petroleum Governance from 1970 to 2018" (London: Platform London and Public and Commercial Services Union, Feb-

ruary 2020), 5, 9. See also Alex Kemp, *The Official History of North Sea Oil and Gas*, 2 vols. (London: Taylor and Francis, 2013).

29. See Andersen, *The Struggle over North Sea Oil and Gas*, 88–94.

30. Ericsson, *Utan omsvep*, 163. Translated from the original Swedish.

31. See, e.g., "Partnerships Jostle for Norway's Subsea Promise," *Offshore Engineer*, January 1, 1984, 29–30.

32. "International Corporate Report," *Wall Street Journal*, April 19, 1984, 1. Kevin Done, "Public Offering by Consafe," *Financial Times*, November 19, 1983, 21. The previous year, Consafe had posted a pretax profit of $50.6 million and had floated shares worth 18 percent of its equity on the Stockholm Stock Exchange.

33. Kevin Done, "Public Offering by Consafe," *Financial Times*, November 19, 1983, 21; David Brown, "Consafe Looks to a Future Based on a Broader International Field," *Financial Times*, April 3, 1985, 35. Ericsson, *Utan omsvep*, 162.

34. "Offshore Orders Generating Confidence for Shipbuilders," *Financial Times*, March 24, 1982, 35.

35. "Knowing How to Compete. Profile: Ake Norling, Governor of Gothenburg and Bohus," *Financial Times*, March 24, 1982, 34.

36. Ibid.

37. Ericssson, *Utan omsvep*, chapter 4.

38. "En ombyggnad hela tiden finnits med i bilden"; "Kan man kanske tillstå att A delvis har rätt."

39. Parley Augustsson to Finnboda, November 15, 1980, Contracts for 409, Finnboda Papers, CfN.

40. Gösta Lind to Parley Augustsson, December 12, 1979, Contracts for 408, Finnboda Papers, CfN.

41. Memorandum re: Sverker Albrektson, November 1, 1979, Contracts for 409, Finnboda Papers, CfN.

42. See Fartygbevis (Ship Certificate) for *Safe Dominia*, October 17, 1981, Sjöfartsverket, Safe Dominia SJZA.

43. JCE, 300 Man Coastel Outline Specification, n.d. [1981], LiG, F2A:375. *Bibby Resolution* Registration, TNA, BT 110/2075/32; *Bibby Venture* Registration, TNA, BT 110/2088. The shipyard was owned by Von Tell. The *Safe Esperia*'s new accommodation blocks were inspected by Swedish officials on March 21, 1983. See Calculation of Tonnage According to the International Convention on Tonnage Measurement of Ships, *Safe Esperia*, March 3, 1981, and Mätbevis (Tonnage Certificate) *Safe Esperia*, March 21, 1983, Sjöfartsverket, Safe Esperia SJZH.

44. See material from Von Tell Nico and Nordelektro in Sjöfartsverket, Safe Esperia SJZH and Safe Dominia SJZA.

45. JCE, 300 Man Coastel Outline Specification, n.d. [1981], LiG, F2A:375.

46. Plans for Gangplank, September 10, 1981, LiG, F2A:375.

47. Invoice from Götmodul, August 7, 1981, LiG, F2A:375.

48. See Certificates and Inspection Reports in Folder B, LiG, F2A:375.

49. Svenska Textilforskningsinstitutet, Report, May 6, 1980, LiG, F2A:375.

50. JCE, 300 Man Coastel Outline Specification, n.d. [1981], LiG, F2A:375.

51. Safe Dominia Fordinelse Mellan Typ 1—Moduler, June 25, 1981, LiG, F3A:450, 096-9.

52. JCE, 300 Man Coastel Outline Specification, n.d. [1981], LiG, F2A:375.

53. Det Norske Veritas, based in Oslo, merged with another major classification society, Germanischer Lloyd, based in Hamburg, in 2013. The combined company is now known as DNV GL.

54. See Certificates from Det Norske Veritas in LiG, F2A:375.

55. Charles Ernest Fayle, *A History of Lloyd's from the Founding of Lloyd's Coffee House to the Present Day* (London: Macmillan, 1928).

56. Frederick Martin, *The History of Lloyd's and of Marine Insurance in Great Britain* (New York: Burt Franklin, 1971 [1876]), chapter 18; Ekaterina Anyanova, "The Changing Role of International Classification Societies in International Shipping Practice," *International Journal of Private Law* 1, nos. 3–4 (2008), 358–67.

57. Anthony D. Muncer, "Classification Societies," in *Encyclopedia of Maritime and Offshore Engineering*, ed. John Carlton, Yoo Sang Choo, and Paul Jukes (London: John Wiley and Sons, 2018), 2054–62.

58. Muncer, "Classification Societies," 2053; Anyanova, "The Changing Role of International Classification Societies." Ten of the most significant societies belong to the International Association of Classification Societies, which, according to Anyanova, "serves as an additional guarantor of the quality and conscientiousness of the fulfilment of their functions," 360–61; International Association of Classification Societies, www.iacs.org.uk.

59. Anyanova, "The Changing Role of International Classification Societies," 359.

60. Det Norske Veritas, Sertifickat for Midlerttidig Klasse, May 23, 1979, Certificates for 409, Finnboda Papers, CfN.

61. Muncer, "Classification Societies," 2057.

62. To do so, it had to get permission from Swedyards (Svenska Varv), which still had title to the old mortgage of 5.6 million Swedish kronor. See Sverker Albrektson and Tor Grotenfelt to Sjöfartsregistret, April 22, 1981, Sjöfartsverket, Safe Dominia SJZA.

63. JCE Consafe Offshore, Coastel Outline Specification, n.d. [1979–1983], Regionarkivet Västra Götalandsregionen och Göteborgs Stad, Göteborg, Sweden, GSA_13-1 /F 1 B/42.

64. David Brown, "Falklands Deadline Draws Near for Swedes," *Financial Times*, November 2, 1982, 6; New York City Board of Correction Minutes (hereafter BOCM), May 10, 1989, www1.nyc.gov.

65. JCE Consafe Offshore, Coastel Outline Specification, n.d. [1979–1983], Regionarkivet Västra Götalandsregionen och Göteborgs Stad, Gothenburg, Sweden (hereafter RVG), GSA_13-1/F 1 B/42; JCE Consafe Offshore, Particulars of the Fleet and Organisation, May 1983, RVG, GSA_13-1/F 1 B/42.

66. Brown, "Falklands Deadline Draws Near for Swedes." 6.

67. On the standardization of the shipping container, see Levinson, *The Box*, chapter 7. See JCE Consafe Offshore, Coastel Outline Specification, n.d. [1979-1983], RVG, GSA_13-1/F 1 B/42, section 2.

68. Twenty-seven people died on the journey from Cameroon to Kingston. Voyage ID 81106, Trans-Atlantic Slave Trade Database, www.slavevoyages.org.

69. Dawn Littler and David Anderson, "Records of Bibby Line," Finding Guide, 2000, National Museums Liverpool Archive Centre, Liverpool, UK. See also Ara-

bella McIntyre-Brown, "Shenanigans in Shipping," Freemagination Blog, www
.wheredoyougetideas.wordpress.com; Arabella McIntyre-Brown, *Time and Tide: 200
Years of the Bibby Line Group, 1807–2007* (Dublin: Capsica Ltd., 2007).

70. Oswald Jones, Abby Ghobadian, Nicholas O'Regan, and Valerie Antcliff, "Dynamic
Capabilities in a Sixth-Generation Family Firm: Entrepreneurship and the Bibby
Line," *Business History* 55, no. 6 (2013), 914; 918. "Bibby Line," *The Red-Duster*, The
Merchant Navy Association, www.red-duster.co.uk. See also Duncan Haws, *Merchant Fleets: The Burma Boats: Henderson and Bibby* (London: TCL Publications,
1996). "Sir Derek Bibby, 69," *The Sunday Times*, May 10, 1992.

71. Jones, Ghobadian, O'Regan, and Antcliff, "Entrepreneurship and the Bibby Line,"
941.

72. Ibid.; "Bibby Line."

73. Britain produced 37.9 percent of the world's shipping fleet in 1950 and only 3.6
percent in 1975. Geoffrey Owen, *From Empire to Europe: The Decline and Revival of
British Industry Since the Second World War* (London: Harper Collins, 2000), 99–110.

74. The offshore contracts, however, turned out to be unprofitable. Lewis Johnman and
Hugh Murphy, *British Shipbuilding and the State Since 1918: A Political Economy of
Decline* (Exeter: University of Exeter Press, 2002), chapter 7, specifically 205–13. See
also Anthony Burton, *The Rise and Fall of British Shipbuilding* (London: The History
Press, 2013), chapter 11.

75. Peter Hill, "Shipbuilders Seek 'Buy British' Aids," *The Times*, November 6, 1975, 20.

76. Stig Tenold, *Norwegian Shipping in the 20th Century: Norway's Successful Navigation
of the World's Most Global Industry* (London: Palgrave Macmillan, 2019), chapter 7.

77. See, for instance, the analysis of a young Tony Blair. Tony Blair, "Thatcherism," *London Review of Books* 9, no. 19 (October 29, 1987), www.lrb.co.uk.

CHAPTER 3: THE SOUTH ATLANTIC

1. Lawrence Freedman, *The Official History of the Falklands Campaign*, vol. II: *War and
Diplomacy* (London: Routledge, 2005), 465.

2. Cited in ibid., 464.

3. *War in the Falklands, 1982* (London: The Stationery Office, 2001), 227.

4. Ibid., 227–32; Freedman, *War and Diplomacy*, chapter 41. See also David Cannadine, *Margaret Thatcher: A Life and Legacy*, chapter 4; Peter Jenkins, *Mrs. Thatcher's
Revolution: The Ending of the Socialist Era* (Cambridge: Harvard University Press,
1988), 159–66.

5. Philip J. Stern, *Empire, Incorporated: The Corporations That Built British Colonialism*
(Cambridge: Harvard University Press, 2023), 318.

6. On images of the Falklands, see Sarah Maltby, *Remembering the Falklands War:
Media, Memory and Identity* (London: Palgrave Macmillan, 2016).

7. "Accommodation requirements" in late February 1983 were 4,629 personnel, with
a reduction to 3,829 by May. B. M. Lane, Falkland Islands: The Coastel Position,
February 25, 1983, TNA, DEFE 47/46.

8. Edward Fursdon, *Falklands Aftermath: Picking Up the Pieces* (Barnsley, UK: Pen and
Sword, 1988), 155.

9. Charles Darwin, *The Voyage of the Beagle* (New York: P. F. Collier and Son, 1909 [1938]), 118.

10. See "The United Kingdom Defence Programme: The Way Forward," June 1981, Cmnd. 8288; Lawrence Freedman, *The Official History of the Falklands Campaign*, vol. I: *The Origins of the Falklands War* (London: Routledge, 2005), chapter 14.

11. World Bank national accounts data and OECD national accounts data files, www.data.worldbank.org.

12. James M. Boughton, *Silent Revolution: The International Monetary Fund, 1979–1989* (Washington, DC: IMF, 2001), chapter 8; Rüdiger Dornbusch and Juan Carlos de Pablo, "Argentina: Debt and Macroeconomic Instability," NBER Working Paper No. 2378, National Bureau of Economic Research, Cambridge, MA, September 1987, www.nber.org; Francisco J. Buera and Juan Pablo Nicolini, *The Case of Argentina*, draft paper, www.manifold.bfi.uchicago.edu.

13. Richard D. Chenette, "The Argentine Seizure of the Malvinas [Falkland Islands]: History and Diplomacy," paper delivered at the War in the Modern Area Seminar, Marine Corps Command and Staff College, Quantico, Virginia, May 4, 1987, www.globalsecurity.org.

14. Ibid., chapter 6; Freedman, *The Origins of the Falklands War*, chapter 1. See also *War in the Falklands, 1982*.

15. Margaret Thatcher in House of Commons, April 3, 1982, in *War in the Falklands, 1982*, 237.

16. On the Falklands and empire, see Exequiel Mercau, *The Falklands War: An Imperial History* (Cambridge: Cambridge University Press, 2019). Mercau notes how the Falklands became associated with conservatism more generally. See, especially, chapter 6.

17. Margaret Thatcher, Speech at Cheltenham, July 3, 1982, Thatcher Archive CCOPR 486/82, www.margaretthatcher.org. See also Jenkins, *Mrs. Thatcher's Revolution*, 164–65; David Edgerton, *The Rise and Fall of the British Nation: A Twentieth-Century History* (London: Penguin, 2019), 426, 432.

18. Thatcher, Speech at Cheltenham.

19. See Mercau, *The Falklands War*.

20. Defence Policy Overseas: Falkland Islands; Accommodation; Location of Coastels, TNA, DEFE 13/1617; Anthony Nicholas, "Hotel Ship for British Troops," *UPI*, October 29, 1982, www.upi.com.

21. Nicholas, "Hotel Ship for British Troops."

22. *Hansard*, House of Commons Debate, November 15, 1982, vol. 32, cc. 40-1W; *Hansard*, House of Commons Debate, February 8, 1985, vol. 72, cc. 739W.

23. Jenkins, *Mrs. Thatcher's Revolution*, and, more generally, Cannadine, *Margaret Thatcher*.

24. Margaret Thatcher, Speech to Conservative Party Conference, October 8, 1982, quoted in Cannadine, *Margaret Thatcher*, 54. See also Edgerton, *The Rise and Fall of the British Nation*, 455.

25. Cannadine, *Margaret Thatcher*, 54.

26. "Military Expenditure (Percent of GDP)—United Kingdom," World Bank Data, www.data.worldbank.org. Data is taken from Stockholm International Peace Research Institute (SIPRI), Yearbook: Armaments, Disarmament and International

Security, 2023. U.S. military spending grew from under 5 percent of GDP in 1979 to nearly 7 percent in the mid-1980s. It was $144 billion at the beginning of the decade and $325 billion by 1990.

27. Stern, *Empire, Incorporated*, 262–63, 317–18.

28. See, for instance, E. J. Hobsbawm, *Industry and Empire* (London: Pelican, 1969); John Darwin, *The Empire Project: The Rise and Fall of the British World System, 1830–1970* (Cambridge: Cambridge University Press, 2009).

29. Jody Freeman and Martha Minow, eds., *Government by Contract: Outsourcing and American Democracy* (Cambridge: Harvard University Press, 2009).

30. See Bill of Sale of the *Safe Esperia*, March 21, 1983, Sjöfartsverket, Safe Esperia SJZH, no. 38. See also Bibby Line Limited Directors' Report and Annual Accounts, 1982, in Sjöfartsverket, Safe Esperia SJZH. Shortly after acquiring the title, the Britain Steamship Company took out two mortgages on the vessel, both from Swedish banks. See *Bibby Resolution* Registration, BT 110/2075/32. See also Falkland Islands: General, Including Construction Work; Coastel Accommodation, TNA, DEFE 47/46.

31. Coastels—Reports, April 7 1983, TNA, DEFE 13/1617. Fursdon, *Falklands Aftermath*, 155. See *Bibby Resolution* Registration, TNA, BT 110/2075/32. The *Safe Esperia* was transported on board the newly constructed MV *Dan Lifter*.

32. *Bibby Resolution* Registration, TNA, BT 110/2075/32; *Bibby Venture* Registration, TNA, BT 110/2088.

33. "Mersey Notes and General News Items," *Liverpool Nautical Research Society Bulletin* 28, no. 2 (April-June 1984), 34.

34. Derek Bibby to A. W. (Jerry) Wiggin, January 31, 1983, TNA, DEFE 13/1617.

35. Bill of Sale of the *Safe Esperia*, March 21, 1983, Sjöfartsverket, Safe Esperia SJZH, no. 38; *Bibby Resolution* Registration, TNA, BT 110/2075/32.

36. *Bibby Venture* Registration, TNA, BT 110/2088. The holding company, Consafe (Jersey) Ltd., formally purchased the vessel for $11 million from Consafe Offshore. By this point, the vessel was mortgaged for about $10 million. Registerutdrag, n.d. [after November 16, 1982], and Bill of Sale, Sjöfartsverket, Safe Dominia SJZA.

37. "Sir Jerry Wiggin, Tory MP—Obituary," *The Telegraph*, March 19, 2025, www.telegraph.co.uk.

38. D. O. Arnold-Foster, "Falkland Islands Accommodation: A Third Coastel," March 1, 1983, TNA, DEFE 47/46.

39. B. M. Lane, "Falkland Islands: The Coastel Position," February 25, 1983, TNA, DEFE 47/46.

40. The assumed inflation rate was around 3 percent, compared to 8 percent the previous year. "Investment Appraisal on Third Coastel Based on Bibby Quotation," February 25, 1983, TNA, DEFE 47/46. Teletype from Derek Bibby to A. W. Wiggin, February 23, 1983, TNA, DEFE 13/1617.

41. See Edgerton, *The Rise and Fall of the British Nation*, 429–32; Anthony Barnett, *Iron Britannia: Time to Take the Great Out of Britain*, rev. ed. (London: Faber and Faber, 2012).

42. *Hansard*, House of Commons Debate, November 4, 1982, vol. 31, cc. 119–214; *Hansard*, House of Commons Debate, March 1, 1983, vol. 38, cc. 122–24.

43. Falkland Islands—Tour Lengths, December 21, 1982, TNA, DEFE 47/46.

44. Points Arising from VCDS(P&L)'s Visit to Falkland Islands, August 9, 1982, TNA, DEFE 47/46.

45. *Hansard*, House of Commons Debate, November 4, 1982, vol. 31, c. 200.

46. Philip Keeble, *Patrolling the Cold War Skies: Reheat Sunset* (Stroud, UK: Fonthill Media, 2017), 152.

47. *Hansard*, House of Commons Debate, March 9, 1983, vol. 38, cc. 889–90.

48. The song, "Coastal 3," was written by Phil Richards. See "1st Battalion: The Argyll and Sutherland Highlanders—Falkland Islands and South Georgia 1986–1987," 2014, www.argylls1945to1971.co.uk.

49. Post about "Coastal Accommodation" in RAF Stanley & Coastel Dwellers (Combined Forces) Falkland Islands Facebook Group, November 4, 2020.

50. Falklands veterans continue to be very active on Facebook; the RAF Stanley and Coastel Dwellers Facebook group has been a great help in the research of this project.

51. Post about "Coastal Accommodation."

52. Dawn Littler and David Anderson, "Records of Bibby Line," Finding Guide, 2000, National Museums Liverpool Archive Centre.

53. The Vessel was slightly more expensive, at £3.5 million. "Coastels," January 7, 1983, TNA DEFE 13/1617.

54. Mike Ricketts, *The Vessel* (Film), 2013, www.youtube.com.

55. *Hansard*, House of Commons Debate, March 9, 1983, vol. 38, c. 889; *Hansard*, House of Commons Debate, January 24, 1984, vol. 52, c. 456. See also Bibby Maritime Limited, Client List, n.d. [2019], www.bibbymaritime.com.

56. "Energy Consumption by Source, World," Our World in Data, www.ourworldindata .org; data comes from Energy Institute Statistical Review of World Energy, 2023.

57. David Brown, "Consafe Looks to a Future Based on a Broader International Field," *Financial Times*, April 3, 1985, 35.

58. Kevin Done, "Swedish Group Granted Debt Moratorium," *Financial Times*, July 17, 1985, 29.

59. "Consafe AB of Sweden Seeks Bankruptcy Protection," *Wall Street Journal*, September 1985, 1. Juris Kaza, "On Election Eve, Sweden Lets an Unprofitable Business Go Under," *Christian Science Monitor*, September 13, 1985, www.csmonitor.com. Ericsson's account of the events is full of recriminations, especially of the Swedish state. See J. Christer Ericsson, *Utan omsvep: Mitt berikande liv med Consafe* (Stockholm: Timbro), 1987, chapter 1.

60. Ericsson, *Utan omsvep*, 191, 214, 222, 242.

61. The *Safe Esperia* became the *Bibby Resolution* on November 29, 1985; *Bibby Resolution* Registration, BT 110/2075/32. "Bibby Line," *The Red-Duster*, The Merchant Navy Association, www.red-duster.co.uk. See also Duncan Haws, *Merchant Fleets: The Burma Boats Henderson and Bibby* (London: TCL Publications, 1996).

CHAPTER 4: THE CARIBBEAN SEA

1. Oswald Jones, Abby Ghobadian, Nicholas O'Regan, and Valerie Antcliff, "Dynamic Capabilities in a Sixth-Generation Family Firm: Entrepreneurship and the Bibby Line," *Business History* 55, no. 6 (September 2013), 941.

2. "Bibby's Flagging-Out Is Condemned by MNAOA," *The Telegraph*, June 1984, in National Museums Liverpool Archive Centre, Liverpool, United Kingdom (hereafter MAL), B/BIBBY/5/11.

3. "Bibby Line," *The Red-Duster*, Merchant Navy Association, www.red-duster.co.uk; Andrew Fisher, "Bibby Line Switches Ship Registration to Hong Kong," *Financial Times*, May 1, 1984, 10.

4. "Bibby's Flagging-Out Is Condemned."

5. "Signpost to British Shipping's Demise," *Liverpool Nautical Research Society Bulletin* 28, no. 1 (January-March 1984), 37.

6. "Employment by economic sector, United Kingdom," Our World in Data, www .ourworldindata.org. See also Geoffrey Owen, *From Empire to Europe: The Decline and Revival of British Industry Since the Second World War* (New York: Harper Collins, 2000).

7. Philip Shore, *Sunset over the Red Ensign: The Decline of British Deepsea Shipping, 1945–1989*, PhD dissertation, University of Kent, Canterbury, UK, January 1990, 4.10. See also Keith Davies, *The Decline of the British Merchant Fleet: Some New Perspectives*, PhD dissertation, University of Warwick, Coventry, UK, 2018.

8. J. McConville, *Industrial Relations in the UK Shipping Industry Since the Second World War*, PhD dissertation, University of Warwick, Coventry, UK, June 1982, 259.

9. Derek P. Richards, "Flagged-Out Implications," in Letters to the Editor, May 1984, *The Telegraph*, 6, Modern Records Centre, University of Warwick, Coventry, UK (hereafter MRC), MSS.441/MNAO/4/3/124.

10. Advertisement for Bibby Line, December 1973, *The Telegraph*, 13, MRC, MSS.441/MNAO/4/3/2.

11. Shore, *Sunset over the Red Ensign*, 4.5.

12. Though, as Keith Davies points out, UK shipowners still were given tax advantages, compared to other British business owners. Davies, *The Decline of the British Merchant Fleet*, 81.

13. "Bibby Line," *The Red-Duster*, 10. See also Duncan Haws, *Merchant Fleets: The Burma Boats Henderson and Bibby* (London: TCL Publications, 1996).

14. Michael Baily, "Shipping Firm Lays Up After 179 Years," *The Times*, May 1, 1984, 28.

15. "Signpost to British Shipping's Demise," *Liverpool Nautical Research Society Bulletin* 28, no. 1 (January–March 1984), 37.

16. For context, see John N. K. Mansell, *Flag State Responsibility: Historical Development and Contemporary Issues* (Berlin: Springer, 2009), 78–79.

17. "Reflag," *Oxford English Dictionary Online*, 2009, www.oed.com.

18. Elizabeth R. DeSombre, *Flagging Standards: Globalization and Environmental Safety, and Labor Regulations at Sea* (Cambridge: MIT Press, 2006), 37, and see chapter 6, more generally, for labor's resistance to flags of convenience.

19. Tonnage registered in the United States went from 25,589,000 to 19,111,000 gross tons over the same period. Liberia moved from 10,079,000 to 70,718,000 gross tons. Hong Kong moved from 318,000 to 2,580,000 gross tons over the period. Ibid., 82–83. UN Conference on Trade and Development (UNCTAD), *2020 Handbook of Statistics* (New York: United Nations, 2020), 78.

20. Jones, Ghobadian, O'Regan, and Antcliff, "Entrepreneurship and the Bibby Line," 941.

21. Shore, *Sunset over the Red Ensign*, 5.39, 6.6.

22. "Coastel: The World's Most Accommodating Floating Unit," Bibby Line Promotional Brochure, n.d. [1980s], MAL, B/BIBBY/4/8.

23. *Bibby Venture* Registration, TNA, BT 110/2088; *Bibby Resolution* Registration, TNA, BT 110/2075/32.

24. "Muscat Dhows Case, Award of the Tribunal," August 8, 1905, *Hague Court Reports*, The Hague, 1916, 96, quoted in DeSombre, *Flagging Standards*, 69. On the Muscat Dhows Case, see Fahad Ahmad Bishara, "'No Country but the Ocean': Reading International Law from the Deck of an Indian Ocean Dhow, ca. 1900," *Comparative Studies in Society and History* 60, no. 2 (2018), 338–66. The notion that ships had a nationality, granted by states through registration, was codified in Article 5(1) of the Geneva Convention on the High Seas in 1958. It was reaffirmed in the UN Convention on the Law of the Sea. See Ademun-Odeke, "An Examination of Bareboat Charter Registries and Flag of Convenience Registries in International Law," *Ocean Development and International Law* 36, no. 4 (2005), 339–62. See also Davies, *The Decline of the British Merchant Fleet*, chapter 3.

25. Bishara, "'No Country but the Ocean.'"

26. S. G. Sturmey, *British Shipping and World Competition* (Liverpool: University of Liverpool Press, 2009 [1962]), chapter 9.

27. E. Kay Gibson, *Brutality on Trial: "Hellfire" Pedersen, "Fighting" Hansen, and the Seaman's Act of 1915* (Gainesville: University of Florida Press, 2006).

28. Boleslaw Adam Boczek, *Flags of Convenience: An International Legal Study* (Cambridge: Harvard University Press), 9–13; DeSombre, *Flagging Standards*, 71–74.

29. W. L. Cornyn of Pacific Freighters, quoted in Rodney Carlisle, *Sovereignty for Sale: The Origins and Evolution of the Panamanian and Liberian Flags of Convenience* (Annapolis: Naval Institute Press, 1981), 10–11; DeSombre, *Flagging Standards*, 72.

30. Carlisle, *Sovereignty for Sale*, chapter 3.

31. On "genuine link," see UNCLOS Article 91.

32. Committee of Inquiry into Shipping, *Report* (London: HMSO, 1970) (Cmnd. 4337), 51.

33. The system of flags of convenience, in the journalist William Langewiesche's words, "constitutes an exact reversal of sovereignty's intent, and a perfect mockery of national conceits. It is free enterprise at its freest." William Langewiesche, "Anarchy at Sea," *The Atlantic*, September 2003. See also Langewiesche, *The Outlaw Sea: A World of Freedom, Chaos, and Crime* (New York: North Point Press, 2004), 4–7.

34. See DeSombre, *Flagging Standards*; Carlos Felipe Llinás Negret, "Pretending to Be Liberian and Panamanian: Flags of Convenience and the Weakening of the Nation State on the High Seas," *Journal of Maritime Law and Commerce* 27, no. 1 (January 2016), 1–28.

35. Doing so carries advantages that go far beyond the tax code. Under existing U.S. law, 75 percent of all onboard personnel serving on a U.S. flagged vessel must be American citizens or residents. Moreover, any U.S. flagged ship engaged in "coastwide trade" must be owned by American citizens and constructed in an American shipyard. Negret, "Pretending to Be Liberian and Panamanian," 16–18.

36. DeSombre, *Flagging Standards*, 72–73. On the United Fruit Company, see Jason M. Colby, *The Business of Empire: United Fruit, Race, and U.S. Expansion in Central*

America (Ithaca: Cornell University Press, 2011); James W. Martin, *Banana Cowboys: The United Fruit Company and the Culture of Corporate Colonialism* (Albuquerque: University of New Mexico Press, 2018).

37. Carlisle, *Sovereignty for Sale*, 2–3. See also Walter LaFeber, *The Panama Canal: The Crisis in Historical Perspective*, rev. ed. (Oxford: Oxford University Press, 1990).

38. Carlisle, *Sovereignty for Sale*, 33.

39. Cf. DeSombre, *Flagging Standards*, 9–10.

40. Quoted in Carlisle, *Sovereignty for Sale*, 120.

41. Stettinius in press release, September 27, 1947, quoted in Carlisle, *Sovereignty for Sale*, 119.

42. Quoted in ibid., 122.

43. Ibid., 129–33. Rodney Carlisle, "The 'American Century' Implemented: Stettinius and the Liberal Flag of Convenience," *Business History Review* 54, no. 2 (1980), 175–91.

44. The fund was administered by the Liberia Foundation; see Carlisle, *Sovereignty for Sale*, 118.

45. "U.S. Liberian Legal Systems," Liberian Registry (LISCR), 2020, www.liscr.com. Several other countries run their registries through private firms based in the United States or Europe. The Marshall Islands' registry, for instance, is run out of Virginia, by International Registries, Inc., a descendent of Stettinius's firm. After Charles Taylor took power in Liberia in 1997, International Registries was replaced by Liberian International Ship & Corporate Registry (LISCR) as the manager of the registry. See Negret, "Pretending to Be Liberian and Panamanian" 22-23; DeSombre, *Flagging Standards*, 79.

46. See "Transfer of British ships to flags of convenience: policy," TNA, MT 73/330.

47. As Ogle has put it, this "archipelago-like landscape of distinct legal spaces . . . allowed free-market capitalism to flourish on the sidelines of a world increasingly dominated by larger and more interventionist nation-states." Vanessa Ogle, "Archipelago Capitalism: Tax Havens, Offshore Money, and the State, 1950s–1970s," *American Historical Review* 122, no. 5 (December 2017), 1432–33.

48. Vanessa Ogle, " 'Funk Money': The End of Empires, The Expansion of Tax Havens, and Decolonization as an Economic and Financial Event," *Past and Present*, August 23, 2020.

49. "Empire Builders," *Sunday Times*, May 24, 1964, 7, quoted in Vanessa Ogle, "Archipelago Capitalism," 1442. Nicholas Shaxson, *Treasure Islands: Uncovering the Damage of Offshore Banking and Tax Havens* (New York: Palgrave Macmillan, 2011).

50. Shaxson, *Treasure Islands*, 88–91. Jeffrey Robinson, *The Sink: Terror, Crime and Dirty Money in the Offshore World* (London: Constable), chapters 1 and 2.

51. Ogle, " 'Funk Money,' " 14-19.

52. As Adam Tooze points out, "The Bahamas is the truly exceptional case of a postcolonial Black-majority state that is also a world-class financial center." Adam Tooze, "The Hidden History of the World's Top Offshore Cryptocurrency Tax Haven," *Foreign Policy*, January 15, 2023.

53. Ibid.

54. Committee of Inquiry into Shipping, 52.

55. Tooze, "The Hidden History"; Shaxson, *Treasure Islands*, 90–91.

56. Nicki Kelly, "Bahamas Makes Waves as a Shipping Registry," *Christian Science Monitor*, May 11, 1983, 10.

57. Langewiesche, *The Outlaw Sea*, 6–7.

58. Ibid., 32, 87–88.

59. "Soldiers' Floating Home Leaves Falklands," *Soldier*, June 1, 1987, 25.

60. Shaxson, *Treasure Islands*, 64–66. On the City, see David Kynaston's four-part *The City of London*, of which volume 4 is most relevant for offshoring. David Kynaston, *The City of London*, vol. 4: *A Club No More, 1945–2000* (London: Penguin, 2015).

61. Quoted in Shaxson, *Treasure Islands*, 136.

62. This is what Nicholas Shaxson calls "Britain's offshore spiderweb." Shaxson, *Treasure Islands*, chapter 5.

63. Nicki Kelly, "Bahamas Makes Waves as a Shipping Registry," *Christian Science Monitor*, May 11, 1983, 10.

64. Ademun-Odeke, "An Examination of Bareboat Charter Registries."

65. DeSombre, *Flagging Standards*, 41–43.

66. See Ryan Cecil Jobson, "States of Crisis, Flags of Convenience: An Introduction," *Small Axe* 24, no. 2 (July 2020), 68–77. The Bahamian dollar is pegged to the U.S. dollar. Neil Hartnell, "Maritime Authority Takes Tax Contributions to $96 Million," *The Tribune* (Nassau), March 12, 2020, www.tribune242.com.

67. "Ship Registry," Bahamas Investment Authority, 2011, www.bahamas.gov.bs.

68. Jones, Ghobadian, O'Regan, and Antcliff, "Entrepreneurship and the Bibby Line."

69. Mansell, *Flag State Responsibility*, chapter 6.

CHAPTER 5: THE RIVER EMS

1. Quoted in Bernhard Rieger, *The People's Car: A Global History of the Volkswagen Beetle* (Cambridge: Harvard University Press, 2013), 188–89.

2. Manfred Grieger and Markus Lupa, *From the Beetle to a Global Player. Volkswagen Chronicle* (Wolfsburg: Volkswagen Aktiengesellschaft, 2015), 82.

3. The figures for Krupp are for the late 1950s. Rieger, *The People's Car*, 192; Steven Tolliday, "From 'Beetle Monoculture' to the 'German Model': The Transformation of Volkswagen, 1967–1991," *Business and Economic History* 24, no. 2 (Winter 1995), 112. See also Volker Wellhöner, *Wirtschaftswunder-Weltmarkt-west deutscher Fordismus: Der Fall Volkswagen* (Münster: Westfälisches Dampfboot, 1996), 181.

4. Grieger and Lupa, *From the Beetle to a Global Player*, 94.

5. Ibid.

6. Bernd Eberstein, *Preußen und China: Eine Geschichte schwieriger Beziehungen* (Berlin: Duncker & Humblot, 2007).

7. On the history of Emden, see Marianne Claudi and Reinhard Claudi, *Goldene und andere Zeiten: Emden, Stadt in Ostfriesland* (Emden: Gerhard, 1982); Bernd Kappelhoff, *Geschichte der Stadt Emden* (Rautenberg: Leer, 1994).

8. This is what Ulrich Jürgens has called Volkswagen's "export-oriented Fordism." See Ulrich Jürgens, "VW at the Turning Point: Success and Crisis of a German Production Concept," in *Des trajectoires des firmes aux modèles industriel*, ed. Groupe d'Etudes et de Recherches Permanent sur l'Industrie et les Salariés de l'Automobile, Université d'Evry-Val d'Essonne (Evry: Université d'Evry-Val d'Essonne, 1994), 94.

9. Over the next two decades, Volkswagen embraced a "modular component kit system, allowing use of the same parts in different models with largely identical technical specifications." The Passat was "closely based" on the Audi 80, and the Polo took its design from the Audi 50. Grieger and Lupa, *From the Beetle to a Global Player*, 116, 130.

10. Ibid., 131, 144–61.

11. According to an article in *Autogramm*, the employee newspaper for the Wolfsburg, Hannover, Braunschweig, Kassel, Emden, and Salzgitter plants, the Vessel was moored in the inner harbor. "Wohnen in einem schwimmenden Hotel," *Autogramm* 7, no. 8 (August 1988). Author's correspondence with Dr. Ulrike Gutzmann, March 4, 2021. Files at the Emden VW plant suggest, instead, that the barge was in the outer harbor.

12. Ibid.; author correspondence with Johann Alberts, February 16, 2021; author's interviews with workers at VW Emdenwerk.

13. Ibid., 79, 109; Ralph Nader, *The Volkswagen: An Assessment of Distinctive Hazards* (Washington, D.C.: The Center for Automotive Safety, 1971), quoted in Tolliday, "From 'Beetle Monoculture' to the 'German Model,'" 114.

14. The exchange rate in 1969 was 4 Deutschmarks to the dollar; by 1975, it was 2.5 to the dollar. Tolliday, "From 'Beetle Monoculture' to the 'German Model,'" 114.

15. Rieger, *The People's Car*, 247–51.

16. Though Volkswagen's employment figures did not meaningfully decrease over the 1980s, VW did cut jobs in the 1990s, from 104,792 wage earners in 1989 to 80,480 a decade later. Grieger and Lupa, *From the Beetle to a Global Player*, 163, 201. On unemployment in West Germany, see Karl-Heinz Paqué, "Unemployment in West Germany: A Survey of Explanations and Policy Options," Kiel Working Paper No. 407, Kiel Institute of World Economics, Kiel, Germany, 1990, www.econstor.eu; Bernd Fitzenberger and Ralf A. Wilke, "Unemployment Durations in West Germany Before and After the Reform of the Unemployment Compensation System During the 1980s," *German Economic Review* 11, no. 3 (August 2010), 336–66.

17. "Das größte Problem," *Nordwest-Zeitung* (Oldenburg), May 5, 1988, 10.

18. Ibid.; Tolliday, "From 'Beetle Monoculture' to the 'German Model,'" 122; Rainer Bombois, "Massenentlassungen bei VW, Individualisierung der Krise," *Leviathan* 4 (1976), 432–63; Rita C-K Chin, *The Guest Worker Question in Postwar Germany* (Cambridge: Cambridge University Press, 2007). The largest group of workers were recruited from Turkey, but VW employed mostly those from eastern Europe and Italy. See Jennifer A. Miller, *Turkish Guest Workers in Germany: Hidden Lives and Contested Borders, 1960s to 1980s* (Toronto: University of Toronto Press, 2018).

19. Jürgens, "VW at the Turning Point," 96. See Jürgens more generally for the particular structure of Volkswagen's labor relations. Eva Brumlop and Ulrich Jürgens, "Rationalisation and Industrial Relations in the West German Automobile Industry: A Case Study of Volkswagen," IIVG Paper dp83-216, Internationalen Instituts für Vergleichende Gesellschaftsforschung / Arbeitspolitik des Wissenschaftszentrums Berlin, September 1983.

20. Ibid.

21. Jonathan Mantle, *Car Wars: Fifty Years of Greed, Treachery, and Skullduggery in the Global Marketplace* (New York: Arcade Publishing, 1995), 102.

22. Quoted in Rieger, *The People's Car*, 252.

23. Grieger and Lupa, *From the Beetle to a Global Player*, 160.

24. Ibid., 145–47.

25. On VW's globalization, see Ludger Pries, "Volkswagen in the 1990s: Accelerating from a Multinational to a Transnational Automobile Company," in *Globalization or Regionalization of the European Car Industry?*, ed. Michel Freyssenet, Koichi Shimizu, and Giuseppe Volpato (London: Palgrave Macmillan, 2013), 51–72.

26. Tolliday, "From 'Beetle Monoculture' to the 'German Model,'" 125; Ulrich Jürgens, Thomas Malsch, and Knuth Dohse, *Breaking from Taylorism: Changing Forms of Work in the Automobile Industry* (Cambridge: Cambridge University Press, 1993).

27. Robert C. Allen, *The British Industrial Revolution in Global Perspective* (Oxford: Oxford University Press, 2009). This view has been challenged by, among others, Jane Humphries. See Jane Humphries, "The Lure of Aggregates and the Pitfalls of the Patriarchal Perspective: A Critique of the High Wage Economy Interpretation of the British Industrial Revolution," *The Economic History Review* 66, no. 3 (August 2013).

28. Eric Hobsbawm and George Rudé, *Captain Swing* (London: Lawrence and Wishart, 1969).

29. Tolliday, "From 'Beetle Monoculture' to the 'German Model,'" 126; Wolfgang Streeck, *Industrial Relations in West Germany: A Case Study of the Car Industry* (New York: Pearson Education, 1984); Wolfgang Streeck, "Successful Adjustment to Turbulent Markets: The Automobile Industry," in *Industry and Politics in West Germany: Toward the Third Republic*, ed. Peter J. Katzenstein (Ithaca: Cornell University Press, 1991). On the German model more generally, see Hyeong-ki Kwon, "The German Model Reconsidered," *German Politics and Society* 20, no. 4 (Winter 2002), 48–72.

30. "Just in Time," *Nordwest-Zeitung* (Oldenburg), April 29, 1988, 2.

31. Ibid. In the original German: "Eine spezielle Technik der Datenfernübertragung ermöglicht, daß Stoßfänger für Stoßfänger in Emden genau in der richtigen Reihenfolge ans Band gelangen."

32. In the original German: "Der Passat aus Emden hatte einen 'Bombenstart.'" See "VW ist gut in Fahrt gekommen: 6,3 Prozent mehr Autos verauft," *Nordwest-Zeitung* (Oldenburg), May 5, 1988, 10.

33. Tolliday, "From 'Beetle Monoculture' to the 'German Model,'" 128.

34. "Zum schwimmende Jugendknast," *Nordwest-Zeitung (Oldenburg)*, February 17, 1989, R2.

35. "Wohnen in einem schwimmenden Hotel." It was also described as a "temporary domicile" (*vorübergendes Domizil*).

36. See Chin, *The Guest Worker Question in Postwar Germany* and Miller, *Turkish Guest Workers in Germany*.

37. "Das sind hier keine Türken," *Der Spiegel*, October 16, 1989, 36-38.

38. "*The Accommodation Review* (Bibby Line Group)," February 1991, MAL, B/BIBBY/4/8.

39. "Aus der Geschichte von f & w: Wohnschiffe," *Fördern und Wohnen*, April 26, 2019, www.foerdernundwohnen.de.

40. "Schicksale auf der 'Bibby Altona,'" *Der Spiegel*, November 29, 2003, www.spiegel.de; "Bibby Altona: Immer wieder gab es Drogen-Razzien," *Das Bild*, April 12, 2008,

www.bild.de. See also "Das Wohnschiff für Fluchtlinge," *Hamburger Abendblatt*, February 6, 2015, www.abendblatt.de. The *Altona* was described as a container ship by Birgit Gärtner, "Die Bibby Altona ist jetzt geschlossen," *Neues Deutschland*, October 2, 2006, www.neues-deutschland.de.

41. Nathaniel C. Nash, "Hamburg Journal: Off a German Shore, Their Lives Lie at Anchor," *The New York Times*, September 11, 1995.

42. Frank Eyssen, quoted in ibid.

CHAPTER 6: THE EAST RIVER

1. Werner Bamberger, "Belgian Line Pier Proving Efficient," *The New York Times*, October 31, 1965.

2. Nelson Rockefeller, Dedication of Pier 36, September 24, 1965, www.wnyc.org.

3. The Port Authority was a multistate group set up by New York and New Jersey in 1921. In the 1940s and 1950s, it had a much closer relationship with New Jersey officials than New York ones. New York City authorities—particularly the powerful planner Robert Moses—were unwilling to yield control over the city's waterfront to the Port Authority. See Jameson W. Doig, *Empire on the Hudson: Entrepreneurial Vision and Political Power at the Port of New York Authority* (New York: Columbia University Press, 2001), chapter 11.

4. Marc Levinson, *The Box: How the Shipping Container Made the World Smaller and the World Economy Bigger* (Princeton: Princeton University Press, 2006), 86–89.

5. In Brooklyn, hiring dropped from 2.3 million in 1965–66 to 930,000 in 1975–76. Levinson, *The Box*, 96. See also Joseph P. Goldberg, "U.S. Longshoremen and Port Development," in *Port Planning and Development as Related to Problems of U.S. Ports and the U.S. Coastal Environment*, ed. Eric Schenker and Harry C. Brockel (Cambridge, MD: Cornell Maritime Press, 1974): 68–81; Marc Levinson, "Container Shipping and the Decline of New York, 1955–1975," *Business History Review* 80 (Spring 2006): 49–80.

6. New York City Board of Correction Minutes (BOCM), January 15, 1987, www1.nyc.gov.

7. Edward Hudson, "Judge Delays Transfer of Inmates to a Barge," *The New York Times*, November 15, 1987.

8. Stephen Ward, "Troop Barge to Be US Prison," *The Independent*, August 15, 1987.

9. Douglas Martin, "Prison Barge Arrives at East River Pier; City to Seek Another," *The New York Times*, October 27, 1987.

10. Elizabeth Hinton, *From the War on Poverty to the War on Crime: The Making of Mass Incarceration in America* (Cambridge: Harvard University Press, 2016), especially chapter 9. See also Clarence Taylor, *Fight the Power: African Americans and the Long History of Police Brutality in New York City* (New York: New York University Press, 2018).

11. Nelson Rockefeller, "State of the State Speech," January 3, 1973, quoted in Julily Kohler-Hausmann, "'The Attila the Hun Law': New York's Rockefeller Drug Laws and the Making of a Punitive State," *Journal of Social History* 44, no. 1 (Fall 2010): 71-95; Alex Vitale, *City of Disorder: How the Quality of Life Campaign Transformed New York Politics* (New York: New York University Press, 2008), chapter 6. Ella

Antell, "Crimes of Youth: Juvenile Delinquency and the Carceral State in New York City, 1920–1978," PhD dissertation, Harvard University, Cambridge, MA, 2020; Douglas J. Flowe, *Uncontrollable Blackness: African American Men and Criminality in Jim Crow New York* (Chapel Hill: University of North Carolina Press, 2020).

12. Today the corresponding figure has risen to about two-thirds of the prison population. See Hinton, *From the War on Poverty to the War on Drugs*, 310 and the rest of chapter 9. David Garland, *The Culture of Control: Crime and Social Order in Contemporary Society* (Chicago: University of Chicago Press, 2002), 14; Michael Tonry, *Malign Neglect: Race, Crime and Punishment in America* (New York: Oxford University Press, 1996).

13. "Incarceration Trends: New York City, NY," Vera Institute, 2020, www.trends.vera.org.

14. Vitale, *City of Disorder*, 125–27; Roger Starr, *The Rise and Fall of New York* (New York: Basic Books, 1985), 114.

15. See Kim Phillips-Fein, *Fear City: New York's Fiscal Crisis and the Rise of Austerity Politics* (New York: Metropolitan Books, 2017), 288, 310.

16. Themis Chronopoulos, *Spatial Regulation in New York City: From Urban Renewal to Zero Tolerance* (New York: Routledge, 2011), chapter 6; Alex Vitale, *City of Disorder*, chapter 3. BOCM, February 17, 1987.

17. John Metzger, Oral History interview with Philip Caruso, August 16, 1994, Edward I. Koch Administration Oral History Project, 1992–1997, Columbia University, www.dlc.library.columbia.edu.

18. Vitale, *City of Disorder*, 40–45; Chronopolous, *Spatial Regulation*, chapter 6.

19. Sharon Zane, Oral History interview with Stanley Brezenoff, April 26, 1993, Edward I. Koch Administration Oral History Project, 1992–1997, Oral History Archives, Columbia University Rare Books Room, New York, NY (hereafter OHA), Audio Part 10, www.dlc.library.columbia.edu. BOCM, October 27, 1986.

20. *Fisher v. Koehler*, 718 F.Supp. 1111 (Southern District of New York 1989); *Fisher v. Koehler*, 902 F.2d 2 (2nd Cir. 1990).

21. BOCM, February 17, 1987.

22. "Department of Correction FY 2023," NYC Comptroller, www.comptroller.nyc.gov.

23. Celestine Bohlen, "Jail Population Reaches a Record," *The New York Times*, September 25, 1988.

24. Author's interview with Michael Jacobson, March 9, 2023.

25. *Fisher v. Koehler*, 692 F.Supp. 1519 (Southern District of New York 1988), 1527, 1532–39.

26. BOCM, October 27, 1986.

27. BOCM, January 15, 1987.

28. Author's interview with Michael Jacobson, March 9, 2023.

29. Robert D. McFadden, "Robert Kasanof Is Dead at 62; Lawyer Led Board of Correction," *The New York Times*, December 2, 1991.

30. Joan Cook, "Rose M. Singer, 94, an Original Member of Correction Board," *The New York Times*, March 16, 1991. "Paid Notice: Deaths Schulte, David A. Jr.," *The New York Times*, November 15, 2005; Robert D. McFadden, "William Booth, Judge and Civil Rights Leader, Dies at 84," *The New York Times*, December 27, 2006.

31. Roma Connable, Oral History interview with Barbara Margolis, August 10, 1994, Edward I. Koch Administration Oral History Project, 1992–1997, OHA, www.dlc .library.columbia.edu.

32. James Forman Jr., *Locking Up Our Own: Crime and Punishment in Black America* (New York: Farrar, Straus and Giroux, 2017); Michael Javen Fortner, *Black Silent Majority: The Rockefeller Drug Laws and the Politics of Punishment* (Cambridge: Harvard University Press, 2015).

33. See Naomi Murakawa, *The First Civil Right: How Liberals Built Prison in America* (New York: Oxford University Press, 2014); Hinton, *From the War on Poverty to the War on Crime*.

34. George L. Kelling and James Q. Wilson, "Broken Windows: The Police and Neighborhood Safety," *The Atlantic* (March 1982).

35. Ibid.

36. Wilson advocated divestment from social welfare programs and investment in law enforcement that would focus on deterrence and the prevention of potential crime. Hinton, *From the War on Poverty to the War on Crime*, 185–87; Vitale, *City of Disorder*, 46–49. See James Q. Wilson, *Varieties of Police Behavior: Management of Law and Order in Eight Communities* (Cambridge: Harvard University Press, 1978).

37. BOCM, February 17, 1987. The tapes were produced by the nonprofit Police Foundation.

38. BOCM, September 3, 1986. John J. DiIulio, *Governing Prisons: A Comparative Study of Correctional Management* (New York: Free Press, 1987). BOCM, September 3, 1986. John DiIulio, "The Coming of the Super-Predators," *Weekly Standard*, November 27, 1995, 23-28; William J. Bennett, John J. DiIulio, and John P. Walters, *Body Count: Moral Poverty—And How to Win America's War Against Crime and Drugs* (New York: Simon & Schuster, 1996). The board advocated "unit management" of prisons, along with DiIulio's ideas. See BOCM, March 14, 1989. On this turn, see Malcolm M. Feeley and Jonathan Simon, "The New Penology: Notes on the Emerging Strategy of Corrections and Its Implications," *Criminology* 30, no. 4 (November 1992): 447-474.

39. BOCM, August 9, 1988, and December 8, 1987.

40. BOCM, March 14, 1988. Jeffrey K. Parker, "Two-Hundred Guards Swinging Clubs and Lobbing Tear Gas Stormed . . . ," UPI, February 18, 1988, www.upi.com.

41. BOCM, February 9, 1988.

42. In 1978, the board had mandated that the Department of Correction provide at least seventy-five square feet of living space per inmate. It lowered that standard in 1985 due to overcrowding. "Minimum Standards," New York City Board of Correction, www1.nyc.gov.

43. BOCM, June 9, 1987.

44. Author's interview with Michael Jacobson, March 9, 2023; NYC Planning "Uniform Land Use Review Procedure," www.nyc.gov.

45. Martin, "Prison Barge Arrives."

46. BOCM, June 9 and July 14, 1987.

47. Hinton, *From the War on Poverty to the War on Crime*, chapter 8. On this process in Los Angeles, see Donna Murch, "Crack in Los Angeles: Crisis, Militarization, and Black Response to the Late Twentieth-Century War on Drugs," *Journal of American*

History 102, no. 1 (June 2015): 162-173. See also Marilynn S. Johnson, *Street Justice: A History of Police Violence in New York City* (Boston: Beacon Press, 2003), chapter 8.

48. See Stephen Graham, *Cities Under Siege: The New Military Urbanism* (New York: Verso, 2011); Peter B. Kraska and Victor E. Kappeler, "Militarizing American Police: The Rise and Normalization of Paramilitary Units," *Social Problems* 44, no. 1 (February 1997): 1-18.

49. About eleven thousand Americans died in prison hulks in New York. See Edwin G. Burrows, *Forgotten Patriots: The Untold Story of American Prisoners During the Revolutionary War* (New York: Basic Books, 2008).

50. "Mayor Michael R. Bloomberg Announces Task Force to Guide Redevelopment of the Brig Site," Press Announcement, July 29, 2004, www1.nyc.gov. Dave Hogarty, "Developing the Brooklyn Brig," Gothamist, April 25, 2007, www.gothamist.com.

51. BOCM, February 14, 1989. Commissioner Koehler noted that the former naval air base in Marine Park, Floyd Bennett Field, "would be perfect" to be used as a camp. Board of Correction Minutes, April 12, 1989.

52. Board of Correction Minutes, September 13, 1990.

53. Martin, "Prison Barge Arrives."

54. Author's interview with Michael Jacobson, March 19, 2023.

55. The official was the Board of Correction's executive director, Richard Wolf. BOCM, November 10, 1987. David W. Dunlap, "Review of a Plan for a Jail Barge Is Drawing Fire," *The New York Times*, August 25, 1988.

56. Ibid. One DOC official asserted that "the chances of an inmate breaking a light fixture in order to commit suicide are remote." See also the reactions of board members when they toured the ship, BOCM, December 8, 1987.

57. BOCM, November 10, 1987.

58. Feeley and Simon, "The New Penology." See also James J. Willis and Stephen D. Mastrofski, "Compstat and the New Penology: A Paradigm Shift in Policing?," *The British Journal of Criminology* 52, no. 1 (January 2012), 73–74; Antell, "Crimes of Youth," 385-387.

59. Feeley and Simon, "The New Penology," 452.

60. BOCM, November 10, 1987; BOCM, April 12, 1988.

61. Vitale, *City of Disorder*, 147–56.

62. Kirk Johnson, "Judge Forbids Inmate Move to Jail Barge," *The New York Times*, October 30, 1987.

63. Ibid.; Kirk Johnson, "Ruling Allows Immediate Use of Barge as Jail," *The New York Times*, February 27, 1988.

64. BOCM, November 10, 1987, and February 9, 1988.

65. BOCM, April 12, 1988.

66. "Prisoners Moving Upstate to Ease Overcrowding," *The New York Times*, August 28, 1988. As elsewhere, the upstate New York facilities brought jobs to economically suffering areas. Ruth Wilson Gilmore, *Golden Gulag: Prisons, Surplus, Crisis, and Opposition in Globalizing California* (Berkeley: University of California Press, 2007); Ryan S. King, Marc Mauer, and Tracy Huling, "Big Prisons, Small Towns: Prison Economics in Rural America," *The Sentencing Project*, 2003, www.sentencingproject.org.

67. BOCM, November 10, 1987, and June 14, 1988.

68. BOCM, May 10, 1988; "Man Is First to Escape from Prison Barge," *The New York Times*, May 1, 1988. Author's interview with Rob Peaco, February 5, 2021.

69. BOCM, January 14, 1989. See also Bohlen, "Jail Population Reaches a Record"; The Vera Institute of Justice, "The Neighborhood Effects of Street-Level Drug Enforcement: Tactical Narcotics Teams in New York," September 1992, www.vera.org. See also Sharon Zane, Oral History interview with Stanley Brezenoff, April 26, 1993, Edward I. Koch Administration Oral History Project, 1992–1997, OHA, Audio Part 10, www.dlc.library.columbia.edu.

70. Celestine Bohlen, "2 More Prison Barges Considered," October 13, 1988, *The New York Times*, October 13, 1988; Maria Laurino, "Battle over Barges," *The Village Voice*, May 16, 1989.

71. BOCM, October 11, 1988; Martin, "Prison Barge Arrives."

72. "Estimate Board Votes Second Prison Barge," *The New York Times*, October 15, 1988; Vitale, *City of Disorder*, 79–80.

73. The ship was embarked in the Netherlands because the harbor in Emden was too shallow for the semisubmersible to get under the barge. "Gevangensschip van Eemshaven naar New York," *Provinciale Zeeuwse Courant*, April 12, 1989, p. 7.

74. Celestine Bohlen, "Jail Influx Brings Plan for 2 Barges," *The New York Times*, March 3, 1989.

75. David M. Kennedy, *Don't Shoot: One Man, A Street Fellowship, and the End of Violence in Inner-City America* (New York: Bloomsbury, 2011), 10; quoted in Forman, *Locking Up Our Own*, 163.

76. Matthew Impelli, "New York City's Most Dangerous Year of Crime Compared to 2022: Analysis," *Newsweek*, October 10, 2023.

77. William N. Evans, Craig Garthwaite, and Timothy J. Moore, "Guns and Violence: The Enduring Impact of Crack Cocaine Markets on Young Black Males," NBER Working Paper No. 2819, National Bureau of Economic Research, Cambridge, MA, July 2018, www.nber.org.

78. Forman, *Locking Up Our Own*, 174–75. ACLU, "Cracks in the System: 20 Years of the Unjust Federal Crack Cocaine Law," October 26, 2006, www.aclu.org.

79. Sharon Zane, Oral History interview with Stanley Brezenoff, April 26, 1993, Edward I. Koch Administration Oral History Project, 1992–1997, OHA, Audio Part 10, www.dlc.library.columbia.edu.

80. BOCM, June 14, 1989. "80 Percent of the Inmates Surveyed by the Substance Abuse Division in March 1989 Reported Using Drugs at Least Once a Week." The Department of Health estimated that about half of all inmates had a history of IV drug abuse and nearly 25 percent were HIV positive. Seventeen percent of all admitted to DOC custody each year required heroin detox. Twenty-eight percent of inmates reported cocaine or crack use.

81. Ibid.

82. "*The Accommodation Review* (Bibby Line Group)," February 1991, MAL, B/BIBBY/4/8.

83. BOCM, April 12, 1988, June 14, 1989, and May 10, 1989.

84. Michael Marriott, "On Prison Barge, All Hands Battle Drugs," *The New York Times*, September 25, 1989.

85. New York State Commission of Correction, *A Report on Corrections in New York*

State—1989, July 1990, Table 29, 103, www.ncjrs.gov. There were forty-four grievances in December 1989 originating on the *Bibby Resolution*.

86. Author's correspondence with New York City Department of Records, December 16, 2020.

87. U.S. House of Representatives, Subcommittee on Criminal Justice, Committee on the Judiciary, "Oversight Hearings on Emerging Criminal Justice Issues (Sentencing Options and Alternatives for Drug-Dependent Offenders," August 15, 1990, 365–67.

88. Author's interview with Maureen Powell. Author's correspondence with members of the Correction History Facebook Group, February 3, 2021.

89. Author's interview with Rob Peaco, February 5, 2021.

90. Celestine Bohlen, "For Inmates, the Living Is Easier on 'The Love Boat,'" *The New York Times*, May 30, 1989.

91. BOCM, November 10, 1987. The *Bibby Venture* was also air-conditioned. See Dunlap, "Review of a Plan for a Jail Barge."

92. Ward, "Troop Barge to Be US Prison."

93. Phillips-Fein, *Fear City*, 19–20 and chapter 16; Twentieth Century Fund, *The Global City* (New York: Twentieth Century Fund, 1981); Robert Schaffer, *Planning and Zoning in New York City: Yesterday, Today and Tomorrow* (New York: Center for Urban Policy, 1993); Chronopoulos, *Spatial Regulation*, chapter 4. On the creation of "global cities," see Saskia Sassen, *The Global City: New York, London, Tokyo* (Princeton: Princeton University Press, 1992, rev. 2013).

94. Rohatyn managed the Municipal Assistance Corporation, which sold bonds to finance the city. Felix Rohatyn, Address to a Conference on a National Policy for Urban America, May 21, 1976, quoted in Phillips-Fein, *Fear City*, 258.

95. Sharon Zane, Oral History interview with Stanley Brezenoff, April 26, 1993, Edward I. Koch Administration Oral History Project, 1992–1997, OHA, Audio Part 10, www.dlc.library.columbia.edu. Edward B. Lazere, Paul A. Leonard, Cushing N. Dolbeare, and Barry Zigas, *A Place to Call Home: The Low Income Housing Crisis Continues* (Washington, DC: Center on Budget and Policy Priorities and Low Income Housing Information Service, 1991); Vitale, *City of Disorder*, chapter 5.

96. "Unemployment Rate in New York," FRED, 2020, www.fred.stlouisfed.org. See also Judith Stein, *The Pivotal Decade: How the United States Traded Factories for Finance in the Seventies* (New Haven: Yale University Press, 2010), especially chapter 11; Dylan Gottlieb, *Yuppies: Young Urban Professionals and the Making of Postindustrial New York*, PhD dissertation, Princeton University, Princeton, NJ, 2020.

97. Greta Krippner, *Capitalizing on Crisis: The Political Origins of the Rise of Finance* (Cambridge: Harvard University Press, 2011), 60–63.

98. Banks also developed certificates of deposit (CDs) and marketed them at American households. Because CDs were not technically accounts, they were not subject to Regulation Q.

99. On the eurodollar market, see also Vanessa Ogle, "Archipelago Capitalism: Tax Havens, Offshore Money, and the State, 1950s–1970s," *American Historical Review* 122, no. 5 (December 2017); Catherine R. Schenk, "The Origins of the Eurodollar Market in London, 1955–1963," *Explorations in Economic History* 35, no. 2 (1998): 221-238. See also Youssef Cassis, *Capitals of Capital: The Rise and Fall of International*

Financial Centres, 1780–2009 (Cambridge: Cambridge University Press, 2006), chapter 6, and Harold James, *International Monetary Cooperation Since Bretton Woods* (New York: Oxford University Press, 1996), especially chapter 12.

100. As Nicholas Shaxson points out, euromarkets allowed banks to effectively dispense with reserve ratios, which made them particularly risky from a financial stability standpoint. Shaxson, *Treasure Islands*, 76–82.

101. Krippner, *Capitalizing on Crisis*, 67.

102. Ibid., 72; Eric Helleiner, *States and the Reemergence of Global Finance: From Bretton Woods to the 1990s* (Ithaca: Cornell University Press, 1994), 136–39.

103. Krippner, *Capitalizing on Crisis*, 87, 97, 104–105; Helleiner, *States and the Reemergence of Global Finance*, 147–49. Stein, *Pivotal Decade*, 266–69.

104. See also Alan Blinder, *After the Music Stopped: The Financial Crisis, the Response, and the Work Ahead* (New York: Penguin, 2013), chapter 3.

105. As New York faced the prospect of bankruptcy in the 1970s, financiers from large firms crept into local government. Their presence—and the austerity budgets it portended—was stipulated by big banks as a prerequisite to issuing more municipal bonds. Kim Phillips-Fein, *Fear City*, part II.

106. Helleiner, *States and the Reemergence of Global Finance*, chapter 7.

107. Ogle, "Archipelago Capitalism." On the Federal Reserve's previous efforts to regulate the eurodollar market, see Helleiner, *States and the Reemergence of Global Finance*, 135–38.

108. In 1984, the federal government removed a 30 percent withholding tax that it had levied on interest payments to foreign bondholders of American bonds. Ibid., 1455.

109. Robert A. Bennett, "America's Debut in Offshore Banking," *The New York Times*, November 22, 1981.

110. Ogle, "Archipelago Capitalism," 1452–53. Shaxson, *Treasure Islands*, chapter 6.

111. Bohlen, "Jail Population Reaches a Record."

112. BOCM, August 9, 1989; Dunlap, "Review of a Plan for a Jail Barge." Maria Laurino, "Prison Barge Blues," *The Village Voice*, August 22, 1989.

113. BOCM, August 9, 1989.

114. David W. Dunlap, "Army Corps Grants One-Year Approval for Prison on Barge," *The New York Times*, August 5, 1989.

115. Author's interview with Rob Peaco, February 4, 2021; author's interview with Maureen Powell, April 1, 2021.

116. Dunlap, "Review of a Plan for a Jail Barge."

117. See Dunlap, "Army Corps Grants One-Year Approval."

118. Russell W. Baker, "New York Seeks Floating Solution," *The Christian Science Monitor*, April 5, 1989, www.csmonitor.com.

119. Bohlen, "For Inmates, the Living Is Easier on 'The Love Boat.'"

120. Mike Ricketts, *The Vessel* (Film), 2013, www.youtube.com.

121. BOCM, February 14, 1989.

122. Carlos Felipe Llinás Negret, "Pretending to Be Liberian and Panamanian; Flags of Convenience and the Weakening of the Nation State on the High Seas," *Journal of Maritime Law and Commerce* 27, no. 1 (January 2016), 18.

123. Celestine Bohlen, "Board Backs Prison Barge Near Pier 40," *The New York Times*, October 28, 1988.

124. BOCM, September 13 and December 12, 1990. "Commissioner's Report," *Correction News* (Summer 1990), www.correctionhistory.org.

125. BOCM, January 9, 1991, and September 13, 1994; Craig Wolff, "Correction Chief Is Faulted by Angry Regulatory Panel," *The New York Times*, December 13, 1990. On Lasker, see Robert D. McFadden, "Morris Lasker, Judge Who Forced City to Clean Up Jails, Dies at 92," *The New York Times*, December 28, 2009; Ted S. Storey, "When Intervention Works: Judge Morris E. Lasker and New York City Jails," in *Courts, Corrections, and the Constitution: The Impact of Judicial Intervention on Prisons and Jails*, ed. John. DiIulio (New York: Oxford University Press, 1990), 138.

126. BOCM, February 21, 1990.

127. René Pierre Meric Jr., *Avondale: A Model for Success, the Story of a Great American Shipyard, 1938–1999* (New Orleans: Philip J. Meric Consulting, 2015).

128. Celestine Bohlen, "$125 Million Jail Barge Is No Mere Ex-Troupship," *The New York Times*, March 22, 1989.

129. BOCM, December 12, 1990, and February 11, 1992. Selwyn Raab, "Bronx Jail Is to Open, Though the Cost Is Steep," *The New York Times*, January 27, 1992.

130. Raab, "Bronx Jail Is to Open." BOCM, May 1994.

131. Luther S. Harris, *Around Washington Square: An Illustrated History of Greenwich Village* (Baltimore: The Johns Hopkins University Press, 2003), chapter 8; Jeffrey Trask, "The 'Loft Cause' or 'Bohemia Gone Bourgeois?': Artist Housing the Private Development in Greenwich Village," *Journal of Urban History* 41, no. 6 (November 2015): 1017-10; Edward Glaeser, Joseph Gyourko, and Raven Saks, "Why Is Manhattan so Expensive? Regulation and the Rise in Housing Prices," *The Journal of Law and Economics* 8 (October 2005): 331-69.

132. The idea to convert Pier 40 into a recreation field as part of a park took off under the Hudson River Park Act of 1998. David W. Dunlap, "Jostling for Position on the Riverfront," *The New York Times*, July 11, 1993. See also Raymond W. Gastil, *Beyond the Edge, New York's New Waterfront* (New York: Princeton Architectural Press, 2002), 126–30.

133. Colette Connor, "Prison Barge Now Illegal," *The Village Underground Press* (September 1991).

134. See Antero Peitila, *Not in My Neighborhood: How Bigotry Shaped a Great American City* (New York: Ivan R. Dee, 2010).

135. Selwyn Raab, "2 Jail Barges to Be Closed and Removed," *The New York Times*, February 15, 1992.

136. BOCM, April 8 and December 9, 1992.

137. "*The Accomodation Review* (Bibby Line Group)," February 1991, MAL, B/BIBBY/4/8.

138. Pamphlet on *Bibby Progress*, n.d. [1990s], MAL, B/BIBBY/4/27.

139. BOCM, July 13, 1994.

140. Author's interview with Michael Jacobson, March 9, 2023.

141. Joe Jackson, "Is Barge Jail in Norfolk's Future? City Hopes to Learn from N.Y. Mistakes," *The Virginian-Pilot*, September 16, 1994.

142. BOCM, July 13, 1994; Esther B. Fein, "A $1.8 Million Bid Wins 2 Empty Prison Barges," *The New York Times*, July 29, 1994. Robert M. Jarvis, "Prison Ships," *British Journal of American Legal Studies* 10, no. 2 (2021), 325.

CHAPTER 7: THE ENGLISH CHANNEL

1. "Unfriendly Berth as Floating Prison Arrives from America," *The Independent*, March 14, 1997.
2. "Floating Prison Has Won Over Tourists and Found the Recipes for Success," *Dorset Echo*, November 28, 2001.
3. See Robert Reiner, *Law and Order: An Honest Citizen's Guide to Crime and Control* (Cambridge: Polity Press, 2007); Emma Bell, *Criminal Justice and Neoliberalism* (Basingstoke: Palgrave Macmillan, 2011); David Garland, *The Culture of Control: Crime and Social Order in Contemporary Society* (Oxford: Oxford University Press, 2001).
4. "United Kingdom: England & Wales," World Prison Brief, 2020, www.prisonstudies .org.
5. See Jonathan Dimbleby interview with Tony Blair, BBC-2, July 4, 1993.
6. The bills were the Criminal Justice Act 1993 and the Criminal Justice and Public Order Act 1994. Bell, *Criminal Justice and Neoliberalism*, chapter 1.
7. David Garland, "The Limits of the Sovereign State: Strategies of Crime Control in Contemporary Society," *The British Journal of Criminology* 36, no. 4 (Autumn 1996): 445-471; Bell, *Criminal Justice and Neoliberalism*, chapter 7.
8. The first privately financed institution (PFI) was contracted in 1996. In 2003, 7 percent of UK prisoners were held in private facilities. Comptroller and Auditor General, "The Operational Performance of PFI Prisons," House of Commons Paper, June 18, 2003, 5.
9. Andrew Ashworth, "Sentencing," in *The Oxford Handbook of Criminology*, ed. Mike Maguire, Rodney Morgan, and Robert Reiner, 4th ed. (Oxford: Oxford University Press, 2007), 990–1023; Bell, *Criminal Justice and Neoliberalism*, 36.
10. "Widdecombe Rejects Abortion Role," June 13, 1998, BBC News.
11. Michael Howard, "Speech to the Conservative Party Conference," Blackpool, UK, October 6, 1993; Bell, *Criminal Justice and Neoliberalism*, 22.
12. Jason Bennetto, "Minister Backs Floating Prison," *The Independent*, March 13, 1997.
13. Private correspondence, March 6, 2021.
14. Chris Blackhurst, "Prisoners May Be Held on Ships," *The Independent on Sunday*, May 23, 1993.
15. "First Inmates Board Ship," *The Times*, June 12, 1997. *Pacific Maritime (Asia) Ltd. v. Holystone Overseas Ltd.*, EWHC 2319, 11 October 2007, paragraph 22.
16. HM Prison Service, *Prison Service Annual Report and Accounts, April 1996–March 1997*, November 1997 (HC 274), 14.
17. Glen Owen, "Emergency Prison Ship Sails into a Storm of Protest," *The Times*, March 14, 1997.
18. James Davie Butler, "British Convicts Shipped to American Colonies," *The American Historical Review* 2, no. 1 (October 1896): 12-23.
19. Diary of Viscount Percival, quoted in Philip J. Stern, *Empire, Incorporated: The Corporations That Built British Colonialism* (Cambridge: Harvard University Press, 2023), 147.
20. Mollie Gillen, *The Founders of Australia: A Biographical Dictionary of the First Fleet* (Sydney: Library of Australian History, 1989).

21. Charles Dickens, *Great Expectations* (New York: Vintage Classics, 2012 [1861]), 38.

22. Owen, "Emergency Prison Ship Sails into a Storm of Protest." See also Mike Ricketts, "Encounters and Spatial Controversies," PhD thesis, University of the Arts, 2015, 118–20.

23. This is what Loïc Wacquant has called a "great penal leap backward." Loïc Wacquant, "Great Penal Leap Backward: Incarceration in America from Nixon to Clinton," in *The New Punitiveness: Trends, Theories, Perspectives*, ed. John Pratt et al. (Cullompton: Willan Publishing, 2005), 3–26.

24. HM Naval Base Portland had existed in Portland since 1923; Portland's harbor was built in the mid-nineteenth century by the navy. "Floating Prison Has Won Over Tourists."

25. Plaque in Portland harbor, accessed by the author, July 9, 2023.

26. As in the United States, new prisons in Britain were often sited in economically depressed regions with rich military histories. Ruth Wilson Gilmore, *Golden Gulag: Prisons, Surplus, Crisis, and Opposition in Globalizing California* (Berkeley: University of California Press, 2007). Even with the navy gone, the barge depended on the military-industrial complex. Its physical upkeep was undertaken by Vosper Thornycroft, a British military contractor later subsumed by BAE. *Pacific Maritime (Asia) Ltd. v. Holystone Overseas Ltd.*, paragraph 22.

27. Owen, "Emergency Prison Ship Sails into a Storm of Protest."

28. Author's interview with Paul Hartley, February 9, 2021.

29. Bennetto, "Minister Backs Floating Prison."

30. Steve Richards, "The New Statesman Interview—Jack Straw," *The New Statesman*, April 3, 1998.

31. Ibid; Bennetto, "Minister Backs Floating Prison"; Patricia Wynn Davies, "Prison Ship Survives Objections," *The Independent*, April 2, 1997.

32. Richard Ford, "Prison Ship Wins Go-Ahead to Take First Inmates," *The Times*, April 2, 1997.

33. "Company," Portland Port, www.portland-port-co.uk.

34. Author's interview with Paul Hartley, February 9, 2021.

35. Ian Burrell, "Fire-Risk Prison Ship Abandoned," *The Independent*, June 27, 1997.

36. Author's interview with Michelle Atkins, March 8, 2021; Ray Bishop, *Outlaw: How I Became Britain's Most Wanted Man*, eBook (London: Virgin Books, 2016)), loc. 1049; author's interview with Ray Bishop, March 24, 2021.

37. Author's interview with James Wild, January 18, 2024; Denholm Engineering, www .denholm-engineering.com.

38. "First Inmates Board Ship."

39. Author's interview with Michelle Atkins, March 8, 2021.

40. "Floating Prison Has Won Over Tourists."

41. Author's interview with Michelle Atkins, March 8, 2021.

42. The monthlong trip was organized annually by a Portland couple. "A Month of Fun for Chernobyl Children," *The Dorset Echo*, August 10, 2002.

43. Bishop, *Outlaw*, loc. 1041; author's interview with Ray Bishop, March 24, 2021.

44. Martin Lea, "It Will Be Lonely This Christmas," *The Dorset Echo*, December 24, 2001.

45. "Weare's Food, Glorious Food," *The Dorset Echo*, June 27, 2002.

46. Steven Shaw, interviewed on June 22, 1999, in Home Affairs Committee, *Fifth Report on Drugs and Prisons*, vol. I, House of Commons, November 9, 1999 (HC 363), 45.

47. Anna Hermann and Caoimhe McAvinchey, "*Inside Bitch*: Clean Break and the Ethics of Representation of Women in the Criminal Justice System," in *The Applied Theatre Reader*, 2nd ed., ed. Nicola Abraham and Tim Prentki (London: Routledge, 2020), chapter 17. The nonprofit was Nacro. Six years later, in 1979, she became the first woman to run a men's establishment, near Bristol. Susan Schonfield, "Susan McCormick Obituary," *The Guardian*, October 27, 2010.

48. James Ellis, "60 Seconds: Dan Treacy," *Metro* (London), March 1, 2006, www.metro.co.uk. See also "HM Prison Weare," *The Encyclopedia of Portland History*, www.portlandhistory.co.uk.

49. Author's interview with Ray Bishop, March 24, 2021.

50. "Weare's Food, Glorious Food."

51. Author's interview with Michelle Atkins, March 8, 2021.

52. "Floating Prison Has Won Over Tourists."

53. "Abuse at Jail Ship Alleged in Report," *The Dorset Echo*, August 7, 2001.

54. "Report on an Announced Inspection of HMP *Weare*," 7–10 June 2004, Appendix II, p. iii, www.webarchive.nationalarchives.gov.uk. In a survey of incarcerated people on the *Weare* in 2004, minority ethnic group respondents reported higher satisfaction with treatment by the staff than white counterparts. Only 6 percent of MEG respondents reported being insulted or assaulted by staff, compared to 19 percent of white respondents.

55. Author's interview with Ray Bishop, March 24, 2021.

56. Author's interview with Michelle Atkins, March 8, 2021.

57. These problems had been flagged by an EU visiting committee in 1997. "Report to the United Kingdom Government on the Visit to the United Kingdom and the Isle of Man Carried Out by the European Committee for the Prevention of Torture and Inhuman and Degrading Treatment or Punishment (CPT) from 8 to 17 September 1997," Council of Europe, Strasbourg, 2000, 39–43, www.refworld.org.

58. "Report on an Announced Inspection of HMP *Weare*." Richard Ford, "Prison Ship 'May Have to Close,'" *The Times*, November 4, 2004; "250 Jobs at Risk if Ship Sold to Capital," *The Dorset Echo*, December 20, 2004; Ben Glass, "Another Prison Ship Would Be Welcome," *The Dorset Echo*, October 24, 2006.

59. "Floating Jail on Brink of Closure," *The Dorset Echo*, July 22, 2005; "Floating Hotel for Refugees," *Sydney Morning Herald*, October 6, 2002, www.smh.com.au.

60. Richard Ford, "Cramped Prison Ship Will Close," *The Times*, March 3, 2005; "Prison Ship Closing by the End of 2005," *The Dorset Echo*, March 10, 2005.

61. "Report on an Announced Inspection of HMP *Weare*."

62. See Loïc Wacquant, *Punishing the Poor: The Neoliberal Government of Social Insecurity* (Durham: Duke University Press, 2009); Elizabeth Hinton, *From the War on Poverty to the War on Crime: The Making of Mass Incarceration in America* (Cambridge: Harvard University Press, 2016); Bell, *Criminal Justice and Neoliberalism*, 151–53; Martin Hewitt, "New Labour and the Redefinition of Social Security," 189–209, in Martin Powell, *Evaluating New Labour* (Bristol: Policy Press, 2002).

63. HM Government, *Reducing Re-Offending Through Skills and Employment* (London: HM Stationery Office, 2005) (Cm. 6702), 11, quoted in Bell, *Criminal Justice and Neoliberalism*, 85.

64. "Report on an Announced Inspection of HMP *Weare*." Ford, "Prison Ship 'May Have to Close'"; "250 Jobs at Risk if Ship Sold to Capital"; Glass, "Another Prison Ship Would Be Welcome."

65. Francis Fukuyama, *The End of History and the Last Man* (New York: Free Press, 1992).

66. Giddens was allegedly Tony Blair's favorite intellectual. By 1998, he led the London School of Economics. Anthony Giddens, *The Third Way: The Renewal of Social Democracy* (Cambridge: Polity Press, 1998), 74–75. See also Anthony Giddens, *Beyond Left and Right: The Future of Radical Politics* (Stanford: Stanford University Press, 1994).

67. Giddens, *The Third Way*, 130.

68. Tony Blair and Gerhard Schröder, "Europe: The Third Way/Die Neue Mitte," Working Documents No. 2, Friedrich Ebert Stiftung, South Africa Office, Johannesburg, South Africa, June 1998, www.library.fes.de.

69. Nick O'Donovan, *Pursuing the Knowledge Economy: A Sympathetic History of High-Skill, High-Wage Hubris* (Newcastle upon Tyne: Agenda Publishing, 2022), chapter 1.

70. Angus Burgin, "The Information Superhighway, the Electronic Frontier, and the Political Economy of the Early Internet," Presentation at the Center for History and Economics, Harvard University, November 29, 2023.

71. Blair and Schröder, "Europe: The Third Way/Die Neue Mitte."

72. Tony Blair, Leader's Speech, Labour Party Conference, Blackpool, October 6, 1996.

73. See Bell, *Criminal Justice and Neoliberalism*, chapter 3.

74. HM Prison Service, *Annual Report and Accounts, April 2003–March 2004*, 2004 [HC 718], 10–11.

75. Shane Bryans, "The Managerialisation of Prisons—Efficiency without a Purpose?," *Criminal Justice Matters* 40, no. 1 (2000): 7-8. See also Shane Clive Bryans, "Prison Governance: An Exploration of the Changing Role and Duties of the Prison Governor in HM Prison Service," PhD thesis, London School of Economics, 2005.

76. In other metrics, HMP *The Weare* was not exceptional. Its positive drug rate (11.9 percent) was about average for category C prisons, as was its yearly cost per bed, which was £21,153, compared to the category C total cost per bed of £21,141. HM Prison Service, *Annual Report and Accounts, April 2003–March 2004*, 86–88.

77. Giddens, *The Third Way*, chapter 3.

78. Blair and Schröder, "Europe: The Third Way/Die Neue Mitte."

79. "Prison Ship Locks Up for Last Time," *The Dorset Echo*, August 12, 2005.

80. "MP Wants Quick Ruling on Prison Ship Future," *The Dorset Echo*, November 6, 2004; "250 Jobs at Risk if Ship Sold to Capital."

81. "Prison Ship Closing by the End of 2005."

82. "250 Jobs at Risk if Ship Sold to Capital."

83. "Prison Ship Locks Up for Last Time."

84. The South West Research Company for the Dorset LEP, "Tourism in Dorset," February 2016, www.visit-dorset.com.

85. "Floating Jail on Brink of Closure."

CHAPTER 8: THE RIVER THAMES

1. *Pacific Maritime (Asia) Ltd. v. Holystone Overseas Ltd.*, EWHC 2319, 11 October 2007, paragraphs 4–5.
2. For more on how these shell companies work, see Kimberly Kay Hoang, *Spiderweb Capitalism: How Global Elites Exploit Frontier Markets* (Princeton: Princeton University Press, 2022).
3. Author's interview with Parley Augustsson, May 12, 2023.
4. "Trimline to Turn Old Prison Ship into Oil Riggers' Paradise," *Daily Echo* (Southampton), February 20, 2007, www.dailyecho.co.uk; Harry Walton, "Prison Ship Could Be on Its Way to Nigeria," *The Dorset Echo*, August 13, 2007.
5. Author's interview with Jon Gale, February 8, 2024.
6. Author's interview with James Wild, January 18, 2024.
7. *Pacific Maritime (Asia) Ltd. v. Holystone Overseas Ltd.*, paragraph 22.
8. Ibid., paragraph 10.
9. Vanessa Ogle, "Archipelago Capitalism: Tax Havens, Offshore Money, and the State, 1950s–1970s," *American Historical Review* 122, no. 5 (December 2017), 1432–1433.
10. See "BP Batam: 45 Years of Developing Batam," *The Jakarta Post*, December 3, 2016.
11. *Pacific Maritime (Asia) Ltd. v. Holystone Overseas Ltd.*, paragraphs 8 and 10.
12. Aristotle, *Politics*, in *Aristotle in Twenty-Three Volumes*, vol. 23, trans. H. Rackham (Cambridge: Harvard University Press, 1932), Book 1.
13. See Jonathan Levy, *Freaks of Fortune: The Emerging World of Capitalism and Risk in America* (Cambridge: Harvard University Press, 2014); William Cronon, *Nature's Metropolis: Chicago and the Great West* (New York: Norton, 1992).
14. First Addendum to Agreement, July 21, 2006, quoted in *Pacific Maritime (Asia) Ltd. v. Holystone Overseas Ltd.*, paragraph 8.
15. Ibid., paragraphs 12 and 13.
16. Ibid., paragraph 14.
17. Ibid., paragraph 17.
18. Ibid.
19. Author's interview with James Wild, January 18, 2024.
20. *Pacific Maritime (Asia) Ltd. v. Holystone Overseas Ltd.*, paragraph 20.
21. Ibid., paragraph 25.
22. Ibid., paragraphs 29 and 31.
23. Gabrielle Kaufmann-Kohler, "Arbitral Precedent: Dream, Necessity or Excuse?," *Arbitration International* 23, no. 3 (2007): 357–78).
24. C. N. Ward-Perkins, "The Commercial Crisis of 1847," *Oxford Economic Papers* 2, no. 1 (January 1950): 75–94).
25. *Robinson v. Robinson*, 1 De G.M. & G (1851), 247.
26. Ibid., 257.
27. Ibid., 247; *Pacific Maritime (Asia) Ltd. v. Holystone Overseas Ltd.*, paragraph 32.
28. Ibid., paragraph 28.
29. The fungibility "operational flexibility" of the vessels was highlighted by the Bibby Line in its promotional materials. See, for instance, Bibby Line Group, "Shallow Water Accommodation," n.d. [1990s], MAL, B/BIBBY/4/18; Bibby Line Group,

"Floating Accommodation Systems," n.d. [2000s], MAL, B/BIBBY/4/25. Marc Levinson, *The Box: How the Shipping Container Made the World Smaller and the World Economy Bigger* (Princeton: Princeton University Press, 2006).

30. The comparison with the grain elevator and the birth of futures markets is striking. See Cronon, *Nature's Metropolis.*

31. *Pacific Maritime (Asia) Ltd. v. Holystone Overseas Ltd.*, paragraph 22.

32. Ibid., paragraphs 34 and 35.

33. Ibid., paragraph 45.

34. Ibid., paragraphs 55–56.

35. Ibid.

36. Ibid., paragraph 63.

37. Ibid., paragraphs 64–68.

38. Ibid., paragraph 75.

39. Ibid.

40. Ibid., paragraph 77; UK Parliament, Arbitration Act 1996, June 17, 1996, Section 44 (5).

41. *Pacific Maritime (Asia) Ltd. v. Holystone Overseas Ltd.*, paragraph 78. UK Parliament, Arbitration Act 1996, June 17, 1996, Section 38 (4). According to the law, the arbitrator had the power to "give directions in relations to any property which is the subject of the proceedings or as to which any question arises in the proceedings, and which is owned by or is in the possession of a party to the proceedings (a) for the . . . detention of the property."

42. *Pacific Maritime (Asia) Ltd. v. Holystone Overseas Ltd.*, paragraph 80.

43. Ibid., paragraph 82.

44. Charlie Caher and Michael Howe, "England & Wales," in Global Legal Group, *International Comparative Guide to International Arbitration*, 12th ed. (Ashford, UK: 2015), 246. Robert Merkin and Louis Flannery, *Arbitration Act 1996* (London: Taylor and Francis, 2014), 177–78. See also Johannes Koepp, Dorine Farah, and Peter Webster, "Arbitration in London: Features of the London Court of International Arbitration," in *International Commercial Arbitration: Different Forms and their Features*, ed. Giuditta Cordero-Moss (Cambridge: Cambridge University Press, 2013), 251, n. 195. "*Pacific Maritime (Asia) Ltd. v. Holystone Overseas Ltd.*—QBD (Com Ct) (Christopher Clarke J)—11 October 2007," *Lloyd's Maritime Law Newsletter* 729, no. 3 (2) (2007), www.lmln.com.

45. "*Pacific Maritime (Asia) Ltd. v. Holystone Overseas Ltd.*," *Arbitration Law Reports and Review* (2007): 677–89.

46. On arbitration in England, see Michael John Mustill, "Arbitration: History and Background," *Journal of International Arbitration* 6, no. 2 (1989): 43–56; V. V. Veeder and Brian Dye, "Lord Bramwell's Arbitration Code, 1884–1889," *Arbitration International* 8, no. 4 (1992): 329–86; Mikaël Schinazi, *The Three Ages of International Commercial Arbitration* (Cambridge: Cambridge University Press, 2021).

47. The 2008 financial crisis is admirably explained in Alan Blinder, *After the Music Stopped: The Financial Crisis, the Response, the Work Ahead* (New York: Penguin, 2013). See also Adam Tooze, *Crashed: How a Decade of Financial Crises Changed the World* (New York: Viking, 2018).

48. Koepp, Farah, and Webster, "Arbitration in London," 263.

49. "A Fond Farewell to the Jascon 27," *Portland Harbour Authority Newsletter* 1, no. 9, February 1, 2010, www.portland-port.co.uk.

CHAPTER 9: THE GULF OF GUINEA

1. On carceral capitalism, see Jackie Wang, *Carceral Capitalism* (Cambridge: MIT Press, 2018).

2. "Fear of Job Losses as Boardroom Crisis Rocks Nigerian Owned West African Ventures," *Business A.M.*, February 20, 2018, www.businessamlive.com.

3. See Tarik Dahou and Brenda Chalfin, "Governing Africa's Seas in the Neoliberal Era," *Oxford Encyclopedia of African Politics* (Oxford: Oxford University Press, 2019).

4. Kyuka Usman, *Nigerian Oil and Gas Industry Laws: Policies, and Institutions*, eBook (African Books Collective, 2017), chapter 3. G. Ugo Nwokeji, *The Nigerian National Petroleum Corporation and the Development of the Nigerian Oil and Gas Industry: History, Strategies, and Current Directions*, James A. Baker III Institute for Public Policy, Rice University, Houston, Texas, 2007.

5. Michael Gould, *The Biafran War: The Struggle for Modern Nigeria* (London: I. B. Taurus, 2012).

6. Nwokeji, *The Nigerian National Petroleum Corporation*, 58.

7. "Oil Rents (Percent of GDP)—Nigeria," World Bank Data, 2020, www.data.worldbank.org.

8. Sarah Burns and Olly Owen, "Nigeria: No Longer an Oil State?," Oxford Martin School Working Paper, August 2019; Olusola Joshua Olujobi, "Nigeria's Upstream Petroleum Industry Anti-Corruption Legal Framework: The Necessity for Overhauling and Enrichment," *Journal of Money Laundering Control* (May 2021), DOI 10.1108/JMLC-10-2020-0119.

9. The federal government receives 52.68 percent, states receive 26.72 percent, and local governments 20.6 percent. R. A. Onuigbo and E. O. Innocent, "State Governors and Revenue Allocation Formula in Nigeria: A Case of the Fourth Republic," *International Journal of Accounting Research* 42, no. 2437 (2015): 1–23).

10. Kaniye S. A. Ebeku, "International Law and the Control of Offshore Oil in Nigeria," *Verfassung und Recht in Übersee* 36, no. 3 (2003): 457–72).

11. Surabhi Ranganathan, "Ocean Floor Grab: International Law and the Making of an Extractive Imaginary," *European Journal of Law* 30, no. 2 (2019).

12. Lotanna Ernest Emediegwu and Augustine Nnoruka Okeke, "Dependence on Oil: What Do Statistics from Nigeria Show?," *Journal of Economics and Allied Research* 2, no. 1 (2017): 110–25.

13. The term *resource curse* was coined by the economist Richard Auty in 1993. Richard Auty, *Sustaining Development in Mineral Economies: The Resource Curse Thesis* (London: Routledge, 1993). See also Jeffrey Sachs and Andrew Warner, "Natural Resource Abundance and Economic Growth," NBER Working Paper No. 5398, National Bureau of Economic Research, Cambridge, MA, 1995, www.nber.org. On Nigeria and the resource curse, see Michael Watts, "Resource Curse?: Governmentality, Oil and Power in the Niger Delta, Nigeria," *Geopolitics* 9, no. 1 (2004): 50–80; Xavier Sala-i-Martin and Arvind Subramanian, "Addressing the Natural Resource

Curse: An Illustration from Nigeria," *Journal of African Economies* 22, no. 4 (2012): 570–615.

14. The average was 65. "Promoting Revenue Transparency: 2011 Report on Oil and Gas Companies," *Transparency International*, www.images.transparencycdn.org. See also Kairn A. Klieman, "U.S. Oil Companies, the Nigerian Civil War, and the Origins of Opacity in the Nigerian Oil Industry," *Journal of American History* 99, no. 1 (June 2022): 155–65. Nwokeji, *The Nigerian National Petroleum Corporation*, 44–54.

15. Klieman, "U.S. Oil Companies."

16. Timothy Mitchell, *Carbon Democracy: Political Power in the Age of Oil* (London: Verso, 2011). As Mitchell notes, this does not mean that oil is incompatible with democracy.

17. Omolade Adunbi, *Oil Wealth and Insurgency in Nigeria* (Bloomington: University of Indiana Press, 2015), 27.

18. Michael Watts, "Empire of Oil: Capitalist Dispossession and the Scramble for Africa," *Monthly Review*, September 1, 2006, www.monthlyreview.org; *Nigeria: Want in the Midst of Plenty*, Africa Report 113, International Crisis Group, 2006, www.crisisgroup.org.

19. Omolade Adunbi, *Enclaves of Exception: Special Economic Zones and Extractive Practices in Nigeria* (Bloomington: Indiana University Press, 2022), 145.

20. Michael Watts, "The Sinister Political Life of Community: Economies of Violence and Governable Spaces in the Niger Delta, Nigeria," Niger Delta Economies of Violence Working Paper No. 3, Institute of International Studies, University of California, Berkeley, 2004.

21. Author's interview with James Wild, January 18, 2024.

22. Ibid.

23. See Adunbi, *Enclaves of Exception*, chapter 3.

24. Hannah Appel, "Offshore Work: Oil, Modularity, and the How of Capitalism in Equatorial Guinea," *American Ethnologist* 39, no. 4 (November 2012): 692–709

25. Adunbi, *Enclaves of Exception*, 92–93.

26. Howard Stein, "Africa, Industrial Policy, and Export Processing Zones: Lessons from Asia," in *Good Growth and Governance in Africa: Rethinking Development Strategies*, ed. Akbar Norman et al. (Oxford: Oxford University Press, 2011), 322–44. "Global Free Zones of the Year 2018—Winners," *Foreign Direct Investment*, October 13, 2018; "A Brief History of Free Zone Legislation in Nigeria," Oil and Gas Free Zones Authority Nigeria, 2020, www.ogfza.gov.ng.

27. T. Mkandawire, "Thinking About Developmental States in Africa," *Cambridge Journal of Economics* 25, no. 3 (May 2001), 306, quoted in Adunbi, *Enclaves of Exception*, 51–55.

28. Watts, "Empire of Oil"; William Easterly, *The White Man's Burden: Why the West's Efforts to Aid the Rest Have Done so Much Ill and so Little Good* (New York: Penguin, 2006).

29. "Onne," Oil and Gas Free Zones Authority Nigeria, 2020, www.ogfza.gov.ng.

30. Stein, "Africa and Industrial Policy."

31. Adunbi, *Enclaves of Exception*, chapter 6.

32. "World Free Zones Economic Outlook," Kiel Institute for the World Economy, 2022, www.ifw-kiel,de.

33. Thomas Farole, *Special Economic Zones in Africa: Comparing Performance and Learning from Global Experience* (Washington, DC: World Bank, 2011).

34. Deinibiteim Monimah Harry, "Value Addition Policy in Nigeria's Export Processing Zones: Lessons from the Asian Economies," *Mediterranean Journal of Social Sciences* 9, no. 3 (May 2018): 165–72. See also Omolade Adnubi and Howard Stein, "The Political Economy of China's Investment in Nigeria: Prometheus or Leviathan," in *China-Africa and an Economic Transformation*, ed. Arkebe Oqubay and Justin Yifu Lin (Oxford: Oxford University Press, 2019), 192–215.

35. Adunbi, *Enclaves of Exception*, 45–50.

36. See Ed Kashi and Michael Watts, *Curse of the Black Gold: 50 Years of Oil in the Niger Delta* (New York: powerHouse Books, 2010).

37. Paul E. Lovejoy and David Richardson, " 'This Horrid Hole': Royal Authority, Commerce and Credit at Bonny, 1690–1840," *Journal of African History* 45 (2004): 363–92.

38. Ibid., 366.

39. So many Africans were sold into slavery from the area along the Bight of Benin between the Volta River and the Niger River delta that the region became known in Europe as the "slave coast." On the slave trade in the Bight of Biafra, see G. Ugo Nwokeji, *The Slave Trade and Culture in the Bight of Biafra: An African Society in the Atlantic World* (Cambridge: Cambridge University Press, 2010). Ibid., 41.

40. "Trans-Atlantic Slave Trade—Database, Map," www.slavevoyages.org.

41. G. Ugo Nwokeji, "Slave Ships to Oil Tankers," in Watts and Kashi, *Curse of the Black Gold*, 64–65. See also Klieman, "U.S. Oil Companies," 158.

42. Anne Ruderman, "The Local and the Coastal," unpublished manuscript.

43. FTI Consulting, "First Report to Creditors," August 10, 2017, www.fticonsulting-emea.com. In 2011, it earned about $415 million in revenue from external customers in Nigeria, Angola, and Equatorial Guinea, compared with about $20 million in revenue from external customers in Australia, the other geographic area in which it operated. PwC, "Sea Trucks Group Limited Consolidated Financial Statements for the Year Ended 31 December 2011," April 27, 2012, p. 37, www.finanznachrichten.de.

44. "Sea Trucks Group Limited," Offshore Leaks Database, International Consortium of Investigative Journalists, www.offshoreleaks.icij.org.

45. The subsidiaries incorporated in the UAE, Australia, and the Netherlands were project management companies. See PwC, "Sea Trucks Group Limited Consolidated Financial Statements," 9. "Sea Trucks Group," *Foreign Affairs* 88, no. 3 (May/June 2009).

46. "Sea Trucks Group—Company Capsule," *World Market Intelligence*, January 20, 2014.

47. "Sea Trucks Group."

48. It had previously issued PwC, "Sea Trucks Group Limited Consolidated Financial Statements."

49. Meg Chesshyre, "Roomans Returns to His Roots," *Offshore Engineer*, September 1, 2012, www.oedigital.com; "Sea Trucks Group," Oil and Gas Netherlands, www.oilandgas.nl.

50. The interest rate on the First Bank of Nigeria loan was 9.5 percent and secured by mortgages on four vessels in the group's fleet. PwC, "Sea Trucks Group Limited Consolidated Financial Statements."

51. Sarka Halas, "Nigeria's Sea Trucks Group Plans Senior Secured Bond," *Dow Jones Institutional News*, March 7, 2013.

52. "U.S. Shale Production," U.S. Energy Information Administration, January 11, 2021, www.eia.gov.

53. The United States became a net gas exporter in 2017. "Natural Gas Explained," U.S. Energy Information Administration, 2022, www.eia.gov.

54. "Gazprom Now Has Own Pipe Laying Vessel—Exec," *Interfax—Russia and CIS Business and Financial Newswire*, May 19, 2016. "This Is How Gazprom Will Bypass US Sanctions in Building Nord Stream-2," May 21, 2016, www.sputniknews.com. The ship, now known as the *Akademik Cherskiy*, did operate in the Baltic for several years. See Benjamin L. Schmitt, "Hot Issue—They're Gonna Need a Bigger Boat: The Curious Voyage of the Akademik Cherskiy," The Jamestown Foundation, March 31, 2020, www.jamestown.org.

55. Adebayo Dawodu, "WAV Condemns Fraudulent Moves by Sea Trucks Group," *The Nigerian Voice*, October 29, 2017, www.thenigerianvoice.com. See also Femi Owolabi, "The Insider: How Expatriates Hijacked a Business Empire from Nigerian Owner," *The Cable*, February 22, 2018, www.thecable.ng.

56. FTI Consulting, "First Report to Creditors." "The beneficiaries of the trust which holds the Company's shares (the 'Equity Beneficiaries') sought to remove the Independent Directors."

57. Ibid.; Owolabi, "The Insider."

58. Owolabi, "The Insider"; Shina Loremikan, "Sea Trucks Group: A Case of Liquidation or a Hostile Takeover?," *The Guardian* (Lagos), March 22, 2018, www.guardian .ng; Peter Ozoho, "Regulators Urged to Wade into Sea Trucks Group's Imbroglio," *This Day* (Lagos), August 30, 2018, www.thisdaylive.com. On Western exploitation of African wealth, see Chalfin and Dahou, "Governing Africa's Seas."

59. Dawodu, "WAV Condemns Fraudulent Moves."

60. Owolabi, "How Expatriates Hijacked a Business Empire."

61. Watts, "Empire of Oil."

62. Mitchell, *Carbon Democracy*.

63. Author's interview with James Wild, January 18, 2024.

64. Nwokeji, *The Nigerian National Petroleum Corporation*, 72. On militant violence, see Adunbi, *Oil Wealth and Insurgency*, especially chapter 6.

65. Nwokeji, *The Nigerian National Petroleum Corporation*, 72–73.

66. Eoin O'Cinneide, "Pirate-Hit Vessels 'not on Nigerian Oilfield,'" *Upstream*, August 6, 2012, www.upstreamonline.com; author's interview with James Wild, January 18, 2024.

67. Appel, "Offshore Work."

68. Tabitha Lasley, *Sea State* (New York: Ecco, 2021), 158.

69. Watts, "Empire of Oil." Today, many ex-militants have become involved in running thousands of illegal and highly toxic "artisanal refineries" using illicitly acquired crude oil. See Adunbi, *Enclaves of Exception*, chapter 5.

70. FTI Consulting, "First Report to Creditors."
71. Ibid.
72. "Public Notice of Sea Trucks Group Limited (In Liquidation)," n.d. [2017–2018], www.fticonsulting-emea.com.
73. Ibid.
74. Order for the Appointment of Provisional Liquidators, Claim No. BVIHC (Com) 71 of 2017, May 5, 2017, www.fticonsulting-emea.com. FTI Consulting, "First Report to Creditors." Emmanuel Okogba, "WAV in the Eye of the Storm: The Story Behind the Dispute with Sea Trucks Group," *Vanguard*, October 24, 2017, www .vanguardngr.com.
75. FTI Consulting, "Sea Trucks Group Limited in Liquidation (the 'Holding Company') Information for Stakeholders," June 15, 2017, www.fticonsulting-emea.com.
76. The chairman, Tom Ehret, continued, "Fundamentally, the Sea Trucks Group is and remains a strong and viable business, well positioned in its markets. We are excited about its prospects and will continue to service clients to the expected high standards." FTI Consulting, Sea Trucks Group Appointment of Provisional Liquidators Press Release, May 8, 2017, www.fticonsulting-emea.com. FTI became the nonprovisional liquidators by order of the Eastern Caribbean Supreme Court of the Virgin Islands, on June 12, 2017. See Order, Claim No. BVIHC (Com) 71 of 2017, June 12, 2017, www.fticonsulting-emea.com.
77. FTI Consulting, "First Report to Creditors."
78. The fifth DP3, operating in Nigeria, was the *Jascon 30*. On May 9, 2017, shortly after provisional liquidation, the Federal High Court of Nigeria in the Port of Harcourt Judicial Division served STG with a notice of arrest in respect of the ship. STG disputed the claim that WAV "has any ownership interest in the J30." FTI Consulting, "First Report to Creditors."
79. The four ships were *Jascon 25, 28, 31,* and *34*. Anne-Marie Causer, "Sea Trucks Group Restructure Following Liquidation," *Maritime Journal*, February 15, 2018, www.maritimejournal.com; Telford Offshore, www.telfordoffshore.com. See also "Notice of a Written Bondholders' Resolution," February 6, 2018, www.stamdata .com.
80. FTI Consulting, "Sea Trucks Group Limited (in Liquidation) Restructuring Press Release," n.d. [July-August 2017], www.fticonsulting-emea.com. In late June 2017, before the formation of Telford Offshore, the bondholders had voted and agreed to provide STG with additional liquidity of $25 million through a new bond that would rank senior to the prior bond. FTI Consulting, "First Report to Creditors."
81. FTI Consulting, "Sea Trucks Group Limited Liquidation Update," October 12, 2017, www.fticonsulting-emea.com.
82. Okogba, "WAV in the Eye of the Storm."
83. 'Femi Asu, "WAV, STG Settle Row as NCDMB, NAPISM Intervene," *Punch*, February 14, 2019, www.punchng.com. Udeme Akpan, "WAV, STG End Rift, Sign Settlement Agreement," *Vanguard* (Lagos), February 19, 2019.
84. Ibid.
85. WAV, "Jascon 27 Accommodation Barge," www.waventures.com.ng.
86. Dawodu, "WAV Condemns Fraudulent Moves."

87. These offshore registries of convenience might be open to shipowners, but they are relatively closed to researchers. As the *Jascon 27*, the Vessel was registered through Monaco, and the *Venture* through Geneva. To find out *exactly* when a ship was reregistered requires paying $200 per ship. Email from SVG—Registry Department Geneva to Author, November 6, 2020.

88. "Venture," Shipphotos.ru, December 5, 2013, www.shipphotos.ru.

CODA: WALVIS BAY

1. On operating "in the gray," see Kimberly Kay Hoang, *Spiderweb Capitalism: How Global Elites Exploit Frontier Markets* (Princeton: Princeton University Press, 2022).

2. See Lynn Berat, *Walvis Bay: Decolonization and International Law* (New Haven: Yale University Press, 1990); Nils Brezelius, *How the Port of Walvis Bay Became Namibian* (Windhoek: Kuiseb Publishers, 2017), 13–14. See also "Walvis Bay: Report of a Fact-Finding Mission, October 1990," NEPRU Working Paper No. 13, August 1992, The Namibian Economic Policy Research Unit, Windhoek, Namibia.

3. The other two ships were the accommodation barge *DSH 1* and the tug *Ima Atisi*. Amarjit Singh Bajwa to Jade McClune, January 7, 2019; author's correspondence with Jade McClune, May 3, 2021; author's interview with John Guard, May 19, 2021.

4. Halani 1—Abandonment ID 00341, SECTOR Database on Reported Incidents of Abandonment of Seafarers, 2021, www.ilo.org.

5. HRAS, "Case Study in Their Own Words: Eight Indian Seafearers Abandoned Off-Shore Walvis Bay, Namibia, Face Fatigue, Lack of Wages and Mental Health Issues," January 2019, 2, www.humanrightsatsea.org; Halani 1—Abandonment ID 00341, SECTOR Database on Reported Incidents of Abandonment of Seafarers.

6. International Maritime Organization, Resolution A.930(22), "Guidelines on Provision of Financial Security in Case of Abandonment of Seafarers," December 17, 2001. See also Lalah Khalili, "Agent Untraceable, Owner not Responding," *London Review of Books* 45, no. 7 (March 2023).

7. "Ship Abandonment," Mission to Seafarers, 2021, www.missiontoseafarers.org; author's interview with John Guard, May 19, 2021.

8. Halani 1—Abandonment ID 00341, SECTOR Database on reported incidents of abandonment of seafarers. The ILO lists 175 vessels abandoned during 2023, but was only notified of 132 abandoned vessels during that calendar year. See also Khalili, "Agent Untraceable."

9. Chris Armstrong, "Abuse, Exploitation, and Floating Jurisdiction: Protecting Workers at Sea," *The Journal of Political Philosophy* 30, no. 1 (March 2022): 3–25.

10. Karen McVeigh, "Abandoned at Sea: The Crews Cast Adrift Without Food, Fuel, or Pay," *The Guardian*, April 12, 2019.

11. HRAS, Case Study in Their Own Words, 2; Halani 1—Abandonment ID 00341, SECTOR Database on Reported Incidents of Abandonment of Seafarers.

12. Jan de Boer to SVG Registry, email, June 4, 2018, in Halani 1—Abandonment ID 00341, SECTOR Database on Reported Incidents of Abandonment of Seafarers. Amarjit Singh Bajwa to Jade McClune, January 7, 2019, author's correspondence with Jade McClune, May 3, 2021.

13. Shiladitya Bose to SVG Registry, email, June 13, 2018, in Halani 1—Abandonment ID 00341, SECTOR Database on Reported Incidents of Abandonment of Seafarers.
14. ILO, Maritime Labour Convention, 2006, www.ilo.org.
15. S. Dulic to Mr. Noh, email, July 20, 2018, in Halani 1—Abandonment ID 00341, SECTOR Database on Reported Incidents of Abandonment of Seafarers.
16. HRAS, Case Study in Their Own Words, 4.
17. Ibid., 4–5.
18. Author's interview with John Guard, May 19, 2021.
19. Statement from International Chamber of Shipping, January 29, 2019, in Halani 1—Abandonment ID 00341, SECTOR Database on Reported Incidents of Abandonment of Seafarers. See also Amarjit Singh Bajwa to Jade McClune, January 7, 2019, author's correspondence with Jade McClune, May 3, 2021.
20. Corinne Vargha to Permanent Secretary, Department of Labour, St. Vincent and the Grenadines, March 27, 2019, in Halani 1—Abandonment ID 00341, SECTOR Database on Reported Incidents of Abandonment of Seafarers.
21. S. Dulic to Jan de Boer, email, January 30, 2019, in Halani 1—Abandonment ID 00341, SECTOR Database on Reported Incidents of Abandonment of Seafarers. Author's correspondence with St. Vincent and the Grenadines Ship Registry, February 2, 2021.
22. "Goeiemann to Retire Next Month," *The Namibian*, February 26, 2020, www.namibian.com.na.
23. International Labour Organization, International Maritime Convention, 2006, Standard A2.5.1—Repatriation, Paragraphs 7 and 8, p. 36.
24. Jan de Boer to Willem Goeiemann, March 20, 2019, in Halani 1—Abandonment ID 00341, SECTOR Database on Reported Incidents of Abandonment of Seafarers.
25. Jonathan Warring to Willem Groeiemann, March 21, 2019, in Halani 1—Abandonment ID 00341, SECTOR Database on Reported Incidents of Abandonment of Seafarers.
26. Author's interview with John Guard, May 19, 2021.
27. Amarjit Singh Bajwa to Jade McClune, April 12, 2019, author's correspondence with Jade McClune, May 3, 2021.
28. Author's interview with John Guard, May 19, 2021.
29. Ibid. "Past Sales," Solution Strategists, www.solutionstrat.com; "Alan: Offshore Supply Ship IMO 7816379," MarineTraffic.com, www.marinetraffic.com. On Bhangavar, see William Langewiesche, *The Outlaw Sea: A World of Freedom, Chaos, and Crime* (New York: North Point Press, 2004).
30. Chris Foote, "Breaking Bad: Uncovering the Oil Industry's Dirty Secret," March 17, 2020, BBC News.
31. Author's interview with John Guard, May 19, 2021.
32. Ibid.
33. Suman Barua et al., "Environmental Hazards Associated with Open-Beach Breaking of End-of-Life Ships: A Review," *Environmental Science and Pollution Research* 25 (2018): 30880–93. On Bhangavar, see Langewiesche, *The Outlaw Sea*. Author's correspondence with John Guard, May 5, 2021.
34. "High Ocean IV, IMO 8638774," Marine MAN, www.ships.jobmarineman.com;

"High Ocean IV," VesselTracking.net, www.vesseltracking.net. Margot Gibbs, "Revealed: How a UK Company Is Using a Caribbean Tax Haven to Cash In on Scrapping Toxic Ships in One of the World's Poorest Countries," *The Independent*, February 20, 2019.

35. "Venture," MarineTraffic.com, www.marinetraffic.com.

36. "Contact," West African Ventures Limited, www.waventures.com.ng.

37. Email from James Wild to author, January 10, 2024; interview with James Wild, January 18. 2024. "Jascon 27," BalticShipping.com, www.balticshipping.com. On using websites to track the vessel, see Mike Ricketts, "Encounters and Spatial Controversies," PhD thesis, University of the Arts, 2015, especially 120–29.

CONCLUSION: INTERNATIONAL WATERS

1. See "HSB-Finnboda Varv Residential Development—Sweden," *World Market Intelligence News* [London], January 13, 2015, www.search.proquest.com. Mikael Josephson, *Finnboda varv och fartygen som byggdes där* (Stockholm: Trafik-Sostalgiska Förlaget, 2020), 124–26.

2. Fogia Products, www.fogia.com.

3. On the culture and despair of British offshore oil, see Tabitha Lasley, *Sea State: A Memoir* (New York: Ecco, 2021).

4. Jillian Ambrose, "Denmark to End New Oil and Gas Exploration in North Sea," *The Guardian*, December 4, 2020.

5. Bruce Morley, "The Effects of Commodity Discoveries on Small Open Economies: Empirical Evidence from the Falkland Islands," *Economies* 7, no. 106 (2019); CIA, "Falkland Islands," *CIA World Factbook*, www.statistical-proquest-com. For a portrait of the Falklands, see Larissa MacFarquar, "How Prosperity Transformed the Falklands," *The New Yorker*, June 29, 2020.

6. "Volkswagen's Global Production Network for Electric Vehicles Grows with Launch of Second German Site in Emden," VW Press Release, May 20, 2022, www.volkswagen-newsroom.com.

7. Fosen Yard Emden, www.nordseewerke.com.

8. Ole Cordsen, "Wirbel um Hotelschiff für Slowaken bei VW," *Ostfriesland Zeitung*, August 20, 2019, www.oz-online.de. Author's conversation with Linda Hallwass, April 28, 2023.

9. "The Floating Pool Lady," n.d., www.floatingpool.org.

10. "Pier 36," DockNYC, www.docknyc.com.

11. "Events," and "Pier 36 NYC," www.pier36nyc.com.

12. "Pier 40," Hudson River Park, www.hudsonriverpark.org.

13. "Bibby Line Group Completes Duke Street Building Sale," Bibby Line Group Press Release, December 1, 2019, www.bibbylinegroup.co.uk.

14. Robin Pagnamenta, "Business Big Shot," *The Times*, August 3, 2009.

15. UK Ministry of Justice "A Royal Opening for the Rolls Building," December 7, 2011, www.gov.uk. Owen Bowcott, "Rolls Building Court Complex Can Make London 'Global Legal Centre,'" *The Guardian*, August 19, 2011.

16. Steven Morris, "'It's Inhumane': Anger at Plan to House Asylum Seekers on Barge

off Dorset," *The Guardian*, April 5, 2023; Aletha Adu, "Home Office to Announce Barge as Accommodation for Asylum Seekers," *The Guardian*, April 3, 2023.

17. UK Home Office, "Factsheet: Asylum Accommodation on a Vessel in Portland Port," www.gov.uk.

18. "The People of Dorset Say No to the Barge," Facebook, www.facebook.com.

19. "The People of Dorset Say No to the Barge," shareable fact sheet, seen posted in Portland on July 8, 2023.

20. Ione Welles and Joe Nimmo, "Bibby Stockholm Barge Migrants Moved After Legionella Bacteria Found," *BBC News*, August 12, 2023.

21. Hannah Appel, "Offshore Work: Oil, Modularity, and the How of Capitalism in Equatorial Guinea," *American Ethnologist* 39, no. 4 (November 2012): 700. Appel has argued that offshore setups "are predicated on the idea that there are spaces where production of profit can evade or minimize contestation." This may be so, but the offshore world is itself a space of ferocious contestation.

22. See Hannah Appel, *The Licit Life of Capitalism: US Oil in Equatorial Guinea* (Durham: Duke University Press, 2019); Omolade Adunbi, *Enclaves of Exception: Special Economic Zones and Extractive Practices in Nigeria* (Bloomington: Indiana University Press, 2022).

23. Philip Mirowski, "Neoliberalism: The Movement That Dare Not Speak Its Name," *American Affairs* 2, no. 1 (Spring 2018): 118–41. Bjarke Saerlund Risager, "Neoliberalism Is a Political Project: An Interview with David Harvey," *Jacobin*, July 23, 2016, www.jacobinmag.com. See also David Harvey, *A Brief History of Neoliberalism* (Oxford: Oxford University Press, 2007); Philip Mirowski and Dieter Plehwe, eds., *The Road from Mont Pèlerin: The Making of the Neoliberal Thought Collective*, rev. ed. (Cambridge: Harvard University Press, 2015); Will Davies, *The Limits of Neoliberalism: Authority, Sovereignty, and the Logic of Competition* (London: Sage, 2014).

24. Daniel Rodgers, "The Uses and Abuses of 'Neoliberalism,' " *Dissent* (Winter 2018).

25. Sam Wetherell similarly highlights the physical, material side of neoliberalism. Sam Wetherell, *Foundations: How the Built Environment Made Twentieth-Century Britain* (Princeton: Princeton University Press, 2020). See also James Vernon, "Heathrow and the Making of Neoliberal Britain," *Past and Present* 252 (August 2021): 213–47.

INDEX

ILLUSTRATION CREDITS

xxi–xxiii: Mapping Specialists LLC

16: Thor Björn Johansson, 1974, Nacka Local History Archive

18: Original plans held by the Swedish Maritime Administration (Sjöfartsverket)

24: Original registration document held in the Norwegian National Archives, AV/RA-S-1627/H/Hd/L0003: Fartøy, B-Bev, s. 125

47: Original plans held in Riksarkivet i Göteborg, F3A:450. 096-9

51 (*top*): Original plans held in Regionarkivet Västra Götalandsregionen och Göteborgs Stad, GSA_13-1/F 1 B/42; (*bottom*): Original plans held by the Swedish Maritime Administration (Sjöfartsverket)

60: Used with permission of Falklands Post

72: FotoFlite

75 (*top* and *bottom*): Nick Barnard

83: Adapted from source held by Modern Records Centre, University of Warwick, MSS.411 MNAOA/4/3. Used with permission of the Bibby Line.

86: Reproduced from "Coastel: The World's Most Accommodating Floating Unit" Bibby Line Promotional Brochure, n.d. [1980s] Archives Centre at the Maritime Museum, Liverpool, B/BIBBY/4/8. Used with permission of the Bibby Line.

97: Christian Hampel, 2024

103: Wikipedia. Created by Wikipedia user Bin im Garten, "Luftbild des Werks, im Hintergrund links der Teil des Hafens, in dem der Autoumschlag stattfindet," 2010. Used under Creative Commons, creativecommons.org/licenses/by-sa/3.0.

104: FotoFlite

106: dpa Infografik

108: Interphoto / Alamy Stock Photo

116: Mapping Specialists LLC

129: Reproduced from *Correction News*, December 1988

133: PA Images / Alamy Stock Photo

155: Flickr. Jack Pease, "Isle of Portland Panorama," 2019. Used under Creative Commons, creativecommons.org/licenses/by-sa/2.0.

156: PA Images / Alamy Stock Photo

160: (*top* and *bottom*): PA Images / Alamy Stock Photos; (*middle*): Jack Sullivan / Alamy Stock Photos

163: John Gale, 2008

167–168: Reproduced from HM Prison Service, *Annual Report and Accounts, April 2003-*

March 2004, 2004 [HC 718]. Used under the Open Government License, www
.nationalarchives.gov.uk/doc/open-government-licence/version/3. Contains public
sector information licensed under the Open Government Licence v3.0.

169: Reproduced from HM Prison Service, *Annual Report and Accounts, April 2003-
March 2004*, 2004 [HC 718]. Used under the Open Government License, www
.nationalarchives.gov.uk/doc/open-government-licence/version/3.

173: Flickr. Flickr User It's No Game, "Royal Courts of Justice," 2014, Used under
Creative Commons, creativecommons.org/licenses/by-sa/2.0.

176: Gigi Sung and Jeff Blossom of the Center for Geographic Analysis, Harvard
University

196: Gigi Sung and Jeff Blossom of the Center for Geographic Analysis, Harvard
University

200: iStockPhoto.com / Modest Franco

214: James Wild, 2017

220: Wikimedia Commons / Flickr. User Sonse, "Sandwich Harbour, Walvis Bay," 2017.
Used under Creative Commons, creativecommons.org/licenses/by-sa/2.0.

223: Reproduced from Jade Lennon, "Ship and Indian crew abandoned for over a year at
Walvis Bay," January 10, 2019, Medium

227: Wikimedia Commons / Planet Labs Inc., "Shipwrecking in Alang, India, 2017-
03-17," 2017. Used under Creative Commons, creativecommons.org/licenses
/by-sa/4.0.

232: Ian Kumekawa, 2023

233: Per Askergren, 2019

234: Linda Halwaß, 2023

238: Ian Kumekawa, 2023